American University Studies

Series VII
Theology and Religion

Vol. 13

PETER LANG
New York · Berne · Frankfurt am Main

In the Ways of Justice Toward Salvation

Gregory J. Polan, O.S.B.

In the Ways of Justice Toward Salvation

A Rhetorical Analysis of Isaiah 56–59

PETER LANG
New York · Berne · Frankfurt am Main

Library of Congress Cataloging in Publication Data

Polan, Gregory J.
In the Ways of Justice Toward Salvation.

(American University Studies. Series VII, Theology and Religion; v. 13)
Bibliography, p.
Includes indexes.
1. Bible. O.T. Isaiah LVI–LIX – Language, style.
I. Title. II. Series.
BS1520.5.P64 1986 224'.1066 85-24082
ISBN 0-8204-0280-X
ISSN 0740-0446

CIP-Kurztitelaufnahme der Deutschen Bibliothek

Polan, Gregory J.:
In the Ways of Justice Toward Salvation: A Rhetor. Analysis of Isaiah 56–59 / Gregory J. Polan. – New York; Berne; Frankfurt am Main: Lang, 1986.
(American University Studies: Ser. 7, Theology and Religion; Vol. 13)
ISBN 0-8204-0280-X

NE: American University Studies / 07

Printed by Lang Druck, Inc., Liebefeld/Berne (Switzerland)

TABLE OF CONTENTS

	Page
ABBREVIATIONS	iii
TRANSLITERATION	v
PREFACE	vii
INTRODUCTION	ix
CHAPTER ONE: Preliminary Considerations	1
I. The Birth and Growth of Rhetorical Criticism in the Study of the Old Testament	1
II. Recent Studies of Isaiah 56-66	10
III. Delimitation of the Text and its Vocabulary Patterns	17
A. Delimitation of the Section and Literary Units	17
B. Selected Patterns of Repeated Vocabulary in Isaiah 56:1--59:20	27
IV. A Method for Analysis	35
CHAPTER TWO: A Rhetorical Analysis of Isaiah 56:1-8	43
Translation of Isaiah 56:1-8	43
I. Overview	44
A. Indications of Unity in Isaiah 56:1-8	44
B. Delimitation of the Strophes	52
II. Close Reading	55
A. Isaiah 56:1-2 -- A Question of Justice and Righteousness	55
B. Isaiah 56:3-7 -- God's New Word Toward Unity	64
C. Isaiah 56:8 -- The Full Community of Israel Gathered by the Lord God	76
III. Application of a Literary Device to Isaiah 56:1-8	79
IV. Summary	89
CHAPTER THREE: A Rhetorical Analysis of Isaiah 56:9--57:21	91
Translation of Isaiah 56:9--57:21	91
I. Overview	94
A. Indications of Unity in Isaiah 56:9--57:21	94
B. Delimitation of the Strophes	101
II. Close Reading	109
A. Isaiah 56:9-12 -- Judgment upon Israel's Leaders	109
B. Isaiah 57:1-2 -- Peace for the Righteous	119
C. Isaiah 57:3-5 -- Mockery and Deception Against God	124
D. Isaiah 57:6 -- A Question of Inheritance	132
E. Isaiah 57:7-10 -- The Way of Harlot Israel: from the Heights to the Depths	137
F. Isaiah 57:11-13 -- A Threat and a Promise	142
G. Isaiah 57:14-19a -- The Way of God's People	147
H. Isaiah 57:19b-21 -- Peace for All but the Wicked	156
III. Application of a Literary Device to Isaiah 56:9--57:21	160
IV. Summary	171

TABLE OF CONTENTS

	Page
CHAPTER FOUR: A Rhetorical Analysis of Isaiah 58:1-14	173
Translation of Isaiah 58:1-14	173
I. Overview	175
A. Indications of Unity in Isaiah 58:1-14	175
B. Delimitation of the Strophes	186
II. Close Reading	191
A. Isaiah 58:1-4 -- Reasons for Judgment	191
B. Isaiah 58:5 -- A Question of Fasting on an Acceptable Day	200
C. Isaiah 58:6-9a -- A Fast the Lord Chooses	206
D. Isaiah 58:9b-12 -- The Way to Salvation	217
E. Isaiah 58:13-14 -- The Holy Day	225
III. Application of a Literary Device to Isaiah 58:1-14	232
IV. Summary	241
CHAPTER FIVE: A Rhetorical Analysis of Isaiah 59:1-20	243
Translation of Isaiah 59:1-20	243
I. Overview	245
A. Indications of Unity in Isaiah 59:1-20	245
B. Delimitation of the Strophes	252
II. Close Reading	257
A. Isaiah 59:1-3 -- Salvation Delayed	257
B. Isaiah 59:4-8 -- The Collapse of Righteousness and Justice	264
C. Isaiah 59:9-13 -- Lament and Confession	275
D. Isaiah 59:14 -- The Situation Reviewed	288
E. Isaiah 59:15-20 -- The Coming of the Redeemer	292
III. Application of a Literary Device to Isaiah 59:1-20	308
IV. Summary	316
CHAPTER SIX: Conclusions	321
I. Poetic Devices	321
II. The Thematic Structure of Isaiah 56-59	323
III. Motifs and Themes in Isaiah 56-59	328
A. Righteousness and Justice	328
B. The Ways of God and of Humanity	330
C. Transgression	332
D. Knowledge	333
E. The Lord who Sees	334
F. The Lord who Comes to Redeem	335
G. From Judgment to Salvation	336
BIBLIOGRAPHY	341
INDEX OF AUTHORS	353
INDEX OF BIBLICAL PASSAGES	355
INDEX OF RHETORICAL DEVICES AND SUBJECTS	359

ABBREVIATIONS OF BOOKS, JOURNALS, AND SERIES

BBET	Beiträge zur biblischen Exegese und Theologie
BDB	F. Brown, S.R. Driver, and C.A. Briggs, eds., A Hebrew and English Lexicon of the Old Testament. Oxford, 1907.
BJ	La bible de Jérusalem (édition 1975)
CE	Christian Education
GHB	P. Joüon, Grammaire de l'hébreu biblique, Rome, 1923 (cited by paragraph from the corrected reprint of 1965)
JNABI	Journal of the National Association of Biblical Instructors (later called, Journal of Bible and Religion)
JSOT	Journal for the Study of the Old Testament
JSOTSup	Journal for the Study of the Old Testament, Supplements
LingBib	Linguistica Biblica, Bonn
PNev	The Prophets (Nevi'im), Jewish Publication Society of America, Philadelphia, 1978 (second edition)
TWOT	R.L. Harris, ed., Theological Wordbook of the Old Testament, Chicago, 1980.
Zor	F. Zorrell and L. Semkowski, Lexicon hebraicum et aramaicum V.T., Rome, 1954.

All other abbreviations of books, journals, and series can be found in Instructions for Contributors to Biblica, 1982.

OTHER ABBREVIATIONS

Col(s).	-	Column(s)	Per.	-	Person
Fem.	-	Feminine	Pl.	-	Plural
Masc.	-	Masculine	Sing.	-	Singular
P. (Pp.)	-	Page (Pages)	Vol(s).	-	Volume(s)

TRANSLITERATION OF HEBREW CONSONANTS

' b g d h w z ḥ ṭ y k l m n s ᶜ p ṣ q r ś š t

The transliteration of Hebrew words gives the consonantal form of the MT except in instances where the vowels are necessary to exhibit sound patterns and where terminology is known in its full written form (as with rîb and hiphᶜil).

PREFACE

The recent trend toward appreciation of literary style and art in the biblical writings has encouraged the development of new methods; among these is rhetorical criticism. Literary critics have begun to ask new questions to understand how each of the books of the Bible stands as a composite whole, how their various parts form a single unity. What are the literary devices which help us comprehend how a text functions as a distinct whole? What are the conventions of style which link its various poems together? And what are the ways that motifs and themes appear as structural devices to show the cohesiveness of a book or collection? These questions are part of the investigative challenge facing those who employ rhetorical criticism in interpreting biblical texts. And it is these questions which this study undertakes in an attempt to better understand the poems of Isa 56-59. This work concentrates on demonstrating elements of Hebrew poetic style and discerning its function in the literary context. The results of analysis show that each of the poems in Isa 56-59 has a unique message but also that the collection of poems forms a structured literary division possessing unity of motifs and themes.

This present work is a slightly revised form of a doctoral dissertation presented to the Faculty of Theology of St. Paul's University, Ottawa, Canada, and defended on 14 November 1984. I wish to express appreciation and gratitude to Rev. Leo Laberge, O.M.I., who served as director of the study. His keen knowledge of the Hebrew Scriptures, his deep insight into the Isaian texts, and his ready availability for consultation have been a constant source of inspiration and encouragement throughout the period of research and writing. I also wish to thank my second reader, Rev. Jean-Pierre Prevost, S.M.M. His expertise and enthusiasm for careful biblical analysis and methodological procedure greatly aided in sharpening my focus, broadening my horizons, and creatively looking at the Hebrew text. A word of gratitude is extended to Rev. Anthony R. Ceresko, O.S.F.S., of the University of St. Michael's College, Toronto, with whom I discussed my project and who eventually served as the external reader of the dissertation. His insightful observations into the stylistics of Hebrew poetry aided in bringing greater clarity to the final draft of the study.

Finally, I wish to thank Rt. Rev. Jerome G. Hanus, O.S.B., Abbot of Conception Abbey who afforded me this opportunity for advanced study in Scripture; throughout this period of study his concern and encouragement have been a great support in bringing this work to completion. To my monastic community, family, students, and friends who have been so supportive, I owe a debt of deep gratitude.

Gregory J. Polan, O.S.B.

16 May 1985
Ascension Thursday
Conception Abbey
Conception, Missouri, U.S.A.

INTRODUCTION

The topic of "method" for the interpretation of biblical texts is becoming quickly the forum for lively debate. While any scientific investigation of biblical writings possesses a literary dimension, the instruments of research which are employed give direction to the kind of study that unfolds; and herein lies the material bringing serious minds into dialogue. Understandably, a variety of methods yields a variety of interpretations; involvement in establishing new and refining old approaches hints that the debate will leave few stones unturned.

Renewed interest in deciphering style, structure, and artistic technique in biblical writings is growing and the result is that new varieties of literary methods are developing. Among such approaches is rhetorical criticism. The fundamental tasks of this method call the critic to discern the limits of literary units according to stylistic devices, to demonstrate the various structural patterns shaping them, and to uncover the functions of diverse literary conventions as vehicles for conveying a message. One could say that the concerns of rhetorical criticism are not new, and this is true to a certain extent; commentators often allude to stylistic devices which aid in explaining a passage. But within the past one hundred years the exegesis of biblical texts has been geared in other directions, giving its rhetorical analysis a position of second place. Now with the recent emphasis on elucidating literary techniques, a discipline like rhetorical criticism is taking its place among other methods.

Rhetorical criticism is a literary approach that seeks to decipher the various techniques which structure a text and which aid in explaining its content.[1]

To note briefly Aristotle's classical notion of rhetoric as the power of persuasion is to note the purpose of a rhetorical study.[2] The discovery of literary conventions in a text assists the reader to see and to comprehend points of climax, relationships among words, and artistic techniques for conveying content. The stylistic manner in which the various devices intermingle and function constitutes a way of persuading the reader that this message is worthy of consideration; the rhetoric presents a captivating guise as an invitation to continue probing the contents of the writing. But the added challenge of this kind of examination takes on an archeological character when the quest is to unearth and to verify style and technique in an ancient literature. Recent studies show the sophisticated and elaborate literary conventions employed by ancient writers;[3] though much has been accomplished in this regard, the task of identifying the style and function of these conventions continues to puzzle and challenge scholars. T.S. Eliot's comments on the analysis of poetry take on added force when applied to biblical writings. He speaks of the interpretation of

---

1. Luis ALONSO SCHÖKEL, a pioneer in the recent resurgence of literary interests, stresses the relationship between structure and meaning. Cf. "Hermeneutical Problems of a Literary Study of the Bible," VTS 28 (1975) 2-7.

2. Cf. ARISTOTLE, Rhetoric (L. Copper, trans.; Englewood Cliffs, NJ: Prentice Hall, 1932) 1; Edwin BLACK, Rhetorical Criticism: A Study in Method (Madison, WI: University of Wisconsin Press, 1978) 10-19.

3. One recent study on chiasm shows its use in Ancient Greek, Roman, Sumerian, Akkadian, Ugaritic, Hebrew, and Aramaic literatures. Cf. John WELCH, ed., Chiasmus in Antiquity: Structures, Analyses, Exegesis (Hildesheim: Gerstenberg, 1981).

poetry as a "raid on the inarticulate."[4] Because of the constantly changing mediums of language and communication, critics are forced to understand qualities of expression once familiar, but now unfamiliar to them. This is true in the study of the Bible where early Hebrew stylistic devices differ considerably from those of the present. The already initiated task continues in probing the Scriptures to discover the mode of fashioning and conveying its contents.

Rhetorical criticism's principle of distinguishing literary units by means of their structural devices opens a door to solving the question of how some of the larger biblical writings like Isa, Jer, and Ezek are constructed. There are literary devices which show the beginning and end of a series of poems; these conventions in style give clues to understanding how a number of literary units are linked. Where the trend in research has been to define small segments of oral and written tradition, literary critics draw attention to the final product of the biblical editor who has shaped the collections of poems into a unified whole.[5] Recent studies show the search for larger units is taking two directions that complement each other. For example with the book of Isa, some exegetes are showing the unity of the corpus by means of themes and motifs which recur in similar patterns at strategic points throughout.[6] These

---

4. Cf. C.A. BODELSEN, T.S. Eliot's Four Quartets: A Commentary (Copenhagen, Denmark: Rosenkilde and Bagger, 1958) 16-20.

5. Cf. John F.A. SAWYER, "A Change of Emphasis in the Study of the Prophets," in Israel's Prophetic Tradition: Essays in Honor of Peter Ackroyd (R. Coggins et al., eds.; Cambridge: Cambridge University Press, 1982) 233-49.

6. Cf. R.E. CLEMENTS, "The Unity of the Book of Isaiah," Int 36 (1982) 117-29; L.J. LIEBREICH, "The Compilation of the Book of Isaiah," JQR 46 (1956) 259-77; JQR 47 (1957) 114-38; John F.A. SAWYER, From Moses to Patmos: New Perspectives in Old Testament Study (London: SPCK Press, 1977) 102-18.

observations suggest greater cohesion among the component parts of Isa and ask for greater literary and theological sensitivity in analysis. The other direction of research shows how poems function as a collection by means of their style, literary structure, genre, and echoing motifs.[7] Such investigations manifest the varied and numerous ways that Hebrew poetry strives to relate a message artistically, subtly, and forcefully. The prophetic books, sometimes viewed as a mélange of texts without order, are being investigated now from a different perspective in order to understand how they convey a message in their present form.

A growing interest in rhetorical criticism as a tool in biblical exegesis and a continuing search for the ways that the poetry in Isa can be delimited combine two subjects of timely interest. Arising from these topics of concern the purpose of this dissertation is twofold: 1) to apply rhetorical criticism to a section of the book of Isa in an attempt to uncover some of its literary devices; and 2) to show how these literary devices establish links within, between, and among the poems in question. The ultimate objective is to discover how the poetic techniques in a section of Isa function to convey its content, its unique message.

Chapter One addresses four topics which lay the groundwork for the study. The initial material presents two pioneers in the resurgence of literary

---

7. Cf. J. Cheryl EXUM, "Isaiah 28-32: A Literary Study," in SBL 1979 Seminar Papers, vol. 2 (P. Achtemeier, ed.; Missoula, MT: Scholars Press, 1979) 123-53; Y. GITTAY, Prophecy and Persuation: A Study of Isaiah 40-48 (Forum Theologiae Linguisticae 14; Bonn: Linguistica Biblica, 1981) see summary on pp. 229-35; L. LABERGE, "The Woe-Oracles of Isaiah 28-33," Église et Théologie 13 (1982) 157-90; W.R. Millar, Isaiah 24-27 and the Origin of Apocalyptic (HSM 11; Missoula, MT: Scholars Press, 1976) see summary on pp. 103-20.

interests in the Bible, James Muilenburg and Luis Alonso Schökel; noting the different facets of investigation they have fostered discloses their influence in having established the basic principles guiding various literary approaches today. The next section centers Isa 56-59 as the poems for analysis; based upon the few signs of unity noted by commentators and the meager rhetorical probing they have received, these chapters represent a textual environment awaiting further research; hence the appropriateness of the study. This is followed by a delimitation of the texts in question and a brief survey of recurring vocabulary which suggests some general signs of continuity among the poems. The Chapter concludes with an explanation of the procedure to be used in the rhetorical analysis.

Chapters Two through Five put rhetorical criticism into practice; each of these chapters discusses one of the defined literary units. In accord with the aims of rhetorical criticism, these Chapters demonstrate the stylistic devices which both structure the individual units and bind them together to form a unified section within Isa 56-66. While previous statements in this Introduction note the importance of discerning "larger units," it is important to stress that this principle applies not only to the collection of poems but also within each poem itself; without a sense of the integrity of each poem the search for coherence among the units would be a futile endeavor. In establishing the unique character of each poem as a unit the search for aspects of similarity among the ensemble follows on solid footing. These Chapters of analysis constitute the heart of the dissertation.

Chapter Six brings the work to a close in drawing several conclusions regarding the poetic style, thematic structure, and the motifs and themes which recur and demonstrate the unity of Isa 56-59. Brief in presentation, this final Chapter demonstrates some of the conclusions that can be drawn from the rhetorical analysis.

Each method of analysis has its limits; no method answers all questions posed to a text. Therefore it is wise to distinguish the restrictions of the method employed in this study. Diachronic exegesis aims to show the development of a text into a final form and to suggest a Sitz im Leben from which it emerges. Being essentially synchronic in nature, this study does not address either of these two questions. While acknowledging the importance of such diachronic inquiry, an investigation of the literary structures of Isa 56-59 isolates the question of stylistic technique allowing the researcher to follow a consistent line of study. While the choice of this method places a limit on the scope of an interpretation of the text, the same choice for one methodological approach presents a rigorous test for its value and potential. It is hoped that this study will exhibit new insights into the interpretation of Isa 56-59 and will encourage the employment of rhetorical criticism in other studies of the Bible.

CHAPTER ONE

PRELIMINARY CONSIDERATIONS

Four preliminary considerations are addressed in this chapter and stand as independent sections. First, rhetorical criticism is considered both in terms of its birth and growth, establishing the principles of the approach used in this study, and also in terms of the pioneers who have fostered a literary approach to the Bible. Second, the need for such a study and the issues at stake are reflected in a survey of what has been accomplished in published studies of Isa 56-66. Third, the context for the study is established by the delimitation of the section, its literary units, and the patterns and context of the recurring vocabulary. Finally, the method of analysis is laid out, specifying the approach used in the four chapters which follow.

I. THE BIRTH AND GROWTH OF RHETORICAL CRITICISM IN THE STUDY OF THE OLD TESTAMENT

Enormous strides have been made in the interpretation of the Bible within the past one-hundred-fifty years. Historical and scientific methods of the nineteenth century have greatly influenced the direction of biblical research.[1] Not only an appreciation for the historical background of a scriptural passage,

---

1. Cf. Ronald E. CLEMENTS, One Hundred Years of Old Testament Interpretation (Philadelphia: Westminster Press, 1976) 4; Martin KESSLER, "A Methodological Setting for Rhetorical Criticism," in Art and Meaning: Rhetoric in Biblical Literature (JSOTSup 19; David J.A. Clines, et al., eds.; Sheffield: JSOT Press, 1982) 9.

but also an interest in its stages of development have dominated the pursuits of research. Form and redaction critics have worked to show the stages of evolution and influence which brought a text to its final shape as found in the canon. Such a heavy concentration on historical questions led scholars to draw attention to the literary construction of prose and poetry of the Bible only as a secondary consideration; however, in the past fifty years reputable scholars have given more attention to specific literary concerns.[2] Even when their intention was not to stress style for its own sake, observations about literary construction sparked both enthusiasm and appreciation for the diverse elements which work together to heighten the impact of a passage. Stemming from this research, a slow but persistent interest has burgeoned into a lively appreciation for the sheer artistry found in the Hebrew Bible.[3]

In North America one of the pioneers of this approach is James Muilenburg. Early studies in literature left a discernible mark on his long career

---

2. Here one could list numerous scholars who, in addition to their historical-critical bent in research, also showed their literary awareness of biblical texts. To be brief here, suffice it to mention two authors. Cf. W.F. ALBRIGHT, "New Light on Early Canaanite Language and Literature," BASOR 46 (1932) 15-20; "The Song of Deborah in Light of Stylistics," VT 1 (1951) 168-80; C.C. TORREY, The Second Isaiah (New York: Charles Scribner's Sons, 1928) especially pp. 183-204.

3. One traces the roots of the modern understanding of the nature of biblical poetry back to Bishop Robert LOWTH in the publication of his Oxford lectures in 1753, De Sacra Poesi Hebraeorum Praelectiones Academicae. See also James MUILENBURG, "Poetry (Biblical Poetry)," Encyclopedia Judaica, vol. 13 (1971-72 ed.) col. 672. The roots for a modern understanding of biblical narrative were awakened only in the twentieth century with the contribution of Martin BUBER, "Leitwortstil in der Erzählung des Pentateuchs," in Die Schrift und ihre Verdeutschung (M. Buber and F. Rosenzweig, eds.; Berlin, 1936) especially pp. 211-38; and E. AUERBACH, Mimesis: The Representation of Reality in Western Literature (Princeton: Princeton University Press, 1953) especially pp. 7-30. For more background on the growth of rhetorical interest in the prose narrative, cf. S. BAR-EFRAT, "Some Observations on the Analysis of Structure in Biblical Narrative," VT 30 (1980) 154, 154 note 1.

as a biblical scholar, and his sensitivity to the literary quality of the Bible may be seen even in his earliest scholarship.[4] It was in his presidential address of 1969 to the Society of Biblical Literature that he adopted the name "rhetorical criticism."[5] Summarizing his results of over thirty years of study on Hebrew literary composition, he describes "rhetoric" in relation to the biblical text as the interworkings of stylistic devices and their functions within a particular literary context.[6] For Muilenburg, the main task of the rhetorical critic is to discover how a particular literary unit is fashioned by means of structural patterns. He insists that the biblical texts are filled with patterns, word repetitions, and verbal sequences that display the Hebrew literary style as sensitively skillful and richly artistic.[7] The work of the rhetorical critic is to reveal the many colored threads which weave the intricate workings of a biblical text into a rich tapestry.

Several articles have been written about the significance and implications of Muilenburg's presidential address.[8] Let it suffice here to

---

4. Cf. James MUILENBURG, "Teaching the Bible from the Literary Angle, " CE (Dec. 1924) 82-87; "The Literary Approach - The Old Testament as Hebrew Literature," JNABI 1, Part II (1933) 14-22; "The Literary Character of Isaiah 34," JBL 59 (1940) 339-65.

5. The 1969 presidential address of James MUILENBURG was published soon after. "Form Criticism and Beyond, " JBL 88 (1969) 8.

6. Cf. MUILENBURG, "Form Criticism," 8.

7. Cf. MUILENBURG, "Form Criticism," 18.

8. Cf. Bernhard W. ANDERSON, "The New Frontier of Rhetorical Criticism," in Rhetorical Criticism: Essays in Honor of James Muilenburg (Pittsburgh Theological Monograph Series 1; J.J. Jackson and M. Kessler, eds.; Pittsburgh: Pickwick Press, 1974) ix-xviii; Richard CLIFFORD, "Rhetorical Criticism in the Exegesis of Hebrew Poetry," in SBL 1980 Seminar Papers (Paul J. Achtemeier, ed.; Chico, CA: Scholars Press, 1980) 17-21; David GREENWOOD

mention two major points he stressed in that speech proposing the practice of rhetorical criticism.

First, Muilenburg calls for the delimitation of the literary unit.[9] Though such a concern may seem to be elementary and not particularly a novel consideration, he introduces here a new way of looking at the literary unit. The tendency of form and redaction critics is to isolate the smallest possible unit for investigation; but Muilenburg asks if what had been called "literary units" is not better understood as "strophes" which are part of a larger literary composition. He advances the idea that a Hebrew literary composition often has several points of climax; thus each of the smaller segments or strophes may be considered as part of a larger whole, which is what he calls a literary unit.[10] It is in appreciation of these distinct points of climax that one can understand the construction and development of the whole literary formulation in relation to its component parts. Muilenburg suggests two concrete ways of deciphering larger units: ballast or climactic lines, and inclusion.[11] But he also points out that not every literary composition is so concretely ordered. Devices of literary style such as shift in thought, motivation to some action, change of speaker or scene,

---

"Rhetorical Criticism and Formgeschichte: Some Methodological Considerations," JBL 89 (1970) 418-26; KESSLER, "A Methodological Setting," 4-5; Roy F. MELUGIN, "Muilenburg, Form Criticism, and Theological Exegesis," in Encounter with the Text: Form and History of the Hebrew Bible (Semeia Studies 8; Martin J. Buss, ed.; Philadelphia: Fortress Press, 1979) 9-10.

9. Cf. MUILENBURG, "Form Criticism," 8-9.

10. Cf. MUILENBURG, "Form Criticism," 9.

11. Cf. MUILENBURG, "Form Criticism," 9. The stylistic device of inclusion is also referred to as "ring composition"; cf. KESSLER, "A Methodological Setting," 4.

or change to a new meter can all be ways of concluding a literary unit. Muilenburg notes that a greater sensitivity to the literature is very important, especially since the more obvious literary devices were not employed by the Hebrew author.[12] Several recent works show the significance of this call for an appreciation of the larger units.[13]

Second, Muilenburg calls for a recognition of the various rhetorical devices which work together to demonstrate the sequence and development in the literary fabric of a passage.[14] He discusses the basic elements of Hebrew rhetoric: the different patterns of parallelism which are basic to understanding structure in Hebrew literary composition; the delimitation of strophes; the regular and irregular metric patterns; the repetition and ordering of vocabulary in both larger and smaller units; and the deictic and emphatic use of particles.[15] An awareness of these literary devices of the Bible enables the interpreter to step into the world of Hebrew rhetoric. For Muilenburg, these are the foundational elements that show the shape of a text and lead to its

---

12. CF. MUILENBURG, "Form Criticism," 9.

13. Cf. Francis I. ANDERSEN and David Noel FREEDMAN, Hosea: A New Translation with Introduction and Commentary (AB 24; Garden City, NY: Doubleday, 1980) 316; Joanna DEWEY, Markan Public Debate (SBLDS 48; Chico, CA; Scholars Press, 1980) 14-17; E.M. GOOD, "The Composition of Hosea," SEA 21 (1966) 21-63; William L. HOLLADAY, The Architecture of Jeremiah 1-20 (Lewisburg: Bucknell University Press, 1976) 17-20.

14. Cf. MUILENBURG, "Form Criticism," 10.

15. Cf. MUILENBURG, "Form Criticism," 10-17. Several of the points discussed by MUILENBURG in this part of his presidential address are explained with greater detail in some of his earlier articles. Cf. "A Study in Hebrew Rhetoric: Repetition and Style," VTS 1 (1953) 97-111; "The Linguistic and Rhetorical Usages of the Particle ky in the Old Testament," HUCA 32 (1961) 135-60.

interpretation.[16] It is also in the awareness of these devices and their functions that the beauty and artistry in the text is perceived; such an approach confirms the notion that an important part of the message is transmitted in the mode of expression.

Another scholar who has fostered a scholarly and enthusiastic approach to the Bible as literature is Luis Alonso Schökel, S.J. Like Muilenburg, he began pursuing biblical interests only after first completing studies in literature. His position as dean, vice-rector, and professor at the Pontifical Biblical Institute in Rome has augmented the range of his influence. Among his many contributions toward a rhetorical approach to the Bible, two stand out as having special significance.

First, at a time when Formanalyse and Gattungsanalyse were the mainstream for scholars' pursuits, Alonso Schökel questioned the exclusiveness of their quest to establish the Sitz im Leben. In a paper delivered at the third Congress of the International Organization for the study of the Old Testament, held at Oxford in 1959, he calls for a reexamination of the Gattungen of oracles; he urges that their placement in a particular literary context also be taken into consideration.[17] Alonso Schökel emphasizes that oracles once proclaimed in a particular setting may well have been altered when set down in their written shape, and then employed later for another context.[18] In their new context,

16. Cf. MUILENBURG, "Form Criticism," 10.

17. Cf. Luis ALONSO SCHÖKEL, "Die stilistische Analyse bei den Propheten," VTS 7 (1959) 154-64.

18. Cf. ALONSO SCHÖKEL, "Die stilistische Analyse," 162.

they have a "literary location" quite distinct from their original setting; Alonso Schökel thus calls for an awareness of an oracle's Sitz in der Literatur.[19] This insight gives rise to a new appreciation of genre analysis in the line of a rhetorical approach.[20] The awareness of Sitz in der Literatur encourages new perspectives toward literary types in the Bible, but also respects the text as it stands--while at the same time noting the author's creativity in its departures from and adherence to traditional structures.[21]

Second, Alonso Schökel is known for his comprehensive study of the stylistics of Hebrew poetry, Estudios de Poética Hebrea.[22] Containing the substance of his dissertation, this work is an analysis of stylistic features of the poetry in selected parts of Isa. It is expanded to include historical background on the research of each aspect of style discussed. What is accounted most significant by rhetorical critics is the systematic and scientific approach which

---

19. Cf. ALONSO SCHÖKEL, "Die stilistische Analyse," 162.

20. The following studies witness to the significance of Alonso Schökel's pioneering question into a fuller scope of genre analysis. ANDERSEN and FREEDMAN, Hosea, 315; Bernhard ANDERSON uses the terminology Sitz im Text in discussing this same issue in "The New Frontier," xiv-xv; J. Cheryl EXUM, "Of Broken Pots, Fluttering Birds, and Visions in the Night: Extended Simile and Poetic Technique in Isaiah," CBQ 43 (1981) 339; Douglas KNIGHT uses the term Sitz in der Rede in discussing the function of a literary genre other than the one of its original setting in "The Understanding of Sitz im Leben in Form Criticism," in SBL 1974 Seminar Papers (George MacRae, ed., Cambridge, MA: SBL, 1974) 108; MUILENBURG, "Form Criticism," 4-5; Wolfgang RICHTER, Exegese als Literaturwissenschaft: Entwurf einer altttestamentlichen Literaturtheorie und Methodologie (Göttingen: Vandenhoeck und Ruprecht, 1971) 149-52.

21. Cf. Roy F. MELUGIN, "The Conventional and the Creative in Isaiah's Judgment Oracles," CBQ 36 (1974) 301-11; Angelo PENNA, Isaia (La Sacra Bibbia 25; Torino: Marietti, 1964) 566.

22. Cf. Luis ALONSO SCHÖKEL, Estudios de Poética Hebrea (Barcelona: Juan Flors, 1963).

he brings to the analysis of Hebrew poetry.[23] Though it is twenty years since the publication of his contribution, no work to date systematically brings together the advancements in Hebrew poetry which have grown from his research and that of others.

Other authors who have contributed to the growth of rhetorical criticism could be enumerated. For the sake of brevity regarding the origins of rhetorical criticism, these two pioneers may be seen to represent the impetus behind much that has been contributed to this approach. The names of James Muilenburg and Luis Alonso Schökel represent two important figures in North America and Europe who have led the way by scholarly writing and enthusiastic probing of the topic.

A final consideration remains in this brief exposé of the development of a rhetorical approach to the Bible: how is rhetorical criticism distinct from the other biblical disciplines that have recently preceded it?

Each methodological approach to the Bible is distinguished by its particular treatment of a text. Form and redaction critics view the text as an entity which is a product of growth and influence over a period of time. Thus emphasis is placed on what lies behind the text in both oral and written stages of development. The process for interpretation is linked to the life setting(s) of the

---

23. Cf. Joseph BLENKINSOPP, "Stylistics of Old Testament Poetry," Bib 44 (1963) 357; GITTAY, Prophecy and Persuasion, 48 note 29; MUILENBURG, "Form Criticism," 7; RICHTER, Exegese, 23-24, 80-82.

text and the traditions which weighed on the intentions of the redactor. Form and redaction criticism are essentially diachronic approaches.

The rhetorical critic, accepting a text as it stands in a final form, seeks to discover the devices which fashion and the structures which establish a literary unit.[24] The focus of attention is directed toward a discernment of stylistic elements for "what a text says is inextricably bound up with how it says it."[25] Rhetorical criticism is essentially a synchronic approach.[26]

---

24. Cf. KESSLER, "A Methodological Setting," 10; MELUGIN, "Muilenburg, Form Criticism," 93; MUILENBURG, "Form Criticism," 8.

25. J. Cheryl EXUM, "Promise and Fulfillment: Narrative Art in Judges 13," JBL 99 (1980) 44. Cf. also, BAR-EFRAT, "Some Observations," 172; James BARR, "Reading the Bible as Literature," BJRL 56 (1973) 21-22, 32; David Noel FREEDMAN, "Pottery, Poetry, and Prophecy: An Essay on Biblical Poetry," JBL 96 (1977) 6-7; Isaac M. KIKAWADA, "Some Proposals for the Definition of Rhetorical Criticism," Semitics 5 (1977) 67; Bezalel PORTEN, "The Structure and Theme of the Solomon Narrative," HUCA 38 (1967) 95.

26. From the very outset of the establishment of rhetorical criticism as an independent approach to biblical interpretation, both Alonso Schökel and Muilenburg state that a literary study of the Bible is meant as a complement to form critical studies. Cf. ALONSO SCHÖKEL, "Die stilistische Analyse," 162; MUILENBURG, "Form Criticism," 18. This point is also emphasized by Bernhard W. ANDERSON, "Tradition and Scripture in the Community of Faith," JBL 100 (1981) 12. The direction which appears to be prevalent among rhetorical critics is that a rhetorical approach to biblical texts is, for the most part, a synchronic process. They view the biblical text in a final form as the work of an editor, one who gives it structure and shape; cf. DEWEY, Markan Public Debate, 18; EXUM, "Of Broken Pots," 331; Henry V.D. PARUNAK, Structural Studies in Ezekiel (Ann Arbor: University Microfilms International, 1979) 111. While rhetorical criticism should not be seen as a rejection of the historical criticism, neither should it be viewed as a subordinate method. Rather rhetorical criticism presents a methodological approach seeking to uncover how the biblical texts are structured and how their patterns demonstrate various means for interpretation. Scholars emphasize that diachronic and synchronic approaches are each distinct and legitimate means to biblical interpretation which, when applied to a text, exemplify integral aspects of that text's meaning. Cf. EXUM, "Of Broken Pots," 339 and note 32; KESSLER, "A Methodological Setting," 4, 12-14; Roger LAPOINTE, "Tradition and Language: The Import of Oral Expression," in Tradition and Theology in the Old Testament (Douglas A. Knight, ed.; Philadelphia: Fortress Press, 1977) 140-41; MELUGIN, "Muilenburg, Form Criticism," 92-96; Walter VOGELS, "Diachronic and Synchronic Studies of Hosea 1-3," BZ 28 (1984) 94-98.

Regardless of what method or approach one applies to a text, there are both values and limitations which accompany it.[27] There is no single method which can display total richness or fullness of message. However as one notes the expanding interest in articles which continue to appear in learned biblical journals, the growth of rhetorical criticism looks promising. Even those who continue to specialize in the historical-critical method urge that equal energies be spent in developing a literary approach to the biblical texts.[28] While the continued growth of rhetorical criticism is encouraged, the challenge of producing quality research will be the determining factor of its position in relation to other methods and approaches to biblical interpretation.

II. RECENT STUDIES OF ISAIAH 56-66

The commentary of Bernhard Duhm, Das Buch Jesaia (1892), set in motion a vigorous search for the delineation of "collections" within the sixty-six chapters of the Isaian corpus.[29] His own separation of Isa into three major "divisions"[30] (1-39, 40-55, 56-66) has, since the turn of the century, substantially

---

27. The values as well as the limitations of rhetorical criticism are noted by those who use the approach. For example, ANDERSEN and FREEDMAN admit that because they choose to work with a final text (MT) many of the problems brought up within Hosea itself remain unsolved by their approach; nonetheless, their literary method explains the texture of the poetry as it stands, itself a valid inquiry. They also comment that their choice of the MT is not a "blind veneration" for it, but a conviction that its poetry is not totally an unsolvable problem. Cf. Hosea, 66-67.

28. Cf. Walter BRUEGGEMANN and Douglas A. KNIGHT, "Why Study the Bible?" quoted in J. KSELMAN, "Design and Structure in Hebrew Poetry," in SBL 1980 Seminar Papers (P. Achtemeier, ed.; Chico, CA: Scholars Press, 1980) 12.

29. Cf. Bernhard DUHM, Das Buch Jesaia. Übersetzt und erklärt, 5. Auflage (Göttingen: Vandenhoeck und Ruprecht, 1922).

30. Unfortunately technical terms for the component parts of Hebrew poetry have not been standardized. For the purposes of this study, the

directed the research towards a solidification of this basic theory.[31] Current scholarly debate continues to discern even more precisely the various collections within 1-39, expanding upon the initial work of Duhm.[32] More recently, there are few who challenge the divisions 40-55 and 56-66.[33]

---

terminology employed here is set forth to avoid confusion in analysis. The sources for the following terms are two: PORTEN, "The Structure and Theme," 95 note 6, and Wilfred G.E. WATSON, "Chiastic Patterns in Biblical Hebrew Poetry," in Chiasmus in Antiquity: Structures, Analyses, Exegesis (John W. Welch, ed.; Hildesheim: Gerstenberg, 1981) 119-21. The following terms are ordered from the smallest to the largest.

1) word: the combination of letters which form an individual unit of thought;
2) colon: a single line of poetry, either standing alone or in parallel with another colon;
3) bicolon: two lines of verse, often made of two parallel cola; the bicolon is the standard unit of ancient Hebrew poetry;
4) tricolon: the formation of three cola functioning together;
5) strophe: the formation of cola and/or bicola and/or tricola bound together by similar motifs and structural patterns;
6) stanza: the combination of one or more strophes;
7) literary unit: the full complement of stanzas and/or strophes acting to display a homogeneous literary context;
8) section: the concert of literary units bound by structural patterns and/or similar themes and motifs;
9) division: the concert of sections bound together by structural patterns and/or similar themes and motifs;
10) literary whole: the concert of divisions bound together by structural patterns and/or similar themes and motifs.

31. A study of the trends which have developed since the theory of B. Duhm is presented in Jacques VERMEYLEN, Du prophète Isaïe à l'apocalyptique: Miroir d'un demi-millénaire d'expérience religieuse en Israël, t. 1 et 2 (Paris: J. Gabalda, 1977-78) 1-26, 451-54.

32. Cf. SAWYER, "A Change in Emphasis," 240-41.

33. One individual who challenges the division of 40-55 and 56-66 is A. MURTONEN, "Third Isaiah -- Yes or No?" Abrn 19 (1980-81) 20-42. In an extensive review of Karl Pauritsch's Die neue Gemeinde (cf. note 34), Murtonen argues that Isa 56-66 is part of the authorship of the same poet of Isa 40-55, but composed at a later time in three stages.

In comparison with Isa 1-39 and 40-55, 56-66 has gained less attention from authors.[34] Perhaps this is because of a past prejudice that there is a lack of coherence in 56-66.[35] As late as 1968 in the Anchor Bible commentary, J.L. McKenzie remarks on Isa 56:9-12, "There is no obvious connection between this poem and 56:1-8; in most of Third Isaiah the pieces are simply strung together."[36] Such statements leave the impression that the poems of the final division of Isa are a mélange of texts, brought together in a haphazard manner.

---

34. This is observable in comparing the number of works written on 40-55 to those on 56-66. Since 1970, two major studies (not including general commentaries on Isa 40-66) have appeared on 56-66: Paul D. HANSON, The Dawn of Apocalyptic, rev. ed. (Philadelphia: Fortress Press, 1979); and Karl PAURITSCH, Die neue Gemeinde: Gott sammelt Ausgestossene und Arme (AnBib 47; Rome: Biblical Institute Press, 1971). Since 1970, nine major studies have appeared on 40-55: Meindert DIJKSTRA, Gods Voorstelling, Predikatieve Expressie van Zelfopenbaring in Oudoosterse Teksten en Deutero-Jesaja (Dissertationes Neerlandicae, Series Theologica 2; Kampen: J.H. Kok, 1980); Pierre GRELOT, Les poèmes du Serviteur (LeDiv 103; Paris: Cerf, 1981); Klaus KIESOW, Exodustexte im Jesajabuch: Literarkritische und motivgeschichtliche Analysen (OBO 24; Fribourg: Editions Universitaires/Göttingen: Vandenhoeck und Ruprecht, 1979); Roy F. MELUGIN, The Formation of Isaiah 40-55 (BZAW 141; Berlin: Walter de Gruyter, 1976); Rosario Pius MERENDINO, Der Erste und der Letzte: Eine Untersuchung von Jes. 40-55 (VTS 31; Leiden: Brill, 1981); Antoon SCHOORS, I Am God, Your Savior: A Form-Critical Study of the Main Genres in Isa 40-48 (VTS 24; Leiden: Brill, 1973); H.C. SPYKERBOER, The Structure and Composition of Deutero-Isaiah (Meppel: Krips Repro. B.V., 1976); Carroll STUHLMUELLER, Creative Redemption in Deutero-Isaiah (AnBib 43; Rome: Biblical Institute Press, 1970); Jean M. VINCENT, Studien zur literarischen Eigenart und zur geistigen Heimat von Jesaja, Kap. 40-55 (Frankfurt: Peter Lang, 1977).

35. Cf. R. ABRAMOWSKI, "Zum literarischen Problem von Jes 56-66," TSK 96/97 (1925) 137; Karl BUDDE, Geschichte der althebräischen Literatur (Leipzig: C.F. Amelangs Verlag, 1906) 176-83; Jacques MARTY, Les chapitres 56-66 du livre d'Isaïe (Paris: P. Geuthner, 1924) xxiii, 170; James MUILENBURG, "The Book of Isaiah, Chapters 40-66," in IB 5 (Nashville, TN: Abingdon Press, 1956) 414; Artur WEISER, Einleitung in das alte Testament (Stuttgart: W. Kohlhammer, 1939) 166-68.

36. Cf. John L. McKENZIE, Second Isaiah: Introduction, Translation, and Notes (AB 20; Garden City, NY: Doubleday, 1968) 154.

More recently two significant studies of Isa 56-66 have emerged, both arguing for the thematic unity of the collection. First, the study of Karl Pauritsch, Die neue Gemeinde, explains how these final chapters of Isa reinterpret the message of Isa 40-55 for the postexilic community of Jerusalem. Pauritsch argues that the Lord's special care reaches out to the lowly because their needs are not met by Israel's covenant community. The poor experience injustice and outsiders rejection, and yet the house of Jacob wonders why the Lord delays his redemptive coming. Pauritsch calls Isa 56-66 a "prophetic awakening book" fostering belief for the lowly and conversion for the unrighteous.[37] Dividing his study into two parts, he first gives the Literarkritik, Formanalyse, and Gattungsanalyse of the twelve literary units; here he presents the historical-critical research since Duhm and furthers this study with his own insights. In the second part he discusses the Sitz im Leben of the individual units, the recurring theological themes, and the redactional origins of the collection. In his theological reflections he notes the different conceptions of God brought out in the poetry and offers an extended exposé on the power of God's message spoken in the postexilic situation.

Second, Paul Hanson's The Dawn of Apocalyptic reconstructs the Sitz im Leben of Isa 56-66 around the irreconcilable differences between hierocratic and visionary groups within the postexilic Israelite community. But more importantly, he shows the outgrowth of the apocalyptic spirit emerging from the prophetic tradition instead of from later Persian influence. Hanson describes his methodology as "contextual typological": the driving concern to establish the

---

37. Cf. PAURITSCH, Die neue Gemeinde, especially pp. 250-52.

context probes the texts to discover the conflicts which gave rise to the writings; the typologies include a consideration of the poetic structure of the strophes, metrical patterns, genre analysis, and various eschatological themes.[38] Hanson's study argues for the integrity of 56-66 by the recurring themes manifesting the interplay between judgment and salvation language as the key which unlocks the situation behind these chapters.[39] Both authors are primarily concerned with historical-critical questions; while displaying a sensitivity to literary concerns, this is not the focus of their attention.

A structural plan for Isa 56-66 was first set forth by Etienne Charpentier.[40] He demonstrates a concentric structure which places Isa 61 at the midpoint, complemented by recurring parallel themes. Though he does not give an explanation for this pattern, close observation shows not only repeated themes, but vocabulary as well.[41] The diagram on page 15 presents his concentric design of Isa 56-66. Since Charpentier's observation on the over-all

38. Cf. HANSON, The Dawn of Apocalyptic, for a brief summary, pp. 209-11.

39. Cf. HANSON, The Dawn of Apocalyptic, 111, 143-44, 187.

40. Cf. Etienne CHARPENTIER, Jeunesse du Vieux Testament (Paris: Fayard, 1963) 79-80.

41. The recurrence of vocabulary in the corresponding parallel poems is demonstrated by P.-E. BONNARD, Le Second Isaïe, son disciple et leurs éditeurs: Isaïe 40-66 (Paris: J. Gabalda, 1972) 317-18; and Rémi LACK, La symbolique du livre d'Isaïe: Essai sur l'image littéraire comme élément de structuration (AnBib 59; Rome: Biblical Institute Press, 1973) 128, 130.

CHARPENTIER'S CONCENTRIC DESIGN OF ISA 56-66

(A) 56:1-8 - Conditions for the entrance to the People of God

(B) 56:9--58 - Reproaches to the wicked; promises to the faithful

(C) 59:1-14 - Two psalms and confession of sin

(D) 59:15-20 - Divine Vengeance

(E) 60:1-22 - The New Jerusalem, fiancée of God

(F) 61:1-11 - The announcement of messianic times. The Spirit of the Lord is upon me.

(E') 62:1-12 - The New Jerusalem, fiancée of God

(D') 63:1-6 - Divine Vengeance

(C') 63:7--64:11 - Two psalms and confession of sin

(B') 65:1--66:17 - Reproaches to the wicked; promises to the faithful

(A') 66:18-24 - Conditions for the entrance to the People of God

structure of Isa 56-66, Raymond Tournay,[42] P.-E. Bonnard,[43] and Rémi Lack[44] have expanded on or modified it according to their particular methodological approaches. Thus the discovery of a concentric design by Charpentier and others

---

42. Cf. Raymond TOURNAY, review of Das Buch Jesaja, Kap. 40-66, by Claus Westermann, in RB 74 (1967) 120-21.

43. Cf. BONNARD, Le Second Isaïe, 318.

44. R. LACK'S concentric design shows similarities to those of Charpentier and Bonnard, but his approach should be recognized as different. While acknowledging a chiastic organization with repeated vocabulary, he also distinguishes anthropological and literary structures; herein Lack specifies complementary sections of semantic fields in Isa 56-58 and 65-66 called "exode sur place" and in 59-64 called "justice et salut." Cf. La symbolique, 125-32.

brings further argumentation for the integrity of the final eleven chapters of Isa based on a literary structure.

Though not always employing a rhetorical method, certain commentators attempt to show how poetic units within Isa 56-66 are joined by repeated vocabulary, motifs and themes. Many distinguish the units in 60-62 as a section, linked by their similar literary style, metric regularity, and redemption themes.[45] A rhetorical study by Fredrick Holmgren expands the limits of 60-62 to include 63:1-6.[46] Also, some call attention to the lament of 63:7--64:11 (MT) and its reply in 65 to the question concluding the prayer;[47] in addition, repeated

---

45. Cf. BONNARD, Le Second Isaïe, 327, 400; Georg FOHRER, Das Buch Jesaja, 3. Band (Zürich: Zwingli Verlag, 1965) 226, 235, 240; MUILENBURG, "The Book of Isaiah," 697; PAURITSCH, Die neue Gemeinde, 103-106, 221; PENNA, Isaia, 599-601; Claus WESTERMANN, Isaiah 40-66 (David M.G. Stalker, trans.; Old Testament Library; Philadelphia: Westminster Press, 1969) 296-98; R.N. WHYBRAY, Isaiah 40-66 (New Century Bible; London: Oliphants, 1975) 229.

It is not the intention of this study to give a complete history of what all commentators since Duhm have said on the poetry of Isa 56-66, but rather to show the more recent trends of interpretation. For that reason, commentaries published since 1950 are utilized; many of these more recent studies explain the interpretations of earlier exegetes and credit their accomplishments. Though the earlier commentaries are cited when applicable, those given in the first half of this note are used most often in this study.

46. Cf. Fredrick HOLMGREN, "Yahweh the Avenger, Isaiah 63:1-6," in Rhetorical Criticism: Essays in Honor of James Muilenburg (Pittsburgh Theological Monograph Series 1; J.J. Jackson and M. Kessler, eds.; Pittsburgh: Pickwick Press, 1974) 133-48. The placement of Isa 63:1-6 has puzzled scholars, wondering if it functions in relation to what precedes or follows it.

47. The first commentator who clearly joins Isa 63:7--64:11 with 65 is Aage BENTZEN, emphasizing a liturgical context for the "question (64:11) - answer (65:1ff)" literary device. Cf. Introduction to the Old Testament, vol. 2 (Copenhagen: G.E.C. Gads, 1948-49) 108. More recent exegetes also note the literary connection between the question-answer device; while not all discuss the larger unit of 63:7--65 with the enthusiasm of Bentzen, they note the stylistic device linking the units together. See BONNARD, Le Second Isaïe, 462,63; FOHRER, Das Buch Jesaja, 257; HANSON, The Dawn of Apocalyptic, 79-81; PAURITSCH, Die neue Gemeinde, 171-72, 222-23; MUILENBURG, "The Book of

vocabulary fosters a sense of unity in 63:7--65.[48] Despite the attempts to encourage the reading of larger sections like 60-62, 60:1--63:6, and 63:7--65, very little has been done to define the remaining material in 56-59.

This brief survey shows that recent exegesis of Isa 56-66, though limited, argues for the integrity of these chapters as a division within the book of Isa. Beyond this, authors point out literary devices which link poems together into sections, exhibiting signs of greater unity within the division. However, only meager attempts surface when trying to discern the inner workings of 56-59.

Rhetorical criticism remains an open avenue for pursuing the question of the literary context and function of Isa 56-59. One of the key functions of a rhetorical approach is to search out the devices which determine the extent of literary units, sections, and divisions so as to discover "how" a text displays its network of interrelating elements.[49] Since no recent attempts have been made to apply this approach to 56-59, the task awaits to be accomplished.

III. DELIMITATION OF THE TEXT AND ITS VOCABULARY PATTERNS

A. Delimitation of the Section and Literary Units

The analysis of any text begins with a consideration of its limits,

---

Isaiah," 744-45; John J. SCULLION, Isaiah 40-66 (Old Testament Message 12; Wilmington, DE: Michael Glazier, 1982) 199-200.

48. Cf. BONNARD, Le Second Isaïe, 462 note 1.

49. Cf. ANDERSEN and FREEDMAN, Hosea, 314; KIKAWADA, "Some Proposals," 67; MUILENBURG, "Form Criticism," 9-10; SAWYER, "A Change in Emphasis," 240-42.

where it begins and ends. A determination regarding the extent of a text's limits depends upon the scientific approach employed. The form critic seeks to discover the smallest possible unit of oral transmission that eventually developed into a written statement. In contrast, a rhetorical approach first looks for the signs that might indicate limits for divisions or sections, and from there moves to establish its component parts.

It has already been noted that 60-62, 60:1--63:6, and 63:7--65 are considered by some commentators as sections within the division of Isa 56-66. The question remaining is whether there are ways of understanding how 56-59 functions in its literary context.

One of the means of establishing the limits of a literary unit, a section, or a division is the rhetorical device of inclusion. Specialists in the study of Hebrew scriptures also point out "distant parallelism" as another device for limiting and uniting literary structures.[50] Distant parallelism is based on the principle that paired words are also able to bring about a sense of inclusion.[51]

---

50. Cf. M.J. DAHOOD and T. PENAR, "Ugaritic-Hebrew Parallel Pairs," in Ras Shamra Parallels, vol. 1 (L.R. Fischer, ed.; AnOr 49; Rome: Biblical Institute Press, 1972) 80. See also Adele BERLIN, "Grammatical Aspects of Biblical Parallelism," HUCA 50 (1979) 17-43; Anthony R. CERESKO, "A Poetic Analysis of Ps 105, with Attention to Its Use of Irony," Bib 64 (1983) 27,35,42; Job 29-31 in the Light of Northwest Semitic: A Translation and Philological Commentary (BibOr 36; Rome: Biblical Institute Press, 1980) 242; William H. IRWIN, Isaiah 28-33: A Translation and Philological Commentary (BibOr 30; Rome: Biblical Institute Press, 1977) 172-73; Shemaryahu TALMON, "The Textual Study of the Bible - A New Outlook," in Qumran and the History of the Biblical Text (Frank M. Cross and Shemaryahu Talmon, eds.; Cambridge, MA: Harvard University Press, 1975) 358; William R. WATTERS, Formula Criticism and the Poetry of the Old Testament (BZAW 138; Berlin:Walther de Gruyter, 1976) 42, 60-80.

51. Cf. DAHOOD, "Ugaritic-Hebrew Parallel Pairs," 80.

The established device of inclusion demonstrates a writer's or editor's propensity for uniting the beginning and end of units or sections in a distinct way.[52] While adhering to the principle that, for the ancient Hebrew writers, repetition is a means of expressing emphasis, continuity, and wholeness,[53] distant parallelism similarly functions as a device demonstrating unity, progression of thought, and stress.[54]

Such an example of distant parallelism and inclusion is found in 56:1b and 59:20a:

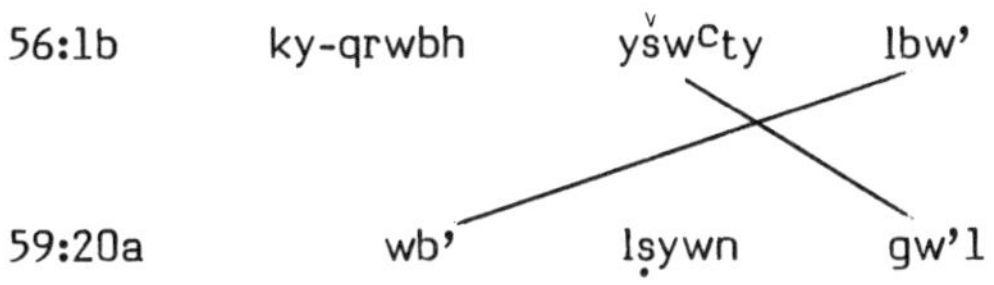

Several points demonstrate the strength of this device in this context. First, the repetition of the root bw' in the literary context is consistent in meaning. In 56:1b, the announcement is made that "soon" (qrwbh) God's salvation is to arrive (lbw'); in 56:1a, the call for just and righteous living is a warning that God's salvation would soon break in upon those being addressed. In 59:20a, the announcement of God's coming is again reiterated. But in 59:20a, the use of bw' is given added strength as a waw consecutive perfect, which refers back to the action which precedes.[55] The verb to which it refers back in 59:19b is the same

---

52. Cf. TALMON, "The Textual Study," 358.

53. Cf MUILENBURG, "A Study in Hebrew Rhetoric," 98-99.

54. Cf. TALMON, "The Textual Study," 358.

55. Cf. GKC, 330 §112a.

verbal root, bw'. Thus the emphasis on God's salvific coming, initially announced in 56:1b, is repeated with force in 59:19b, 20a.

Second, there is also the employment of the parallel roots yšᶜ//g'l in 56:1b and 59:20a respectively.[56] The uses of these words in their individual contexts exhibit a similarity in thought; both examples are concerned with an aspect of a deliverance which comes to those who practice just and right deeds. In 56:1-2, the announcement of a forthcoming deliverance is couched amid admonitions to act righteously; but importantly, the call to such observance is founded on the understanding that God's salvation is at hand (56:1b).[57] In 59:20 the proclamation of God's advent is accompanied by the reminder that the Redeemer comes to those who turn away sin in their lives. Preceding this in 59:18, a description of God's recompense (šlm, twice) according to their deeds (gml, thrice) also highlights the relationship between "observance" and the "approaching salvation." Thus the announcement of God's salvific coming (yšwᶜty, 56:1b) and his arrival as Redeemer (gw'l, 59:20a) are linked to the actions and deeds of those being addressed.

Third, the repeated and parallel terms are inverted in a chiastic fashion. In examples of distant chiastic parallelism, S. Talmon suggests the possibility that literary inversion may intend to exhibit some kind of reversal in the movement of the text;[58] the literary inversion may serve to point out a

---

56. Isa offers several examples of the parallel pair yšᶜ//g'l at 49:26; 60:16; 63:9.

57. Cf. John J. SCULLION, "ṢEDEQ-ṢEDAQAH in Isaiah cc. 40-66," UF 3 (1971) 342.

58. Cf. TALMON, "The Textual Study," 360.

change or development in the contents of the textual material framed by this device. A closer look at the grammatical structure facilitates an appreciation of what is happening in the inverted distant parallelism. In 56:1b, the use of the participle (qrwbh) plus the infinitive (lbw') indicates a sense of duration;[59] the import of the verbal structure indicates that God's salvation is about to happen soon, is coming near. While in 59:19b-20a the imperfect (ybw') and waw consecutive perfect (wb') indicate an action of progressive duration,[60] the sense conveys that God continues to draw near and now is coming to Zion as the redeeming one. Though it remains difficult to discern the use of the imperfect and waw consecutive perfect, the use of a participle in 59:19bb (nssh is in the same bicolon with ybw') could serve to favor a translation of the verb to the present tense in English. Also the use of the emphatic particle ky in 59:19b breaks the consecutive relation with the preceding verb in 59:19a, which is in the imperfect (wyyr'w), and is probably best translated by the English future tense. Thus a sense of movement and development is brought out in the grammatical syntax of the inverted parallelism: the initial announcement of God's "soon to happen" arrival in 56:1b is reiterated in 59:19b-20a, but is now presented as the progressive and present coming of God as Redeemer to those who turn away transgression. The development of this emphasis on "the Lord's coming" is taken one step further in the new section which begins at 60:1; here the section begins with the statement that the people's light (an image of salvation, cf. Isa 58:8) has already come (b'; prophetic perfect).[61] The eleven uses of the root bw' in 60:1-

59. Cf. GKC, 315 §107d.

60. Cf. GKC, 315 §107d.

61. Cf. MUILENBURG, "The Book of Isaiah," 698.

22 witness to a new development of thought begun in 56:1 and completed in 59:20: it is because of the Lord's salvific coming (b' ; 60:1) that all peoples will now come (from the root bw' ; cf. 60:4,4,5,6,9,11,13,17,17,20) to Israel, the City of the Lord.[62]

The example of distant parallelism in 56:1b and 59:20 is only an initial beginning to the study of 56-59 as a section in the division 56-66. By itself, the example of distant parallelism only isolates a conjectured beginning and end to a section; the significance of this device can only be rightly examined in relation to the continuing attempt to discover if the theme of God's salvific coming is supported by the structure of the literary units and the motifs found therein. Thus the distant parallelism should not be considered the sole element defining the limits of this section; rather it offers an initial step toward such delimitation. The study now procedes to the delimitation of the literary units of 56:1--59:20.

First Literary Unit. Isa 56:1,8 are marked by typical expressions of beginning and conclusion: kh 'mr YHWH (Thus says the Lord, v. 1) and n'm 'dny YHWH (an oracle of the Lord God, v. 8). The formula kh 'mr YHWH, followed by the twofold imperative, represents a strong initial statement for this unit and section calling for the practice of justice and righteousness. Vv. 1,8 are also linked by a distant parallelism with lbw'//mqbṣ, showing the Lord's salvific action in his coming to and gathering of the people.[63] Commentators call 56:1-8

---

62. Cf. MUILENBURG, "The Book of Isaiah," 697.

63. Isa has several examples of bw'//qbṣ as parallels at 43:5; 49:18; 60:4; 66:18.

a literary unit bound by the motifs of sabbath observance (vv. 2,4,6), foreigners and eunuchs invited to become part of the Israelite community (vv. 3,4,6), and the Lord's promises to those who observe his decrees (vv. 2,5,7,8).[64]

56:1-8 is separated from what comes before it in 55:12-13 by a change in the tone of the language. According to Muilenburg, 55:12-13 forms the perfect climax to the whole of 55, while 55:1-13 serves as an inclusion to 40:1-11.[65] This is supported by an emphasis on God's word (dbr, cf. 40:8; 55:10-11) and the new exodus vocabulary and imagery (cf. 40:3-5; 55:12-13). The words of comfort in 55:12-13 change in 56:1-2 to instruction and admonition.[66] Three terms distinguishing motifs in 56:1-8 are not found in the preceding section 40-55: šbt (sabbath; 56:2,4,6; cf. also 58:13,13; 66:23); nkr (foreigner; 56:3,6; cf. also 60:10; 61:5; 62:8); srys (eunuch; 56:3,4). These words represent motifs particular to 56-66, also separating 56:1-8 from what precedes.

56:1-8 is separated from what follows it in 56:9ff by a striking change in tone and an absence of repeated or similar vocabulary. The instructive and promise-oriented language of 56:1-8 gives way to harsh words of condemnation and judgment in 56:9-12. Thus, 56:1-8 stands apart from what precedes and follows it, and is distinct in its motifs of sabbath, foreigners, and eunuchs.

---

64. Cf. BONNARD, Le Second Isaïe, 343-44; FOHRER, Das Buch Jesaja, 185-87; HANSON, The Dawn of Apocalyptic, 388; MUILENBURG, "The Book of Isaiah," 652-53; PAURITSCH, Die neue Gemeinde, 31-32; WESTERMANN, Isaiah 40-66, 315-16; WHYBRAY, Isaiah 40-66, 196.

65. Cf. MUILENBURG, "The Book of Isaiah," 650-51.

66. Cf. WESTERMANN, Isaiah 40-66, 310.

Second Literary Unit. How to delimit the literary unit beginning at 56:9 is a divided question among commentators. The majority distinguish two literary units for the final verses of 56 and all of 57: 56:9--57:13 and 57:14-21.[67] Their reasons for this division are based on the difference in both thematic material (judgment in 56:9--57:13 and salvation in 57:14-21) and in literary style (terse in 56:9--57:13 while expansive and repetitive in 57:14-21). A smaller group of commentators suggests one literary unit: 56:9--57:21.[68] Their position is based on a literary pattern of antithesis which divides the unit into three parts.[69] 56:9--57:1 is a denunciation of the lack of proper leadership among the leaders of Israel, while 57:2 changes to a promise of peace for the righteous. 57:3-13b decries the ways of and punishment for idolatrous practices, while 57:13c pledges the inheritances of the land and God's holy mountain to those who trust in him. 57:14-19 proclaims the gifts of redemption, while 57:20-21 presents a threat to the wicked.

In addition to the above literary characteristics showing the unity of

---

67. Cf. FOHRER, Das Buch Jesaja, 190-91; HANSON, The Dawn of Apocalyptic, 77-78, 187; PAURITSCH, Die neue Gemeinde, 52, 62, 66, 72, 219-20; VERMEYLEN, Du prophète Isaie, 458-59, 461-62; WESTERMANN, Isaiah 40-66, 302; WHYBRAY, Isaiah 40-66, 199-200. For a commentator who chooses 56:9--57:13 as a literary unit, but hints at a larger unit, cf. MUILENBURG, "The Book of Isaiah," 659-60, 670.

68. Cf. BONNARD, Le Second Isaïe, 367; W.H. IRWIN, " 'The Smooth Stones of the Wady'? Isaiah 57:6," CBQ 29 (1967) 32 note 11; PENNA, Isaia, 565-66; TORREY, The Second Isaiah, 429-30. Also TOB makes special reference to the literary unity of 56:9--57:21 on p. 864 note (b).

69. Although L. ALONSO SCHÖKEL does not call 56:9--57:21 a literary unit, he hints this in his remarks about the antithetical patterns of the literary context; cf. "Isaias III," in Profetas I: Introducciones y comentario (L. Alonso Schökel and J.L. Sicre Diaz, eds.; Madrid: Ediciones Cristiandad, 1980) 354; cf. also BONNARD, Le Second Isaïe, 325-26; IRWIN, "The Smooth Stones," 32 note 11; TOB, 864 note (b).

56:9--57:21, the verb ykl (to be able) serves as an inclusion, found at the beginning (56:10b) and the end (57:20a) of the unit. In 56:10b ykl describes the watchmen of Israel as dumb dogs, unable to bark (l' ywklw lnbḥ); in 57:20a the same verb portrays the wicked as the tumultuous sea, unable to rest (ky hšqṭ l' ywkl). Both examples demonstrate the incapacities of the leaders and the wicked ones.

The repetition of bṣc (covetousness) in 56:11c and 57:17a also unites the beginning and end of the unit. In 56:11c, the shepherds are accused of turning in their own ways, the way of avarice (lbṣcw). In 57:17a, it is the avarice (bṣcw) of the people which angers the Lord and causes him to strike them. The significance of bṣc in this context is heightened by the fact that these are the only two times it appears in the whole of Isa. The uses of this term here center the motif of avarice or covetousness in this context. Thus, the three patterns of antithesis, the inclusion with ykl, and the contextual uses and placements of bṣc all work together to support the literary unity of 56:9--57:21.

Third Literary Unit. The delimitation of 58 has been generally marked by a tendency to view the literary unit as 58:1-12 and to disregard 58:13-14 as unrelated thematic material about the sabbath.[70] However, an appreciation for the marks of a literary structuring of the text reveals an

70. Cf. FOHRER, Das Buch Jesaja, 212; HANSON, The Dawn of Apocalyptic, 101; Leslie J. HOPPE, "Isaiah 58:1-12, Fasting and Idolatry," BTB 13 (1983) 45; Hans KOSMALA, "The Form and Structure of Isaiah 58," ASTI 5 (1967) 69, 79-80; PAURITSCH, Die neue Gemeinde, 73,221; VERMEYLEN, Du prophète Isaïe, 465; WESTERMANN, Isaiah 40-66, 340.

inclusion marking the limits of the literary unit.[71] The references to yᶜqb (Jacob) in 58:1,14 frame the passage. In 58:1, the command is given to declare to the house of Jacob (wlbyt yᶜqb) their sins, while 58:14b closes with a promise that God will feed them with the inheritance of Jacob (nḥlt yᶜqb). Also the final colon in 58:14bb contains a solemn expression of conclusion, ky py YHWH dbr (for the mouth of the Lord has spoken).

Fourth Literary Unit. The unity of 59:1-20 is attested to by the majority of recent commentators.[72] 59:1 opens with an unresolved question regarding God's power to save and willingness to hear the people's plea. It is not until 59:19-20 that a resolution is reached when the announcement of God's coming is made. This is further strengthened by an example of distant parallelism in 59:1,20 with yšᶜ//g'l;[73] in 59:1, the question is asked whether the hand of the Lord is too short to save (mhwšyᶜ), while in 59:20 it is announced that he will come to Zion as its Redeemer (gw'l). The movement of the poem begins with an inquiry into the absence of God's saving power toward his people and concludes with the announcement of his arrival as the redeeming one. 59:20 concludes with a traditional way of ending an oracle, n'm YHWH.

---

71. Cf. Elizabeth ACHTEMEIER, The Community and Message of Isaiah 56-66: A Theological Commentary (Minneapolis: Augsburg Publishing House, 1982) 59-60: MUILENBURG, "The Book of Isaiah," 677.

72. Cf. BONNARD, Le Second Isaïe, 326-27, 395-96; FOHRER, Das Buch Jesaja, 223 note 32; HANSON, The Dawn of Apocalyptic, 113; MUILENBURG, "The Book of Isaiah," 686; PAURITSCH, Die neue Gemeinde, 94; VERMEYLEN, Du prophète Isaïe, 471; WESTERMANN, Isaiah 40-66, 345, 352.

73. Cf. note 56.

The verse which follows in 59:21 stands apart from what precedes by virtue of its break with the poetic rhythm and a change to the first per. sing. characteristic of this poem's movement or style.[74] The progression of the text from a search for salvation in 59:1 to the coming of the Redeemer in 59:20, coupled with the distant parallelism in 59:1,20 (yšᶜ//g'l), supports the establishment of 59:1-20 as a literary unit.

By means of inclusion, distant parallelism, repeated vocabulary, and literary patterns, the process of defining Isa 56-59 and its component units is begun. Noting these devices only sets in motion the initial stage of analysis, but nonetheless defines the parameters of the study. 56:1--59:20 is thus divided into four literary units: 56:1-8, 56:9--57:21, 58:1-14, and 59:1-20.

B. Selected Patterns of Repeated Vocabulary in Isaiah 56:1--59:20

A final consideration remains in the establishment of 56:1--59:20 as a literary unit: an analysis of patterns of repeated vocabulary. It is James Muilenburg who emphasizes the importance of the repetition of words in a literary context when analyzing Hebrew literature. In doing this he accentuates the synthetic character of biblical literature by demonstrating how it seeks to center motifs and themes by means of repetition, to express totality in recurring significant words, and to show movement and stress more clearly by recalling vocabulary at the significant points in the narrative or poem.[75] Apart from this

---

74. Some commentators view 59:21 as a "bridge" between 59 and 60, or a way of summarizing the theme of covenant; cf. MUILENBURG, "The Book of Isaiah," 696; PAURITSCH, Die neue Gemeinde, 94; SCULLION, Isaiah 40-66, 168-69. What remains consistent among these various views is that 59:21 does not belong to the poetry of 59:1-20.

75. MUILENBURG, "A Study in Hebrew Rhetoric," 99.

rhetorical device, single uses of vocabulary and unique expressions in a literary context provide an avenue for discovering vehicles of creative expression.

A word of caution is necessary. The fact that words reappear in each of the literary units does not signify a unity among them; rather, when a repeated word remains consistent in meaning or expands a similar motif then a chain of thought between the passages is established. The following consideration of selected patterns of vocabulary attempts a bird's-eye view of some of the more obvious and easily explained word repetitions demonstrating a similarity in their different literary contexts. The discovery of such affinities gives rise to the possibility that certain motifs are repeated, thus pointing to a sense of continuity among the literary units.[76] The explanations which here compare the words in their contexts are intended to be brief and painted with broad strokes; however, even such an overview can help point out the motifs which weave their way through the literary units and constitute links binding the passages together. The intention here is simply to demonstrate patterns of vocabulary in support of the sections and literary units as this study proposes them.

---

76. A study of Jonathan MAGONET on the book of Jonah verifies the importance of repeated words for defining and encapsulating larger literary units. Cf. Form and Meaning: Studies in Literary Techniques in the Book of Jonah (BBET 2; Bern: Herbert Lang, 1976) 13-22.

In literary studies of the biblical writings, authors often easily interchange the terms "motif" and "theme." In this study I distinguish between them. "Themes" refers to the principal elements of unity in the poem, while "motifs" refers to the various ideas which, in concert with one another, establish the themes. For example, the motifs of "the Lord's guidance, comfort, and protection" may work together as a theme of "salvation." Distinguishing between motifs and themes helps in defining the main signs of unity in the poems.

The following words are found in at least three of the four literary units of 56:1--59:20. The radicals of the verbs are listed according to their appearance in the section.

Word	56:1-8	56:9--57:21	58:1-14	59:1-20
1) špṭ (to judge)	56:1		58:2,2	59:4,8,9,11, 14,15
2) ṣdq (to be righteous)	56:1,1	57:1,1,12	58:2,2,8	59:4,9,14, 16,17
3) bw' (to come)	56:1,7	57:2	58:7	59:14,19,20
4) yd^{c} (to know)		56:10,11,11	58:2,3	59:8,8,12
5) drk (to step)		56:11; 57:10, 14,14,17,18	58:2,13	59:8,8
6) pš^{c} (to transgress)		57:4	58:1	59:12,12, 13,20
7) šwb (to turn)		57:17	58:12,13	59:20
8) r'h (to see)		57:18	58:3,7	59:15,16

The root špṭ appears nine times in the context of 56:1--59:20; eight of these occurrences are as a noun (mšpṭ), most often translated "justice." The word first appears in the opening verse of the section at 56:1 in parallel with ṣdqh; the pair mšpṭ//ṣdqh appears five other times in the section (cf. 58:2a,2b; 59:4a,9a,14a). The initial use of mšpṭ is in a context calling for the observance of justice (56:1a). The remaining eight occurrences point out that justice is not practiced. In 58:2b,2c God announces that the house of Jacob seeks him like a nation (kgwy) which does not forsake justice, asking for righteous judgments; however, the description of the people's wicked deeds shows that justice is lacking. The use of _'yn_ with _mšpṭ_ in 59:4,8,11,15 repeats like a refrain through 59 that there is no justice. In metaphorically describing the downfall of virtue, justice is said to be both far off (59:9) and turned away (59:14) from the people. Thus a consistent motif, initiated by a call to practice justice (56:1), continues throughout the section with a description of its absence.

Forms of the root _ṣdq_ appear thirteen times in 56:1--59:20. In 56:1, _ṣdqh_ appears twice, each time with a different parallel noun. As already mentioned in the consideration of _mšpṭ_, outside of 56:1a _ṣdqh_ appears five other times with _mšpṭ_ as its parallel, in which contexts the usual translation of _ṣdqh_ is "righteousness." As has been shown in its use with _mšpṭ_, the examples where the parallel terms are found together convey a sense that the practice of righteousness is lacking (58:2a,2b; 59:4,9,14). A similar use of _ṣdqh_ is found in 57:12 where the parallel words _ṣdqtk//mcśyk_ are used in a rhetorical question aimed at exposing a lack of righteous actions. The double use of _hṣdyq_ in 57:1,1 refers to the person who practices righteousness and walks in uprightness (_hlk nkḥw_, 57:2), an image of the _ṣdyq_ standing in sharp contrast to the irresponsible leaders of Israel discussed in 56:9-12. In 56:1b, _ṣdqty_ is parallel to the noun _yšwcty_, and the salvific sense which is conveyed in its parallel noun encourages the translation of _ṣdqh_ in this context as "deliverance."[77] In that bicolon the particle _ky_ tells why justice should be observed: because the Lord's salvation and deliverance are soon to be revealed. It can also be observed that the parallel words of 56:1b (_yšwcty//ṣdqty_) are also found twice as pairs in 59:16b,17a. The sense of _ṣdqh_ in 56:1b is brought out well in the imagery describing the Divine

---

77. Cf. SCULLION, "_ṢEDEQ-ṢEDAQAH_," 342.

Warrior: his own arm brings him salvation and his deliverance (wṣdqtw; 59:16b) upholds him, while he clothes himself in a breastplate of deliverance (ṣdqh; 59:17a) and a helmet of salvation. In 58:8, the use of ṣdqk bears a close resemblance to the idea of God's deliverance and saving presence.[78] The imagery of a grand procession for the new exodus is employed to show God's deliverance (ṣdqk) leading those who fast authentically, according to the Lord's instructions, with the glory of the Lord (kbwd YHWH) as their rear protector (cf. similar imagery in Isa 52:12; Ex 14:19). Thus the two uses of ṣdqh in 56:1a,1b serve as a guide for understanding the twofold use of the word in 56:1--59:20: the call to practice righteousness in 56:1a displays both the exercise of righteousness (57:1) and its lack (57:12; 58:2; 59:4,9,14); the announcement of God's approaching deliverance in 56:1b is explained in the imagery of both the new exodus of 58:8 and the Divine Warrior (59:16,17).

The root ydᶜ is found eight times in three of the literary units. Its striking feature is its employment with the negative l' six out of eight times (56:10,11,11; 58:3; 59:8,8); such a frequent repetition fosters the understanding that a "lack of knowledge" constitutes a motif. Deficiency of knowledge is first attributed to the leaders of Israel (56:10,11,11), but then the people accuse God of being without a knowledge of their acts of humiliation (58:3). In 58:2a, the reference to the people's delight in knowing God's ways (wdᶜt drky) is countermanded in 58:2b by the use of kgwy (like a people) to suggest that they are not who they claim to be; the truth is that they lack a knowledge of God's ways.[79] In 59:12b, the people acknowledge their sinfulness (wᶜwntynw ydᶜnwm);

---

78. Cf. SCULLION, "ṢEDEQ-ṢEDAQAH," 343.

79. Cf. SCULLION, "ṢEDEQ-ṢEDAQAH," 343.

thus there is a consistent motif of a "lack of knowledge" in the use of *yd*^{c} except in 59:12 where the people admit to their transgressions.

Like *yd*^{c}, *drk* appears in the second, third, and fourth literary units. The word is used ten times, nine in the noun form, best translated as "a way." The contexts of *drk* exhibit a similar meaning expressing a *modus operandi*. The literary contexts show that there are directions of behavior which lead to God's judgment and anger (56:11; 57:10,17,18; 59:8,8) and likewise to salvation and blessing (57:14,14; 58:13). In 58:2 *drky* expresses God's inclination to act in a certain manner, as if the divinity also has a *modus operandi*; God remarks that the people take pleasure in believing they know how he functions or operates. As the recurrences of *drk* distinguish between the paths to judgment or salvation, they also identify the ways of humanity as distinct from those of the divinity.

The root *pš*^{c} occurs six times in the final three literary units. In 57:4, it expresses a sense of the deep-rooted nature of sin which is in the people being addressed; it refers to them as "children of transgression" (*yldy-pš*^{c}), a sinfulness inherited from their ancestors. In 58:1, the literary unit begins with the appeal to declare to the people their transgression after which the text proceeds to explain their wrong-doing. Emphatic placement at the beginning of the passage demonstrates its importance and suggests the motif that will follow in the succeeding lines. In 59:12,12,13, the triple uses of the word in such close proximity center the motif of "transgression" in the midst of a confession of sinfulness. The significance of *pš*^{c} is underscored again by its use in the last line of the literary unit, which is also the last line of the section (59:20), here recalling that the Redeemer comes to those who turn away pšᶜ. Though used only six times, pšᶜ is employed with emphasis and is found in strategic places.

The uses of šwb reflect the choice one makes in following one's own will toward sin (57:17; 58:13) or walking in the ways of God (58:12; 59:20).[80] From what is already presented, the contexts where šwb appears echo the similar motif with drk where one's actions lead toward judgment or salvation. The closing verse of the section (59:20) reflects this, announcing that the Redeemer comes to Zion to those turning away sin (wlšby pšᶜ).

Of the five uses of r'h, four have reference to God. In 57:18 and 59:15,16, God sees a situation in need of reform and reacts with redemptive power to transform it: in 57:18 the Lord brings healing, and in 59:16 his own arm brings salvation and deliverance. In 58:3, God is accused by the people of not seeing (wl' r'yt) their practice of fasting. The other use of this word in 58:7 gives an admonition; after the people's complaint, they are told to cover the naked person when they see him (tr'h). The connection between the two uses of r'h in 58 presents an interesting reversal: as they complain that God does not see their fasting, they are told in response to keep their eyes open so as to see the needs of another individual and to care for that need. Those who accuse God of not seeing are themselves dimsighted.

---

80. At first sight, the example of 58:12 is obscure; further discussion of it follows in Chapter Four, pp. 222-23.

It has already been shown that bw' is used consistently in 56:1 and 59:19,20, relating to the Lord's coming.[81] Also in the opening literary unit, 56:7 explains that the Lord will bring (whby'wtym) to his holy mountain those foreigners who hold fast to the covenant; the hiphᶜîl of bw' shows God's mercy in opening his special place to outsiders, and what is more God will bring them there. Similarly in 58:7 the hiphᶜîl of bw' appears again with the Lord commanding the house of Jacob to bring (tby') the wandering humbled ones into their home. As YHWH opens his house of prayer in kindness to foreigners, so are his people to open their house to those in need. There are two further repetitions of bw' in 57:2 and 59:14. At 57:2 the righteous person is described as entering (ybw') into peace. Elaborating in a metaphorical manner on the collapse of virtue among the people, 59:14 declares that uprightness is unable to enter (lbw') the public square. Neither instance of bw' appears related to those previously noted; the uses of bw' in 57:2 and 59:14 are considered further in the close reading of the literary units. However, the uses of bw' in 58:7 and 59:19,20 are redolent of the motifs related to the Lord's salvific coming in 56:1,7.

Although the above considerations of patterns of repeated vocabulary are brief and broadly sketched, the words show a relatively similar sense as found in their literary contexts. Thus, the consistent use of recurring words considered above demonstrates some of the motifs which are present within 56:1--59:20 and argues for its unity as a section within 56-66.

---

81. This is explained on pp. 19-22.

D. A METHOD FOR ANALYSIS

Analysis of each of the literary units may now be discussed in the light of three facets of a rhetorical approach: 1) Overview of the literary unit, 2) Close Reading of the individual strophes, and 3) application of a literary device to the unit;[82] finally, a "summary" notes the major findings of the rhetorical analysis. This formal analysis of the literary units constitutes Chapters Two through Five. Chapter Six completes the study with conclusions drawn from the discussion of the biblical texts and methodology; here also the theological motifs and themes of Isa 56-59 are presented.

Preceding each chapter of analysis is a translation of the literary unit based on the MT.[83] To highlight the major inclusion of a literary unit the repeated words or distant parallels appear in italics. To emphasize the repetitions within each literary unit, repeated words are given in capital letters; the important repetitions between literary units are underscored. Consider the following verses as an example.

---

82. The terms "Overview" and "Close Reading" are used by Jerome WALSH in his analysis of the prayer of Jonah; cf. "Jonah 2:3-10: A Rhetorical Critical Study," Bib 63 (1982) 219. Following a similar procedure in analysis, A. CERESKO uses the terms "macrostructure" and "microstructure" as a similar means of designating the larger and smaller structural elements; cf. "A Poetic Analysis," 24, 29. And J. Kenneth KUNTZ employs a related approach in a twofold study of Isa 51:1-16 with "the poem as a whole" and "analysis of individual strophes;" cf. "The Contribution of Rhetorical Criticism to Understanding Isaiah 51:1-16," in Art and Meaning: Rhetoric in Biblical Literature (JSOTSup 19; David J.A. Clines, et al., eds.; Sheffield: JSOT Press, 1982) 143, 151.

83. The translation of Isa 56-59 presented here is prepared by the author of this study; texts other than Isa 56-59 are taken from the RSV unless otherwise indicated.

56:1 THUS SAYS THE LORD:
KEEP justice and PRACTICE RIGHTEOUSNESS,
For soon is my salvation to *COME*
and my DELIVERANCE to be revealed.

The verb "*COME*" forms an inclusion with "*GATHERS*" in 56:8. The expression "THUS SAYS THE LORD" and the verbs "KEEP" and "PRACTICE" are repeated in this literary unit (56:1-8); the words "RIGHTEOUSNESS" and "DELIVERANCE" (both from the root ṣdqh) are repeated in this literary unit and also are important in at least one other context in 56-59. The words "justice" and "salvation" are significant elsewhere in 56-59 and their employment here establishes links within the section. As much as is possible for a correct rendering of the vocabulary, the same word is used to translate a Hebrew root. For example, among the different expressions for "sinfulness," pšᶜ is consistently translated "transgression," ḥṭ' is "sin," and ᶜwn is "perversity." The reason for such consistency is to alert the reader to the recurrence of Hebrew roots and expressions in the translation. But where a single root can have two meanings (as ṣdqh in 56:1 as "righteousness" and "deliverance"), a translation according to the literary context prevails. Also the Hebrew word order is retained as much as possible. Such an approach tends to stifle the English poetic style and rhythm; this limitation is acknowledged. However, highlighting repeated words and their ordering enables one to more clearly discern the structural elements of the MT in an English translation.

Overview. The Overview of the literary unit involves two steps. The first is to note the signals which argue for the integrity of the literary unit. Examples of repeated phrases and vocabulary, inclusions, distant parallelism, and examples of recurring literary techniques place in relief the elements which work together in a wider context. The second step discerns the strophes of the literary unit. Muilenburg defines a strophe as "a series of bicola or tricola with a particular beginning and a particular close, possessing unity of thought, structure, and style."[84] Thus the delimiting of the strophes displays the thought-units and exhibits the manner in which the literary unit is constructed. The patterning of motifs, repetitions of vocabulary, and the various grammatical and syntactic styles all work together in defining the strophes.

Close Reading. Close Reading of the strophes involves a study of the varied structural patterns in their local setting (the strophe). Different techniques of assonance, various kinds of parallelism, patterns of repetition, metric stability or change, and other poetic devices as well work together to deepen the interpretation already begun in the establishment of the strophes.[85] These smaller structural patterns are sometimes referred to by rhetorical critics as "microstructures";[86] a close reading shows how the various microstructures interact with each other.[87] The close reading also discusses vocabulary in the strophe which is repeated in other literary units of the section, establishing a

---

84. Cf. MUILENBURG, "Poetry (Biblical Poetry)," col. 675.

85. One might well ask whether there can be a clear line of distinction between the structural patterns discussed in the "overview" and those in the "close reading." Charles CONROY alludes to this question when he notes that there can be overlapping of the descriptions of structural patterns. Cf. Absalom, Absalom! Narrative and Language in 2 Sam 13-20 (AnBib 81; Rome: Biblical Institute Press, 1978) 93.

86. Cf. CERESKO, "A Poetic Analysis," 6; CONROY, Absalom, Absalom, 93; KESSLER, "A Methodological Setting," 4-5; KSELMAN, "Design and Structure in Hebrew Poetry," 2.

87. Cf. Stephen ULLMANN, Language and Style: Collected Papers (Oxford: B. Blackwell, 1964) 127.

network of ties among the poems of 56-59.[88] Despite the emphasis on repetition, unique stylistic features and vocabulary are also a part of deciphering the macrostructures.[89] The concert of various literary devices working together as components constitutes the texture and fiber of the literary unit, the parts in union with the whole.[90]

Application of a Literary Device to a Unit. Findings from an overview and close reading are brought to bear on the discernment of a literary device or pattern for a reading of the unit. Rhetorical critics are quick to point out that the structures found in literary units are particular; variety and creativity in the patterning of structural devices are the trademark of Hebrew poetry.[91] At the very heart of the rhetorical approach is an openness to what the text itself reveals; its analysis tries to uncover the shape of a literary unit as a singular expression.[92] It is in the very process of gathering data and analyzing it that one comes to discover patterns in a text. There are numerous ways the

---

88. At times the repeated vocabulary can indicate links with the larger division of Isa 56-66, or the whole 1-66. These ties are also important to note because 56-59 is only one segment of a larger editorial composition, the book of Isa. Cf. ANDERSEN and FREEDMAN, Hosea, 119-20, 133-34; MAGONET, Form and Meaning, 13.

89. Cf. ANDERSEN and FREEDMAN, Hosea, 138; HOLLADAY, The Architecture of Jeremiah, 21.

90. Cf. KESSLER, "A Methodological Setting," 4-5.

91. Cf. MELUGIN, "Muilenburg, Form Criticism," 93-94.

92. HOLLADAY writes, "[. . .] one cannot be at all sure what to look for when he embarks upon a search for shape or structure [. . .] it is simply not possible to specify in detail the kinds of signs to look for by which one may establish structure. [. . .] for rhetorical criticism analyzes what is unique and distinctive about a given unit of material, and therefore a description of its rhetorical form must inevitably proceed inductively, on the basis of the specificities before us." Cf. The Architecture of Jeremiah, 20-21.

patterns can be discerned. Somewhat common are concentric designs in which points of relationships are established at the beginning and end of the literary unit; from there other relational elements converge in an ordered way until they arrive at a point of focus in the passage, generally in the middle. However, biblical poets shaped their texts by numerous other devices; a few examples include balanced parallelism, chiasm, the use of imagery, antithesis, and wordplay.[93] It is also important to note that often more than one structural pattern can be at play in one literary unit.[94] This final step of the rhetorical analysis will demonstrate one literary device for the reading of the passage.

Interpretation of biblical texts according to a rhetorical method has grown in the past fifteen years.[95] The method is yet young and needs time for further verification of devices as structures in ancient poetry. F. I. Andersen and D. N. Freedman emphasize that their study of Hosea, grounded in the search for literary devices, is an "approach" to the text and not a "provable conclusion."[96] They set out with the presupposition that the fourteen chapters of the prophet are a literary composition, a finished product of an editor. Their

---

93. Cf. Bonnie P. KITTEL, The Hymns of Qumran: Translation and Commentary (SBLDS 50; Chico, CA: Scholars Press, 1981) 28-29.

94. On the subject of "overlapping" or "superimposed" structures, cf. CERESKO, "A Poetic Analysis," 39-44.

95. In addition to the works already cited, the following can also be considered. Lawrence BOADT, Ezekiel's Oracles Against Egypt: A Literary and Philological Study (BibOr 37; Rome: Biblical Institute Press, 1980); Georg BRAULIK, Die Mittel deuteronomischer Rhetorik: Erhoben aus Deuteronomium 4:1-40 (AnBib 68; Rome: Biblical Institute Press 1978); Jack R. LUNDBOM, Jeremiah: A Study in Ancient Hebrew Rhetoric (SBLDS 18; Missoula, MT: Scholars Press, 1975).

96. Cf. ANDERSEN and FREEDMAN, Hosea, 316.

task is to discover the literary texture of the MT which they have before them. Despite the limitations which any method has when applied to a text, the task of those trying to discern the structural patterns of the ancient Hebrew writings is still one of discovery, trial and error, and probing; guidelines for the practice of rhetorical analysis are still being formed. In *The Design of Poetry*, Charles B. Wheeler writes,

> Where do the rules of interpretation come from? No single authority. Rules are developed through trial and error as readers confront typical problems. Whatever method produces valid results is duly recognized as worthy of adoption for future use, but it takes a great many successful applications of a given method to turn it into anything like a rule. By combining a large number of these cases according to the features they have in common, we can see a pattern of judgment at work, and this pattern can then be used as a guide for future decisions.[97]

Acknowledging its limitations, it is hoped that this rhetorical study of Isa 56-59 makes a modest contribution to the on-going work in rhetorical criticism and research in Isaiah. This present work does not claim to be exhaustive in pointing out literary devices, but simply attempts to show structural elements which argue for the integrity of the text under consideration.

And finally, a method so heavily centered on the question of structure naturally raises the question: was so subtle a pattern in the mind of the Hebrew poet, or are rhetorical critics engaging in artistic eisegesis? Answers could be varied; however, the careful and discerning application of stylistic analysis to the poetry of the Bible continues to justify greater

---

97. Charles B. WHEELER, *The Design of Poetry* (New York: W.W. Norton, 1966) 267-68.

appreciation for the sensitivity of the Hebrew author. C. H. Whitman confirms the skill and subtlety which characterize the poetry of ancient civilizations:

> The human mind is a strange organ, and one which perceives many things without conscious or articulate knowledge of them, and responds to them with emotions necessarily and appropriately vague. An audience hence might feel more symmetry than it could possibly analyze or describe. The second point is that poets sometimes perform feats of virtuosity for their own sakes and without much hope of understanding from their audiences, for one of the minor joys of artistic creation is the secret which the artist buries in his work, the beauty (if such indeed it be) which he has deliberately concealed amid the beauties which he has tried to reveal and express.[98]

Rhetorical critics admit that much is still uncertain about the numerous and varied ways the Hebrew poets structured their oral and written language. The quest for better mining techniques to unearth the riches of the Bible's poetry continues; the challenge remains great but the treasures produced thus far promise a satisfying reward.

---

98. C.H. WHITMAN, Homer and the Heroic Tradition, quoted in KSELMAN, "Design and Structure," 11.

CHAPTER TWO

A RHETORICAL ANALYSIS OF ISAIAH 56:1-8

Translation of Isaiah 56:1-8

1 THUS SAYS THE LORD:
KEEP justice and PRACTICE RIGHTEOUSNESS,
For soon is my salvation to *COME*
and my DELIVERANCE to be revealed.
2 Blessed is the person who DOES this,
and the individual who HOLDS FAST to it:
KEEPING the SABBATH, NOT PROFANING IT
and KEEPING his HAND from DOING any evil.

3 INDEED, LET NOT THE FOREIGNER SAY,
the one who JOINS HIMSELF to the LORD SAY:
"Surely the LORD will separate me from his PEOPLE."
And INDEED, LET NOT THE EUNUCH SAY:
"Behold, I am a withered tree."
4 For THUS SAYS THE LORD:
To the EUNUCHS who KEEP my SABBATHS,
choose that in which I am pleased,
that is, HOLDING FAST MY COVENANT,
5 I will PLACE for them within my HOUSE,
and even within my walls a NAME-MONUMENT,
better than sons and daughters,
An EVERLASTING NAME I will PLACE upon it,
which will not be cut-off.
6 Also the FOREIGNERS who JOIN THEMSELVES to the LORD
to minister to him, to love the NAME of the LORD,
and to be his servants,
ALL KEEPING the SABBATH, NOT PROFANING IT,
that is, HOLDING FAST MY COVENANT,
7 I will BRING them to my holy mountain,
I will make them joyful in my HOUSE OF PRAYER;
Their burnt offerings and their SACRIFICES
will be acceptable upon my SACRIFICIAL ALTAR,
For my HOUSE, a HOUSE OF PRAYER it shall be called for
ALL PEOPLES.

8 An oracle of the LORD God,
who *GATHERS* the outcasts of Israel:
"Others I will *GATHER* to him, unto his *GATHERED* ones."

I. OVERVIEW

A. Indications of Unity in Isaiah 56:1-8

The occurrences of word repetition in 56:1-8 are numerous despite its short span of eight verses. Attention is given first to the vocabulary which links motifs in the wider context of the poem by means of repetition. Each of the following five words appears at least three times in vv. 1-8: *YHWH* (the Lord), *šmr* (to keep), *ᶜśh* (to do, to practice), *ḥzq* (to hold fast), and *šbt* (the sabbath).

The divine name *YHWH* recurs seven times (vv. 1a,3a,3b,4a,6a,6b,8a) and can be viewed from two perspectives. First, *YHWH* appears three times in the context of speech formulas common to the prophetic writings: *kh ʼmr YHWH* (vv. 1a,4a) and *nʼm ʼdny YHWH* (v. 8a). These repetitions are a reminder that it is God's word which is given;[1] structurally, the literary unit is framed by the affirmation that this message comes from the Lord.[2] A fuller expression of the divine name in v. 8a concludes the unit (*ʼdny YHWH*), giving emphasis to the

---

1. WESTERMANN's research on the expression *kh ʼmr YHWH* as a "messenger formula" identifies the word of the prophet as the word of God; cf. *Basic Forms of Prophetic Speech* (H.C. White, trans.; Philadelphia: Westminster Press, 1967) 93-95. See also, PAURITSCH, *Die neue Gemeinde*, 49.

2. MUILENBURG explains how different forms of the divine name often serve as structural elements in limiting a unit or strophe; cf. "A Study in Hebrew Rhetoric," 106.

final verse. The usual placement of n'm YHWY is at the very end of a verse (cf. Isa 3:15; 19:4; 54:17; 59:20) while here it is at the beginning of v. 8 and it is immediately followed by a colon which even lengthens the description of the speaker (mqbṣ ndḥy yśr'l) portraying him as the one who gathers. This departure from the usual manner of concluding draws attention both to God's message of assurance and to the Lord God who will bring his words to fulfillment.

Second, the other repetitions of YHWH express a motif of unity between God and his people. In 56:3ab the foreigner is described as one who joins himself to the Lord (hnlwh 'l-YHWH). Following this description of v. 3a, a word of contrast appears in v. 3b; whereas v. 3a speaks of "joining" (lwh), v. 3b speaks of "separating" (bdl). The opposing words are both posited in relation to YHWH; but note that the foreigner who joins himself to the Lord should not say (w'l-y'mr) that the Lord will separate him from his people. The impact of the unity in the contrasting words is further stressed by ᶜmw (his people) in v. 3b; the joining of oneself to the Lord implies oneness with his people. The expression of union with the Lord in v. 3a is repeated in v. 6a (hnlwym ᶜl-YHWH), recalling and emphasizing the motif. This somewhat vague concept of "joining oneself to the Lord" is then explained in v. 6a by a series of three infinitives; among these manifestations of avowal in v. 6b, "to love the name of the Lord" is given. Here the divine name ('t-šm YHWH) once more appears in a context in which oneness with God is expressed, and further clarified with a vocabulary of intimacy (wl'hbh, to love) and service (lšrtw, to minister to him).[3]

---

3. G. WALLIS notes that in 56:6 the two ideas of "love" and "action/service" are brought together to describe those who faithfully follow Yahweh. Cf. "'hb," TDOT 1, 106.

Both the literary contexts, with the words of assurance from Yahweh and the expressions of unity, witness to a God bound close to the life of his people.

A key word occurring five times is šmr (vv. 1a,2ba,2bb,4b,6c). Following the messenger formula is v. 1a, šmrw initiates the literaty unit on a note of command: keep justice. This placement of šmrw in v. 1ab, then followed by four more uses of the verb, shows that it functions as a "signpost" of an important motif;[4] the immediate command to "keep justice" sets in motion a "call to observance" which unfolds in various ways in the poem. The three occurrences of šmr in tandem with šbt demonstrate the importance of keeping the sabbath (vv. 2ba,4b,6c) as a primary concern. Also, šmr appears twice with cśh in vv. 1ab,2bb. These words in concert express a positive and a negative admonition, calling for the practice of justice (v. 1ab) and the desistance from evil (v. 2bb). Together these words in their respective cola distinguish two ways of observance: what one should do (v. 1ab) and what one should refrain from doing (v. 2bb). And finally, beyond the repetition of the verb itself, the theme of observance is underscored in the different exhortations to choose what is pleasing to God (v. 4b), to minister to him, to love his name, to become his servants (v. 6b), and to hold fast to the covenant (vv. 4c,6c). In noting this theme and its consistent recurrence in 56:1-8, one remembers that this is the opening poem of 56-66. Rhetorical critics draw attention to the significance of the opening literary unit of a section or division to introduce the key themes

4. G. BRAULIK discusses a similar use of šmr in Deut 4 where, beginning the chapter, it initiates a key idea that is repeated several times; the subsequent repetitions reinforce this initial motif. Cf. Die Mittel, 88-89.

which guide the movement of subsequent chapters.[5] The implication of the call to observe what God commands will only be better appreciated as the analysis of the subsequent literary units unfolds.

Located in the opening verses, ^c^śh recurs three times (vv. 1a,2a,2b). As noted in the previous paragraph, ^c^śh appears twice with šmr, in vv. 1ab,2bb, supporting the twofold call to do right and to avoid evil. The other occurrence is in v. 2aa, showing that a share in "blessedness" depends on a particular way of acting, of performing a specific action (y^c^śh-z't): v. 2aa continues the emphasis given to observing what God commands. Both šmr and ^c^śh recur three times in the opening two verses, displaying a sense of symmetry in highlighting the theme.

The verb ḥzq appears three times (vv. 2a,4c,6c) and each occurrence is in the hiph^c^îl. The hiph^c^îl's causative sense is sometimes employed with verbs which express the receiving of a concrete or abstract quality;[6] thus "causing one to be strong" is expressed in the qualitative action of "holding fast" to something, remaining firm in its practice. With this in mind, the macarism of v. 2a grows in intensity with the progression of the bicolon's reading: Blessed is the person who does (y^c^śh) this, / and the individual who holds fast (yḥzyq) to it.

---

5. J. Cheryl EXUM discusses the importance of Isa 28 in the interpretation of the collection Isa 28-32; cf. "Whom Will He Teach Knowledge?: A Literary Study of Isa 28-32," in Art and Meaning: Rhetoric in Biblical Literature (JSOTSup 19; David J.A. Clines, et al., eds.; Sheffield: JSOT Press, 1982) 133-35. MUILENBURG notes the importance of Isa 40:1-11 as an opening poem to 40-55 in his comments on 55:1-13; cf. "The Book of Isaiah," 642.

6. Cf. GKC, 144 §53c,f. Gesenius specifies ḥzq as one of these verbs.

The thought pattern moves beyond mere "practice" to an expression of qualitative observance marked by a tenacious fidelity. The other two uses of ḥzq (vv. 4c,6c) are exact repetitions occurring with bryty (my covenant). The use of the hiphcîl coupled with the placement of wmḥzyqym bbryty at the conclusion of the exhortations of vv. 4,6 highlights the call to the foreigners and eunuchs for faithful adherence to God's covenant.[7] In the occurrences of ḥzq, the call to "hold fast" addresses a general audience explaining the way to be counted among the blessed (v. 2a), and a particular audience of eunuchs and foreigners inviting them to embrace the observance of God's covenant (vv. 4c,6c). The extremes of the general and the particular addresses show the expansive invitation of God to live in fidelity to his word; this quality of faithful adherence is a prerequisite to sharing in blessedness (v. 2a) and God's promises (vv. 5,7). A consistent progression of thought for ḥzq carries through the literary unit: a general address of intense concern for holding fast to the exhortations of v. 2, and a more specific concern for adherence to the covenant is given to the eunuchs and foreigners in vv. 4,6.

The three uses of šbt, consistently in tandem with šmr (vv. 2b,4b,6c), focus attention on observance of the sabbath; even the recurring sibilant sound of the s in both words forms an alliteration stressing the motif.

v. 2b) šmr šbt mḥllw

v. 4b) yšmrw 't-šbtwty

v. 6c) kl-šmr šbt mḥllw

---

7. M. WEINFELD notes that this is the only time this expression appears as a way to describe adherence to the covenant. Cf. "bryt," TDOT 2, 261.

Several observations can be made about the literary contexts in which šbt appears. First, vv. 2b,6c are very similar, marked by an almost word-for-word repetition in the cola where they appear. Likewise their literary contexts are similar in addressing their exhortations to a broad audience: v. 2b stands in the context of a macarism which also serves as a general admonition;[8] v. 6a begins as a word to foreigners but broadens its scope in v. 6c addressing all who keep (kl-šmr) the sabbath from profanation.[9] In contrast to this, v. 4b is solely directed to the eunuchs. Second, vv. 2b,6c speak of keeping the sabbath from its profanation (mḥllw); though mḥllw can be interpreted in different ways, it is probably a technical term by reason of its consistent use with šbt in other contexts of the scriptures.[10] The several uses of šbt with ḥll indicate that what

---

8. E. LIPINSKI explains v. 2 as an "admonition" clothed in the literary genre of a macarism; cf. "Macarisme et psaumes de congratulation," RB 75 (1968) 356-57. See also, PAURITSCH, Die neue Gemeinde, 49.

9. Cf. PAURITSCH, Die neue Gemeinde, 37.

10. Cf. Walther ZIMMERLI, Ezekiel, 1 (Hermeneia; R.E. Clements, trans.; F.M. Cross and K. Baltzer, eds.; Philadelphia: Fortress Press, 1979) 410. The profanation of the sabbath (expressed, ḥll with šbt) also appears in Ez 20:13,16,21,24; 22:8; 23:28.

In Ex 31:14-17 the profanation (ḥll) of the sabbath is explained as laboring on the holy day of the Lord.

> You shall keep (wšmrtm) the sabbath because it is holy for you; everyone who profanes it (mḥllyh) shall be put to death; whoever does any work on it, that soul shall be cut off from among his people. Six days shall work be done, but the seventh day is a sabbath of solemn rest, holy to the Lord [. . .] observing the sabbath (l^{c}śwt 't-hšbt) through their generations as a perpetual covenant. It is a sign ('wt) for ever between me and the people of Israel that in six days the Lord made heaven and earth, but on the seventh day he rested and was refreshed. (Ex 31:14-17)

Also in Neh 13:15-18, certain men are remonstrated for work they do on the sabbath; the question is posed to them, "what is this evil thing you are doing, profaning the sabbath (wmḥllym 't-ywm hšbt)?" Ez 20:12-13 repeats the vocabulary of Ex 31:17 by noting the sign ('wt) of the sabbath as the bond of union between God and his people, and then describing their rebellion as a great profanation of the sabbath (w't-šbtty ḥllw m'd).

is meant by profanation of the sabbath is work done on the holy day of the Lord. And third, the uses of šbt distinguish not only an exhortation calling for observance, but also a practice which promises blessing. In v. 2 the keeping of the sabbath is one of the criteria by which one is counted among the blessed (’šry);[11] the eunuchs who keep the sabbath are secured a place within God's house and given an everlasting name (v. 5); the foreigner and all who keep the sabbath are brought into God's house of prayer and made joyful there (v. 7). While the inheritance of the promises is not contingent upon sabbath observance alone, a call for its satisfaction appears in the contexts which look forward to a share in blessing (vv. 2, 4-5, 6-7); thus the sabbath observance stands as a key practice for sharing in blessings which come to God's people.

The general movement of the literary unit stresses the theme of observance particularly by the repetitions of šmr, ḥzq, and ᶜśh. But beyond these recurrences the poetry draws attention to other motifs by another device of repetition in which the same words appear two or three times in close proximity. In eight verses, this device presents itself seven times.

1) šmr (vv. 1,2,2)
2) ᶜśh (vv. 1,2,2)
3) ’mr (vv. 3,3,3)
4) šm (vv. 5,5)
5) byt (vv. 7,7,7)
6) zbḥ (vv. 7,7)
7) qbṣ (vv. 8,8,8)

---

11. Cf. Waldemar JANZEN, "’ašrê in the Old Testament," HTR 58 (1965) 222, especially note 22.

In their literary contexts these repetitions function as a means of highlighting a specific motif in the movement through the poem.[12] While among these repetitions the first two (šmr, ᶜśh) focus attention on a theme that carries through the unit, the other repetitions interject motifs which complement the scope of the poem's main point(s); the interaction between the theme(s) and the motifs broadens the dimensions by which the themes develop.

And finally, the distant parallelism of lbw'//mqbṣ framing the poem in vv. 1b,8a argues for its unity.[13] Helpful for an appreciation of this example of distant parallelism is 66:18 where the words appear in tandem at the close of the division.

> I am coming to gather (b' lqbṣ) all nations and tongues; and they shall come (wb'w) and see my glory.

Here a clear relationship exists between the Lord's coming and his gathering all nations and tongues: he comes to gather them that they might see his glory. Similar to 66:18, 56:1,8 frames the literary unit with the announcement of the coming of the Lord's salvation (v. 1b) and his gathering of many peoples (v. 8). Specific to this literary context, the threefold use of qbṣ in v. 8 develops the scope of God's coming salvation announced in v. 1 to include the gathering of Israel, her outcasts, and others. The stylistic placement of these parallels at the beginning and end of the poem focuses attention on God's forthcoming salvific action and provides an avenue for appreciating more fully the emphasis on

---

12. Cf. MUILENBURG, "A Study in Hebrew Rhetoric," 101-102.

13. Examples of bw'//qbṣ as parallel pairs are found in Isa 43:5; 49:18; 60:4; 66:18. In 66:18a, this rendering follows the RSV, emending b'h to b', as found in the LXX, Syriac and Vulgate.

observance: it is the advent of deliverance (v. 1b) and the gathering of many peoples (v. 8) which calls for the faithful practice of righteousness (v. 1) and covenant responsibilities (vv. 4,6). The roots bw' and qbṣ form an inclusion as parallel words. Thus the theme of salvation frames the literary unit, stressing God's redemption which is soon to come.

B. Delimitation of the Strophes

Among the commentators who specify a strophic division for 56:1-8, the majority fall into two patterns: 1) vv. 1-2, 3-8;[14] and 2) vv. 1-2,3-7,8.[15] The following consideration of the strophic delimitation surveys their views, proposes several rhetorical devices to assist in the discernment of limiting the strophes, and then presents the strophic plan accepted here.

In discussing the reasons for distinguishing vv. 1-2 as a strophe, exegetes note the initial admonition to "keep justice and practice righteousness" of v. 1 moves to a concretization of those words with specific actions in v. 2, further explaining the opening exhortation.[16] Also, vv. 1-2 adhere to a distinctive poetic character with parallel construction in the bicola and a rhythmic balance of 3+2, while in vv. 3-7(8) these characteristics are less in

---

14. Cf. BONNARD, Le Second Isaïe, 342-44; PENNA, Isaia, 551; WESTERMANN, Isaiah 40-66, 305.

15. Cf. PAURITSCH, Die neue Gemeinde, 32; SCULLION, Isaiah 40-66, 150-52; WHYBRAY, Isaiah 40-66, 196-99. Similar, yet varying, MUILENBURG specifies the strophic division as 56:1 (Proem), 2-3, 4-5, 6-7, 8 (Conclusion); cf. "The Book of Isaiah," 654-59.

16. Cf. PAURITSCH, Die neue Gemeinde, 33; WESTERMANN, Isaiah 40-66, 310; WHYBRAY, Isaiah 40-66, 197.

evidence.[17] A final point, not noted by commentators, is the example of inclusion found in vv. 1ab,2bb with šmr and ^{c}śh.

v. 1ab) šmrw mšpṭ w^{c}św ṣdqh

v. 2bb) wšmr ydw m^{c}śwt kl-r^{c}

Not only are the two verbal roots repeated, but they are words which establish the theme of observance at the beginning of the literary unit.[18] The opening words of the strophe start on a note of admonition and then conclude in a similar way, rounding off the strophe in a typically Hebraic manner.[19]

The delimitation of the next strophe is governed by several rhetorical devices. The introduction of two individuals in v. 3 (the foreigner and eunuch) begins a pattern leading into vv. 4-7 with a message directly related to them. The repetition of the words for the foreigner and eunuch in the plural at vv. 4b,6a sets up a chiastic structuring of the verses.[20]

---

17. Cf. PAURITSCH, Die neue Gemeinde, 32; PENNA, Isaia, 551.

18. This example of inclusion, coupled with the other signs of unity, argue against Muilenburg's separation of vv. 1 and 2.

19. J. LUNDBOM discusses inclusion as a common device of the ancient Hebrew authors which serves to establish continuity and sense of closure in a deliberate manner. Cf. Jeremiah, 16-17.

20. Cf. MUILENBURG, "The Book of Isaiah," 653; PAURITSCH, Die neue Gemeinde, 32.

In the following diagram the letters A and B, when repeated, show the reiteration of the same Hebrew root. Similar other patterns occur with parallel words or corresponding motifs, but are distinguished by a prime factor next to the letter as in A'; this shows that the structure has corresponding elements other than or in addition to Hebrew roots.

(A) bn-hnkr (v. 3a)

(B) hsrys (v. 3c)

(B) lsrysym (v. 4b)

(A) wbny hnkr (v. 6a)

The structure begins in v. 3a by naming the foreigner (A) and eunuch (B). In vv. 4-5 the message to the eunuchs (B) consists of an exhortation in the style of "conditions" (v. 4) which, when put into practice, lead to an inheritance of the enumerated "promises" (v. 5); the same progression from "conditions" (v. 6) to "promises" (v. 7) characterizes the message to the foreigners (A). Together the chiasm and the "conditions-promises" pattern argue that the strophe concludes at the end of v. 7. In addition, the formula n'm 'dny YHWH in v. 8a breaks the flow of the "conditions-promises" pattern and introduces the final message of the unit.[21] The triple repetition of qbṣ in v. 8a stylistically stresses the salvific gathering of the peoples by the Lord God. The distant parallelism with lbw'//mqbṣ in vv. 1,8 strengthens the salvific tone of the final verse by solemnly explaining the advent of the Lord as a redemptive act of gathering the peoples.

In light of the above considerations vv. 1-2 and 3-7 are read as strophes with v. 8 as a concluding verse. Generally one expects to find more balance and symmetry in the length of strophes than is seen here. Also, though

---

21. For a discussion of the formal literary style with the divine name in v. 8a, refer to pp. 43-44. Also PAURITSCH calls v. 8aa a "formula of transition" (Überleitungsformel) signalling the end of the unit in a forceful manner with the addition of a final promise of Yahweh; cf. Die neue Gemeinde, 37.

poetic style is evidenced in vv. 3-7, this strophe exhibits irregularity in meter.[22] Despite the lack of balance in length between the strophes and the sometimes uneven metrical patterns, a number of rhetorical features in 56:1-8 indicate its unity: 1) the recurring theme of "a call to observance" fostered by the repetitions of šmr, ᶜśh, and ḥzq; 2) the framing theme of "salvation" supported by the parallel pair bw'//qbṣ (vv. 1,8) and the assuring word of Yahweh (vv. 1,4,8); 3) the thrice-repeated motif of the sabbath; and 4) the consistent literary device of repetition in which words appear in close proximity.

II. CLOSE READING

A. Isaiah 56:1-2 -- A Question of Justice and Righteousness

Following the messenger formula of 56:1aa, the remaining cola of v. 1 demonstrate an ordering of the nouns in an ABCB pattern: A) mšpṭ; B) ṣdqh; C) yšwᶜty; B) wṣdqty. This example of a recurring word in close parallel relationship to other words was first pointed out by S. Gevirtz in his study of Gen 27:29.[23] Directed by the findings of Gevirtz, B. Porten and U. Rappaport expand the number of examples in their article on Gen 9:7;[24] and beyond the citing of new instances, they discuss the function of the pattern in its literary context.

---

22. One could suggest that vv. 3-7 should be called a stanza with three strophes consisting of vv. 3 (a word of exhortation to the foreigner and eunuch), 4-5 (message to the eunuchs), and 6-7 (message to the foreigners), showing more balance.

23. Cf. Stanley GEVIRTZ, Patterns in the Early Poetry of Israel (Chicago: University of Chicago Press, 1963) 43-44.

24. Cf. B. PORTEN and U. RAPPAPORT, "Poetic Structure in Genesis IX:7," VT 21 (1971) 363-69.

Most recently, J. Kselman further elucidates this feature of patterning with fifteen more examples;[25] among these he cites Isa 56:1.

Most important in the discovery of such rhetorical patterns is the discernment of their function. Among the several observations regarding the ABCB pattern in Gen 9:7, Porten and Rappaport offer two of a more general nature which can be asked of other similar sequences: 1) does the pattern assist in establishing the context by means of a theme or themes which run through the passage? and 2) do the words of the pattern occur elsewhere together?[26] To initiate the study of the ABCB pattern's function in this literary context, these questions are directed to the text.

56:1 displays a movement beginning with "exhortation" (keep mšpṭ and practice ṣdqh, v. 1ab) and proceeding to a "salvation announcement" (for soon yšwᶜty is to come, wṣdqty to be revealed, v. 1b). A relationship between the exhortation (v. 1ab) and the salvation announcement (v. 1b) is established by the particle ky introducing a motive clause;[27] the particle ushers in the reason why one should heed the imperative: for salvation is soon to come. Also as Whybray suggests, the repetition of ṣdqh in vv. 1ab,1bb draws together two ideas by a single word;[28] the practice of righteousness (ṣdqh, v. 1ab) is motivated by

25. Cf. John KSELMAN, "The ABCB Pattern: Further Examples," VT 32 (1982) 224-29.

26. Cf. PORTEN and RAPPAPORT, "Poetic Structure," 368.

27. Cf. MUILENBURG, "The Linguistic and Rhetorical Usages," 152.

28. Cf. WHYBRAY, Isaiah 40-66, 196-97; see also LACK, La symbolique, 224; WESTERMANN, Isaiah 40-66, 309-10. When paired with yšwᶜh, ṣdqh is translated "deliverance" to bring out the parallelism describing God's

God's deliverance (wṣdqty, v. 1bb) which is to be revealed. This progression of thought from "exhortation" to "salvation announcement" in the ABCB pattern repeats itself in vv. 4-5,6-7.[29] V. 4 exhorts the eunuchs to keep God's sabbaths, to choose what is pleasing to him, and to hold fast to his covenant; the repetition of yšmrw (v. 4b) echoes the initial call to observance (v. 1a), here establishing the conditions by which one shares in God's promises (v. 5). The exhortations (v. 4) move to the promises (v. 5) held out to the eunuchs; they are given the assurance that they will forever be remembered within God's house by a name-monument. Then the foreigners (v. 6) are exhorted to minister to the Lord, to love his name, and to be his servants; finally in v. 6c the admonition to keep the sabbath and hold fast to God's covenant expands to include all. The promise of entry to God's holy mountain and the acceptance of their sacrifices follow in v. 7. A diagram shows the similarity between the opening verse of the literary unit and the word to the eunuchs and foreigners.

I.	(A)	Exhortation (v. 1ab)
	(B)	Salvation Announcement (v. 1b)
II.	(A')	Exhortation to the Eunuchs (v. 4)
	(B')	God's Promises to them (v. 5)
	(A')	Exhortation to the Foreigners (v. 6a-b) and All (v. 6c)
	(B')	God's Promises to them (v. 7)

One may question whether in the B/B' elements of the above diagram there is a relationship between the salvation announcement and God's promises. The promises of vv. 5,7 speak of incorporation into the people of God: for the

---

saving act (see the translation of 56:1b; 59:16b,17a). Cf. SCULLION, "ṢEDEQ-ṢEDAQAH," 342.

29. Some commentators note the influence of v. 1 on the general movement of the literary unit. Cf. MUILENBURG, "The Book of Isaiah, 654; VERMEYLEN, Du prophète Isaïe, 457.

eunuchs it is a place within the house of God which endures and will not be cut off; for the foreigner it is being brought to God's holy mountain. Incorporation into the community is the work of God, expressed by the first per. sing. verbs in vv. 5,7; God establishes a place of honor within the confines of those he calls his own, the people who are the recipients of his mercy and love. Also, the concrete expression of God's salvific action in v. 8 (his act of gathering) can also be related to the expressions of uniting other people into the community of Israel. In accepting such an approach to God's redemptive action, the concept of salvation in 56:1-8 is expressed in the assurance of the Lord's gathering of peoples together and the incorporation of new members into the community of God's favor. Thus the movement of the ABCB pattern in v. 1 with the pattern of exhortation-salvation announcement echoes twice in the related pattern of exhortation-promise in vv. 4-5,6-7.

The words of the ABCB pattern form an ordered progression through several chapters of 56-66. However what is distinctive about their occurrence is that they appear in pairs: mšpṭ with ṣdqh (A and B); yšw^{c}h with ṣdqh (C and B). The following diagram shows their progression through Isa 56-66.

The AB and CB Word Pairs of 56:1 in 56-66

I. mšpṭ//ṣdqh (A and B)	II. yšw^{c}h//ṣdqh (C and B)
56:1a (mšpṭ//ṣdqh)	56:1b (yšw^{c}ty//wṣdqty)
58:2b (ṣdqh//wmšpṭ)	
58:2c (mšpṭy//ṣdq)	
59:4a (bṣdq//nšpṭ)	
59:9a (mšpṭ//ṣdqh)	
59:14a (mšpṭ//wṣdqh)	

59:16b (wtwšc//ṣdqtw)

59:17a (ṣdqh//yšwch)

61:10b (yšc//ṣdqh)

62:1b (ṣdqh//wyšwcth)

63:1c (bṣdqh//lhwšyc)

A structural pattern spanning such a distance makes it difficult to come to any clear significance of its function and influence in these chapters without a thorough study of the passages in question. Nevertheless, several observations can be made.[30] First, the ABCB pattern in 56:1 appears to function in an "introductory" manner to present key words that appear several times in tandem in 56-66, and which follow a consistent pattern of occurrence in separating the elements of AB (mšpṭ//ṣdqh) from CB (yšwch//ṣdqh). Second, the AB and CB elements appear in a plan recalling the ABCB pattern of 56:1; instead of consistent repetitions of the pattern of 56:1, a series of five instances of AB precedes another five of CB. One notes that, as in 56:1, the series of AB is followed by CB. And third, beyond the confines of 56-66, the AB and CB patterns are found in a similar series covering the rest of Isa as shown in the following diagram.

I. mšpṭ//ṣdqh (A and B) II. yšwch//ṣdqh (C and B)

Isa 1:27 (bmšpṭ//bṣdqh)

5:7 (lmšpṭ//lṣdqh)

5:16 (bmšpṭ//bṣdqh)

9:6 (bmšpṭ//bṣdqh)

30. This diagram includes any occurrences of mšpṭ//ṣdqh and yšwch//ṣdqh in a parallel construction in 56-66.

16:5 (špṭ//ṣdqh)

26:9 (mšpṭyk//ṣdq)

28:17 (mšpṭ//wṣdqh)

32:1 (lṣdq//lmšpṭ)

32:16 (mšpṭ//wṣdqh)

33:5 (mšpṭ//wṣdqh)

45:8 (ṣdq//yšc)

45:21 (ṣdyq//wmwšyc)

46:13 (ṣdqty//wtšwcty)

51:5 (ṣdqy//yšcy)

51:6 (wyšwcty//wṣdqty)

51:8 (wṣdqty//wyšwcty)

Such an example confirms the word pairs mšpṭ//ṣdqh (AB) and yšwch//ṣdqh (CB) as being important in the context of Isa. The fact that AB and CB fall into the widely accepted division of Isa 1-39, 40-45 respectively, suggests that there may be some way in which these pairs function as key words in their literary contexts and could even be considered a structuring device by reason of their patterned recurrence throughout Isa.[31]

Such observations have implications beyond the scope of this study; nevertheless, cognizance of certain questions is necessary in a continuing

31. MUILENBURG writes, "Sometimes the repeated word or line indicates the structure of the poem, pointing to the separate divisions;" cf. "A Study in Hebrew Rhetoric," 99. On a somewhat larger scale, MAGONET shows how specific repeated words build the movement in Jonah and provide a structure for a reading of this prophetic book; cf. Form and Meaning, 13-38. Despite the size of the book of Isa, it is not inconceivable that key words or expressions are specific to the divisions within the whole.

analysis of 56-59. How do the parallel pairs *mšpṭ//ṣdqh* and *yšwʿh//ṣdqh* function in 56-59? How do the individual words of the ABCB pattern (*mšpṭ*, *ṣdqh*, *yšwʿh*) function in 56-59? Answers to these questions can be found only in an analysis of the chapters which contain them; still, such inquiries open up the possibility of understanding more fully how the elements of the ABCB pattern recall motifs throughout the ensuing chapters and may even be influential in the structuring of 56-59.

The verbs *šmrw* and *wʿśw* accompany the AB pair of v. 1ab and then each is repeated twice in the context of v. 2. The significance of *šmr* and *ʿśh* is demonstrated in the overlapping chiastic structure which these verbs form in vv. 1-2.

(A) šmrw (v. 1ab) ⟶ (B) wʿśw (v. 1ab)

(B) yʿśh (v. 2aa) ⟶ (A) šmr (v. 2ba)

(A) šmr (v. 2bb) ⟶ (B) mʿśwt (v. 2bb)

Chiasm abounds in the biblical writings and is accepted by more and more specialists of Hebrew prose and poetry as a common device functioning in various ways in different contexts.[32] Chiasm is a form of inverted parallelism.[33] This basic understanding suggests that the inversion of words may

---

32. Cf. LUNDBOM, *Jeremiah*, 17; John W. WELCH, "Introduction," to *Chiasmus in Antiquity: Structures, Analyses, Exegesis* (John W. Welch, ed.; Hildesheim: Gerstenberg, 1981) 9.

33. Cf. James L. KUGEL, *The Idea of Biblical Poetry: Parallelism and Its History* (New Haven: Yale University Press, 1981) 19-20; LUNDBOM, *Jeremiah* 17; TALMON, "The Textual Study," 358; WELCH, "Introduction," 9-10.

serve to direct one's attention to an inversion of ideas taking place in a text, or even to a simple movement from one idea to another.[34] The aspect of transition appears to be at the heart of what an overlapping chiastic movement signals. The first AB appears in an exhortation, a general call to right-living, with concern for justice and righteousness. But in the macarism of v. 2a one sees a shift to admonition with a demonstrative pronoun as object: blessed is the person who does this (z't). There is a movement from a general to a specific urging, though yet unidentified.[35] The specification of z't appears in v. 2ba with šmr šbt mḥllw, the referent to y^{c}śh-z't of v. 2aa; the relationship of v. 2aa to v. 2ba is supported by the parallels y^{c}śh/šmr. Then v. 2bb signals a shift with the pair wšmr/m^{c}śwt back to exhortation, treating a general call to keep the hand from doing evil. But an aspect of v. 2bb distinguishes it from v. 1ab: while v. 1ab calls for the practice of justice and righteousness in a positive command, v. 2bb reverses the general exhortation by placing it in a negative construction with mn in m^{c}śwt.[36]

---

34. Cf. TALMON, "The Textual Study," 360; WELCH, "Introduction," 10.

35. The use of z't and bh at the end of each colon in v. 2a is an example of the rhetorical device "delayed identification." Cf. M. DAHOOD, "Poetry, Hebrew," in IDBSup, 671-72. Vv. 2a,2b are structured to bring emphasis to the delayed identification by placing the demonstrative pronoun and the pronominal suffix with preposition at the end of each colon in v. 2a, and then repeating the participle šmr at the beginning of each colon in v. 2b. The emphasis given by the recurrences of šmr and their placement in key positions in the bicolon suggests that they are the referents of z't and bh; the delayed identification then points to two aspects of observance which are each designated by šmr in v. 2b. The PNev translation (p. 483) adopts this interpretation by placing a colon at the end of v. 2a to designate the description of v. 2a which follows in v. 2b. Contra, PAURITSCH who sees v. 2a as referring back to v. 1a; cf. Die neue Gemeinde, 34; also contra MUILENBURG who sees v. 2a as referring back to v. 1a and also to v. 2b; cf. "The Book of Isaiah," 654-55.

36. For the connotation of mn as a negative, cf. GKC, 382-83 §119v-w.

(A) General admonition (positive):
observance by practice of justice (v. 1ab)

(B) Specific admonition:
observance of the sabbath (vv. 2aa,2ba)

(A') General admonition (negative):
observance by desistance from evil (v. 2bb)

A general admonition initiates the strophe with a positive call to carry out just actions (A), concludes with a negative command to keep one's hand from evil (A'), and frames the call to proper sabbath observance (B).[37]

In 56:2a 'nwš and bn-'dm are in parallel positions within the bicolon, both as subjects of participles. The TDOT gives the usual meaning of both 'dm and 'nwš in OT usage as a general reference to the human person, a mortal being.[38] Within the larger context of Isa, 51:12 brings together the same words of 56:2 as parallels, once again denoting human individuals with an emphasis on their mortality.

> I, I am he that comforts you;
> who are you that you are afraid of man (m'nwš) who dies,
> of the son of man (wmbn-'dm) who is made like grass?
> (Isa 51:12)

Two other examples of these parallel pairs referring to humanity are found in Job 25:6 and Ps 8:5.

---

37. WESTERMANN comments on the "awkward parallelism" in v. 2b with a concrete and a particular command; cf. Isaiah 40-66, 310. However, when one accepts the repetitions as a structuring device, a sense of movement can be seen in the strophe.

38. Cf. F. MAASS, "'dm," TDOT 1, 75; "'nwš," TDOT 1, 346.

How much less man ('nwš), who is a maggot,
and the son of man (wbn-'dm), who is a worm. (Job 25:6)

What is man ('nwš) that you remember him,
the son of man (wbn-'dm) that you care for him? (Ps 8:5)

The clear parallel construction with 'nwš and bn-'dm in 56:2a and the three other (and only) examples of these pairs suggest that this macarism is couched in language suggesting it to be a general address.

The opening strophe bears the marks of careful construction with an overlapping chiastic structure, bound by the parallel pairs šmr//ᶜśh. The opening imperatives of v. 1ab and the use of 'nwš//bn-'dm in v. 2a distinguish the strophe as a general address, opening the section with a call to practice with ways of righteousness, to observe the sabbath, and to restrain from doing evil. The placement of the ABCB pattern in v. 1 and the subsequent use of the word pairs in 56-66 distinguish the importance of 56:1, setting forth the command to practice justice and the announcement of the Lord's imminent coming as significant motifs.

B. **Isaiah 56:3-7 -- God's New Word Toward Unity**

In 56:3a w'l-y'mr begins the new strophe with a negative and a jussive. But what is more important is the w's function in this literary context; textual consideration may shed light on the inquiry. The MT introduces the foreigner and eunuch in parallel fashion in vv. 3a,3c, w'l-y'mr; 1QIsaª differs in not employing the w in v. 3a, but doing so in v. 3c. The LXX is the same as 1QIsaª with mē legetō ho allogenēs in v. 3a, and with kai mē legetō ho eunouchos in v. 3c. In 1QIsaª and the LXX a connective element between v. 2 and v. 3 is not present, while a w/kai connects v. 3c with what immediately precedes. This suggests that the w of w'l-y'mr in v. 3a is more and/or other than a bridging device between the verses or strophes. There are several ways that the opening w of v. 3a can function in an emphatic manner: 1) it forcibly introduces a new and longer strophe while also drawing attention to the special message for the foreigner and eunuch; and 2) it isolates the two main individuals of the strophe in a distinctive way with an exact repetition w'l-y'mr in vv. 3a,3c. Similar examples of balance by means of repetition are found in this literary unit to confirm such a device.[39] As v. 3a begins a new strophe and introduces two new characters into the poem, there is insufficient reason to read the opening w as a connective element; rather the arguments favor it as an emphatic waw distinguishing the two main persons (the foreigner and eunuch) to whom the message is addressed. The emphasis is expressed in translation with "indeed."

The expression w'l-y'mr initiates the triple repetition of 'mr in vv. 3aa,3ab,3ca. Three repetitions of a word in close proximity draw attention to a developing motif. A particular emphasis is given to 'mr in v. 3a as the bicolon begins with it (w'l-y'mr) and concludes with it (l'mr). The opening colon begins with an injunction "not to speak" directed to the foreigner; the second colon goes on to describe him as one who has joined himself to the Lord concluding with an infinitive repeating the admonition not to speak (l'mr). The l sounds with 'mr in v. 3a accentuate the repetition and link the opening and closing words of the bicolon. In v. 3c the eunuch is introduced into the strophe like the foreigner is, with an emphasis on what he should not say. The build-up

39. Note šmr šbt mḥllw in vv. 2ba,6ca; wmḥzyqym bbryty in vv. 4cb,6cb.

of the three occurrences of 'mr in v. 3 is reversed in v. 4a. The reason for the prohibition against what the foreigner and eunuch say is given in v. 4a: ky kh 'mr YHWH, for the Lord says something quite different. The ky functions climactically to introduce the Lord's message, correcting the words of the eunuch and foreigner and offering them both a word of exhortation and promise.[40] In vv. 3-4 the word of God is contrasted with the human word. As the word of the foreigner is centered on separation (v. 3b), the word of God offers welcome to his holy mountain and house of prayer (v. 6); as the word of the eunuch describes his destination as decay (v. 3c), the word of God invites him to be the recipient of an everlasting name within the house of the Lord (v. 5).

The naming of the bn-hnkr and hsrys in v. 3 sets in motion the two groups that are the recipients of God's word in vv. 4-7. These words set up a chiastic pattern and serve as a structuring device for the strophe, vv. 3-7 expanding upon what was already proposed on pp.52-53.

(A) w'l-y'mr bn-hnkr (v. 3a)
    (B) w'l-y'mr hsrys (v. 3c)
        (C) ky kh 'mr YHWH (v. 4a)
    (B) lsrysym (v. 4b)
(A) wbny hnkr (v. 6a)

There are two ways in which the chiasm functions to demonstrate a reversal or inversion taking place in the strophe. First, the words of the foreigner and

---

40. MUILENBURG notes the emphatic use of the particle in this context; cf. "The Linguistic and Rhetorical Usages," 144.

eunuch are set aside and the word of God becomes the turning point (C) by which the doom of v. 3 is changed into guidance and hope in vv. 4-7. The significance of the Lord's message is also manifested by the longer second half of the chiasm in vv. 4-7;[41] the word of exhortation and promise (vv. 4-7) overshadows that of separation (v. 3). Second, the change from the singular to the plural in the two AA and BB elements indicates a wider audience for the message; instead of continuing the command to a single foreigner and eunuch (v. 3), the word of exhortation and promise widens to include eunuchs and foreigners generally. The words of the foreigner and eunuch speaking of exclusion from the community become words of acceptance when the word of God intervenes to invite eunuchs, foreigners, and all (kl, v. 6c) as his people.

In 56:3ab the foreigner is designated as one who hnlwh ʼl-YHWH (joins himself to the Lord); when introduced into the poem again at v. 6a the similar expression hnlwym ᶜl-YHWH distinguishes the foreigners. It is difficult to distinguish the character of this expression from the immediate context alone; two examples outside Isa using similar vocabulary help clarify lwh in 56:3a,6a. In Zech 2:15a (MT) the Lord tells the daughter of Zion to rejoice because he will dwell in her midst; the text further announces the coming of other nations who will be joined to the Lord.

> And many nations shall join themselves (wnlww) to the Lord (ʼl-YHWH) in that day, and shall be my people (ly lᶜm); and I will dwell in your midst [. . .] (Zech 2:15)

41. EXUM shows a similar example of an ABCB'A' pattern in Isa 28:14-22, where the expanded B'A' segments demonstrate a greater emphasis. Cf. "Whom Will He Teach Knowledge," 124.

Beyond the repetition of wnlww, ly l^{c}m echoes in Isa 56:3b telling the foreigner he will not be separated from God's people (^{c}mw). While Zech 2:15 repeats the basic formula of the covenant found in Lev 26:12, Jer 7:23; 31:33, Ez 11:20 and numerous other places, Isa 56:3b alludes to that same union with God's people (^{c}mw) by joining themselves to him. Further, in Jer 50:5 the exiles returning from Babylon emphasize that their union with God is to be an everlasting covenant.

> They shall ask the way to Zion, with faces turned toward it, saying, "Come, let us join ourselves to the Lord (wnlww ʼl-YHWH) in an everlasting covenant (bryt ^{c}wlm) which will never be forgotten.
> (Jer 50:5)

As the Jeremian passage brings together wnlww ʼl-YHWH with bryt, so is a similar repetition found in Isa 56:6. The expressions hnlwym ^{c}l-YHWH and wmḥzyqym bbryty frame v. 6 with the description of the foreigners at the beginning and a final word of exhortation to hold fast to God's covenant. Thus the repetitions of hnlwh/ym ʼl-YHWH in vv. 3a,6a both attest to a union in a covenant relationship.

From the literary context it is clear that the foreigner fears exclusion from the people of God, the community of Israel (v. 3b); similarly, the concern of the eunuch (v. 3c) is that his memory will no longer live on in progeny.[42] Beyond these cares expressed in v. 3, Deut 23:3 (MT) excludes the eunuch from participation in the Lord's assembly of worship and Deut 23:4-7 does

42. The image of the eunuch as a withered tree expresses his inability to produce fruit in offspring. As WHYBRAY points out, the succession of descendants who bear the family name is a sign of God's blessing, while its discontinuance removes the recollection of the individual from the land of the living. Cf. Isaiah 40-66, 198.

likewise for the foreigner. An understanding of these restrictions enhances appreciation of the promises which are offered to these groups later in this strophe.

The expression wmḥzyqym bbryty appears in vv. 4cb,6cb. Its conspicuous placement at the end of verses draws attention to it.[43] The NAB, NEB, RSV, and TOB translate the w of wmḥzyqum as a simple connective, "and." However, the repetition of the expression at the end of both instructions to the eunuchs and foreigners may be a signal that it functions as a summary statement of what precedes. D.W. Baker discusses further examples of the waw explicativum, one of which is a concluding statement which brings a preceding list to its resolution;[44] in such literary contexts the w is intended to serve as a link to sum up what has just been stated. The examples of wmḥzyqym bbryty in vv. 4cb,6cb are analogous to such a literary situation. The word to the eunuchs in v. 4 mentions observing the sabbath, choosing that in which the Lord delights, and concludes with holding fast to the covenant; both the keeping of the sabbath and deciding to act according to what delights the Lord are expressive of adherence to a relationship in covenant. In v. 6 the address to the foreigners follows the same progression of ideas with a concern to minister to the Lord, to love his name, and to be his servants, then moving to a more inclusive call (kl-šmr) for keeping the sabbath;[45] especially after this longer list of actions

---

43. MUILENBURG notes its climactic position in vv. 4cb,6cb; cf. "The Book of Isaiah," 657.

44. Cf. David W. BAKER, "Further Examples of the Waw Explicativum," VT 20 (1980) 131.

45. The l for the infinitives in v. 6b punctuates the bicolon with the exhortations to the foreigners; then in v. 6c the bicolon has participles moving with the change to the more inclusive audience introduced by kl.

describing avowal to Yahweh, would the final w indicate the link which introduces the summarizing explanatory statement. With the acceptance of the waw explicativum for vv. 4cb,6cb, the translation reads similar to what one would expect if it were a relative clause, " [...] that is, holding fast my covenant."[46]

Several scholars suggest that yd wšm of v. 5a is an example of hendiadys, expressing the image of a memorial monument.[47] Based on the use of yd in 1 Sam 15:12 and 2 Sam 18:18 where the monument (yd) perpetuates the name (šm) of Saul and Absalom respectively, so also in Isa 56:5 does a monument keep in lasting memory the eunuchs who will not live on in descendants. Albright comments on the archeological findings of Yadin at Hazor where the carving of upraised hands and forearms in memorial stelae commemorate those who have died; these impressions, set in stone, witness to a manner of preserving the memory of those who die without offspring.[48]

In v. 5 Scullion suggests that the connotation of ntn plus l is "to put, to place" instead of the usual translation "to give."[49] Other verbs of "locating"

---

46. Cf. GKC, 488 §155n. Gesenius describes the explicative waw as functioning in the manner of an independent relative clause.

47. Cf. PAURITSCH, Die neue Gemeinde, 36; SCULLION, Isaiah 40-66, 152; M. WEINFELD, Deuteronomy and the Deuteronomic School (Oxford: Clarendon Press, 1972) 193 note 4; WHYBRAY, Isaiah 40-66, 198; WESTERMANN, Isaiah 40-66, 314.

48. Cf. W.F. ALBRIGHT, "The High Places in Ancient Palestine," VTS 4 (1957) 251.

49. Cf. J.J. SCULLION, "Some Difficult Texts in Isa 56-66 in the Light of Modern Scholarship," UF 4 (1973) 105-106.

like gwr and mṣ' which often employ the preposition l favor translating ntn in these words; moreover, Scullion quotes Dahood, who demonstrates how in Jer 48:9a tnw ṣyṣ lmw'b means "put salt on Moab," serving as an image of the evident ruin which awaits it.[50] In v. 5a the object which is placed within God's house, and even within his walls,[51] is the name-monument (yd wšm); likewise in v. 5b 'tn lw, the referent of lw is yd wšm specifying that the everlasting name is placed upon the name-monument.[52] Thus in 56:5 the literary context suggests a reading of ntn plus l as "to place."

The repetitions in v. 5 form a chiasm which has the expression "better than sons and daughters" at its center.

(A) wntty lhm

(B) yd wšm

(C) ṭwb mbnym wmbnwt

(B) šm ᶜwlm

(A) 'tn-lw

While the repeated words stress the action of God's "placing" and the promise of a name-monument, the structure draws attention to the C element which qualifies it as something greater than descendants. In focusing attention on this promise, one is made aware of how significant its message is; departing from the

---

50. Cf. SCULLION, "Some Difficult Texts," 105-106.

51. The translation of wbḥwmty follows SCULLION reading the w as emphatic, highlighting an even more significant entrance into the house of God. Cf. "Some Difficult Texts," 106.

52. Cf. SCULLION, "Some Difficult Texts," 106.

traditional understanding that descendants are a sign of favor from God, the previous lines of exclusivity are broken down and the expanse of the Lord's mercy is extended. The eunuchs who were formerly excluded from a share in the community's worship (Deut 23:2) are now invited within the walls of God's house, and their names are inscribed on a monument to endure and not to be cut off. Fidelity to the covenant (Isa 56:4) becomes the criterion for sharing in God's promise (56:5), transcending the ties of kinship and blood.

Following the description of the foreigners as those who join themselves to the Lord in v. 6a, v. 6b is punctuated by an alliteration with l to emphasize the series of infinitives.[53] With the repeated sound pattern the line distinguishes three ways in which the foreigners manifest their avowal: to minister to the Lord, to love his name, and to be his servants. The end of the line emphasizes the l with its occurrence at the beginning of each of the three elements (lhywt lw l^{c}bdym); the continuation of the already initiated sound pattern adds a note of distinction to the idea of becoming a servant of the Lord amidst the short list of instructions. The motif of "God's servants" is developed later in this division of Isa in the style of an eschatological title for the people who have been faithful to God's command and inherit his promises.

> Thus says the Lord:
> "As the wine is found in the cluster,
>   and they say, "Do not destroy it for there is a blessing in it,"
> So will I do for my servant's sake (lm^{c}n ^{c}bdy),
>   and not destroy them all.
> I will bring forth descendants from Jacob,
>   and from Judah inheritors of my mountains;
> My chosen shall inherit it,
>   and my servants (w^{c}bdy) shall dwell there. (Isa 65:8-9)

---

53. Cf. MUILENBURG, "The Book of Isaiah," 658.

Therefore, thus says the Lord:
Behold, my servants (ᶜbdy) shall eat, but you shall be hungry;
behold, my servants shall drink, but you shall be thirsty;
behold, my servants shall rejoice, but you shall be put to shame;
behold, my servants shall sing for gladness of heart,
but you shall cry out for pain of heart, and shall wail for anguish of spirit.
You shall leave your name to my chosen for a curse, and the Lord God will slay you;
But his servants (wlᶜbdyw) he will call by a different name. (Isa 65:13-15)

You shall see, and your heart shall rejoice;
your bones shall flourish like the grass,
And it shall be known that the hand of the Lord
is with his servants (ᶜbdyw),
and his indignation is against his enemies. (Isa 66:14)

The emphasis given to the motif of God's servants in the exhortation of v. 6b distinguishes a word which indicates those who, through their loyalty and obedience to God, are the recipients of his redeeming care. The significance of this is that those people who had once been outsiders to Israel are now offered a place among God's chosen ones.

The chiasm which governs the promises of v. 5 is similar to the structure of v. 7. Though there is not a center point, a pattern of inversion is apparent in v. 7.

(A) bbyt tplty

(B) wzbḥyhm

(B) ᶜl-mzbḥy

(A) byt-tplh

The verse begins with whby'wtym announcing that the Lord will bring the foreigners to his holy mountain. The opening verb of v. 7 forms a link with lbw' of 56:1b; the initial proclamation of the Lord's approaching salvation is now specified in God's causative action (note the hiph^{c}îl) bringing in the foreigners and all to his holy mountain.[54] The movement toward God's holy mountain in v. 7 touches on two aspects of that place: as a house of prayer (A) and a place of sacrifice (B). An ABBA pattern gives primary weight to the AA elements which frame the structure.[55] In 56:7 emphasis falls on the idea that God's holy mountain is seen first as a house of prayer and second as a place of sacrifice; the significance of byt-tplh in v. 7c is also supported by its climactic position with the particle ky and the repetition of byt clarifying that God's house is a house of prayer for all peoples.[56] The ABBA pattern clarifies the position regarding the importance of God's holy mountain as a promise to the foreigners: it is primarily a pledge to joyful participation in God's dwelling as a house of prayer and secondarily as a place where their sacrifices will be acceptable. In the Bible there are several correctives to making sacrifice the key focus of religious practice; warnings are given against practices of sacrifice to the exclusion of

54. The same kind of play on the idea of "the Lord's coming" and its effects is found in Isa 60 were bw' occurs eleven times and dominates the chapter with the universal movement to Zion. It is because the light and glory of the Lord have come (b', 60:1) that the sons of Israel are brought (lhby', 60:9b) from afar and that men bring (lhby', 60:11b) the wealth of nations to Zion. Cf. MUILENBURG, "The Book of Isaiah," 697.

55. John WELCH discusses the extremes in a chiastic pattern as the dominant ones. Cf. "Introduction," 10.

56. Stylistically this is done with the repetition of byt and the final words of the link opening up the promise to include all peoples. Here it would appear that ky functions both to emphasize the conclusion of the strophe and to highlight the line itself. Cf. SCULLION, "Some Difficult Texts," 107.

other essentials of authentic faith. In Ps 50, God does not chide the people for their sacrifices; their burnt offerings are acceptable in his presence. But what God desires more is another kind of sacrifice.

> I do not reprove you for your sacrifices (zbḥyk);
> your burnt offerings (wᶜwltyk) are continually before me [. . .]
> Offer to God a sacrifice of thanksgiving (zbḥ twdh)
> and pay your vows to the Most High [. . .]
> He who brings thanksgiving as his sacrifice (zbḥ twdh) honors me,
> to him who orders his way aright, I will show the salvation of God. (Ps 50:8,14,23)

Qoheleth, in warning against thoughtless worship, places the value of listening before that of sacrifice when coming to the house of the Lord.

> Guard your steps when you go to the house of God; to draw near to listen (lšmᶜ) is better than to offer the sacrifice (zbḥ) of fools. (Qoh 4:17)

While not objecting to sacrifice, Jesus teaches that an action toward reconciliation must precede that of offering at the altar.

> So if you are offering (prospherēs) your gift at the altar, and there remember your brother has something against you, leave your gift there before the altar and go; first be reconciled (diallagēthi) to your brother, and then come and offer (prosphere) your gift. (Mt 5:23-24)

Isa 56:7 does not oppose sacrifice to prayer, but it does set up a priority as to which of the two promises in connection with God's holy mountain is more important. The promise made to the eunuchs, in relation to their being given a place within God's house and walls, is not specifically sacrificial. Thus while one would understand allusions to sacrifice with words like byt, zbḥ, and ᶜwlh in vv. 5,7 the structural patterns therein do not give primary considerations to it.

Even though the eunuchs and foreigners are important characters helping to establish the structure of vv. 3-7, the three uses of 'mr (v. 3) and ky kh 'mr YHWH (v. 4) focus attention on the authoritative word of God which countermands the voices of the outsiders in v. 3 and issues both exhortation and promise in vv. 4-7. The fuller elaboration of the strophe's structure with midpoint at v. 4a (cf. pp. 65-66) argues further for the reading of vv. 3-7 as a strophe, stressing the Lord's word as the integrating element of the strophe. Thus both the exhortations (vv. 3-4,6) and the promises (vv. 5,7) have as their goal to extend the bonds of covenant to outsiders, to offer a share in God's blessings, and to unite all peoples in YHWH.

C. Isaiah 56:8 -- The Full Community of Israel Gathered by the Lord God

Several remarks have already been made regarding v. 8 and establishing its function in its literary context: n'm 'dny YHWH is a concluding formula bringing the unit to an end in a solemn and emphatic manner; the triple occurrence of qbṣ follows a pattern of repetition found elsewhere in the unit; and the distant parallelism of lbw'//mqbṣ brings together the opening and closing of the poem on the theme of salvation. A few observations remain in the consideration of 56:8.

The redemptive tone of 56:8 is supported by the examples of distant parallelism with lbw'//mqbṣ in vv. 1b,8. The eschatological image of God's gathering is used by the prophets to depict God as a shepherd who brings back those who have been separated from the flock.[57] The expression ndḥy yśr'l of v. 8a also appears in Ps 147:2 and Isa 11:12, though employing synonymous verbs for "to gather" (ykns, w'sp, respectively), both examples are in literary contexts which suggest the bringing together of dispersed Israelites.[58] Within a literary context which addresses the separation of foreigners and eunuchs from the community, an eschatological vision of God's gathering would appropriately make mention of those who may belong to the community but are separated from it in some way. Furthermore, among those to be assembled, mention is first made of those who are presently being gathered (present participle, mqbṣ), the outcasts of Israel; in the ordering of the verse's elements priority of place is given to those of Israel who are dispersed.

The threefold repetition of qbṣ underscores God's salvific action of uniting the people, of drawing them together. The aspect of unity brought out in v. 8 echoes earlier examples of God's desire to join people into the covenant community. In v. 3 the Lord tells the foreigner not to say that he will be separated from God's people. In v. 5 the eunuchs are promised an everlasting name inscribed upon the monument within God's house, never to be cut off. Neither among the Israelites nor among other peoples are there to be outcasts, for the Lord God comes to gather all, to unite all people as a community in covenant.

---

57. PAURITSCH notes Jer 23, Ez 34, and Isa 40 as examples; cf. Die neue Gemeinde, 37-38.

58. In Ps 147 the poem begins with a mention of the outcasts of Israel and broken-down Jerusalem, but then a description of the strengthening of Jerusalem's gates and blessing their sons within it follows in vv. 12-13; here Jerusalem is fortified and her outcasts are gathered. Isa 11:12 is specific in designating the ndḥy yśr'l as those to be assembled from the four corners of the earth.

The introduction of the name ysŕ'l in v. 8 identifies one of the groups being gathered. The importance of ysŕ'l is seen in the references made to it in each occurrence of qbṣ. In v. 8ab the piᶜel participle designates the present action of the speaker 'dny YHWH as the one gathering the outcasts of Israel (mqbṣ ndḥy ysŕ'l). In v. 8b, 'qbṣ ᶜlyw emphasizes that the Lord will gather others to him (that is, Israel). And the final word in v. 8b (lnqbṣyw) is a niphᶜal plural participle with a third per. masc. sing. suffix again designating "the ones of him" (that is, Israel) who are being gathered. The "gathering" motif expresses that it is an action of uniting others to Israel. Thus the concluding verse of the literary unit not only emphasizes qbṣ but also ysŕ'l with three referents to it.

The placement of ysŕ'l at the end of the literary unit brings a new name into focus at a climactic point in the poem.[59] The three references to Israel in ndḥy ysŕ'l, 'qbṣ ᶜlyw, and lnqbṣyw focus attention on the act of God's gathering: it is an assembling of the outcasts of the community and others into Israel. Israel is God's own people (ᶜmw, 56:3b), those redeemed from affliction by his steadfast mercy (cf. 63:7-9). It becomes apparent in reading this unit that the bonds of unity are concretized both in the people's willingness to heed God's word and in their reception of his blessings. From beginning to end, the admonitions of 56:1-7 recall the basic manifestations of union with God as his people: observance of justice (v. 1), practice of righteousness (v. 1), obedience

---

59. MUILENBURG notes the importance given to names in the OT literature. The distinctive character of Hebrew names suggests a great deal in a literary context by attention given to an individual or the tradition connected with an important personage. A name in a climactic position of a poem adds a dimension of concreteness which rescues its interpretation from diffusion. Cf. "A Study in Hebrew Rhetoric," 106.

to his word (vv. 1,3-4), avoidance of evil (v. 2), fidelity in keeping the sabbath (vv. 2,4,6), and strict adherence to his covenant (vv. 4,6). Likewise the promises of God show magnanimous gifts of blessing: salvation and deliverance (v. 1), perpetual remembrance within the community for the eunuch (v. 5), joyful participation in the Lord's assembly for all (v. 7). In v. 8 the name yśr'l, included as a specification of the outcasts, also serves as a reminder that the admonitions and promises given above concentrate on incorporation into a specific group, the community of Israel. Thus, the gathering which the Lord announces is a union of those who walk in the ways of God which are also the ways of the true Israel, awaiting the promises of salvation soon to come.

III. APPLICATION OF A LITERARY DEVICE TO ISAIAH 56:1-8

It has already been shown that several literary devices are at work within 56:1-8 which demonstrate its unity including repetition, distant parallelism, and chiasm. The question remains: is there a literary device at work throughout 56:1-8 which helps to understand how the literary unit functions as a whole?

The ABCB pattern of 56:1 suggests that the literary unit, or at least its opening verse, has an introductory character by initiating key words which recur at parallels through 63:1 in a consistent ordering.[60] The parallel pair bw'//qbṣ of 56:1,8 appears in tandem at 66:18, establishing links with the final verses of the division. These repetitions both at the beginning and conclusion of

60. See pp. 57-58.

56-66 hint that these two extremes may function as "bookends" for the final division of Isa; for this to be substantiated, further examples of repeated vocabulary expressing or expanding upon similar motifs need to be demonstrated.

Examining the vocabulary of 56:1-8 and 66:18-24, a considerable number of repeated words appears in these two pericopes. The following diagram shows the recurrences of eight words and how they form a pattern which unites the beginning and conclusion of this division in Isa.

		56:1-8		66:18-24
1) bw'	vv.	1,7	vv.	18,18,20
2) 'nwš		2		24
3) šbt		2,4,6		23,23
4) byt		5,7,7,7		20
5) šm		5,5,6		22
6) hr-qdšy		7		18
7) qbṣ		8,8,8		18
8) yśr'l		8		20

The task remains to examine these repeated words in their literary contexts and to determine if there are relationships which can be determined from them.

In 56:1 the word of the Lord announces that his salvation is soon to come (lbw'); this idea is complemented in 66:18a with the proclamation by God that he is coming (b', as in LXX) to gather all nations and tongues. The initial announcement that salvation is to come, beginning the division in 56:1b, also begins the final unit in 66:18-19, but now with the fulfillment of that proclamation in the redemptive context of God's glory being manifested to all peoples. In 56:7 the Lord brings (whby'wtym; in the hiph^c^îl, he causes them to come) the foreigners to the Lord's holy mountain. A new development of 56:7 takes place in 66:18b,20; those who have been gathered by the Lord come (wb'w) to see his glory, and then in turn they will bring (whby'w; in the hiph^c^îl, they will cause to come) all the brethren from the nations to God's holy mountain in Jerusalem. As God brings the foreigners to his holy mountain ('l-hr qdšy, 56:7), so will the nations who have been gathered still bring others to the Lord's holy mountain Jerusalem (^c^l hr qdšy yrwšlm, 66:20). The uses of bw' show both consistency and development in their literary contexts: the verb announces both God's coming and his act of bringing foreigners to his holy mountain who will subsequently bring others there. Similarly, hr-qdšy is consistently the place to which the foreigners and nations are brought (56:7; 66:20), further specified as Jerusalem in 66:20.

The macarism of 56:2 has 'nwš as a general term for a mortal being, stating that blessing comes to the one who follows the given precepts. In 66:24 h'nšym specifies the mortal aspect of those who have rebelled against God and have experienced death. A strong note of contrast exists between these two examples of 'nwš, but when seen in the larger interworking of the literary units they function well to bring out a message. While 56:1-8 opens the division with a call for an observance of God's ways and a firm holding to his covenant, 66:18-24 is set entirely in the context of why that call to follow God's precepts is given, namely because of his coming (56:1b) and his rendering of deliverance (wṣdqty, 56:1bb). While 56:2 exhorts the 'nwš with a promise of blessing to follow God's decrees, 66:24 relates the sentence of death which comes to the h'nšym who have rebelled against God (hpš^c^ym by). Thus these references to the human individual demonstrate both the exhortation to observance and the recompense for rebellion; by the repetition of ’nwš the call to blessedness in obedience and the price of death in disobedience are brought into contrast at the beginning of 56:1-8 and at the end of 66:18-24.

The occurrences of šbt in 56:2,4,6 are each in tandem with šmr, emphasizing a regard for sabbath observance. Beyond this observation, one also notes the all-embracing audience to whom the teaching is addressed: the general context of the macarism (v. 2), the eunuchs (v. 4), and the foreigners with all who would keep it (v. 6). Similarly the salvific context of 66:22-23 also looks to a universal honoring of God when all Israel's descendants (v. 22) and all flesh (v. 23) will come to worship before the Lord from new moon to new moon and from šbt bšbt. Two aspects of these uses of šbt show a development when compared in their literary contexts. First, the emphasis given to keeping the sabbath in 56:2,4,6 is strengthened by the vision of new heavens and a new earth where each šbt remains a day when the Lord is worshipped (66:22-23).[61] Even in the creation of a new world, the sabbath is a day set aside for the honoring of God. Second, the exhortation to observe the sabbath was given both to God's people and outsiders in 56:1-8; participation in the practice of avowal to God is open to all who would accept it (56:6c). Similarly the vision of worship to Yahweh in 66:22-23 includes kl-bśr who come into his presence.[62] The sabbath observance remains an expression by which all people show their union with the community of God's elect.

---

61. Cf. BONNARD, Le Second Isaïe, 493-94.

62. SCULLION sees kl-bśr in 66:23 as a reference to the Gentiles; cf. Isaiah 40-66, 210. But one notes the repetition of kl-bśr in 66:24 where the reference is to all humanity. The close occurrence of these words would suggest a common reading of the expression as a reference to all humanity.

In 56:5 the promise of a place within God's house (bbyty) is an assurance that the eunuchs holding fast to God's covenant will share in the life of the community of Israel; it is within the house and its walls that their names are inscribed onto the monument assuring them that the inscription of the names remains eternal (šm ᶜwlm) and will not be effaced. Likewise in 56:7 bbyt tplty is a promise made to the foreigners that God will bring them there; their entry to the house of prayer is an approval of their union with the Lord. In 56:7c the strophe concludes on a note of expansion, announcing that God's house will be called byt-tplh (a house of prayer) for all peoples. A similar context in 66:20 shows all the brethren from all the nations being brought to God's holy mountain; the repetition of mnḥh in v. 20 emphasizes the image of an acceptable offering as the worldwide procession draws toward byt YHWH.[63] The uses of byt, while being a promise for the future and a vision of hope, are also ways of showing acceptance into the life and activity of God's people by receiving a name-monument within the walls of his house (56:5), by offering an acceptable sacrifice in the house of prayer (56:7), and by participating in the worship of Yahweh (66:20-23).

In 56:6 the word of instruction to the foreigners includes special concern for the name of the Lord as a means of expressing loyalty toward him in covenant; this same respect for God's name is found elsewhere in 56-66 (cf. 57:15; 59:19; 60:9; 63:12,14,16). In 56:5, the promise made to the eunuchs of an eternal name (šm ᶜwlm) within God's house is a benefit assuring their lasting remembrance in the community. Likewise in 66:22, wšmkm is an image that

63. Cf. WESTERMANN, Isaiah 40-66, 427.

designates a remembrance of descendants that will remain (y^cmd); the perdurance of the zr^ckm wšmkm is compared to the creation of the new heavens and new earth which will stand before the Lord (^cmdym lpny). Though the contexts are different in relating to the eunuchs (56:5) and then to descendants (66:22), the image of šm as a lasting remembrance and presence is consistent.

The repetition of qbṣ in 56:8,8,8; 66:18 has already been discussed in connection with the parallels bw'//qbṣ. Beyond this, several points can be made to further demonstrate the ties between the repetitions. In considering the movement of 56:1-8, the initial announcement of God's forthcoming salvation is given at the beginning of the poem (v. 1b), and then further explains and culminates in the redemptive gathering of Israel and the others. Linked by the repetition of qbṣ, 66:18 continues where 56:8 concluded. In 56:8 God promises "I will gather" ('qbṣ) Israel and the dispersed, and in 66:18 God announces "I am coming to gather" (b' lqbṣ) all nations and tongues; the passage proceeds to describe the approach of the scattered nations (66:20). The gathering of the nations initiates the movement toward the Lord's holy mountain where his glory is revealed and his renown declared. Thus the gathering announced in 56:8 is the point at which 66:18 begins and further develops the redemptive action of Yahweh's gathering.

In 56:8 yśr'l is in construct with ndḥy referring to the outcasts of Israel. The bny yśr'l of 66:20 is part of a description comparing the approach of the brethren from among all the nations ('t-kl-'ḥykm mkl-hgwym) to a procession of Israelites who bring offerings to the Lord. In 66:20 'ḥykm (your brothers) echoes an earlier occurrence in 66:5 ('ḥykm) where the word carries the connotation of membership in the same community; those who have seen the Lord's glory will then bring back members of the Israelite community who are dwelling apart from the place of God's holy mountain.[64] The two occurrences of ysŕ'l are similarly found in literary contexts (56:8; 66:20) which draw attention to those who share in the fellowship of Israel by belief and birth and yet are separated; but in both occurrences the outcasts will be gathered (56:8) and the brethren from the nations will be brought (66:20) to the house of the Lord (56:7; 66:20). Thus the appearances of ysŕ'l at the beginning and end of this division in Isa focus attention on separated members of the Israelite community whom the Lord wishes to assemble at his holy mountain.

It can be seen that the recurrence of vocabulary in 56:1-8 and 66:18-24 not only brings together the repetition of words, but also a complementarity of ideas and a maturation of certain motifs initiated at the beginning and developed at the end. In typical Semitic fashion, 56:1-8 and 66:18-24 frame 56-66 with reiteration of key words and ideas. Lawrence Boadt notes that the closing half of an inclusion made up of a cluster of repeated words may represent a "recapitulation."[65] Such a literary device harmonizes the two ends of the poem or composition by recalling earlier motifs, distinguishing them as key. Rather than focusing on only one word, recapitulation distinguishes several words and establishes stronger ties with the opening. Thus one manner of reading 56:1-8 is as a pattern of inclusion with 66:18-24; the eight elements of

64. Cf. Helmer RINGGREN, "'ḥ," TDOT 1, 190; WESTERMANN, Isaiah 40-66, 427.

65. Cf. Lawrence BOADT, "Isaiah 41:8-13: Notes on Poetic Style and Structure," CBQ 35 (1973) 24-25, 30-31.

inclusion provide a way of understanding the architecture and style of 56:1-8 as an integral part of the structure of 56-66, with 66:18-24 as its recapitulation.

When dealing with literature of some length as in 56-66, rhetorical critics distinguish between two types of inclusion. An "internal" inclusion has repeated words which recall and develop similar motifs within the material they frame.[66] "External" inclusion has repeated words functioning only in the literary context of the inclusion, but not in the material framed by the repetitions.[67]

Among the words of inclusion discussed above, six recur again within the material framed (56:9--66:17). The following considerations show how they function outside the inclusion. 1) The emphasis given to the Lord's coming (bw') in 56:1,7 and 66:18 echoes again in 59:19,20 (ky-ybw', wb') depicting his advent to Zion in a theophany of rushing winds and water. Also, the whole of Isa 60 focusses on the arrival of Yahweh's glory in Jerusalem and how this, in turn, begins the movement of the nations toward the holy city. In 63:1 the Divine Warrior comes (b') from his combat with Edom, announcing salvation and deliverance. 2) Both 56:2,4,6 and 66:23 call for the proper sabbath (šbt) observance, depicting it as a day of special worship even in the creation of the new heavens and new earth. The same respect for the sabbath is noted in 58:13, where one is told how to act on the holy day and the blessings that accrue to those who follow the precepts. 3) The repetitions of byt in 56:5,7 and 66:20 describe the house of the Lord as a place of gathering and worship for those

---

66. Cf. Henry van Dyke PARUNAK, "Oral Typesetting: Some Uses of Biblical Structure," Bib 62 (1981) 158.

67. Cf. PARUNAK, "Oral Typesetting," 158.

counted among God's people. Similarly in 60:7 and 64:10, byt refers to the place of God's presence where he is praised. 4) Within the inclusion the recurrences of šm distinguish both love for God's name (56:6) and promise of an enduring name for those counted among God's people (56:5; 66:22). Concern for God's holy name is a key theme in the lament of 63:7--64:11, with six references to it (63:12,14,16,19; 64:1,6; see also 60:9; 65:1). References to the bestowal of a new name upon the people occur at 62:2 and 65:15. 5) God will bring to his holy mountain (hr-qdšy) those who are faithful to his commands (56:6-7). This same motif repeats in 57:13 where those who take refuge in God inherit his holy mountain. Also in 65:11 the significance of hr-qdš is stressed where forgetting God's holy mountain is parallel with forsaking the Lord; to be unmindful of God's holy mountain is a manifestation of disavowal to the God of Israel. 6) In 56:8 Israel (yśr'l) is the recipient of God's gracious act of gathering. Similarly in 63:7 the house of Israel recounts the abundance of God's steadfast kindness; marked by the glory which the Lord bestows upon Israel, the nations refer to Zion as the Holy One of Israel (60:9,14). The contexts in which yśr'l appears bespeak the special relationship between God and Israel.[68]

Six of the eight words in the inclusion repeat similar motifs within the poems they frame. Though not all the words of the inclusion are there, the majority exemplify marks of affinity. The brief survey of the words suggests that 56:1-8 and 66:18-24 form an internal inclusion.

---

68. Cf. J.J.M. ROBERTS, "Isaiah in Old Testament Theology," Int 36 (1982) 136.

The purpose of 56:1-8 becomes clearer, for in noting the examples of inclusion and their function one can better perceive the introductory character of this literary unit. The motifs of God's coming salvation, his gathering of other peoples unto Israel, entry to the Lord's holy mountain, and reverence for the sabbath each figure into the opening and closing units of 56-66. As an introduction, the different motifs set the tone for the succeeding chapters by distinguishing its key ideas. Several commentators presenting a genre analysis of 56:1-8 describe it as a "prophetic torah" accentuating a call for observance of God's decrees;[69] particularly here, the text stresses the essentials for life in the Israelite community. While not dealing specifically with genre analysis, the Overview and Close Reading of this study also show the emphasis given to observance in the structure of the unit. But it can also be noted that the literary device of inclusion in this introductory unit stresses various motifs related to redemption: the Lord comes to gather the nations and all will have access to his house upon his holy mountain. So while a parenetic thrust begins 56-66, this is complemented by images of salvation. Lest one weigh too heavily the call to observance, it needs to be pointed out that the instruction points toward the reception of God's redemptive promises: keep justice for soon is my salvation to come (56:1). The elements of inclusion function to accent the theme of salvation in this opening unit; this network of motifs at the beginning sets the stage for the unfolding of the deliverance Yahweh offers, awaiting the further description of the magnanimous event. Fidelity to God's word assures redemptive blessings. What remains to be seen in the subsequent literary units of 56-59 is if the theme

---

69. Cf. ACHTEMEIER, The Community and Message, 34; MUILENBURG, The Book of Isaiah," 652-53; PAURITSCH, Die neue Gemeinde, 45-46; SCULLION, Isaiah 40-66, 150.

of salvation continues to remain consonant and to develop along the lines set out in the introduction at 56:1-8.

IV. SUMMARY

Isa 56:1-8 is marked by several elements which show its unity. The repetitions of vocabulary focus attention on the theme of observance (šmr, ᶜśh, ḥzq), especially in relation to the sabbath. The opening verse expresses a concern for the practice of justice and righteousness because of the approach of salvation. This twofold development of an exhortation followed by a salvation announcement repeats twice in the admonitions and promises made to the foreigners and eunuchs. The theme of salvation frames the unit in v. 1b and v. 8 by the announcement of its coming and a concluding word about the Lord God's redemptive gathering of many peoples.

This first literary unit of 56-66 functions in two ways as an introduction. First, the ABCB pattern initiates this section of Isa with words that occur in a structured order in the succeeding literary units; the pattern of vocabulary suggests that these are key words whose repetitions unite the literary units in their movement from chapter to chapter. The analyses of the succeeding poems will test this hypothesis. Second, 56:1-8 and 66:18-24, as literary units, form an internal inclusion for this final division of Isa by the repetitions which also echo in the poems they frame.

Both the strophes in vv. 1-2 and 3-7 are set in chiastic structures. The overlapping chiasm with šmr//ᶜśh stresses the theme of observance by a movement from a "general" to "specific" and back to a "general" admonition. The foreigner and eunuch introduce two characters in v. 3, the names of which demonstrate an inverted pattern in vv. 4-5 and 6-7, centering the word of God in v. 4a as the turning point, contrasting the words of separation in v. 3 to the words of exhortations and promise in vv. 4-7.

The themes of observance and salvation interact in the poem to emphasize both the reason for the call to observance (the approach of salvation, v. 1) but also the redemptive action of God which is open to those who heed his word and put it into practice (vv. 4-5,6-7,8).

CHAPTER THREE

A RHETORICAL ANALYSIS OF ISAIAH 56:9--57:21

Translation of Isaiah 56:9--57:21

Stanza I

56:9 ALL BEASTS of the field,
COME to devour;
ALL BEASTS of the forest!
10 EACH of his watchmen are blind,
they are without KNOWLEDGE;
EACH of them are dumb DOGS,
they are *UNABLE* to bark,
Dreaming, RECLINING,
LOVING to sleep.
11 Yes, the DOGS have an insatiable appetite,
they do not KNOW satisfaction;
And look, they are shepherds,
they do not KNOW DISCERNMENT;
EACH of them turns in his own WAYS,
each one COVETOUS for his own gain.
12 "COME, let me bring wine,
and let us fill ourselves with strong drink;
Tomorrow will be like today,
yet even greater."

57:1 The RIGHTEOUS ONE has perished,
and NO ONE TAKES IT TO HEART;
People of steadfast kindness are TAKEN AWAY,
and no, there is NO ONE with DISCERNMENT.
But, from the presence of evil he is TAKEN AWAY,
the RIGHTEOUS ONE,
2 he enters into PEACE.
They rest upon their COUCHES,
who WALK in uprightness.

Stanza II

57:3 BUT YOU, COME FORWARD, here,
sons of the sorceress,
OFFSPRING of the adulterer and the harlot.

4 AGAINST WHOM do you mock,
AGAINST WHOM do you open wide your mouth
and wag your tongue?
YOU, are you not CHILDREN of transgression
and OFFSPRING of deceit,
5 Burning with passion for the oaks
UNDER every green tree,
Slaughtering CHILDREN in the VALLEY
UNDER the ledges of the rocks?

6 Among the stones of the VALLEY is your portion;
THESE, THESE are your lot;
INDEED, to them you poured out a drink offering,
you caused it to be offered UP as a sacrifice;
WITH these things, am I to be COMFORTED?

7 UPON a MOUNTAIN towering and LOFTY,
you have SET UP YOUR COUCH,
INDEED, you WENT UP there
to OFFER a SACRIFICE.
8 Behind the door and the doorpost
you have SET UP your symbol;
Departing from me, you revealed yourself and WENT UP;
you spread wide YOUR COUCH.
You made treaty for yourself with them,
you LOVED their COUCH,
you gazed upon STRENGTH.
9 You lavished oil upon the king
and INCREASED your perfumes;
And you sent your messengers AFAR OFF,
you DESCENDED to the deepest depths.
10 With the EXTENT of your WAY you were wearied,
but you did not SAY, "it is hopeless."
You found LIFE in this STRENGTH,
and therefore you did not flag.

11 And WHOM did you dread and FEAR
when you deceived me?
BUT ME, you did not remember
nor PLACE UPON YOUR HEART.
Have I, I, not been silent long enough?
BUT ME you did not FEAR.
12 I, I will proclaim your RIGHTEOUSNESS
and your ACTIONS.
And they will not profit you,
13 will not save you when you cry, your collection of idols.
The WIND shall sweep EACH of them away,
a mere breath takes them off.
But the one who takes refuge in me shall INHERIT the land,
and shall possess MY HOLY MOUNTAIN.

Stanza III

57:14 And he will SAY:
BUILD UP, BUILD UP, CLEAR the WAY,
REMOVE any obstacle from the WAY of my people.
15 For thus SAYS the EXALTED and LOFTY One,
the One ABIDING forever whose name is HOLY,
I ABIDE in a LOFTY and HOLY place,
But also with the CONTRITE and HUMBLE of SPIRIT,
TO REVIVE the SPIRIT of the HUMBLE,
TO REVIVE the HEART of the CONTRITE.
16 FOR not endlessly will I contend,
nor continually will I be ANGRY,
FOR the SPIRIT proceeds from me
and I have MADE the breath of life.
17 Because of the perversity of his COVETOUSNESS, I grew ANGRY,
and I struck him, I hid myself from him and was ANGRY.
But he WALKED, turning in the WAY of his own HEART.
18 His WAYS I have seen, but I will HEAL him;
I will lead him and restore FULL COMFORT to him
and his mourners,
19 creating the fruit of the lips.

19b PEACE! PEACE to those who are FAR and NEAR,
SAYS the Lord, and I will HEAL them.
20 But the WICKED are like an AGITATING sea
which is *UNABLE* to be calm;
And its waters AGITATE mire and slime.
21 There is no PEACE, SAYS my GOD, for the WICKED.

I. OVERVIEW

A. Indications of Unity in Isaiah 56:9--57:21

The major argument in establishing the unity of 56:9--57:21 is the literary device of antithesis recurring at three points of transition in the poem. This literary characteristic binds together what some commentators believe are several diverse literary units.[1] Beyond this, an inclusion with ykl in 56:10b and 57:20a marks the beginning and end of the poem with a motif describing the inabilities of the irresponsible leaders and wicked ones.

Beyond these signs of unity, one notices that repeated words are also numerous in this section; for so lengthy a literary unit, it is also important to show that the repeated words which recur in its different parts throughout establish continuity and coherence of thought. This Overview considers the twice used expression śm ^{c}l-lb (to take to heart), and the repeated words bṣ^{c} (to covet), drk (a way), škb (to recline), ṣdqh (righteousness), and šlwm (peace).

The expression śm ^{c}l-lb occurs twice at 57:1ab and 57:11bb.

---

1. See Chapter One, p. 24.

57:1ab) w'yn 'yš śm ᶜl-lb

57:11bb) l' śmt ᶜl-lbk

Three points of similarity unite these two cola: 1) the use of a negation ('yn with the noun 'yš, and l' with the verb śmt); 2) the repetition of the verb śwm; and 3) the repetition of lb with the preposition ᶜl. The sense of these expressions is quickly passed over by commentators.[2] Beyond a literal translation of 57:1ab used by NAB, NEB, RSV, and TOB ("no one lays it to heart"), the BJ expresses it "et personne ne s'en inquiète"; this general sense of ᶜl-lb expresses a lack of concern toward the righteous individual's calamity.[3] But in comparing the parallel structure between vv. 1a and 1b, a fuller sense of the expression can be appreciated. As the parallel structure of 57:1aa and 57:1ba (hṣdyq//w'nšy-ḥsd) distinguishes the just individuals, so the structure of 57:1ab and 57:1bb (w'yn 'yš śm ᶜl-lb//b'yn mbyn) presents the people's lack of concern as rooted in their want of discernment. Similarly in 57:11b the parallel structure assists in uncovering the sense of the phrase; there is the negative l' with the second per. fem. verb which shows a parallel relationship between the two cola (l' zkrt//l' śmt). B.S. Childs points out that the use of the parallel verbs zrk//śwm at 57:11 extends the interpretation of this bicolon beyond the notion of

---

2. While commentators note the lack of concern shown to the plight of the righteous one, their concern rests with showing parallel passages dealing with similar troubles afflicting the upright (Ps 12:2 and Mic 7:2); cf. FOHRER, Das Buch Jesaja, 193-94; MUILENBURG, "The Book of Isaiah," 664; SCULLION, Isaiah 40-66, 155; WESTERMANN, Isaiah 40-66, 319; WHYBRAY, Isaiah 40-66, 201. In addition, despite his extended consideration of the word, H.W. WOLFF does not consider the meaning of lb in 57:1,11; cf. Anthropology of the Old Testament (Margaret Kohl, trans.; Philadelphia: Fortress Press, 1974) 40-58.

3. Cf. FOHRER, Das Buch Jesaja, 193-94; MUILENBURG, "The Book of Isaiah," 664; WHYBRAY, Isaiah 40-66, 201.

mere concern to include a sense of awareness;[4] this aspect of awareness includes the notions of perception, cognizance, and knowledge. As God addresses the people in 57:11b, the parallel construction of the verbs suggests that they have not even been cognizant of him; he says, "but me, you did not remember, nor place upon your heart." In 57:1a and 57:11b there is a similarity in meaning between the two expressions, while the two recipients are distinct: 57:1a addresses a lack of concern toward the righteous individual, while 57:11b reproves the accused for want of an awareness toward God.

In addition lb recurs in 57:17b in a similar manner, pointing to the human individual's inner workings of awareness and discernment. The expression bdrk lbw describes a particular way of thinking or acting guided by the promptings of one's heart.[5] "In the way of his heart" characterizes the activity of the will which guides one's actions and discerns a mode of behavior; Wolff speaks of it as "conscience."[6] Thus, the repetitions of lb in 57:1,11,17 all point to the inner workings of discernment giving rise to one's actions, while forms of the repeated expression śm ᶜl-lb distinguish the lack of concerned awareness toward the righteous (57:1) and toward God (57:11).

The repetition of bṣᶜ in 56:11 and 57:17 centers the motif of covetousness in this literary unit as these are the only recurrences of this word

---

4. Cf. Brevard S. CHILDS, Memory and Tradition in Israel (SBT 37; London: SCM Press, 1962) 58.

5. The expression bdrk lbw (in the way of his heart) of 57:17b resonates with Prov 16:9, lb ʼdm yḥšb drkw (a man's heart plans his way); both Isa 57:17b and Prov 16:9 show the heart as an instrument in the discernment of one's actions.

6. Cf. WOLFF, Anthropology, 51.

in all of Isa. In 56:11 lbṣᶜw describes the shepherds of Israel who are to care for their flock but have all turned in their own ways (klm ldrkm pnw), each of them after his own gain (ʼyš lbṣᶜw mqṣhw); instead of being concerned for those entrusted to their care, they see to their own needs.[7] In 57:17 God grows angry at the perversity of the people's covetousness (bᶜwn bṣᶜw qṣpty); because this people has walked in its own way, God strikes it and hides himself from it. In the repetitions of bṣᶜ, drk occurs with them.

56:11c) klm ldrkm pnw / ʼyš lbṣᶜw mqṣhw

57:17a-b) bᶜwn bṣᶜw qṣpty [. . .] wylk šwbb bdrk lbw.

The combination of bṣᶜ and drk shows in both instances how covetousness has become "the way" the shepherds and the people have chosen to act. Thus, the "way of covetousness" appears as a pervasive influence attributed both to the shepherds (leaders) and to the people.

Among the examples of repeated vocabulary, the six repetitions of drk distinguish it as a key word appearing throughout the literary unit (cf. 56:11; 57:10,14,14,17,18). The uses of drk have similar meanings, expressing a modus operandi, a manner in which individuals choose to act. In 56:11; 57:10,18, drk is found with pronominal suffixes distinguishing a manner of acting attributed to some group: the shepherds turn in their own way (ldrkm, 56:11c); those accused

---

7. The names "watchmen" and "shepherds" of 56:10-11 distinguish titles referring to different roles of leadership within the community of Israel. Commentators present varying views as to whether these names refer to the offices of king, priest, or prophet; cf. HANSON, The Dawn of Apocalyptic, 187; WESTERMANN, Isaiah 40-66, 317. A general reference to the watchmen and shepherds as leaders of the Israelite community suffices for the purpose of this study.

of wrong-doing were weary in their way (*drkk*, 57:10a); despite the manifestation of God's anger, the people continue to walk in the way of their own heart (*bdrk lbw*, 57:17a); though the Lord has seen his people's ways (*drkyw*, 57:18a), he will bring healing. This same emphasis is given to *drk* when found in the construct form: the way of my people (*mdrk ^{c}my*, 57:14). In 57:14ab "the way" spoken of refers to following in the paths of God's law leading to salvation; the Lord calls for their construction so that his people might live according to his commands and will.[8] From the examples cited, one can distinguish two aspects of *drk* as a *modus operandi*: 1) a motif of "waywardness" speaking about those who walk in their own ways instead of God's (cf. 56:11; 57:10,17,18); and 2) a motif of "salvation" calling for the removal of all obstacles that would prevent God's people from walking in his ways (57:14aa,14ab). Together these two aspects of *drk* provide an opposition between the ways of humanity and the ways of God.

The root *škb* appears five times in the context of the literary unit, four of them in a pejorative sense. In 56:10 the watchmen are described as reclining (*škbym*) and loving to sleep; such an account of guardians serves as an indictment against them. The uses of *mškb* (couch) in 57:7a,8b,8c highlight a

---

8. Cf. MUILENBURG, "The Book of Isaiah," 670-71; ROBERTS, "Isaiah in OT Theology," 142; P. VOLZ, *Jesaja II* (Kommentar zum Alten Testament 9; Hildesheim/New York: Georg Olms, 1932) 217-18; WESTERMANN, *Isaiah 40-66*, 328; WHYBRAY, *Isaiah 40-66*, 208-209. The uses of *drk* in 57:14aa and *mdrk ^{c}my* in 57:14ab demonstrate the poetic device "delayed identification," where for the sake of effect, the full clarification of a word is not immediate. In 57:14ab, *mdrk ^{c}my* (from the way of my people) elucidates the initial *drk* of v. 14aa and also distinguishes it from 56:11 and 57:10 where the contexts of *drk* are different. For further examples of this device see CERESKO, "A Poetic Analysis," 30; DAHOOD, "Poetry, Hebrew," 671-72; *Psalms III* (AB 17C; Garden City, NY: Doubleday, 1970) 52, 56.

motif of idolatrous practices, shrouded in the language of adultery and sexual immorality. In striking contrast to these three uses of mškb, 57:2 depicts the couch as a place of rest for those who walk in uprightness.[9] The converse sense of mškb for the upright in 57:2, as opposed to its relation to the irresponsible (56:10) and idolatrous (57:7,8), brings out an antithetical application of the word. The Hebrew poet was fond of such kinds of opposition which distinguish between good and evil, distress and joy, salvation and judgment in veiled or less obvious ways; similar examples of literary style allowed for subtle correspondence and striking contrasts.[10] The antithetical development and character of this literary unit has been discussed on p. 24 of Chapter One; a build-up of other literary features of contrast serves to demonstrate a literary style present in this passage. An awareness of the contrasting elements already mentioned encourages an open eye for more examples in this literary context.

The three repetitions of the root ṣdq in 57:1a,1c,12a recall one of the key words beginning the section in 56:1a. In 57:1 the righteous one (hṣdyq) appears from two perspectives: as the one who perishes (v. 1a) and as the one who is taken away from evil, entering into peace (vv. 1c,2a). Despite the lack of concern shown at the passing of the righteous, blessing comes to him who is

---

9. Cf. William L. HOLLADAY, Isaiah: Scroll of a Prophetic Heritage (Grand Rapids, MI: William B. Eerdmans, 1978) 168.

10. Cf. Richard CLIFFORD, "The Function of Idol Passages in Second Isaiah," CBQ 42 (1980) 454. Clifford shows the contrast in 41:1-10 between the fear (yr') which grips the coastlands and Yahweh's call to his people not to fear for he is with them; the futile encouragement (ᶜzr) of the unbeliever contrasts with the strength and encouragement the Lord gives his people; the maker of idols fastens (ḥzq) it together with nails but it is the Lord who takes his servants from the ends of the earth; and finally, the useless words ('mr) of the idolator are no match for the words of the victorious Lord.

counted among the upright (v. 2). The synonyms distinguishing the righteous one portray him as one who walks in the ways of the Lord; he is among those who show steadfast mercy (v. 1b) and practice uprightness (v. 2b). In contrast to this, the use of ṣdqh in 57:12 attacks the feigned practice of righteousness with a sarcastic threat made by the Lord; what the people of 57:11-12 consider as righteous will not save them from harsh judgment. Thus within the literary unit another contrast appears distinguishing the blessings coming to those who practice righteousness (57:1-2) and the harsh judgment to those who falsify it (57:12).

There are four recurrences of šlwm in 57:2,19a,19a,21. In the context of 57:2a "peace" is a blessing for it is a movement away from the presence of evil (v. 1c). The literary context of v. 2 suggests that šlwm carries a connotation of "rest," noting its parallel structure with v. 2ba: the righteous one enters into peace and the upright rest upon their couches. A similar sense of "peace" repeats in 57:20-21 but in a contrasting manner: there is no peace for the wicked who are like a tumultuous sea that is unable to rest. While in 57:1-2 šlwm is a blessing accompanying the righteous one's departure from the presence of evil, the absence of šlwm in 57:20-21 depicts punishment for the wicked. In 57:19 "peace" is connected to the Lord's action of healing. The repetition of the word heightens the promise of well-being and rest which šlwm carries here.[11] Thus, the concept of peace in the literary unit appears as the Lord's salvific blessing (57:2,19), but offered to the righteous (57:1-2) and denied

---

11. Cf. MUILENBURG, "The Book of Isaiah," 675.

to the wicked (57:20-21). The motif of "peace" links the opening and closing of the unit, as do ykl and bṣ^{c}.[12]

B. Delimitation of the Strophes

The major antitheses dividing the literary unit (56:9--57:2, 57:3-13, 57:14-21) are the starting point for the verification of the strophes. Each of the three parts is considered separately for an analysis of the structural elements aiding in the discernment of strophes.

56:9--57:2. There are several stylistic devices demonstrating links in these verses. An example of distant parallelism with 'th//bw' frames these verses in 56:9 and 57:2b.[13] This pair further demonstrates the antithesis: as the wild beasts are called to come ('tyw) and devour the leaders, the righteous one enters (ybw') into peace.[14] Another example of distant parallelism is yd^{c}//byn in 56:10a and 57:1b.[15] Both cola lament the absence of knowledge and discernment among the watchmen (56:10a) and the general populace (57:1b).

---

12. Commentators do not note šlwm, ykl, or bṣ^{c} and their similar contexts for establishing ties and lengthening the span of the literary unit.

13. For examples of the parallel pair 'th//bw', cf. D.N. FREEDMAN, "The Poetic Structure of the Framework of Deuteronomy 33," in The Bible World: Essays in Honor of Cyrus H. Gordon (Gary Rendsburg, ed.; New York: KTAV Publishing House, 1980) 38-39; IRWIN, Isaiah 28-33, xv, 78-79; Lorenzo VIGANO, Nomi e titoli di YHWH, alla luce del semitico del Nord-ovest (BibOr 31; Rome: Biblical Institute Press, 1976) 147-48. Beyond the examples given in these references, the following others can be noted; Job 3:25; Cant 4:8; Prov 1:27; Isa 41:22c, 23a; 41:25; 44:7.

14. Cf. p. 109.

15. Cf. FISCHER, Ras Shamra Parallels, I, 197-98.

This parallel pair in 56:10a and 57:1b initiates and concludes a series of negative descriptions occupying a consistent placement in the second colon of the bicolon structure. Note the pattern of negative expressions:

56:10a) l' yd^{c}w (they are without knowledge)

56:10b) l' ywklw lnbḥ (they are unable to bark)

56:11a) l' yd^{c}w śb^{c}h (they do not know satisfaction)

56:11b) l' yd^{c}w hbyn (they do not know discernment)

57:1a) w'yn 'yš śm ^{c}l-lb (there is no one who takes it to heart)

57:1b) b'yn mbyn (no, there is no one with discernment).

With the ten bi- and tricola that these verses span, six carry the development that begins with a statement and then is countered by the negative l' (56:10a,10b,11a,11b) or 'yn (57:1a,1b). The recurring reminder of the deficiencies in knowledge, satisfaction, discernment and concern bespeaks a bleak message pervading these verses. Further, several repetitions echo motifs. The recurrences of byn in 56:11b and 57:1b call to mind the lack of discernment among the shepherds and the people. The reiteration of škb presents a contrast in 56:10c and 57:2b; words of harsh judgment come against the watchmen who dream and recline (škbym, 56:10c) instead of guarding the people, while blessing issues for the upright who rest upon couches (mškbwtm, 57:2b) as reward for righteous living.

Though the ties among these verses are clear, several other structural devices help in the consideration of smaller strophic units. The repetition of the verb 'tyw (to come) in 56:9,12a functions as an inclusion, framing the description of the watchmen and shepherds. By means of repetition, the prophets often present a play on words to bring out a point with clarity or to demonstrate a turn in events; such a device is at work with this inclusion. Hanson expresses it well when he speaks of 56:12 as the "carpe diem philosophy" of the leaders which backfires on them.[16] The summons of the watchmen and shepherds "to come" and drink, to seize the moment, is going to be the same summons to the beasts (56:9) which will be their ruin. The repetition of the same verb in its command form and the example of "punning" bring a sense of closure to 56:12, concluding the judgment against the leaders of Israel. A shift in characters also takes place between 56:9-12 and 57:1-2; the watchmen and shepherds occupy the focus of attention in 56:9-12, while the fate of the righteous and upright ones is of importance in 57:1-2. Furthermore, an allusion to the destiny of both groups represented adds a dimension of symmetry to the consideration of each one: the leaders face a bitter end at the teeth of wild beasts (56:9), while the righteous enter into peace freed from the presence of evil (57:1c-2).

The examples of distant parallelism, repetition, and negative constructions verify the links in 56:9--57:2. However, the inclusion with *'tyw* and the self-contained descriptions of the leaders and the righteous, and their distinct fates recommend a division into strophes. These points suggest that 56:9--57:2 is a "stanza" composed of two strophes (56:9-12, 57:1-2).

57:3-13. In contrast to the previous stanza, 57:3-13 demonstrates a regular 3+2 *qinâ* rhythm; despite the few usual variations for emphasis, the

16. Cf. HANSON, *The Dawn of Apocalyptic*, 188.

uniform meter suggests the integrity of these verses. Beyond this, the use of rhetorical questions throughout witnesses to a consistent literary device at work.

v. 4a) Against whom (ᶜl-my) do you mock?

v. 4b) Against whom (ᶜl-my) do you open wide your mouth?

v. 4c) You, are you not (hlw'-'tm) children of transgression?

v. 6c) With such as these (hᶜl-'lh) am I to be comforted?

v. 11a) Now whom (w't-my) do you dread and fear?

v. 11c) Have I not (hl' 'ny) been silent long enough?

The rhetorical questions set up a literary context where the speaker is often the focus of attention; the interrogative my (vv. 4a,4b,11a) and personal pronoun in hl' 'ny (v. 11c) expect answers verifying the abuse and neglect the speaker has received.[17] In v. 6c, the h- interrogative functions as a negative assertion cast in the form of a rhetorical question, the speaker declaring his disconsolation with the actions stated in v. 6a-b.[18] Commentators concerned with genre analysis point out the characteristics of a courtroom scene (rîb) where the speaker acting as judge, plaintiff, and jury in vv. 3-13 is the Lord.[19] In light of this, the rhetorical questions function to enhance an argumentative literary style where the speaker establishes his just suit and forces those addressed to acknowledge

---

17. C. CONROY distinguishes between "my questions" looking for a particular response, and "hlw' questions" seeking an answer in the affirmative or negative; cf. Absalom, Absalom, 137. See also GKC, 476 §151a.

18. Cf. GKC, 474 §150d.

19. Cf. HANSON, The Dawn of Apocalyptic, 200; W. Eugene MARCH, "Prophecy," in Old Testament Form Criticism (John H. Hayes, ed.; San Antonio, TX: Trinity University Press, 1974) 166-68; MUILENBURG, "The Book of Isaiah," 669; PAURITSCH, Die neue Gemeinde, 64; WHYBRAY, Isaiah 40-66, 202.

their wrong doing (v. 4c).[20] Finally, in addition to the contrast of vv. 13a-b,13c, the parallel pair ḥlq//nḥl in 57:6a,13c adds another example of contrast: while a portion (ḥlqk, 57:6a) of smooth stones goes to those who practice idolatry, an inheritance of the land (ynḥl-'rṣ, 57:13c) issues to those who manifest fidelity to Yahweh.[21] The word-play with nḥl (meaning either "valley" or "inheritance") in bḥlqy-nḥl (stones of the valley, v. 6a) and ynḥl-'rṣ (will inherit the land, v. 13c) further brings out the difference between the recompense for the idolators and the faithful.[22]

In addition to the signs of unity in 57:3-13, several shifts in the speaker indicate a possible division into smaller units. The second per. masc. pl. verbs dominate in vv. 3-5. Then in vv. 6-10 there is a change to second per. fem. sing. verbs; within the prophetic writings the description of adulterous practices appears in this verb system to suggest that the message is addressed to a harlot.[23] Another change occurs in vv. 11-13 where there is a mixture of first per. sing. (vv. 11c, 12a), second per. fem. sing. (v. 11a-b), third per. masc. pl. (vv. 12b,13a), and third per. masc. and fem. sing. (vv.13b-c) verbs. The variation in speakers shows groupings into vv. 3-5, 6-10, and as a mixed construction vv. 11-13.

---

20. Some commentators point out that the rhetorical question is often used for effect in trial speeches; cf. SCHOORS, I Am God, Your Savior, 202, 204, 215; MUILENBURG, "The Book of Isaiah," 388. KUNTZ shows the importance of rhetorical questions as a stylistic feature in Isa, particularly his study of Isa 51:1-16; cf. "The Contribution of Rhetorical Criticism," 149.

21. On the parallel pair ḥlq//nḥl, see examples in Deut 32:9; Jer 5:19; Ezek 48:29.

22. Cf. HANSON, The Dawn of Apocalyptic, 187.

23. Cf. HANSON, The Dawn of Apocalyptic, 198.

To further support this division of 57:3-13 into three groupings, the repetition and organization of pronouns also function as a structuring device.[24] The following chart distinguishes the repetitions and their placement in context.

(A)	v. 3a) w'tm	(B)	v. 6a) hm, hm	(C)	v. 11a) w't-my
	v. 4a) ^{c}l-my		v. 6b) lhm		v. 11b) w'wty
	v. 4b) ^{c}l-my		v. 6c) 'lh		v. 11ca) 'ny
	v. 4c) w'tm		v. 8c) mhm		v. 11cb) w'wty
					v. 12a) 'ny

The pronouns appearing in 57:3-13 form three patterns coinciding with the change of speakers. In A the courtroom scene begins with the second per. masc. pl. personal pronoun emphasizing the ones summoned for trial (v. 3a) and an acknowledgement of their identity (vv. 3,4c) by the address made to them, "and you." The reiteration of the interrogative pronoun (my) draws attention to the speaker Yahweh, the one they offend. The pronouns in vv. 3-5 distinguish the two parties involved with emphasis, the accused and the judge Yahweh. In B the demonstrative pronouns center around v. 6 with another occurrence in v. 8c. With vv. 6-10, the practices of idolatry are described; Muilenburg believes the repeated pronouns draw attention to the inheritance coming from illicit conduct, further emphasizing the relationship between deed and recompense.[25] Scholars

24. ALONSO SCHÖKEL shows how the accumulation of verbal forms, pronouns, and pronominal suffixes not only function to structure a poem, but also provide order, movement, and development of motifs and themes; cf. Estudios de Poética Hebrea, 90, 116. Others in rhetorical criticism confirm this; see ANDERSEN and FREEDMAN, Hosea, 126-27, 265, 381-82, 516; David J.A. CLINES, I, He, We, and They: A Literary Approach to Isaiah 53 (JSOTSup 1; Sheffield: The University of Sheffield, 1976) 37-40; KUNTZ, "The Contribution of Rhetorical Criticism," 146-47.

25. Cf. MUILENBURG, "The Book of Isaiah," 666.

remain divided as to whether v. 6 belongs to v. 5,[26] or to vv. 7ff;[27] this demands further investigation in the Close Reading of the verse. At least for the present purposes, the change in speaker and the recurring demonstrative pronouns suggest it be placed with vv. 7ff. In C the mixture of interrogative and personal pronouns accentuates the speaker Yahweh, focusing attention on him in this final word of judgment. The pronouns in their full form stress God in his address: Now whom did you fear [. . .] but me you did not remember [. . .] have I not been silent long enough, yet me you did not fear (v. 11). Thus while the regular meter, the repeated rhetorical questions, and distant parallelism show the unity of these verses, the shift in speaker and patterned placement of pronouns suggest that 57:3-13 is a stanza composed of three strophes (vv. 3-5, 6-10, 11-13).

57:14-21. The repetitions of ʼmr in vv. 14,21 enclose a predominantly salvation-oriented message proclaiming a way for God's people (v. 14) with healing, comfort, and guidance (v. 18). Another two recurrences of ʼmr in vv. 15a,19b further reiterate God's promise of redemptive intervention in reviving the humble (v. 15) and offering peace (v. 19). The localization of ʼmr, four times in this final part of the unit with God as the speaker, highlights these final verses as a divine word of salvation. To further show the congruous character of this motif, thirteen first per. sing. verbs (ʼškwn, 57:15b; ʼryb [. . .] ʼqṣwp, 57:16a; ᶜśyty, 57:16b; qṣpty wʼkhw hstr wʼqṣp, 57:17a; rʼyty wʼrpʼhw wʼnḥhw wʼšlm, 57:18b; wrpʼtyw, 57:19b) occur in

26. Cf. BONNARD, Le Second Isaïe, 357, 359; PENNA, Isaia, 558, 566; among translations, see JB and NAB, following the strophic division of vv. 3-5, 6-10.

27. Cf. MUILENBURG, "The Book of Isaiah," 665-66; WESTERMANN, Isaiah 40-66, 321; WHYBRAY, Isaiah 40-66, 203-204.

which God is the speaker. There is also a general metric shift from the 3+2 of vv. 3-13 to 3+3 in vv. 14-21, with a few variations for emphasis.

Several stylistic devices suggest a division into strophes. The emphasis given to the repetition of the opening words in v. 14 (slw, slw) recurs in v. 19b (šlwm, šlwm). Beyond the repetition of initial words, the opening sibilant sounds of s and š followed by l indicate a pattern of alliteration; since this structured assonance begins this final section in v. 14, its recurrence could signal another division in v. 19b. In addition, vv. 14,19b stand out as expansive lines of 4+4 (also v. 15a) and 4+3 respectively. Often changes in rhythm serve to introduce something new or to show a transition taking place in the text.[28] And finally, the triple use of šlwm in 57:19-21 focuses on an earlier motif (cf. 57:2) in these final verses. The repetition of "peace" expands on the redemptive character of this blessing in showing its relationship to healing (v. 19b) and echoes the previous announcement that its bestowal comes to the righteous and not the wicked (57:20-21). Thus while an emphasis on God's salvific word carries through the unit, recurring patterns of assonance, expanded meter, and focus on a concluding motif suggest that 57:14-21 is a stanza composed of two strophes (vv. 14-19a, 19b-21).

Beyond the major literary device of contrast dividing the unit into three parts (56:9--57:2, 57:3-13, 57:14-21) and the inclusion with ykl, the repeated vocabulary discussed above exhibit both continuity and development of

---

28. Cf. Robert GORDIS, "The Structure of Biblical Poetry," in Poets, Prophets, and Sages: Essays in Biblical Interpretation (Bloomington, IN: Indiana University Press, 1971) 70; MUILENBURG, "Form Criticism," 12.

thought. The repeated śm ᶜl-lb shows the lack of concern for both the righteous one (57:1) and for God (57:11). The repetition of bṣᶜ, appearing only in this literary unit within Isa, describes a way of acting ascribed to the leaders within Israel and to the people. The uses of drk, škb, ṣdqh, and šlwm build on the literary characteristic of antithesis distinguishing between the ways of God (57:14) and of humanity (56:11; 57:10,18), the couch of blessed rest (57:2) and of idolatry (57:7), authentic (57:1) and inauthentic (57:12) righteousness, and peace for the upright (57:2) but not for the wicked (57:20-21). Diverse structural elements consisting of inclusion, distant parallelism, repetition, metric regularity, assonance, and use of rhetorical questions all assist in the division of this unit into three stanzas with strophes.

II. CLOSE READING

A. Isaiah 56:9-12 -- Judgment upon Israel's Leaders

The opening verse begins the strophe with a tricolon in an ABA pattern.[29]

(A) kl ḥytw śdy

(B) 'tyw l'kl

(A) kl-ḥytw byᶜr

29. Cf. WATSON, "Chiastic Patterns," 126.

In the AA elements the repetition of kl ḥytw not only frames the middle colon but also signals an example of "merism."[30] In 56:9 the merism stands out with the repetition of kl (all), calling all beasts of the field and forest; the summons presents an image of numerous wild animals called to a feast.[31] The B element is the center of focus stressing the call, "come to devour." As earlier noted, the imperative verb 'tyw forms both an inclusion and a pun with its repetition in 56:9,12a; its placement in the middle of this chiasm further shows its importance in this opening verse. A final point distinguishing v. 9 is its internal structure as a tricolon amidst a strophe and stanza of bicola. As L. Boadt points out, the lack of symmetry and style in poetic verse often draws attention to itself and is an external manifestation of a significant message being presented.[32] As noted on p. 101, the distant parallels 'th//bw' in 56:9 and 57:2 signal a contrast. Further, a contrast exists in the movement from the previous literary unit stressing the coming of salvation (56:1,7) to this new unit highlighting the coming of punishment (56:9) amidst words of judgment. Thus the opening verse artistically shifts the reader from the admonition-salvation imagery in 56:1-8 into that of judgment-punishment in 56:9-12.

---

30. Cf. WATSON, "Chiastic Patterns," 126. Merism is a device employed in biblical literature naming two (or more) components within a given species that connote the whole genus, giving the expression(s) an exhaustive character, representing fullness; often these expressions are polar expressions. See also DAHOOD, Psalms III, xiv; A.M. HONEYMAN, "Merismus in Biblical Hebrew," JBL 71 (1952) 14.

31. For another example of śdh and y^{c}r expressing totality, see Ezek 39:10.

32. Cf. BOADT, "Isaiah 41:8-13," 26-27.

In 56:9 the call to the beasts of the field and the forest can be enigmatic at a first reading. The question arising is, to devour whom? Thus far 56:9 is seen as an announcement of punishment for the leaders and contrasts with the blessing for the righteous in 57:2. However, 56:9 is interpreted by some commentators as a call by God to come and make waste of the people left without guardians, described in 56:10-11.[33] The reasoning behind a solution to the vague opening verse led scholars to discover an answer in Jer 12:9b which closely resembles Isa 56:9.

Jer 12:9b) lkw 'spw kl-ḥyt hśdh / htyw l'klh.
Go, assemble all the wild beasts, / bring them to devour.

Here the object of the devouring is Israel, God's heritage (nḥlty, Jer 12:7,8,9); because his heritage lifts up its voice against the Lord (Jer 12:8), he abandons it calling the beasts of the field to come and devour. Jer 12:10 proceeds describing the shepherds (rᶜym; see also Isa 56:11) who destroy God's vineyard, his portion (Jer 12:10).

Though employing similar vocabulary and imagery, Isa 56:9-12 and Jer 12:7-9,10-13 describe different situations and are distinct literary contexts. Isa 56:9-12 is not an indictment against the people as is Jer 12:7-9; the Isaian text is an indictment against Israel's leaders. Rhetorical critics point out that one must be careful in stepping out of the literary context to explain a text that is vague; although grounded in tradition, the prophets were creative in their use

33. Cf. FOHRER, Das Buch Jesaja, 192; MUILENBURG, "The Book of Isaiah," 661; SCULLION, Isaiah 40-66, 155; WHYBRAY, Isaiah 40-66, 200.

of familiar images and vocabulary.[34] While aware of how a particular phrase or set of images is used in another context, the unique literary context that is before one should be evaluated for its particular message, possibly reshaping an old idea for a new literary environment. Though it is difficult to be certain if the call to devour is also directed against the neglected people, the announced punishment can be taken as a proper recompense for the irresponsible leaders who disregard their responsibility. This opening verse reads as a judgment against the watchmen and shepherds, naming the penalty for their remiss stewardship.

Several commentators remark on the uneven structure in 56:10-11 with four bicola describing the watchmen (ṣpw, 56:10a) and only two bicola describing the shepherds (r^{c}ym, 56:11b).[35] However a closer look at the internal structure may reveal a smoother reading of vv. 10-11 than suggested.

There is an absence of the usual w connecting bicola in the strophe except in 56:11a,11b,12b. The w of whyh in 56:12b connects the two bicola by concluding the thought begun in v. 12a. The two uses of w in 56:11a,11b are somewhat different. Some suggest the w of whklbym is emphatic in this context;[36] the grammatical structure of the preceding bicolon in 56:10c does not connect easily with 56:11a since 56:10c is a series of participles which describe

---

34. The study of MELUGIN points out how "typical" aspects of a text are modified to present another understanding of a passage; cf. "The Conventional and the Creative," 301-11.

35. Cf. MUILENBURG, "The Book of Isaiah," 663; WESTERMANN, Isaiah 40-66, 318.

36. Cf. SCULLION, "Some Difficult Texts," 108; TORREY, The Second Isaiah, 432-33.

the klbym of 56:10b. Besides, the repetition of the root klb in 56:11a forms a link with its first use in 56:10b. Thus the w of whklbym functions as a way to stress the second use of klb; hence the translation, "yes, the dogs."

The whmh of 56:11b needs clarification as to its meaning and function. Some translators follow BHK or BHS which suggest an emendation reading wᵉgam hārōᶜim (and also the shepherds) instead of the Massoretic whmh rᶜym;[37] however the MT remains the preferred reading for this study despite the initial challenge it presents. The w with the personal pronoun hmh (they) in 56:11b can have whklbym (the dogs) of 56:11a as its referent. The bicola in v. 11a-b have a similar parallel structure with an acknowledgement of who is spoken about, followed by a negative statement about them.

v. 11a)	(A)	the dogs have an insatiable appetite
	(B)	they do not know satisfaction;
v. 11b)	(A')	they are shepherds
	(B')	they do not know discernment

This same pattern appears in 56:10a-b.

v. 10a)	(A)	his watchmen are blind
	(B)	they are without knowledge
v. 10b)	(A')	each of them are dumb dogs
	(B')	they are unable to bark

The parallel pattern of vv. 10a-b, 11a-b demonstrates a similar manner of introducing both the watchmen and the shepherds based on internal structuring of the bicola. Such parallel organization then suggests that v. 11b functions with v. 11a, following suit with v. 10a-b. In his discussion of 56:11b, J. Scullion

37. Cf. RSV; WESTERMANN, Isaiah 40-66, 316.

furthers the argumentation by noting Dahood's proposal of hmh as an expletive or particle of surprise.[38] Dahood demonstrates several examples in the Psalms where hmh either does not make sense as a personal pronoun, or works well as both pronoun and expletive together; it is not uncommon for the biblical text to have a word carrying more than one meaning or allusion.[39] In accepting its dual role in 56:11b, whmh displays an example of "delayed identification," where the derogatory image of "dogs" applied to the watchmen in 56:10a is later applied to the shepherds also.[40] In v. 11a the dogs are described as having an insatiable appetite and not knowing satifaction; then v. 11b identifies who the dogs are: "and look, they are shepherds, they do not know discernment." Further unifying the verse, the motif of "covetousness" in v. 11c resonates with the description of the dogs in v. 11a who are without satisfaction; their insatiable appetite and lack of satisfaction keep them covetous for their own needs.

Looking again at the larger context of 56:10-11, the "dogs" of 56:10b,11a are an image describing both leaders; but in the unfolding of the poem their titles as watchmen and shepherds, and their descriptions as dogs present a chiastic structure.

---

38. M.J. DAHOOD suggests hmh is a variant form of hnh borrowed from the Ugaritic hm; cf. "The Language and Date of Psalm 48(47)," CBQ 16 (1954) 16. In his commentaries on the Psalms he shows other examples in Pss 9:8; 27:2; 37:9; 38:11; 43:3; 56:7; 59:4; 107:23.

39. M.J. DAHOOD shows this in relation to hmh; cf. Psalms I (AB 17A; Garden City, NY: Doubleday, 1966) 166-67, 191.

40. For more information on "delayed identification," see DAHOOD, "Poetry, Hebrew," 671-72.

(A) His watchmen (56:10a)
  (B) they are dumb dogs (56:10b)
  (B) the dogs have an insatiable appetite (56:11a)
(A') They are shepherds (56:11b)

From the above considerations a sense of balance is restored to the reading of 56:10-11 with a three-bicola description of both the watchmen (v. 10) and the shepherds (v. 11), and with two descriptions of Israel's leaders both presented in the imagery of dogs (v. 10b, 11a).

A further indication of the symmetry in vv. 10,11 is the distant parallelism with ydᶜ//byn in 56:10a,11b.[41] In the bicola naming the two groups of leaders, a word from the parallel pair occurs.

56:10a)	ṣpw	/	l' ydᶜw
56:11b)	rᶜym	/	l' ydᶜw hbyn

The titles "watchmen" and "shepherds" in concert with the parallel words add to the sense of balance in each description of the leading groups: both lack knowledge and discernment. Not only does the pair show structural sensitivity but also distinguishes the leadership in Israel as lacking in a key component of faith. The opening verses of Isa lament a similar situation.

The ox knows (ydᶜ) its owner
  and the ass its master's crib;
But Israel does not know (l' ydᶜ)
  my people does not understand (l' htbwnn). (Isa 1:3)

---

41. On the parallel pair ydᶜ//byn, see note 15 in this Chapter.

As O. Kaiser notes, an Israelite conception of knowledge is not purely intellectual but also relational.[42] In Isa 1:3, Israel does not have a proper sense of affinity with its Master the Lord. In Isa 56:10-11, the leaders of Israel do not have a proper sense of their relationship to those entrusted to their care: though watchmen, they love to slumber; though shepherds, they seek their own gain. Their lack of knowledge and discernment witnesses to the breakdown of their call and its responsibilities.

Several examples of sound patterns enhance an effective reading of this strophe. In 56:9 there is the threefold use of the radicals kl and the repetition of the word ḥytw; the sound of kl ḥytw initiates the first and third cola with the second colon concluding on the kl sound in the infinitive l'kl. When the sound repetitions are placed in relief the message is boldly displayed.

56:9) kl ḥytw	/	l'kl	/	kl ḥytw
All beasts	/	to devour	/	all beasts!

The sound motif of kl continues to recur another six times in the following two verses. The words ^{c}iwrîm kullām in 56:10a initiate a recurring sound pattern with -îm and -ām at the end of words in the first colon of the bicolon carrying through 56:10-11. Note the following recurrences:

56:10a	[. . .] ^{c}iwrîm kullām [. . .]
56:10b	kullām k^{e}lābîm 'ill^{e}mîm / lō' yuk^{e}lû [. . .]
56:10c	hōzîm šōk^{e}bîm [. . .]
56:11a	w^{e}hakk^{e}lā bîm [. . .]

---

42. Cf. Otto KAISER, Isaiah 1-12 (R.A. Wilson, trans.; Old Testament Library; Philadelphia: The Westminster Press, 1972) 8.

56:11b [. . .] ro^c^îm [. . .]

56:11c kullām l^e^darkām [. . .]

As the repetition of kl in 56:9 emphasizes the total ensemble of wild beasts, so the repetition of klm specifies that each of the watchmen (56:10a), each of the dogs (56:10b), and each of the shepherds (56:11b,11c) are included in the description; the effect is not only in the recurrence of the word but also in the sound, as it punctuates the opening bicola of 56:9,10b,11c.[43] Then the recurring -ām, -îm in 56:10-11 serves as a motif bringing back the sound pattern which initiates the description of the leaders in 56:10a.[44]

There is also a pattern in the use of the negative l' in the second cola of several bicola (56:10ab,10bb,11ab,11bb) and the more specific repetition of l' yd^c^w in 56:10ab,11ab,11bb. Here again the recurring sound enforces the motif of a lack of knowledge.

In 56:10b each word in the bicolon contains a l and the combination of kl as radicals occurs three times. It is effective here with the root of the word "dog" being klb.[45] In 56:11b the description of the sleeping watchmen is marked

---

43. J.C. EXUM stresses that there is an intimate connection between "thought rhythm" and "sound rhythm" figuring into the interpretation of Hebrew poetry; cf. "Of Broken Pots," 340.

44. Thomas P. McCREESH designates a recurrent combination of sounds, whether vowels, consonants, or both as a "motif"; cf. "Poetic Sound Patterns in Proverbs 10-29" (Ph.D. dissertation, Catholic University of America, 1982) 30.

45. The repeated l breaks the accents of the harsher consonants, toning down the guttural sounds that would hint at a barking sound; this aids in creating the image of a mute dog.

by a predominance of the ō, û, and final m sounds. The open breathlike sound of the ō, û and the humming sound of the final m suggest an example of onomatopoeia, depicting their sleep. Other examples of ō, û, m, plus š, imitating sounds of slumber, can be cited.

Ps 4:5 rigzû wᵉʼal-teḥᵉṭāʼû / ʼimrû bilbabkem /
ᶜal-miškabkem wᵉdommû;

Isa 14:18b kullam šākbû bᵉkābôd / ʼiš bᵉbêtô

The effects of assonance not only bring a sense of order to the strophe, but also refine the different images with force and deftness.

The final verse at 56:12 brings the strophe to a conclusion not only by its repetition of ʼtyw and sarcastic implication, but also by climaxing what has been stated about the leaders; now on the lips of the leaders, they confirm what is stated above and condemn themselves. Instead of being concerned about the responsibilities of watchmen (56:9) and shepherds (56:10), their attention is fixed on wine (yyn, 56:12a) and strong drink (škr, 56:12a); though their cry is that tomorrow will be like today, "great beyond measure" (gdwl ytr mʼd, 56:12b), these shepherds are like dogs that are never satisfied (lʼ ydᶜw śbᶜh, 56:11a). This final verse caps a theme of judgment initiated from the beginning. In 56:9 the summons to the wild beasts announces the punishment awaiting the irresponsible leaders. The descriptions of the watchmen and shepherds in vv. 10-11 elaborate on the charges brought against them. A tone of judgment prevails showing how the leaders fail in carrying out the fundamental tasks of their offices: watchmen characterized by their slumber and shepherds distinguished by their avarice. Their want of knowledge and discernment addresses the poverty of their care for others; they do not know their calling. And finally, the leaders' invitation to share in their revelry without concern for tomorrow displays their ignorance that time is all important, for divine judgment now awaits them.

B. Isaiah 57:1-2 -- Peace for the Righteous

The internal structure of 57:1a-b demonstrates an ABA'B pattern.

(A) The righteous one has perished
 (B) and no one (w'yn) takes it to heart
(A') People of steadfast kindness are taken away
 (B) and there is no one (b'yn) with discernment

The AA' cola note the threatening situation of the upright: the righteous one perishes ('bd) and the people of steadfast kindness are taken away (n'spym). The BB cola explain the lamentable circumstances regarding the upright: there is neither concern (w'yn 'yš śm ᶜl-lb) nor discernment (b'yn mbyn) for what is happening. The repetitions of w'yn and b'yn in the second cola assume an emphatic role stressing the absence of solicitude by anyone with regard to the situation. This is further established by the w of w'yn acting as an adversive connection to stress the surprise at the incongruity of the situation in 57:1aa and the response to it in 57:1ab;[46] the b of b'yn is an emphatic particle strengthening the phrase to which it belongs.[47] In the larger context of the stanza 56:9--57:2, the lack of people with concern (57:1ab,1bb) resonates with the irresponsible leaders (klm, cf. 56:10a,10b,11c) demonstrating another link in

---

46. Cf. GKC, 484-85 §154a.

47. Cf. SCULLION, "Some Difficult Texts," 109.

the strophes. The repetition of mbyn in 57:1b echoes the shepherds' lack of discernment (l' yd^{c}w hbyn, 56:11b) and the watchmen's want of knowledge (as a distant parallel with l' yd^{c}w at 56:10a). The relational aspect of yd^{c}//byn in 56:10a,11b returns in 57:1a-b where the want of discernment translates into a poverty of concern for the plight of the upright.

In 57:1 a chiastic word pattern with hṣdyq and 'sp carries through the verse.

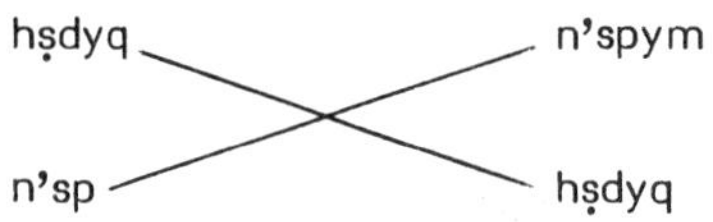

The careful construction of the chiasm in 57:1 demonstrates several emphases in the strophe. One notes the verse is framed by hṣdyq at its limits; this placement at the beginning and end of the verse gives the word a position of priority in the literary context.[48] Such a use of hṣdyq helps to accentuate the contrast with the leaders discussed in 56:10-11, referred to as dogs. In the chiasm itself the vocabulary discusses the state of the righteous (57:1aa,1ba,1ca), not those who lack concern (57:1ab,1bb). Thus the chiasm draws attention to the situation of the righteous as the primary consideration of the strophe; this further supports the contrast with the irresponsible leaders who were the focus of 56:9-12.

48. N.W. LUND argues that the constitutive words/elements of a chiastic structure distinguish important words; cf. Chiasmus in the New Testament (Chapel Hill, NC: University of North Carolina Press, 1942) 44; see also MUILENBURG, "The Book of Isaiah," 664.

The construction of the bicola in 57:1-2 provides a clue for understanding the function of the chiasm. The particle ky in 57:1c shows an adverse movement taking place in the text;[49] the placement of the particle between the two middle elements of the chiasm also serves to demonstrate its purpose of being a "signpost" of a transition. Several authors observe that a chiasm can indicate a reversal, transformation, or some kind of alternation in the ideas or motifs that are taking place in the text.[50] The inversion of the words in a chiasm may suggest an inversion of a situation in the text; this is further enhanced by the repetition of the same words but in reversed order signalling change and yet balance.[51] The change implies a possible reversal of ideas, and balances a complementary part of the previous notion. This appears to be the function of the chiasm in 57:1. The opening two bicola of 57:1 state the lamentable situation of the righteous one (hṣdyq) and the people of steadfast kindness who are being taken away (n'spym); but the third bicola (57:1c,2a) ushers in a change by showing that their passing away is a blessed event because the righteous one is taken away (n'sp hṣdyq) from evil. 57:2 then expands upon this reversal of events by explaining the passing away as an entry into peace (šlwm) and rest (ynwḥw).

---

49. MUILENBURG explains that the particle ky can indicate opposition following a negative expression in the text; cf. "The Linguistic and Rhetorical Usages," 139. With regard to this comment, one notes the use of b'yn in 57:1bb, followed by ky in 57:1c.

50. Cf. Anthony R. CERESKO, "The Function of Chiasmus in Hebrew Poetry," CBQ 40 (1978) 2-6; TALMON, "The Textual Study," 358-64.

51. Cf. WELCH, "Introduction," 9.

The change indicated in the chiasm at 57:1c continues its description in 57:2a; the movement away from evil (hr^{c}h) and into peace (šlwm) develops the notion of reward for the righteous. Other examples attest to the opposing character of r^{c}h and šlwm to express a single idea. In a description of the Lord as creator of all, Isa 45:7 expresses totality by use of merism; the examples of contrast are light and darkness, prosperity (šlwm) and woe (r^{c}h). Here the extremes of imagery build the idea of Yahweh as a cosmic authority, in control of all things.

> I form the light and create the darkness,
> I make prosperity and create woe:
> I, the Lord, do all these things. (Isa 45:7, NAB)

And in Jer 29:11 the Lord speaks through the prophet to assure the people of his deep and abiding concern for them in their captivity with a vision of their forthcoming release. Once again the polarities expressed by šlwm and r^{c}h (with a negative) depict God's love as wholly directed toward restoration.

> For I know the plans I have for you, says the Lord, plans for welfare and not for evil, to give you a future and a hope. (Jer 29:11)

These examples support the opposition which hr^{c}h and šlwm present in 57:1c,2a, demonstrating the polarities in the movement from evil toward peace. Serving as a merism, these words show the reward for the righteous, a transformed situation away from evil into peace (cf. also 57:19b-21).

In 57:2a the righteous one enters (ybw') into peace. As earlier noted, ybw' forms an example of distant parallelism with 'tyw of 56:9. This parallel pair further confirms the contrast between the opening and closing of the stanza in presenting two images of "coming." Even before considering these words in their literary context, the previous uses of bw' in 56:1,7 began this section and division of Isa looking forward to the coming of God's salvation and deliverance. Moving to the next literary unit, a similar "coming" motif recurs, this time set in judgment and punishment (56:9,12) and reward and blessing (57:2). In the contrast of the distant parallels 'th//bw', one can see an affinity between the uses of bw' in 56:1,7 and 57:2a; both recurrences echo God's redemptive action. The call to practice righteousness (56:1) reflects the understanding that salvation is approaching; similarly in 57:2, the righteous individual is rescued from evil and given entry into peace. Especially in light of the contrast brought out by the distant parallelism in 56:9 and 57:2, the use of bw' in 57:2 resonates with its earlier uses in 56:1,7.

Several commentators mention the difficult reading of 57:2 with ybw' as a singular verb, followed by ynwḥw as a plural verb, and concluding with a singular active participle.[52] However, the change in the person of the verbs can be understood more easily and the poetic freedom appreciated when considering the whole of 57:1-2. In 57:1a the subject of the verb is a singular noun (hṣdyq); in 57:1b it is a plural noun in construct (w'nšy-ḥsd). Then in 57:1c, it is again a singular noun (hṣdyq); the subject of 57:1c is also the "subject understood" of ybw' in 57:2a. The subject of 57:2ba is not identified in the text, but the verb indicates a third per. pl. subject; the referent of the verb is likely 'nšy-ḥsd of 57:1b. And the singular participle of 57:2bb refers back to hṣdyq of

---

52. Cf. SCULLION, Isaiah 40-66, 155; WESTERMANN, Isaiah 40-66, 320; WHYBRAY, Isaiah 40-66, 201.

In 57:2 ybw' šlwm is ambiguous with a possible reading of šlwm as the subject or the direct object. Based on the parallelism in 57:1c and 57:2a, šlwm is taken as the direct object. Cf. HANSON, The Dawn of Apocalyptic, 192 note (k); SCULLION, "Some Difficult Texts," 109.

57:1a,1c. When considering the parallel construction of hṣdyq (57:1a) and 'nšy-ḥsd (57:1b), the opening cola speak both of an individual and a group; the importance of this distinction is highlighted by the alternating forms of singular and plural verbs, especially in those without a subject. One also notes that the subject of the verbal root 'sp is both the 'nšy-ḥsd (57:1b) and hṣdyq (57:1c); the similar use of the same verb links the passive activity of being taken away to both the individual and the group. The description refers both to the individuals and to a collective body who can be called "people of steadfast kindness"; their fate is common (57:1a,1b) but so is their reward (57:1c,2a,2b). Thus, it appears that the free alternation of hṣdyq and 'nšy-ḥsd as the subjects permits a free alternation of the verbs between singular and plural, understanding the mutual situation and reward which belong both to ḥsdyq and 'nšy-ḥsd.

The strophe begins with the statement explaining the unfortunate situation of the righteous; but in 57:1c,2a this ill-fated circumstance is explained as a reward because he is rescued from evil. Despite the neglect shown them, the righteous know God's blessing in their passage from the presence of evil to peace; those who walk in uprightness come to rest from their trials.

C. Isaiah 57:3-5 -- Mockery and Deception Against God

The opening words of 57:3 begin this strophe on a note of contrast. Hanson explains w'tm as a term of transition in Isa 56-66 demonstrating a movement from a word of salvation to judgment;[53] w'tm quickly moves the

53. Cf. HANSON, The Dawn of Apocalyptic, 188.

reader from the rewards of the righteous in 57:2 to a summons to appear before the judge in 57:3. The w'tm functions in a similar fashion with 65:10 describing the place of rest for the flocks of those seeking the Lord, and 65:11 breaking in with a harsh word against those forsaking him.

65:10 Sharon shall become a pasture for flocks [. . .]
for my people who have sought me.
65:11 But you (w'tm) who forsake the Lord [. . .]

The antithesis between the words of salvation and judgment continues in Isa 65.

65:13 Therefore, thus says the Lord God:
Behold, my servants shall eat,
but you (w'tm) shall be hungry;
behold, my servants shall drink,
but you (w'tm) shall be thirsty;
behold, my servants shall rejoice,
but you (w'tm) shall be put to shame;
65:14 behold, my servants shall sing for gladness of heart,
but you (w'tm) shall cry out for pain of heart [. . .]

Among its several functions in 57:3 w'tm makes a contrast between the upright of 57:1-2 and the wicked in 57:3-5. The w of w'tm also connects the poetry of 57:3 with the preceding stanza; this manner of uniting the stanzas similarly recurs in 57:14 with w'mr.[54] And finally, with its emphatic position opening the stanza and strophe, w'tm signals the movement from the word of promise in 57:2 into another judgement scene.

54. Cf. HANSON, The Dawn of Apocalyptic, 186, 188.

It is generally agreed by commentators that 57:3-5 is constructed as a trial speech, a rîb.[55] Though it is not the intention of this study to take up the literary genre, several points can be gleaned from such an approach and aid in distinguishing the literary character of vv. 3-5.[56] The component elements constituting the structure of a trial speech help one to appreciate how its descriptive language distinguishes a theme of judgment.[57]

The strophe begins with a summons to court.[58] The word qrbw calls the accused to come before the judge to begin the process of the lawsuit. This same verbal root (qrb) is found in other judgment scenes/speeches (cf. Deut 25:1; Isa 34:1; 41:1b); this way of calling forth the accused to approach the judge paints a vivid image of a courtroom scene where a trial is about to begin. In connection with this summons, the titles of address given the defendants are made in an accusatory manner carrying a sense of incrimination and reproach.[59]

---

55. Cf. BONNARD, Le Second Isaïe, 357; FOHRER, Das Buch Jesaja, 196-97; HANSON, The Dawn of Apocalyptic, 188-89; MUILENBURG, "The Book of Isaiah," 664; PAURITSCH, Die neue Gemeinde, 64; WESTERMANN, Isaiah 40-66, 321; WHYBRAY, Isaiah 40-66, 202.

56. Such a use of literary genre is viewed as a means of appreciating the Sitz in der Literatur not Sitz im Leben; cf. ALONSO SCHÖKEL, "Die stilistische Analyse," 162.

57. While one speaks of the "component elements" of a trial speech, it should also be noted that there is not a complete consensus on this topic; the debate continues. To enter into this discussion would extend beyond the scope of this study. Rather, drawing on various studies of the rîb, a brief survey of its stylistic devices and vocabulary depicting the progression of a trial speech follows.

58. Cf. J. HARVEY, Le plaidoyer prophétique contre Israël après la rupture de l'alliance: Etude d'une formule littéraire de l'Ancien Testament (Bruges/Paris: Desclée De Brouwer, 1967) 61.

59. Cf. Kirsten NIELSEN, Yahweh as Prosecutor and Judge (JSOTSup 9; Sheffield: University of Sheffield, 1978) 15.

Terms like *bny* (sons, 57:3), *zr^{c}* (offspring, 57:3,4), and *yldy* (children, 57:4) express a motif of descendants/family/generations connoting that those summoned to court come from a long line of sinful people, a generation born of transgressors.[60] The vindictive character of such language heightens the harshness of this judgment scene at its outset.

The rhetorical questions function as a kind of cross examination beginning the actual proceedings of the trial.[61] In 57:4 the verbs used in the questioning are in the second person, another characteristic of the trial speech.[62] The manner of questioning in the second per. focuses attention on the defendants and the charge brought against them; this is effectively done in 57:4 with a motif of assonance brought out with the initial *t* and the final *û* sound for each of the verbs. The sounding of the verbs brings forth an accusation in 57:4: you mock, you open wide your mouth, and you wag your tongue. In the MT a sense of rapid questioning is achieved by a regular 3+2 rhythm and by the short cola found in 57:3-5. Thus the rhetorical questions and the stylistic devices of 57:3-5 (especially v. 4) support a theme of judgment in this trial speech.

---

60. Cf. HANSON, *The Dawn of Apocalyptic*, 197-98. In the description of the descendants, a textual difficulty occurs in 57:3b with *wtznh*, often emended to *wznh* (and the harlot). SCULLION offers a solution and keeps the MT, showing how *wtznh* can be a participle with the preformative *t-*; he cites several examples of *similar* participles and discusses the LXX reading of v. 3b as *sperma moichōn kai pornēs* to build his case. Following his lead, the translation of *wtznh* reads "and the harlot," accepting it as a participle. Cf. "Some Difficult Texts," 110.

61. Cf. HARVEY, *Le plaidoyer prophétique*, 23, 61.

62. Cf. SCHOORS, *I Am God, Your Savior*, 182.

Some scholars begin the actual indictment for crimes at v. 5.[63] Here the h- interrogative continues the question from v. 4 but now specifies the offenses. The account of crimes describes acts of adultery and child slaughter, which in the biblical writings generally represent offences of idolatry.[64] In deciphering the constitutive elements of the genre, one senses the gradual progression in the judgment scene from the summons, to the cross-examination, and finally to the indictment.

In reading through the strophe different kinds of transgressions represent a varied vocabulary of "sin" in vv. 3-5. In v. 3 the people are addressed according to the two categories of sorcery (bny ^{c}nnh) and of adultery (zr^{c} mn'p wtznh). Those who are summoned before the judge are specified as descendants of generations involving themselves in practices deplorable before the Lord. The accusations of vv. 7-8 present a description of idolatrous practices on a high mountain; here the portrait of a harlot is displayed, setting up a bed and bargaining with lovers. The imagery of vv. 7-8 helps to better appreciate the names of "adulterer" and "harlot" appearing in v. 3b.

In v. 4 the rhetorical question introduces a new series of evil deeds, leaving behind the sins of sorcery and adultery. The verb tt^{c}ngw expresses an act of mockery followed by the disparaging gestures of a wide open mouth and a wagging tongue. These different acts of ridicule portray signs of mockery; set

---

63. Cf. ACHTEMEIER, The Community and Message, 44; HANSON, The Dawn of Apocalyptic, 198; HARVEY, Le plaidoyer prophétique, 62; PAURITSCH, Die neue Gemeinde, 64.

64. Cf. WESTERMANN, Isaiah 40-66, 322.

in the context of a rhetorical question, God asks them whom they are taunting. In the address of v. 4c, two more words for sin appear in construct: children of transgression (yldy-pšᶜ) and offspring of deceit (zrᶜ šqr). The vocabulary of sin in vv. 4a-b and 4c does not initially seem to be similar; however, when viewed in the larger context of 56-59 word repetitions help to establish connections between the vocabulary in vv. 4a-b and 4c. In Isa 59 šqr appears twice, both instances in tandem with the verb "to speak" (dbr).

59:3b) Your lips speak deceit (dbrw-šqr).

59:13b) Conceiving and murmuring deceitful words (dbry-šqr).

These examples from Isa 59 describe "deceit" primarily as a spoken expression of deception. Both passages also make use of the organs of speech to depict the manner of deception.

57:4b-c) Against whom do you open wide your mouth (ph)
and wag your tongue (lšwn)?
Are you not children of transgression,
the offspring of deceit (šqr)?

59:3b) Your lips (śptwtykm) speak deceit (šqr),
your tongue (lšwnkm) murmurs dishonesty.

The mention of "tongue" and "lips" in relation to "deceit" at 59:3 suggests a way of understanding how the motif of "mockery" in 57:4b can be linked to "deceit" with "mouth" and "tongue" as instruments of the action. Furthermore, the repetitions of šqr and the similar organs of speech found in 57:4 and 59:3 demonstrate links between the literary units and coherence of motifs. Beyond the immediate context of Isa 56-59, šqr appears with lšwn (tongue) and ph (mouth) in other passages of the Bible as an expression of verbal deceit.[65]

---

65. Cf. Pss 31:19; 63:12; 109:2; 120:2; Jer 9:2,4.

In the description of 57:5 the two expressions introduced by *tḥt* stand in apposition to the colon preceding each of them. The expression *tḥt kl-^{c}ṣ r^{c}nn* (under every green tree) in 57:5a often speaks of adulterous practices of fertility rites and cult prostitution in the biblical texts;[66] Jer 2:20; 3:6 specifically relate this expression of adultery to whoring (*znh*).[67] The expression *hnḥmym b'lym* (burning with passion for the oaks) suits the adulterous connotations which go with "under every green tree." The slaughter of children is mentioned in 57:5b, but the expression accompanying it (*tḥt s^{c}py hsl^{c}ym*) is found nowhere else in relation to child sacrifice. However, 2 Kgs 21:6/2 Chr 33:6 and Deut 18:10,14 distinguish the slaughter of children as an act of sorcery (*^{c}nn*).[68] According to biblical texts sacrificing children is both an Assyrian and a Phoenician practice of witchcraft intended to appease the God Molech.[69] Distinguishing child sacrifice as an act of sorcery links v. 5b with v. 3a where *^{c}nnh* appears. Similarly the imagery of v. 5a (burning with passion for the oaks) echoes the adultery motif of v. 3b (offspring of the adulterer and the harlot). Here one sees the repeating motifs of adultery and sorcery at the opening and closing of the strophe.

---

66. Cf. John BRIGHT, *Jeremiah* (AB 21; Garden City, NY: Doubleday, 1965) 15; Paul-Eugène DION, "Did Cultic Prostitution Fall into Oblivion during the Postexilic Era? Some Evidence from Chronicles and the Septuagint," *CBQ* 43 (1981) 41-48; HANSON, *The Dawn of Apocalyptic*, 197-98.

67. Cf. BRIGHT, *Jeremiah*, 15.

68. The verb *^{c}nn* (to practice sorcery) appears only eight times in the OT (Lev 19:26; Deut 18:10,14: 2 Kgs 21:6/2Chr 33:6; Isa 2:6; 57:3; Jer 27:9; Mic 5:11); three of these (four including 57:3) are in reference to child sacrifice. With so few occurrences of *^{c}nn* in the OT, the several examples in relation to child sacrifice suggest this is the sense here, especially in context with 57:5.

69. Cf. John L. McKENZIE, "Molech", in *Dictionary of the Bible* (Milwaukee: Bruce Publishing Company, 1965) 583. Some translations of *lammelek* in 57:9 read "to Molech" because of the reference to sorcery in 57:3; cf. RSV; notes in BJ and TOB.

In viewing the "sin" vocabulary of the strophe, an ABA' pattern occurs aiding an appreciation of the strophe's development.

(A) Sorcery and Adultery (v. 3)
- sons of the sorceress and offspring of the adulterer and the harlot

 (B) Mockery and Deceit (v. 4)
 - whom do you mock with open mouth and wagging tongue?
 - are you not children of transgression, offspring of deceit?

(A') Adultery and Sorcery (v. 5)
- burning with passion for the oaks and slaughtering children in the valley.

The AA' elements frame the strophe with language of sorcery and adultery. In v. 3 (A), those summoned before the judge receive names based on their ancestry steeped in sin; then in v. 5 (A'), the attributions of sorcery and adultery in v. 3 obtain concrete points of reference as the indictment specifies their passion for the oaks and murder of children. Here the accusations of sorcery and adultery refer to different idolatrous practices manifesting external acts of disloyalty to Yahweh. In an ABA' pattern like the above, the B figure is often a key to unlocking the significance of the framing elements. Though he does not deal with the structure of these verses, Westermann provides a clue in understanding this pattern. He comments that the gestures of mockery and contempt in v. 4 exhibit the true nature of rebellion that the violations display.[70] Based on the ABA' pattern, the B element places at the heart of the strophe what idolatry is--nothing less than gestures of contempt and mockery against the Lord. Furthermore, the "deception" motif in the B element is parallel with *pš^{c}*

---

70. Cf. WESTERMANN, *Isaiah 40-66*, 322.

(transgression), a general word denoting a broken relationship with God caused by rebellion against him.[71] Thus the core of the idolatry exposed in this strophe accentuates the revolt against God compounded in the mockery and deception these actions represent.

D. Isaiah 57:6 -- A Question of Inheritance

The initial organization of the strophes for this stanza is based on a change of speaker in 57:6, from second per. masc. pl. to second per. fem. sing. A cursory look at commentaries and translations reveals that the placement of v. 6 is an unsettled question. Some scholars follow the verb pattern as the initial approach of this paper suggests, separating v. 5 from v. 6.[72] Others join vv. 5-6 because of the recurring nḥl and motifs of idolatrous practices;[73] further, Westermann unites vv. 5-6 seeing v. 6a as the "pronouncement of sentence" for the crimes of v. 5.[74]

The opinions of commentators suggest that words in v. 6 look back to v. 5, while other words look ahead to vv. 7ff; v. 6 concludes a development in the text by threatening a sentence of punishment (among the stones is your portion, these are your lot) while also looking to a continued description of the

71. Cf. H.G. LIVINGSTON, "pšᶜ," TWOT 2, 741-42.

72. Cf. BONNARD, Le Second Isaïe, 357, 359; PENNA, Isaia, 558, 566; among translations, see JB and NAB following a strophic division of vv. 3-5, 6-10.

73. Cf. MUILENBURG, "The Book of Isaiah," 665-66; WHYBRAY, Isaiah 40-66, 203-204.

74. Cf. WESTERMANN, Isaiah 40-66, 321.

transgressions now in the second per. fem. sing. A. Ceresko discusses the "hinge" as a verse looking both ways in a poem, to what precedes and to what follows, summarizing the progress to this point and hinting at what is to come.[75]

In 57:6 several points look back at what precedes. The repetition of the root nḥl (valley) in 57:5b (bnḥlym) and 57:6a (nḥl) shows a relationship between a transgression and its consequences; the slaughter of children in the valleys (bnḥlym) brings the smooth stones of the valley (bḥlqy-nḥl) as an inheritance.[76] The effect of the inheritance repeats in 57:13c when contrasted with the inheritance (ynḥl-'rṣ) of those who take refuge in the Lord. In v. 6 nḥl both looks back to v. 5 and sets the stage for v. 13c.

In addition, there is an example of paronomasia built on a chiastic sound pattern appearing in 57:5a and 57:6c.[77]

57:5a)	hnḥmym	b'lym
57:6c)	h^{c}l 'lh	'nḥm

75. Cf. CERESKO, "Poetic Analysis," 36. Also, H. van Dyke PARUNAK discusses the "hinge" as a transitional unit in a text; his examples represent literary units indicating a change in the progression of a text. However, in principle the hinge functions in the same way, whether as a verse or a literary unit. Cf. "Transitional Techniques in the Bible," JBL 102 (1983) 540-46.

76. Patrick D. MILLER shows numerous examples in prophetic literature where a correlation is made between a "sin" and its "consequences" by the repetition of the same verbal root. Cf. Sin and Judgment in the Prophets: A Stylistic and Theological Analysis (SBLMS 27; Chico, CA: Scholars Press, 1982) pp. 4-6 give background on this device of repetition.

77. Several authors discuss examples of chiastic sound patterns; cf. John KSELMAN, "Semantic-Sonant Chiasmus in Biblical Poetry," Bib 58 (1977) 219-23; LUNDBOM, Jeremiah, 68-69; WATSON, "Chiastic Patterns," 132; "Further Examples of Semantic-Sonant Chiasmus," CBQ 46 (1984) 31-33.

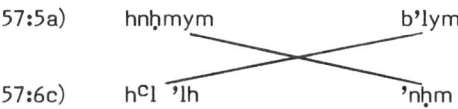

In 57:5a the words are ḥmm (to burn) and ʼlym (oaks), while in 57:6c they are nḥm (to comfort) and ʼlh (these, a demonstration plural pronoun). Though different words, a similarity in sound characterizes the pairs. An opposition emerges between the "oaks" of 57:5a and the speaker "God" of 57:6c in these two sound patterns; is God to be comforted (ʼnḥm) by these things, their burning (hnḥmym) passions for the oaks. The rhetorical question in 57:6c further expresses the disgust of the speaker, as if the loathsome practices could be a consolation. Does the distance between vv. 5a and 6c diminish the effect of the play on words and sounds? The sound patterns stand at the extremes of the two verses in question, framing them. Further, the basic 3+2 meter and bicolon structure are broken in 57:6c accentuating the final colon and drawing attention to it.[78] The conspicuous placement of word and sound patterns, and the final break in rhythm at 57:6c stress these two cola and suggest an example of paronomasia at work.

In 57:6 there are words anticipating the message that unfolds in the following verses. The repetition of the root ᶜlh (to go up) in 57:6b recurs at 57:7b,8b. The use of hᶜlyt mnḥh in 57:6b introduces a motif of sacrifice with movement upward, an ascent; yet the place is not mentioned, its identification is delayed. When the new strophe begins in 57:7a the place is designated as a towering and lofty mountain (hr-gbh wnśʼ). The effect of the designated place is enhanced by the use of "metonymy," where an expression is substituted for a specific place or object;[79] here the "towering and lofty mountain" suggests

---

78. MUILENBURG notes that a break in the rhythm can serve to draw attention to a line; cf. "Form Criticism," 12. See also, GORDIS, "The Structure of Biblical Poetry," 70.

79. "Metonymy" is listed among several literary devices by KUNTZ, "The Contribution of Rhetorical Criticism," 142.

Jerusalem or another high shrine.[80] In 57:7b the motifs of "ascent" and "sacrifice" reappear with gm-šm ᶜlyt / lzbḥ zbḥ. The harlot is described in v. 8b as ascending (wtᶜly) the mountain, an image of departure from God.

A structural pattern initiates the bicola at 57:6b,6c,7a,7b with a chiasm of an adverb and preposition.

(A) gm (v. 6b)

(B) hᶜl (v. 6c)

(B) ᶜl (v. 7a)

(A) gm (v. 7b)

The repetition of these elements links the material of 57:6b,6c with 57:7a,7b.[81] The adverb gm also begins the bicola where the ascent is noted by hᶜlyt (v. 6b) and ᶜlyt (v. 7b). Following C.J. Labuschagne who reads gm as a particle of emphasis, the stress given to the bicola describing the ascent further unites vv. 6b and 7b.[82]

One also notes the triple use of the third per. pl. subj. personal pronoun in 57:6a (hm, hm), 57:6b (lhm) and 57:8c (mhm). While one must be

---

80. Cf. HANSON, The Dawn of Apocalyptic, 199; WHYBRAY, Isaiah 40-66, 204. Other passages highlight the notion of "ascent to Jerusalem"; cf. Pss 24:3; 122:4; Isa 2:3.

81. MUILENBURG shows how particles can act as a means of exposing the texture of poetry by connecting words or cola that may not appear associated; cf. "The Linguistic and Rhetorical Usages," 135-36.

82. For further clarification and examples of emphasis by gm, see C.J. LABUSCHAGNE, "The Emphasizing Particle gam and its Connotations," in Studia Biblica et Semitica pro Theodoro Christiano Vriezen (W.C. van Unnik and A.S. van der Woude, eds.; Wageningen: H. Veenman, 1966) 193-203, especially the summary on pp. 202-203.

careful not to assign too much weight to the use of individual pronouns, it is important to distinguish their antecedents; it is the antecedent which can link verses together by showing how a pronoun refers to something or someone mentioned. Manfred Weise does a textual study comparing the MT and LXX to discern how the Greek text interprets the Hebrew with its double personal pronoun in of 57:6.[83] The LXX reads

57:6) Ekeinē sou hē meris, houtos sou ho klēros [. . .]

Weise points out according to the rules of Greek syntax that when ekeinos and houtos come together in this fashion, most often ekeinos finds its referent in what precedes if the pronoun is in an emphatic position, as it is here.[84] In such cases houtos finds its antecedent with what is more remote in the literary context, preceding the first referent. Applying this rule to the LXX, a chiasm forms with ekeinos referring to 57:5b and houtos to 57:5a. Such a textual consideration of the LXX provides a way for interpreting the repetition of hm. The duplication of hm in this colon could be a way fo emphasizing bḥlqy-nḥl as its antecedent, but also possibly is a more subtle link with what precedes 57:6 establishing a stronger emphasis for a hinge verse reiterating the inheritance according to one's deeds. Following the grammatical suggestion from the LXX, the double hm of the MT could not only emphasize but also point to the "lot" (gwrlk) of 57:6a to include both of the illicit practices portrayed in 57:5b and 57:5a. This gives a more complete picture of the "inheritance" and "lot" of 57:6a

83. Cf. Manfred WEISE, "Jesaja 57:5f," ZAW 72 (1960) 25-32.

84. Cf. WEISE, "Jesaja 57:5f," 27.

as referring back to both the actions done under every green tree (57:5a) and the slaughter done under the recesses of the rocks (57:5b).

Several points argue for reading 57:6 as a hinge verse. V. 6c looks back to v. 5a with the chiastic sound pattern playing on both words and sounds, with this structuring device framing vv. 5-6. The double hm of v. 6a also recalls the sorcery and adultery of vv. 5a,5b. The verb ^{c}lh in v. 6 anticipates the ascent of the towering mountain in 57:7b,8b where the word repeats. Finally, in v. 6 nḥl both looks back to v. 5 to show what inheritance comes from idolatrous practices, and looks forward to the announcement of inheritance in v. 13c for those who trust in the Lord. The motif of inheritance is key in interpreting v. 6 to appreciate the contrasting recompenses issuing from infidelity and from devotion to God.

E. Isaiah 57:7-10 -- The Way of Harlot Israel: from the Heights to the Depths

The repetitions of ^{c}lh in 57:7b,8b highlight the ascent of the towering mountain; further, the intensive particles gm (57:7b) and ky (57:8b) draw attention to the bicola where the ascent is mentioned.[85] The description of the mountain in v. 7a as "towering and lofty" heightens the motif of ascent. In contrast to the description of the ascent up the mountain, 57:9 tells of a descent where messengers are dispatched afar off (^{c}d-mrḥq), even to Sheol (^{c}d-š'wl). The repetition of the preposition ^{c}d in 57:9b unites the two images of the

85. MUILENBURG points out that a particle stresses the whole bicolon; cf. "The Linguistic and Rhetorical Usages," 135-36. The placement of m'ty (from me, v. 8b) at the beginning of the bicolon, with the particle, stresses that the ascent up the mountain for sinful activities is a departure from God (the speaker).

descent and stresses the motif. D.W. Thomas gives examples in biblical poetry where š'wl functions as an adjective rather than designating a place or condition.[86] He shows how the expression qšh kš'wl, describing jealousy in Cant 8:6, is best rendered "profoundly cruel," instead of "cruel as the grave" (RSV); similarly in Ps 18:6 he translates hbly š'wl as "terrible pains" in lieu of "the cords of Sheol" entangled me.[87] Based on the imagery in the strophe and its contrasting character, the designation of ᶜd-š'wl as the underworld and its parallel ᶜd-mrḥq in v. 9a, š'wl may also function as an adjective here expressing the extent of the descent (wtšpyly); the translation of ᶜd-š'wl in v. 9b then reads "to the deepest depths." Thus the progression of thought in the strophe presents a broad sweep of imagery, from an ascent to a high and lofty mountain to a descent into the deepest depths.

Alonso Schökel explains that in Hebrew poetry antithesis is a literary device expressing different aspects of a text's message; polar expressions can denote totality, change, opposition, and even unity.[88] The Sitz in der Literatur discerns the antithesis and its function in the world of the text. In this strophe the movement to the high and lofty mountain (57:6-8) and then to the deepest depths (57:9-10) expresses the extent to which the harlot goes in her actions; the polarities seen in the contrast of hr-gbh wnś' (57:7a) and ᶜd-š'wl (57:9b), hᶜlyt/ᶜlyt/wtᶜly (57:6b,7b,8b) and wtšpyly (57:9b), express the vast dimensions

---

86. Cf. D. Winton THOMAS, "A Consideration of Some Unusual Ways of Expressing the Superlative in Hebrew," VT 3 (1953) 222-24.

87. Cf. THOMAS, "A Consideration of Some Unusual Ways," 223.

88. Cf. Luis ALONSO SCHÖKEL, "Poésie hébraïque," in DBSup VIII, col. 75.

that measure Israel's pursuit of sinful activity. The figurative language expounds upon the extremes that she journeys in her movement away from God; she has travelled the limits and yet in the end she is not languished (<u>ᶜl-kn</u> <u>l'</u> <u>ḥlyt</u>, 57:10). Hanson describes her as the "untiring whore," knowing no flagging in the ways of infidelity.[89]

Another element demonstrating unity in this strophe is the repetition of <u>yd</u> in 57:8c,10b. In the contexts where <u>yd</u> repeats, it is difficult to be certain of its interpretation; authors present varying views of its uses in 57:8c,10b.[90] However, for the purposes of this study, how this word functions as a structuring device is the issue at stake. In 57:8c,10b <u>yd</u> appears at the end of the two descriptions of the ascent (57:7-8) and the descent (57:9-10). In both instances the word's use as an euphemism is clear; it says something more than what the usual sense of the word carries. But this same word appears in both accounts of

---

89. Cf. HANSON, <u>The Dawn of Apocalyptic</u>, 200.

90. M. Delcor provides a summary of the various ways <u>yd</u> is explained by commentators; he then builds an argument for its reading in Isa 57:8,10 as an euphemism for the male sexual organ based on archeological, stylistic, and comparative philological studies. Cf. "Two Special Meanings of the Word <u>yd</u> in Biblical Hebrew," <u>JSS</u> 12 (1967) 230-40. Another study appears about the same time by Aloysius FITZGERALD, comparing the Hebrew <u>yd</u> with Arabic and Ugaritic cognates; cf. "Hebrew <u>yd</u> = 'love' and 'beloved,' " <u>CBQ</u> 29 (1967) 368-74, especially pp. 371-72.

Despite the several studies on the meaning of <u>yd</u> in 57:8,10, uncertainty still remains. And yet the ambiguity of this word heightens its impact in the literary context, suggesting several images. EXUM addresses the question of ambiguity in another poem of Isa. "Figurative language embraces ambiguity. In fact, much of its power derives from its plurisignificance, from its ability to be suggestive of multiple meanings. But to observe that figurative language is not precise is not to claim that it cannot capture and convey meaning with deftness." Cf. "Of Broken Pots," 333. Thus the choice of "strength" for <u>yd</u> brings to the translation a sense of the ambiguity found in the MT while also carrying connotations in the literary context.

her wanderings; in the heights and in the depths, yd is present. Furthermore yd appears in climactic literary contexts. In 57:8c the bicolon structure changes to a tricolon; this alternation in rhythm signals a special message.[91] The concluding colon of v. 8c refers to yd as the object of the harlot's gaze. Similarly in 57:10b yd ends a description of the descent, focusing on the untiring pursuit and engendering of life which yd gives the harlot. Thus as a structuring device yd appears in climactic points of the harlot's ascent and descent, bringing a sense of balance to the descriptions by means of a common euphemistic word.

The repetitions in vv. 7-8 portray the accusations of adultery with deftness. The recurrence of śmt in the second cola of 57:7c,8a places the verbs in close proximity to one another. The reiteration of the verb brings two ideas together; "setting up the couch" refers to adultery and "setting up your symbol" (zkrwnk) to idolatry. Most commentators accept zkrwn as a phallic object, a trinket of a harlot's trade.[92] Often zkrwn is a memorial stone, but in this context of licentious language, a pun can be read here since zkr also refers to a male individual; the kind of "object" which the harlot displays distinguishes an adulterous and idolatrous practice. In reading the two cola at vv. 7ab,8ab the even syllable count and end-rhyme function as vocal gestures to stress the setting up of couch and symbol: śamt miškāb̄ek(v. 7a) and śamt zikrônēk(v. 8a).

---

91. On the importance of the tricolon, see note 32 of this Chapter.

92. Cf. HANSON, The Dawn of Apocalyptic, 200; MUILENBURG, "The Book of Isaiah," 667; WESTERMANN, Isaiah 40-66, 324; WHYBRAY, Isaiah 40-66, 204.

In addition, _mškb_ recurs in vv. 7a,8b,8c. The "couch" as a motif of adulterous practices appears in a step-wise movement, unfolding the procedure of the harlot.

v. 7a) You set up your couch

v. 8b) You spread wide your couch

v. 8c) You loved their couch.

The verbs accompanying _mškb_ present a sense of gradation moving from the setting up of the couch on the lofty mountain, to enlarging the couch and finally to loving it. Also the pronominal suffixes with _mškb_ show an expansion in the harlot's activity, moving from "your" couch in vv. 7a,8b to include "their" couch in v. 8c. The repetitions of _ᶜlh_, _śm_, and _mškb_ are part of a network of motifs which present descriptive images of Israel's idolatrous practices on the lofty mountain.

Each of the cola in 57:9 begins with the same vocalization _wat_- and concludes with a terminal _-î_ (_wattāšurî_, _wattarbî_, _watteᵉšalleᵉḥî_, _wattašpîlî_). In 57:10 the verbs have a terminal _t_, further accentuating the direct address spoken to the accused in their trial scene. Also the second cola in vv. 10a-b have a negative _l'_; this negative points out the accusation that Israel was unwilling to remedy the situation. In v. 10a she is accused of being weary, but the negative shows her refusal to say it is hopeless; in v. 10b she is indicted with finding new life in the idolatry, and therefore would not cease practicing it.

The repetition of _drk_ in 57:10a echoes its earlier occurrence in 56:11c distinguishing a _modus operandi_. The example in 56:11c narrates how Israel's leaders follow their own pursuits to the neglect of those under their care. Now in 57:10a drkk can be seen as a word summarizing the different ways that harlot Israel manifests a disregard for God. In v. 8b the Lord says that the idolatrous acts on the lofty mountain are a means of departing from him; here the particle ky and the emphatic personal pronoun m'ty stress the withdrawal away from the divinity. In v. 8c God accuses her of entering into treaty with others;[93] she chooses to establish a pact with another than the Lord who brought her into being as his people. This mention of drkk in 57:10a brings back into focus the theme of judgment begun in 57:3 by describing the "ways" of Israel's wanderings, the paths of departure from God spanning the heights and the depths. The account of Israel's ways in 57:7-10 continues the trial scene, announcing the extent to which she goes in her own path away from God.

F. Isaiah 57:11-13 -- A Threat and a Promise

Following upon the long indictment of crimes in vv. 5-10, two further elements of the trial speech are noted by Harvey. In v. 11 an accusatory address in the form of a rhetorical question shows the lack of gratitude and concern by the harlot Israel for God;[94] she has no dread nor fear in deceiving God. One sees a similarity in v. 11a with v. 4, both using the interrogative pronoun my. But in v. 11b the answer to the preceding question comes quickly with the emphatic personal pronoun: but me, you did not remember. Then in v. 12 the threats

---

93. HANSON gives several examples with krt means "making a treaty" without bryt; cf. The Dawn of Apocalyptic, 193 note (tt).

94. Cf. HARVEY, Le plaidoyer prophétique, 62.

conclude the trial speech announcing the fate of the idolators.[95] The power of Yahweh distinguishes itself in the description of the "collection of idols" who are unable to bring deliverance to their worshippers in time of need (vv. 12b-13b); a mere wind sweeps away the unfaithful ones who put confidence in anything other than Yahweh. Distinct in this trial speech is the early hint of a threat in v. 6 explaining the inheritance accruing to those engaging in idolatry; then in vv. 12b-13 that threat expands in the closing words of the trial speech, contrasting the fate of the idolators (vv. 12b-13b) with the inheritance of the faithful (v. 13c).

The rhetorical question of v. 11a and its immediate answer in v. 11b focus attention on the speaker. In addition, a series of first per. personal pronouns pulsates through vv. 11-12 (w'wty in v. 11b, 'ny in v. 11ca, w'wty in v. 11cb, and 'ny in v. 12a). Though the speaker (Yahweh) is the focal point here, the accused is also referred to with repeated second per. fem. sing. verbs and second per. sing. pronominal suffixes continuing the manner of address from the indictment in vv. 6-10. The repeated use of consistent verb forms, pronouns, and pronominal suffixes displays the movement back and forth between the speaker and the accused.

57:11a	Whom did you dread [. . .] when you deceived me;
57:11b	Yet me, you did not remember, nor place upon your heart;
57:11c	Have I not been silent [. . .] yet me you did not fear;
57:12a	I, I will proclaim your righteousness and your activities,
57:12b	but they will not profit you,
57:13a	When you cry [. . .] let your collection [. . .] save you.

95. Cf. HARVEY, Le plaidoyer prophétique, 62.

One sees a loosely alternating pattern with "I," "me," "you," and "your" in vv. 11-13; but what appears more important is the character of the literary style which the pronominal pattern shows. The nature of the accusation takes on a personal tone with the rapid change from "me" to "you."[96] The accusatory address and threat are not incriminating words from an uninvolved speaker; on the contrary, the emphatic pronouns and the pronominal suffixes function to underscore the position of a God deeply affronted by the lack of concern shown him as he threatens the idolators with their just fate.

The opening verbs in 57:11a (*d'gt*, *wtyr'y*) begin a motif centering around a lack of regard toward God; the question *w't-my* presumes that some other god is the recipient of the reverence due the God of Israel. Following these opening verbs, the negative *l'* appears in each cola of 57:11b,11c. The four negatives work in a parallel construction for the bicola. In 57:11b the lack of remembrance (*l' zkrt*) is reflective of the want of concern toward God (*l'-śmt ^{c}l-lbk*); God has been patient in remaining silent about these things (*hl' 'ny mḫšh*) yet there has been no fear toward him (*w'wty l' tyr'y*). A negative returns in 57:12b. But in 57:12b what is the subject of the verb *yw^{c}ylwk*? The RSV follows the verse structure connecting 57:12b with the two nouns of 57:12a (your righteousness and your activities); here the *w* of *wl' yw^{c}ylwk* is taken as an adversive *waw* rendered "but they (your righteousness and your doings) will not help you." But Scullion suggests that the root *y^{c}l* in the *hiph^{c}îl* resembles other passages where this same verb demonstrates the weakness of idols;[97] thus

---

96. Cf. WESTERMANN, *Isaiah 40-66*, 324.

97. Cf. SCULLION, "Some Difficult Texts," 114. The passages to which he refers are Isa 44:9,10; Jer 2:8; Hab 2:18.

he decides qbwṣyk (your collection of idols) of 57:13a is the subject of ywᶜylwk in 57:12b. Scullion's point is well taken for then the build-up of negatives in 57:11b,11c only reaches its climax with a concluding negative in 57:12b, where the final wl' does double duty acting both for ywᶜylwk and yṣylk of v. 13. Such a powerful conclusion brings the argument begun in 57:11a full circle: the idols whom Israel dreads and fears (57:11a) will neither be able to help nor save her (57:12b,13a). Further, Dahood cites 57:12 as an example of delayed identification where the verb ywᶜylwk only later specifies what will not profit Israel, namely your collection of idols (qbwṣyk).[98] The poetry then proceeds to 57:13b describing the helplessness of the idols whom Israel reveres; this is Israel's allotment, helpless idols!

In 57:12a ṣdqtk rings with a note of sarcasm. From the beginning of the stanza at 57:3 the progression through the trial speech explains the extent that the harlot Israel goes in departing from God's ways. Now in 57:12, to culminate the recital of indictment, God threatens to announce her righteousness, a righteousness based on her actions. Such actions of idolatry, such a lack of concern for God can hardly be counted as righteous; this becomes clear as the threat of vv. 12b-13b is given. A note of contrast also rests in relation to the earlier use of ṣdq. In 57:1-2 the righteous one (hṣdyq) suffers from lack of concern (w'yn 'yš śm ᶜl-lb), yet is rewarded with a promise of peace. In 57:11-12 God suffers from lack of concern (l'śmt ᶜl-lbk), and for this the unrighteous receive a threat of punishment.

---

98. Cf. DAHOOD, "Poetry, Hebrew," 672.

The occurrence of ṣdqtk and mᶜśyk as parallel words in 57:12a recalls the use of these words in the opening bicolon of this section at 56:1a, wᶜśw ṣdqh (practice righteousness). The opening command of this section calls for the practice of righteousness because God's salvation and deliverance are soon to be revealed (56:1). While 56:1a calls for the observance of righteousness, 57:12 marks its absence by threatening to reveal the poverty of righteous actions by Israel. The want of true righteousness brings judgment (57:12b-13b) instead of deliverance (56:1b; 57:13c).

Muilenburg finds 57:12-13 to be an "excellent transition" to 57:14-21, yet does not explain his comment.[99] The final considerations of this strophe address the vocabulary and poetic architecture of these verses to build on Muilenburg's intimation.

The vocabulary of v. 13 recalls earlier motifs in the stanza. The distant parallelism with ḥlqk//ynḥl in 57:6a,13c opposes the worthless portion of idolatrous stones with the inheritance of the land; the allusion made here distinguishes between the recompense of the idolators (v. 6a) and of the faithful (v. 13c). The gift of the land is a central promise of God for Israel, a sign of the Lord's enduring blessing.[100] An inheritance of the land and of God's holy mountain sharply contrasts with an allotment of idolatrous stones (vv. 13c,6). Also the paronomasia with bḥlqy-nḥl (stones of the valley) and ynḥl-'rṣ (shall inherit the land) plays on the threat to the idolators and the promise to the

99. Cf. MUILENBURG, "The Book of Isaiah," 660.

100. Cf. Walter BRUEGGEMANN, The Land (Overtures to Biblical Theology 1; Philadelphia: Fortress Press, 1977) 4-6.

faithful.[101] A further contrast lies in the two images of hr in this stanza; in v. 7 the mountain depicts the place of idolatry while in v. 13c it is an inheritance of blessing. The contrasting uses of hr is considered later in this Chapter. Thus the distant parallelism, paronomasia, and repetitions strengthen the antithesis in v. 13c by opposing a recompense of no value (v. 6) to an inheritance of central importance in the faith of Israel (v. 13c), and contrasting the mountain of idolatry (v. 7) with the mountain of inheritance; as in 57:2, the antithesis in 57:13c strongly concludes the stanza.

The specification of the mountain as "holy" in v. 13c distinguishes it as being set apart. A vocabulary of "holiness" continues in 57:15 in a description of the Lord whose name and dwelling place are set apart; this solemn vocabulary in v. 13c leads into the final stanza where it recurs in a context where the predominant theme is salvation. The 3+2 rhythm of vv. 11-13b slightly expands in v. 13c only then to continue the Lord's promise of redemption in v. 14 with a meter of 4+4. Thus it is that v. 13c functions as a point of transition contrasting with the previous words of judgment and also anticipating a motif among the promises of salvation dominating the final stanza.

G. Isaiah 57:14-19a -- The Way of God's People

The word drk appears twice in v. 14, linking this stanza with the previous two but also identifying a contrast with its two previous occurrences. In 56:11 and 57:10 drk describes a way of living and acting which is cause for

---

101. See p. 105 and note 22 of this Chapter.

judgment; it depicts one following a manner of living which is not consonant with the ways of God. This same word begins the final stanza announcing the establishment of a way for God's people. But distinct from its earlier uses, this is to be a modus operandi by which their actions distinguish them as God's own people (mdrk ᶜmy, 57:14ab). This opening verse looks forward to a redemptive transformation where God's way prevails over humanity's. Several literary devices set off v. 14 in solemn fashion. Four imperatives (slw, slw, pnw, hrymw) mark the bicolon with a note of urgency. The expansive 4+4 meter contrasts the verse with the regular 3+2 rhythm of vv. 3-13b. And finally, the repeated s, l, m, and r assonance coupled with the recurring open ō and û vowels signal majesty and grandeur; Alonso Schökel shows it to be a typical Isaian sound pattern of splendor and amplitude.[102]

Two examples of inverted parallelism mark the structure of 57:15.[103]

1) 57:15a-ba

(A) rm (v. 15a)
    (B) škn
        (C) wqdwš
(A) mrwm (v. 15ba)
        (C) wqdwš
    (B) 'škwn

2) 57:15bb-c

(A) dk'
    (B) wšpl-rwḥ
    (B) rwḥ-šplym
(A) ndk'ym

---

102. Cf. ALONSO SCHÖKEL, Estudios de Poética Hebrea, 116.

103. Cf. Anthony R. CERESKO, "The A:B::B:A Word Pattern in Hebrew and Northwest Semitic with Special Reference to the Book of Job," UF 7 (1975) 79.

The first example in 57:15a-ba is not a pure chiasm; however, there is an inversion of the BC elements so the example is noted for the sake of completeness. Also the three repeated elements (ABC) of the structure show an equal distribution in the description of God (v. 15a) and his dwelling place (v. 15ba). The depiction of God and his dwelling demonstrates a sense of balance among the repeated vocabulary. The words contained in the structure describe a transcendent God, incomparable to any other being; not only is his being (šmw) distinguished as holy (set apart) but also the place of his dwelling. The language characterizes a God and his habitation as other worldly, set apart from humanity.

The second chiasm in 57:15bb,15c focuses on the image of a people contrite and humble of spirit (dk' wšpl-rwḥ); but in considering the pattern of the chiasm, one keeps in mind that the structure is governed by the verb 'škwn in 57:15ba. The description is an immanent one continuing the exposition of God's dwelling; the immanence is underscored by the description of a people who are not lofty and exalted (57:15a) but who are brought low and made humble (57:15bb). The imagery found here recalls the same verbal roots explaining the great extent to which the harlot Israel went in her infidelity in the strophe 57:7-10. It is up to a high and lofty (wnś', 57:7a) mountain that she ascended only to complete the journey by a descent (wtšpyly, 57:9b) to the deepest depths (^{c}d-š'wl). The same vocabulary describes the exalted (wnś', 57:15a) God inhabiting eternity yet also dwelling with the humble of spirit (wšpl-rwḥ, 57:15c) who are in need of being revived (lhḥywt, 57:15c). The words narrating the extent of Israel's infidelity are recast in 57:15 to show the transcendent and immanent dwellings of God. A sense of contrast emerges from such a comparison, opposing the extent of Israel's sinful wandering with the extent of God's transcendent and immanent dwelling. While cast in contrast, the repetitions establish links between the two stanzas.

Often a chiasm marks a transition in a text, but here it appears that the double chiasm distinguishes the movement of the verse from a description of a transcendent to an immanent presence of God. Brought together by the governing verb *'škwn* (57:15b), God announces his dwelling both in a lofty place and with humble folk; the God who is exalted exalts the humble with whom he dwells, bestowing new life upon them.

Another look at 57:15 suggests still one more structure here. Each chiasm divides v. 15 into three cola; but if one reads 57:15 as a series of three bicola, several more patterns emerge. The verb *'mr* in 57:15a governs the bicolon describing who is speaking; the disclosure of the speaker gives emphasis to the word. God continues in 57:15a the salvific thrust of the message begun in 57:14. Similarly in 57:15b the verb *'škwn* functions for both cola and therein God announces his dwelling in the high and holy place and among the contrite and humble of spirit; the bicolon deals with the motif of God's twofold dwelling. Finally in 57:15c the bicolon is marked with the repetition of *lhḥywt* at the beginning of each colon; this emphatic repetition builds on the preceding colon and explains God's purpose in dwelling with the humble: to give them life, to revive them. Thus the development which works through a reading of each bicolon of 57:15 progresses from the announcement of a salvific word from the God of holiness, to a statement of the Lord's twofold dwelling, to a disclosure of God's intention to bring life to the humbled. Thus in 57:15 an overlapping of two structures appears based on its division into three cola each forming a chiasm, and into three bicola distinguishing three motifs (God's redemptive word, dwelling, and action).

Muilenburg notes that the double ky in 57:16a,16b connects these verses with the infinitives in the preceding bicolon, showing that the motive behind God's judgment and anger is directed to restoring life.[104] Beyond this, the internal structure of 57:15c,16a,16b demonstrates how these verses are bound together; note the similar organization of the bicola.

v. 15c)	lhḥywt rwḥ šplym (A) (B) (C)	/	wlhḥywt lb ndk'ym (A) (B') (C')
v. 16a)	ky l' l^{c}wlm 'ryb (A) (B) (C)	/	wl' lnṣḥ 'qṣwp (A) (B') (C')
v. 16b)	ky rwḥ mlpny y^{c}ṭwp (A) (B) (C)	/	wnšmwt 'ny ^{c}śyty (A') (B') (C')

In 57:15c the repetition of the AA elements at the beginning of each colon emphasizes the action of restoring life with the similar infinitive form. The correspondence between the BB' words comes from their grammatical use as nouns in construct and also as a parallel pair.[105] Beyond this the literary context sees rwḥ//lb as life-giving components of the human person; in v. 15c the purpose of God's dwelling is to revive. Lastly, the CC' words describe the similar attitudes distinguishing the people with whom God dwells, the humble and contrite.[106] The rhyme of the final -îm also links these words. The internal structure of v. 15c shows an ABCAB'C' pattern.

---

104. Cf. MUILENBURG, "The Book of Isaiah," 673; "The Linguistic and Rhetorical Usages," 148.

105. For examples of the parallel pair rwḥ//lb, see Isa 65:14; Ezek 18:31; 36:26.

106. This is the only example of špl and dk' as parallels. Such a careful use of vocabulary heightens the contrasting uses of špl in 57:9 and 57:15.

In 57:16a a similar pattern of correspondence imitates the previous bicolon. Each colon begins with the repetition of the negative l' (AA). Following the negations are adverbs (BB') expressing a great length of time (forever, continually). And finally, the verb concludes each colon (CC') in the first per. sing. imperfect, displaying a motif of anger. The progressions from a negative to an adverb underscore in each colon that God's wrath has a limitation, it will not last forever. As in v. 15c, 57:16a has an internal parallel structure of ABCA'B'C'.

And in 57:16b the AA' words begin each colon with vocabulary describing the constitutive components of life: spirit and breath.[107] In both instances, God is the source of these fundamental origins of a human being's vital powers. The BB' words emphasize from whom the blessings of life flow. The preposition mn in mlpny indicates that the spirit proceeds from God's presence; the emphatic personal pronoun 'ny emphasizes the speaker (God) announcing his salvific work of creating the breath of life. Lastly, the verbs (CC') conclude each cola as in v. 16a. As in the previous two bicola, v. 16b shows an internal parallel structure of ABCA'B'C'.

The repetition of an internal structure in vv. 15b-16b draws these bicola together suggesting that their similar organization presents an inner logic binding them together; the repeated internal structure acts as a device to unite the bicola. As Muilenburg suggests, the infinitives of 57:15c give a context to

---

107. Cf. WOLFF, Anthropology, 33.

what is found in 57:16.[108] The fostering of new life (vv. 15c,16b) springs from the severe blow dealt to God's people in his anger (v. 16a); when God contends with them, he alone can restore the breath of life that animates them. But also, v. 15c specifies that the redemptive revitalization comes to those who are humble and contrite.

The double recurrence of the root qṣp in 57:17a both stresses the motif of God's wrath and brings to mind its earlier use of 57:16a. The repetition of qṣp appears at the conclusion of the two cola, giving a sense of symmetry to the bicolon. The reason of God's rage is presented at the beginning of the bicolon; the alliteration of b, ᶜ, and ō in baᶜᵃwōn biṣᶜô draws attention to these words and marks them off in the bicolon. The reason for God's anger recalls the earlier motif of covetousness (lbṣᶜw in 56:11c). In 56:11b,11c the shepherds are indicted for their lack of discernment and for turning in their own ways. The final colon (56:11) then concludes, ʾyš lbṣᶜw mqṣhw (each of them covetousness for his own gain). In 57:17 two motifs recur that are found in 56:11, covetousness and walking in one's own way. These two elements explain God's anger and show what gives rise to their punishment. The recurrence of vocabulary brings together the beginning and end of this somewhat long literary unit. The initial uses of bṣᶜ and drk in 56:11 are in a context of judgement and punishment, while at the end punishment gives way to a promise of salvation for the Lord will heal and lead the people regardless of their ways (57:18). Despite the wanderings of his people, God commands that a way (drk [. . .] mdrk ᶜmy, 57:14) be prepared so that the people can walk in the paths of the Lord.

---

108. Cf. MUILENBURG, "The Book of Isaiah," 673.

The MT of 57:18-19 is marked by irregular rhythm and verbal forms that are difficult to interpret. In his study of the use of ʼnḥhw in 57:18b, J. Kselman demonstrates a congruity found here by means of the metaphors that are employed.[109] In opting for the MT instead of a revocalization to waʼanīḥēhû (from nwḥ, to give rest), Kselman shows how wʼnḥhw (I will lead him) has a counterpart in wylk šwbb bdrk lbw (he walked turning in the way of his own heart); he also demonstrates that ʼkhw (I struck him) in v. 17 has a counterpart in wʼrpʼhw (I will heal him) in v. 18. But it is possible to extend Kselman's argument one step further by pointing out a third example of congruence among the metaphors in vv. 17-18. Notice the relation between hstr wʼqṣp (I hid myself and was angry) and wʼšlm nḥmym lw (I will restore full comfort to him). A similar example of movement from "anger" (qṣp) to "comfort" (nḥm) is found in Zech 1:2,15,17. The opening words of this chapter express God's displeasure with Israel by a double use of qṣp: "angry, angry is the Lord with your fathers" (Zech 1:2, translation mine). Yet God remains jealous for Jerusalem (v. 14) and when the nations increase Zion's disaster the Lord grows exceedingly angry (qṣp, v. 15 twice) with them. God's anger turns to the nations and Jerusalem receives his comfort (nḥm, vv. 16-17 twice).[110] Similarly in Isa 57:17-18 the vocabulary qṣp and nḥm appear and, coupled with the other metaphors, describe God's modulation from an expression of anger to a restoration of comfort. Together

---

109. Cf. John S. KSELMAN, "A Note on wʼnḥhw in Isa 57:18," CBQ 43 (1981) 539-42.

110. In his commentary, Charles FEINBERG notes the relationship between the uses of qṣp in Zech 1, and also how Zech 1:1-16 relates to the series of eight night visions of which vv. 14-17 are a part. Cf. God Remembers: A Study of Zechariah (Portland, OR: Mullnomah Press, 1979) 13-15.

with the other examples, this addition shows the interworking of metaphors to express the movement from punishment to blessing in vv. 17-18.

v. 17		v. 18
'khw (I struck him)	- - -	w'rp'hw (but I will heal him)
w'qṣp (and I was angry)	- - -	w'šlm nḥmym lw (and/but I will restore full comfort to him)
wylk šwbb (he walked turning	- - -	w'nḥhw (and/but I will lead him).

The correspondences noted here underscore the progressive drive toward the Lord's intervention with the gifts of salvation; the language of punishment gives way to divine reconciliation in healing, guidance, and full comfort.[111] And yet coupled with the words of redemption is God's righteous response to the insult of Israel's straying; in justice the Lord's anger flares up and he strikes the wayward ones. But the One who once gave them life (57:15-16) will restore that gift in healing, guidance, and comfort (57:18).

Expressions of salvation and redemption dominate this strophe; though the text reveals the sin of covetousness and disregard for God's ways, its thrust points toward the bestowal of redemptive blessings. The use of drk recalls an earlier motif of wandering from God's path but in 57:14 presents an image of God's intervention announcing the preparation of ways enabling Israel to be known as God's people (ᶜmy, 57:14). Those straying and in need of healing (57:17-18) are the same ones to be revived (57:15c). So even if one has sinned, the expectation of God's redemptive hand can only be hoped for if one is humble

111. Cf. KSELMAN, "A Note on w'nḥhw," 541.

and contrite (57:15), for with such people does God abide, reviving, healing, leading, and comforting them.

H. Isaiah 57:19b-21 -- Peace for All but the Wicked

Two elements in this strophe create links with the previous one: the repetition of rp' in 57:18b,19b and a recurring sound pattern. In 57:18b the Lord's healing of wayward Israel is an act of restoration; despite the punishment inflicted for Israel's covetousness, Yahweh renews them with healing, guidance, and comfort. In 59:19b, Yahweh's offer of peace also includes healing, continuing the idea of restoration into the final strophe. Other examples of rp' and šlwm in concert bear a similarity to the idea of restoration found in vv. 16-19. In the Fourth Servant Song of Isa the chastisement borne by the servant brings wholeness and healing to those who have committed iniquities.

> But he was wounded for our transgressions,
> he was bruised for our iniquities;
> Upon him was the chastisement that made us whole (šlwmnw)
> and with his stripes we are healed (nrp'-lnw). Isa 53:5

In Jer 33 the revivification of Jerusalem after the onslaught of the Babylonians looks forward to healing and abundance of peace.

> Behold, I will bring to it (i.e., Jerusalem) health and healing (wmrp'), and I will heal them (wrp'tm) and reveal to them an abundance of peace (šlwm) and truth. (Jer 33:6; translation mine.)

Thus from the immediate context of 57:15-18 and the other examples noted, one can see how the use of rp' and šlwm in 57:19b continues the motif of salvific restoration into the final strophe.

A repeated sound pattern links 57:18b with 57:19b-21; the recurring <u>š</u>, <u>l</u>, and final <u>m</u> form a "motif" of sound that links words and ideas.[112] The following elements from the text demonstrate the reiterated sound pattern.

v. 18b) w'šlm (and I will restore)

v. 19b) šlwm šlwm (peace, peace)

v. 21) w'yn šlwm (and there is no peace)

The motif of restoration coming with <u>w'šlm</u> (v. 18b) shows that God will act on behalf of the humble and contrite; despite his anger the Lord will restore full comfort. The dual use of <u>šlwm</u> in v. 19b, so similar in sound to <u>w'šlm</u> of v. 18b, links the notion of restoration with the gift of peace. The final expression in v. 21, announcing no peace for the wicked (<u>w'yn šlwm</u>), demonstrates the lack of restoration for the wicked. This closing comment about the wicked echoes v. 15b-c noting that God's restoration comes to the humble and contrite; peace, healing, and new life come to those walking in the way of the Lord.

The rhythm and sound patterns of 57:19b-21 indicate the transition in the message occurring in these verses. The predominance of the <u>ā</u> and <u>ô</u> patterns in 57:19b gives a sense of solemnity and grandeur to the bicolon;[113] in comparison to the previous cola, a broadening of the line at v. 19b connotes the majesty of the salvific proclamation. There appears to be a pattern in 57:19b, moving back and forth between the <u>ā</u> and <u>ô</u> vowel sounds:

---

112. See note 44 of this Chapter.

113. See note 102 of this Chapter.

57:19b ā-ô-ā-ô-ā-ā-ā-ô-a-ā-ô / ā-a (ʼādônay) u-ᵉ-ā-î.

Then in 57:20 the r and š sounds highlight the key word that begins and concludes vv. 20-21, hršᶜym (the wicked ones): ngrš, wygršw, rpš. The repetition of these sounds draws attention to a new focal point, the wicked. These sounds of the verses witness to a change in the movement in the text: the ā and ô sounds of 57:19b express a lightness and splendor in rhythm, while 57:20-21 with the repeated r and š sound of hršᶜym and a regular change of vowels produce a heavy and laborious rhythm. Thus the interworking of rhythm and sound patterns communicate the glory of the salvific promise in 57:19b, and form a contrast to the dismal announcement of the wicked ones' fate in 57:20-21.

The expression lrḥwq wlqrwb (to the far and to the near) in v. 19b is a merism.[114] These polar expressions heighten an understanding of the restoration being offered; peace is extended to all. Then in v. 20 the w of whršᶜym functions in an adversive manner to specify that the wicked stand outside the magnanimous offer of restoration. Nonetheless, the merism of v. 19b distinguishes the expansive offer of God's salvation.

In 59:20-21 several repetitions highlight special features in the text focusing on a key idea concerning the wicked. The repetitions form a chiastic structure with a focal point that recalls an earlier motif.

---

114. This poetic device is discussed in note 30 of this Chapter.

(A) whrš^{c}ym

(B) kym ngrš

(C) ky hšqṭ l' ywkl

(B) wygršw mymyw

(A) lrš^{c}ym

The opening words about the wicked ones in v. 20aa set the stage for the unfolding description of them and their fate. The positioning of hrš^{c}ym at the beginning and end of the structure focuses attention on the wicked ones (AA). As noted earlier, the w of whrš^{c}ym in v. 20aa connects these verses with the preceding in an adversive manner, differentiating between those who will and those who will not be the recipients of peace. Two points of contrast distinguish the wicked ones: the w in v. 20aa clarifies the merism of v. 19b specifying the exclusion of a certain group from "those near and far"; also the negation 'yn in v. 21 eliminates the wicked ones from the blessing of peace. The BB words work together comparing the wicked to tumultuous waters. In v. 20aa ngrš as a niph^{c}al participle describes the sea as agitated while in v. 20b the same root (wygršw) depicts the waters agitating mire and slime with a qal imperfect verb; the movement from the first to the second B points out the effect of the agitated water, stirring up mire and slime. Alonso Schökel notes the accumulative effect of the imagery depicting the wicked; the turbulent waters, wind, muddy depths, and darkness represent a biblical conception of horror.[115]

Finally, the key to the chiastic pattern in C centers the expression ky hšqṭ l' ywkl. The particle ky accentuates the result of the preceding

---

115. Cf. ALONSO SCHÖKEL, Estudios de Poética Hebrea, 290.

colon;[116] the consequences of the wicked being like tumultuous water is that they are unable to be calm. At the center of the chiasm is the verb of inclusion for the poem, ykl. Its place as the focal point of the structure shows its importance, further strengthening the inclusion despite the distance between repetitions. As 56:10b describes the inability of Israel's leaders to fulfill their task as watchmen, so the motif returns in 57:20 now characterizing the inability of the wicked to find rest. Further connecting the opening and closing stanzas, this time with contrast, is the distant parallelism with nwḥ//šqṭ in 57:2b,20a.[117] In 57:2, despite the neglect shown them, the upright will rest (ynwḥw) upon couches as reward for righteous living; in 57:20 the wicked are portrayed as agitated water that is unable to be calm (hšqṭ), a penalty for their way of living. Thus the C element of the chiasm brings the poem to a conclusion recalling two ideas from the opening stanza: the inclusion with ykl (56:10b; 57:20) presents another aspect of the inabilities of those not walking in God's ways; and the distant parallelism of nwḥ//šqṭ differentiates the reward of rest for the upright and the punishment of disquietude for the wicked.

III. APPLICATION OF A LITERARY DEVICE TO ISAIAH 56:9--57:21

One of the initial arguments for the unity of 56:9--57:21 points out three examples of contrast in the poem: as a literary device, antithesis demonstrates a way of perceiving how the various strophes can be read as part of

---

116. Cf. MUILENBURG, "The Linguistic and Rhetorical Usages," 137.

117. For examples of the parallel pair nwḥ//šqṭ, see 2 Chr 4:5(MT); Job 3:13; 3:26; Isa 14:7.

a whole. The close reading of the strophes further illustrates how the antitheses occur at points of major transition in the poem, concluding each of the three stanzas. Muilenburg notes that poems often have several points of climax, emphasizing more than one idea or motif;[118] together these turning points highlight different aspects of a similar theme. In this literary unit, 57:2 and 57:13c contrast the redemptive reward that comes to the righteous and faithful ones as compared with the punishment awaiting the wicked as found in 57:20-21; beyond the relationship of reward and punishment, the general literary contexts building up to the antitheses distinguish themes of judgement and salvation.

The contrasts found at the conclusions of the stanzas present a broad way of seeking how this device unites the poem, saving it from the sense of dispersion that most commentators see here.[119] But the question remains, are there links among the stanzas that demonstrate a greater sense of unity for the reading of the whole poem? Two points in the preceding analysis briefly mention the repetition of vocabulary that serves to further demonstrate contrasts between stanzas. On pp. 98-99, the consideration of the word for "couch" (_mškb_) illustrates how it appears in two quite different settings and displays a dissimilarity in their usages; in 57:2 the description of the couch denotes a reward for the upright ones while in 57:7 the couch symbolizes an instrument of the harlot's trade bringing her judgment. On pp. 149-50 reference is made to the ambiguity rising from the two uses of _špl_ at 57:9b,15b-c; the same verbal root portrays the harlot's descent (_wtšpyly_) to the deepest depths and the Lord's

118. Cf. MUILENBURG, "Form Criticism," 9.

119. See p. 24 and notes 67 and 68 of Chapter One.

promise of new life to the contrite of spirit (wšpl-rwḥ). These two examples of repetitions with differing meanings form links between the stanzas; but to be certain that this is a literary device at work and not two isolated instances, it is important to find more examples continuing this kind of wordplay. As noted at the beginning of this Chapter, beyond the key words noted in the Overview, the Chapter has several other examples of repetition; these recurrences can be considered in order to determine if this device of wordplay is operative in the poem.

Before returning to the poem itself, a few points of clarification should be made about the kind of wordplay noted above. The most common term describing the various types of wordplay is "paronomasia."[120] There are a variety of ways in which the biblical authors compose their plays on words. Akin to the above description is a form of wordplay called "metaphony," where the root of a word is repeated, but in its recurrence a change in meaning is introduced, often with a vowel mutation while the stem remains the same;[121] J.J. Glück maintains that in Semitic languages where the basic meaning of a word is conveyed by the radicals, the modification of the vowels signals a modification of thought.[122] This style of paronomasia creates a sense of ambiguity, for a single word either carries more than one connotation or its uses display contrasting situations; yet by their common root, these words stand

---

120. Cf. J.J. GLÜCK, "Paronomasia in Biblical Literature," Semitics 1 (1970) 50-78; J.M. SASSON, "Wordplay in the OT," IDBSup, 968-701.

121. Cf. GLÜCK, "Paronomasia," 61-66; SASSON, "Wordplay in the OT," 967.

122. Cf. GLÜCK, "Paronomasia," 61.

in relationship with one another. In Isa 1:19-20 the verb ’kl (to eat) has two meanings for the same people.

If you are willing and obedient
you shall eat (tō’kēlu)
But if you refuse and rebel,
you shall be devoured (t^{e}’ukk^{e}lu) by the sword,
for the mouth of the Lord has spoken. (Isa 1:19-20)

Depending upon their response in obedience, the people of Judah will either be blessed with eating the produce of the land or will be punished with being eaten (figuratively) by the sword. The juxtaposition of the two uses of the same verbal root with differing connotations engenders a sense of incongruity suggesting that a play on words may be taking place, calling for reflection on these links of opposition.

In 56:9--57:21 several repeated words express incongruity and/or contrast when viewed in relation to one another. The following repeated words are considered in an effort to understand how they function in the poem: mškb (couch, 57:2,7-8), hlk (to walk, 57:2,17b), qrb (to draw near, 57:3,19b), nḥm (to comfort, 57:6c,18b), rḥq (to be far away, 57:9b,19b), hr (mountain, 57:7,13c), špl (to descend, 57:9,15), ḥyh (to live, 57:10,15c), ᶜśh (to make, 57:12,16b), and rwḥ (wind or spirit, 57:13b,15c,16b).

The recurrences of mškb in 57:2,7,8 represent two differing images of couches. In 57:2 the couch depicts a reward for the righteous, giving them rest from the evil they endure. The following stanza presents an indictment for idolatrous practices, cast in a language of adultery. In 57:7-8 mškb appears three times as the couch of the harlot's trade; the imagery crescendoes as she sets up her couch, enlarges it, and loves it. The heightened use of mskb in vv. 7-8 as an instrument of the harlot's covenant with idolatry contrasts with the same word in v. 2 as a recompense for upright living; the repetition opposes a message of blessing for the righteous with an indictment for the unfaithful.

The two uses of hlk in 57:2,17b carry a metaphorical sense of "walking" to depict a manner of acting, similar to drk in this unit. However the two examples of this word portray contrasting applications. In 57:2 hlk is an active participle expressing a way of life directed toward acting in an upright manner; the participle describes a modus operandi of those who are given respite from evil because of the way they live their lives. The root hlk in 57:2 portrays a manner of living which brings a reward of rest for following the paths of uprightness. But in 57:17b the description of the corporate Israel shows one who walks (wylk) in the way of his own heart, the way of covetousness; this way of acting brings God's anger. The vocabulary in 57:17b suggests a movement away from God's decrees with šwbb: but he walked turning in the way of his own heart. Israel turns from one way to another causing God to hide himself in anger. The contrasting uses of hlk highlight not only the pathways of uprightness and evil, but also the reward for righteousness and the departure of God in the face of injustice.

In 57:3 the trial scene begins with the command for the accused to draw near (qrbw) before the judge. For acts of idolatry, Israel faces accusation, indictment, and threats. In 59:19b God offers peace and healing to those who are far off and near (wlqrwb). Despite the anger God exercises for their departure according to their own ways, the Lord brings healing and consolation; this promise is held out to all, those near and far. The two uses of qrb present God calling the accused to draw near for judgment and offering gifts of redemption to those far and near.

The recurrences of nḥm in 57:6c,18b contrast the lack of consolation which God receives from idolatrous Israel with the bestowal of full comfort the Lord offers to his people. In 57:6, a hinge verse, the references to idolatrous practices display the honor given to other gods, replacing the reverence due to God; and in reaction to such profanations, is he to be comforted? In 57:17-18 the text describes how, despite its departure from his ways, God heals, leads, and restores full comfort (nḥmym) to wayward Israel. The two uses of "comfort" portray a God whose goodness transcends the bounds of what is expected; even though he does not receive the consolation of the reverence due to him, he promises to bestow full comfort upon his people.

In the pursuits of idolatry at 57:9b the harlot sends messengers afar off (ᶜd-mrḥq) and herself descends to the deepest depth (ᶜd-šʾwl); as noted, these expressions show the length to which Israel would go in her infatuation with other gods. The same root, rḥq, appears at the outset of the final strophe distinguishing the extent of God's offer of salvation (57:19b); peace and healing are offered to those far off (lrḥwq) and near. The expedition into the ways of idolatry in 57:9 contrasts with God's magnanimous offer of salvation in 57:19b; the extent of the journey into sin is set against the expansive offer of God's peace. In comparing the two uses of rḥq one sees the absurdity of sending a messenger far off which, in the end, brings no deliverance (57:13a) while a share in God's redemptive gifts extends to the farthest limits to include all. Further, the span of the harlot's wanderings wearies her (57;10) while rest and healing characterize the offer to those far off and near (57:19b-21); it is the wicked who are without rest, denied peace (57:20-21). In the repetitions of rḥq a contrast comes to light in the exaggerated quest for what is futile (57:9) as opposed to the magnitude of God's offer to those who reject wickedness.[123]

The repetitions of hr in 57:7,13c display traditional biblical images referring to Jerusalem.[124] Portrayed as towering and lofty (v. 7), the ascent up the mountain recalls other passages noting its height as the peoples stream toward it (cf. Ps 122:4; Isa 2:2; Jer 3:16; Mic 4:2); specified as God's holy place (v. 13c), the expression hr-qdšy occurs several times in Isa as a gathering place for worship of Yahweh (cf. 27:13; 56:7; 66:20). However the two uses of hr, while denoting the same place, present it as both a place of harlotry (v. 7) and a place of blessed inheritance (v. 13c). In one stanza the contrasting employment of this word suggests that the holy place destined as the inheritance for those confiding in Yahweh has been turned into a site of idolatry. The literary contexts where hr recurs oppose the indictment for judgment to the promise of inheritance.

The verb wtšpyly in 57:9 describes the journey of Israel in the ways of idolatry; the descent explained here characterizes the lengths to which the unfaithful one is willing to go, that is to the deepest depths. The repetition of špl in 57:15b,15c portrays God's immanent dwelling with those who are contrite

---

123. The merism lrḥwq wlqrwb in v. 19b has counterparts of contrast, further stressing its use in the announcement of peace and healing.

124. See pp. 134-35 and notes 79 and 80 in this Chapter.

and humble of spirit (wšpl-rwḥ). The transgression involved with Israel's descent specifies a lack of fear, concern, and righteousness toward God in 57:11-12; in contrast to what God expects of those with whom he abides is a sense of contriteness and humility (57:15). The incongruity between the two situations described in 57:9,15 is found in the "kind of descent" that is life-giving: while it is the humble (or bowed down, as the verb implies) individual who is revived by God (57:15), it is the one descending in search of another god who is left to be delivered by useless idols (57:13).

In 57:10 the unfaithful one is said to have found life (ḥyt) in her pursuits and despite the extent of her travels, she does not flag. This verse suggests that it is in idolatry that Israel seeks to be enlivened; this idea is countermanded later in 57:13 where the collection of idols is characterized as useless in delivering anyone. In 57:15c the double use of lhḥywt at the beginning of each colon stresses the action of God to restore life to the spirit of the humble and the heart of the contrite; rwḥ and lb are components of the human person fostering life. The need for revitalization comes as a result of God's anger (57:16a); the giver of life is the One from whom the breath of life proceeds (57:16b). The ambiguity, lying in the repetition of ḥyh, presents two sources of life, one which is false and one which is true; the life sought from idolatry fails to bring deliverance (57:13a) while the life sought by the humble and contrite brings healing, guidance, and full comfort (57:18) emanating from the author of life.

The root ᶜśh is found in 57:12,16. The literary context of 57:12 sets out to strike a hard blow against the transgressors; in a statement of biting sarcasm God tells them that their deeds are far from righteous and their activities (w't-m^{c}śyk) useless in providing assistance for them. What they do (w't-m^{c}śyk)--their efforts, their confidence in idolatry--all these things do not help them as they stand before the judge. In contrast, ^{c}śyty in 57:16b is linked with the idea of creation. This motif carries a redemptive tone as the One who made the breath of life (v. 16b) revives the humble and contrite (v. 15); the author of life bestows his life upon those in need of revitalization. The activities (w't-m^{c}śyk) of the accused bring them to judgment, while the actions of God (^{c}śyty) depict a work of salvation; the actions of the accused do not bring the merit of deliverance for them, while the actions of God bring forth redemption in fostering new life. The deliverance in this repetition emerges as the same word describes deeds which fail to bring salvation in times of need (57:12-13) and a deed which brings forth new life, opposing the idolatrous works of humanity to the creative work of God.

A final example comes from the root rwḥ in 57:13b,16b. In 57:13b the fate of the unrighteous is described as the judgment scene comes to a close; those who put their confidence in idols will see that these are gods of no strength for they cannot save in moments of need. So weak are these idols that the wind (rwḥ), like a mere breath, sweeps them away. But in 57:16b the same word describing the wind which drives away these gods then portrays the life-giving spirit by which God animates the humble and contrite. These uses of rwḥ bring into contrast the futility of placing one's confidence in impotent gods while the only God who can bestow life stands ready to enliven the spirit of the humble (rwḥ šplym, 57:15c) with his own animating spirit. Once again God's promise to give of his own animating spirit to humanity contrasts with the useless benefits of idolatrous practices.

These ten examples of paronomasia demonstrate a literary device running through the poem. The following chart shows the ties of contrast between and in the stanzas and the context in which they are found.

	Word	Stanza I	Stanza II	Stanza III
1)	mškb (a couch)	57:2 (a promise)	57:7-8 (a judgment)	
2)	hlk (to walk)	57:2 (a promise)		57:17b (a judgment)
3)	qrb (to draw near)		57:3 (a judgment)	57:19b (a promise)
4)	nḥm (to comfort)		57:6 (a judgment)	57:18 (a promise)
5)	rḥq (to be far off)		57:9 (a judgment)	57:19b (a promise)
6)	hr (a mountain)		57:7 (a judgment)	
			57:13 (a promise)	
7)	špl (to descend)		57:9 (a judgment)	57:15 (a promise)
8)	ḥyh (to live)		57:10 (a judgment)	57:15 (a promise)
9)	^{c}śh (to do)		57:12 (a judgment)	57:16 (a promise)
10)	rwḥ (wind, spirit)		57:13 (a judgment)	57:15,16 (a promise)

In considering the function of the wordplays discussed above there is a common thread uniting all of them: the difference between the ways of humanity and the ways of God. The ways of humanity lead toward judgment while the ways of God promise different aspects of redemption.[125] The character of such a contrast takes on parenetic implications, placing the riches of God's redemptive gifts in contrast with the impoverished way of life apart from God. Further, the repetitions in contrast point out the salvific promises accruing to those whose trust is in Yahweh as opposed to the judgment coming to those whose strength resides in idols. By means of the wordplays one sees that the drk ^{c}my (way of my people, 57:14) is the path of blessing, the road to peace; the wordplays demonstrate the futility of any practice of idolatry for such activities warrant accusation, indictment, and punishment.

From a stylistic point of view, these repetitions effecting wordplays perform several functions. First, they link the stanzas with the recurrence of verbal roots. Their ambiguous character returns the reader/listener to the previous use of the word to struggle with the implications of their divergent meanings. Second, these examples of paronomasia give continuity to the progression of throught from stanza to stanza. The ten patterns establish the device as a means of appreciating how the message can be interpreted, i.e. by means of wordplay. Paronomasia becomes a tool for understanding how the stanzas progress and work together as a whole. And third, the compositional structure by means of antithesis as wordplay focuses attention on a key idea expressed by drk (appearing six times) and by the contrast between words of judgment and of promise. The poem tries to persuade one to comprehend the invaluable greatness of living as God's people, according to the way of his

---

125. R. CLIFFORD similarly shows how repetition as wordplay functions in the "idol passages" of Isa 40-55 to reinforce the description of Yahweh's power to restore Israel in opposition to the uselessness of the various other gods. Cf. "The Function of Idol Passages," 454, 456-57, 464.

commands and promises. The harsh words of judgment give way to the promise of redemption for those who walk in uprightness, following the way of God's people.

IV. SUMMARY

The three stanzas comprising this literary unit focus on the themes of judgment and salvation, the first two focusing on the indictment and punishment of irresponsible leaders and idolatrous individuals, and the concluding one on the promise of redemptive gifts. Despite the commentators who divide 56:9--57:21 into several units, a rhetorical analysis demonstrates numerous links among the stanzas arguing for its integrity. Typical of biblical literature, the beginning and end repeat a similar motif by an inclusion with *ykl*; the only occurrences of *bṣ*^{c} in Isa recur in the opening and closing stanzas, reiterating the way of covetousness which leads to manifestations of God's wrath (56:9-11; 57:16-18). Furthermore, the repetition of vocabulary throughout recalls the motifs of concern for God and the just one, righteousness, and peace: the key word *drk* further clarifies the themes of judgment and salvation, distinguishing between the ways of God and of humanity. Literary devices of inclusion, distant parallelism, rhetorical questions, repeated pronouns, and sound patterns aid in distinguishing the strophes and stanzas.

The close reading of the individual strophes demonstrates the various parallel patterns. For example, by an appreciation for the uses of *w* in 56:11, a sense of balance is restored to the description of the watchmen and shepherds in 56:10-11, each party characterized in three bicola; in 57:3-5 the vocabulary of sin forms a pattern distinguishing the heart of idolatry as a mockery of God. The repetitions of ṣdq (57:1,12) and hr-qdšy (57:13c) show ties with the previous literary unit (56:1-8), encouraging a sense of continuity in the progression through 56-59. The consideration of 57:6 as a hinge verse offers a solution to the disputed question of its placement and function. Several chiastic structures show movement and isolate key ideas by their patterning; in the final verses of the poem, the chiasm not only centers the element of inclusion (ykl) but also clarifies an element of distant parallelism uniting the final verses of the poem with an earlier motif in 57:2, the tranquil rest of the righteous.

The literary device of contrast marks the transition from stanza to stanza. Beyond this, ten examples of paronomasia add to the stylistic manner of uniting the stanzas by means of repetition; the patterned wordplays between and in the stanzas further demonstrate how another manner of contrast is at work uniting the various parts of the poem and highlighting the difference between the ways of God and of humanity.

CHAPTER FOUR

A RHETORICAL ANALYSIS OF ISAIAH 58:1-14

Translation of Isaiah 58:1-14

1 CALL OUT with full throat, do not hold back,
like a trumpet LIFT HIGH your VOICE;
Proclaim to my people their transgression,
to the HOUSE of *JACOB* their sins.
2 Yet me, DAY after DAY they seek,
in KNOWING my WAYS, THEY TAKE PLEASURE,
Like a nation with RIGHTEOUSNESS, it has ACTED
and the JUSTICE of its GOD it did not forsake;
They ask me for RIGHTEOUS JUSTICE,
in drawing near to GOD, THEY TAKE PLEASURE.
3 "Why do we FAST and you do not SEE,
HUMBLE OURSELVES and you do not KNOW?"
BEHOLD, on the DAY of your FAST you FIND PLEASURE
and all your workers you tyrannize.
4 BEHOLD, while continuing to contend and to quarrel, you FAST,
and to strike with a WICKED fist.
You are not FASTING as on a DAY
when you make heard ON HIGH your VOICE.

5 IS THIS the FAST I CHOOSE,
a DAY when a person HUMBLES ONE'S SELF?
IS it to bow like a rush one's head,
and sackcloth and ashes to lie upon?
IS THIS what you CALL a FAST,
and a DAY acceptable to the LORD?

6 Rather IS NOT THIS the FAST I CHOOSE:
To loosen the fetters of WICKEDNESS,
to unfasten the thongs of the YOKE,
To SET FREE the oppressed,
for thus every YOKE you shall shatter?
7 IS IT NOT to divide among the HUNGRY your bread,
the wandering HUMBLED ones you should bring into your HOUSE,
When you SEE someone naked to clothe him,
and from another human being, not to hide yourself?
8 THEN it shall break forth like the dawn, YOUR LIGHT,
and your healing quickly shall rise up,
And it shall walk before you your DELIVERANCE,
and the GLORY of the LORD will protect you from behind.

9 THEN you shall CALL OUT and the LORD will answer;
you shall cry out, and he will say, "HERE I am!"

IF you turn away from your midst the YOKE,
the REPROACHING finger and the evil WORD.
10 IF you give to the HUNGRY of YOURSELF,
and the SELF of the HUMBLED one you SATISFY.
Then it shall rise from the darkness, YOUR LIGHT,
your obscurity like high noon
11 Then he shall lead you always, the LORD,
he shall SATISFY in desert places your SELF,
and your bones he shall make strong.
Then you shall be like a garden well-watered,
and like a spring of WATER,
whose WATERS do not deceive.
12 Then they shall rebuild from you the ruins of old,
the foundations of GENERATION upon GENERATION you shall LIFT UP,
And you shall be CALLED the mender of the breach,
the RESTORER of the paths in which to abide.

13 IF you TURN BACK from the SABBATH your foot,
from DOING your PLEASURE on my HOLY DAY,
If you CALL the SABBATH a DELIGHT,
the HOLY (day) of the LORD HONORABLE,
If you HONOR it by not ACTING in your own WAYS
from FINDING your own PLEASURE, and SPEAKING and SPEAKING.
14 THEN you shall take DELIGHT in the LORD,
and I shall bring you to mount the heights of the land,
And I shall nourish you with the inheritance of *JACOB* your father,
for the mouth of the LORD has SPOKEN.

I. OVERVIEW

A. Indications of Unity in Isaiah 58:1-14

As in the two previous literary units, examples of repeated vocabulary in Isa 58 are numerous, already suggesting its integrity. It is through the recurrence of words that chains of thought carry through a poem and develop motifs; whether manifesting similarities and/or contrasts, repetitions point out important ideas by the accumulation of references to them.[1] To initiate the analysis, this Overview considers recurring vocabulary at the beginning and end of the poem and then words appearing at least five times in the unit: ywm (a day), ṣwm (to fast), YHWH (the Lord), qr' (to call out), and npš (a person, the self).

The tendency to separate vv. 13-14 from the rest of 58 prevails among scholars who contend these verses introduce a "sabbath" motif which is incongruous to the basic theme of fasting.[2] However, beyond the inclusion of y^{c}qb in 58:1b,14b, four other words recur in vv. 2 and 13 arguing for the integrity of vv. 13-14 which conclude the poem by recalling the opening motifs

---

1. Cf. MUILENBURG, "A Study in Hebrew Rhetoric," 99.

2. For those commentators separating vv. 13-14 from the rest of Isa 58, see Chapter One, note 70, on p. 25.

of the poem. The following chart specifies the inclusion and other repetitions within the opening and closing verses.

1) y^{c}qb (Jacob) vv. 1b,14b
2) ywm (a day) vv. 2a,2a,13a
3) drk (a way) vv. 2a,13a
4) ḥpṣ (to take pleasure) vv. 2a,2c,13a,13c
5) ^{c}śh (to do, to act) vv. 2b,13a,13c

The elements of inclusion with y^{c}qb demonstrate contrast with a summons to declare to the house of Jacob their transgression and sins in v. 1 and a promise of blessing with the inheritance of their father Jacob in v. 14. This recurrence of the name of Jacob frames the poem and signals a change from an initial announcement of judgment for sin to a proclamation of blessing for those following God's precepts. Further, supporting this inclusion, Muilenburg notes how important names in the biblical tradition serve as structuring elements;[3] here the name of Jacob marks off the beginning and end of the unit.

The four words of v. 2 do not repeat in v. 13 in a parallel or inverted pattern but simply recur as groups of words clustered together. A similar manner of bringing repetitions together is discussed in Chapter Two as recapitulation;[4] this literary device often brings together words from the beginning of a unit at its end as a means of summarizing and reinforcing key motifs. The diagram below shows how the vocabulary from v. 2 appears in v. 13, sometimes combining the repeated words.

---

3. Cf. MUILENBURG, "A Study in Hebrew Rhetoric," 106.

4. For a discussion of the literary device, see BOADT, "Isaiah 41:8-13," 24-25, 30-31.

	V. 2		V. 13
(A)	ywm ywm (v. 2a)	(DC)	^{c}śwt ḥpṣyk (v. 13a)
(B)	drky (v. 2a)	(A)	bywm qdšy (v. 13a)
(C)	yḥpṣwn (vv. 2a,2c)	(DB)	m^{c}śwt drkyk (v. 13c)
(D)	^{c}śh (v. 2b)	(C)	ḥpṣk (v. 13c)

Similar to the change in the literary contexts with *y^{c}qb* in vv. 1,14, these four words also demonstrate a divergence in usages between the opening and closing of the poem. To establish the two literary contexts where the repetitions appear, note that in v. 2 God explains what the house of Jacob is doing while in v. 13 God gives directives for what the people *should* do. The *ywm ywm* in A of v. 2 describes the people's "day after day" search for God, while A in v. 13 does not concern itself with daily practices but gives directives for observance of *the* holy day, the sabbath. The B element in v. 2 refers to the *ways* of God whereas in v. 13c the DB elements combine to warn against *acting* in one's own *way* on the sabbath. The people are said to take *pleasure* in both knowledge of and access to God at C of v. 2, but are cautioned later against *doing* and finding one's *pleasure* on the sabbath in DC and C of v. 13.[5] The description of the nation which *acts* righteously in D of v. 2b changes to prescriptions for sabbath observance expecting restraint from *doing* one's pleasure and *acting* in one's own way on the holy day in DC and DB of v. 13.

While too early in the analysis to understand fully the ties among the elements of inclusion and recapitulation, they display relationships of contrast

---

5. This warning against acting according to one's pleasure on the sabbath is supported in the denouncement of seeking one's own pleasure on the day of fasting in v. 3b.

framing the poem. Furthermore, the establishment of such structures suggests that they signal the sabbath day, the ways of God and humanity, and the seeking of one's own pleasures as important motifs in the unit. Thus from the vantage point of rhetorical analysis, vv. 13-14 play a role as part of structural components distinguishing the unit's beginning and end, arguing against those who excise them.

A stylistic feature for certain vocabulary in this poem is the recurrence of ywm, ṣwm, and YHWH seven times each.

1) ywm (vv. 2a,2a,3b,4b,5a,5c,13a)
2) ṣwm (vv. 3a,3b,4a,4b,5a,5c,6a)
3) YHWH (vv. 5c,8b,9a,11a,13b,14a,14b)

Despite numerous commentators alluding to the significance of sevenfold repetitions or patterns, this rhetorical device for these words passes unnoticed.[6] Beyond the enumerated repetition of a word seven times for emphasis, studies show the ancients regarded certain numbers as special for underscoring a message; the numbers three, seven, ten, and forty are significant in biblical literature.[7] The repetition of words or ideas according to these special numerations can serve also as a device for structuring and as a symbolic way of expressing perfection, excellence, and/or completion.[8] A consideration of these

6. ALONSO SCHÖKEL notes the seven occurrences of ṣwm in Isa 58, but not the other two words; cf. "Isaias III," 357.

7. Cf. Marvin POPE, "Number," IDB 3, 563.

8. Several commentators show examples of sevenfold repetitions or patterns as a means of structuring. Cf. Umberto CASSUTO, A Commentary on the Book of Genesis (Israel Abrahams, trans.; Jerusalem: Magnes Press, 1961-64) 12-17; David Noel FREEDMAN and C.F. HYLAND, "Psalm 29: A Structural Analysis," HTR 66 (1973) 241; Arvid S. KAPELRUD, "The Number Seven in

words in their context follows to discern their function.

Several patterns appear demonstrating how ywm and ṣwm function together. Consider the following diagrams showing the ordering of these words in the poem.

Diagram I			Diagram II			Diagram III		
58: 2aa	ywm	(A)	58:5aa	ṣwm	(B)	58:6a	ṣwm	(B)
2aa	ywm	(A)	5ab	ywm	(A)	13a	bywm	(A)
3aa	ṣmnw	(B)	5ca	ṣwm	(B)			
3ba	bywm	(A)	5cb	wywm	(A)			
3ba	ṣmkm	(B)						
4aa	tṣwmw	(B)						
4ba	tṣwmw	(B)						
4ba	kywm	(A)						

The ordering of the words in Diagram I does not manifest any clear pattern of parallelism or inversion in the ensemble of elements. However, a pattern of ywm and ṣwm in the same colon appears in vv. 3ba and 4ba. At v. 3ba, bywm ṣmkm appears in construct representing the idea of fasting as relegated to a specific day when its practices are carried out: on the day of your fast. Similarly in v. 4b the act of fasting is consigned to a day, a day when one wishes to have his voice heard by God on high. Thus the two examples where ywm and ṣwm function together designate fasting as a practice done on a specific day.

In Diagram II the two words in question again appear together, but this time one in each colon of the bicola at vv. 5a,5c. In vv. 5a,5c an internal

---

Ugaritic Texts," VT 18 (1968) 494-95; Richard Green MOULTON, The Literary Study of the Bible (London: D.C. Heath and Co., Publishers, 1899) 110-12; MUILENBURG, "A Study in Hebrew Rhetoric," 106; Marvin POPE, "Seven" IDB 4, 295; J.H. STECK, "The Stylistics of Hebrew Poetry," Calvin Theological Journal 9 (1974) 20.

structure repeats where the opening colon begins with a question about fasting (is this the kind of fast I choose [. . .] is this what you call a fast) followed by a description relating it to a practice done on a specific day (a day when a person humbles one's self [. . .] a day acceptable to the Lord). The same motif from vv. 3ba,4ba repeats in vv. 5a,5c, characterizing the exercise of fasting as something performed on a special day.

An appreciation for the split between ṣwm and ywm in 58:5a,5c further develops in Diagram III. The words ṣwm and ywm each appear only once more, ṣwm initiating an explanation of the fasting which God chooses and the benefits given to those who follow it (vv. 6-12), and ywm initiating an explanation of proper sabbath observance and the benefits accruing to those who follow it (vv. 13-14). After the references to fasting as "a day" on which practices are carried out (58:3b,4b) and to the kind of fasting observances limited to "a day" (58:5a,5c), the word ywm does not appear at all in the description of the fasting that God chooses (vv. 6-12); this signals a move away from the previous contexts which consign fasting to a practice done on a particular day. On the contrary, the verbal system describing the fast God chooses is built on a series of infinitives in vv. 6-7; the infinitives stress a mode of action, a way of living, to be put into practice, not something merely done on a single or specific day.[9] Thus one can see a movement in the text away from understanding fasting as a practice done during a designated time to perceiving fasting as a mode of acting, as a way of life; and on the other hand, the

9. Cf. GKC, 94 §40b; 109-10 §49a-b; 348 §123b.

recurrence of ywm in 58:13a draws attention to the day which is holy (58:13a,13b), the sabbath.

Both Alonso Schökel and Muilenburg point out that when a term is employed often in a literary context (and this is especially applicable to repetitions of seven) its final use receives the emphasis and displays an example of excellence, perfection, authenticity, and completion of the topic in question.[10] In its seventh and final occurrence, the word is brought to its summit of meaning and there reveals its significance in the literary context. The pattern in which ṣwm and ywm appear throws weight on the final time that each word is found; after a series of placements together (vv. 3b,4b,5a,5c), they no longer appear in tandem but rather are separated with ṣwm in v. 6a and ywm in v. 13a. In v. 6a an explanation of the kind of fasting God chooses unfolds; similarly, v. 13a begins the observances for the day of holiness and honor, the sabbath. Thus the seventh and final occurrences of ṣwm and ywm in this literary unit take on special force as they introduce the expressions of authentic and perfect fasting, and observance of the day "par excellence," the sabbath.

The seven occurrences of ywm and ṣwm and their patterns within the text function as a structuring device as well as aid in the interpretation of the text. In vv. 3b,4b,5a,5c fasting is presented as a practice relegated to a day's involvement, but the final occurrence of ṣwm in v. 6a initiates a new concept of this traditional custom geared more to a mode of living than a ritual execution of actions on an appointed day. Also the final occurrence of ywm in v. 13a,

---

10. Cf. ALONSO SCHÖKEL, "Isaias III," 357; MUILENBURG, "A Study in Hebrew Rhetoric," 108.

without any reference to a day of fasting, explains that the sabbath is the day set aside for special observances. Thus the final uses of ṣwm and ywm structure the text to signal the kind of fasting and sabbath customs that God prefers.

The seven occurrences of the root ṣwm in 58 distinguish it as a key word. The importance of ṣwm is further underscored by the close proximity and interchange of the radicals ṣ and m which keep the "sound" of fasting present to the listener: ṣmkm tmṣ'w (v. 3b), wmṣh tṣwmw (v. 4a), tṣmḥ (v. 8a), wᶜṣmtyk (v. 11b), and wkmwṣ' (v. 11c).[11] The significance of ṣwm is also heightened here, Isa 58 being the only literary context where the word appears in all of Isa. Thus Isa 58 presents a statement on this practice, so closely associated with Israelite religion, expanding beyond the usual confines of actions directed toward penance; this Isaian concept of fasting is developed more in detail in the Close Reading of the strophes.

The divine name YHWH appears first in 58:5c and six more times in the verses explaining the fasting and sabbath observances which reap the blessings of salvation (58:8b,9a,11a,13b,14a,14b).[12] Two observations can be made regarding the placement of the divine name in this literary context. First, the use of YHWH is primarily related to God's redemptive action toward those

---

11. CERESKO notes a similar example of where the radicals r and ṣ appear in nine examples within Ps 105, stressing the importance of the root 'rṣ; this kind of sound-motif reinforces the basic repetitions of the word. Cf. "A Poetic Analysis," 28.

12. The divine name appears equally three times in the strophes related to the blessings of authentic fasting and three times in the strophe about the sabbath. Regarding the importance of the pattern of three, see POPE, "Number," 563-64.

who observe the given precepts: the glory of the Lord (kbwd YHWH, v. 8b) will protect them from behind; when they call out, the Lord (wYHWH, v. 9a) will answer; the Lord (YHWH, v. 11a) shall lead them continually; the sabbath is referred to as the holy day of the Lord (lqdwš YHWH, v. 13a); they shall take delight in the Lord (ᶜl-YHWH, v. 14a); the assurance that all the blessings given will come to pass is founded on the understanding that this word of promise comes from the mouth of the Lord (ky py YHWH dbr, 58:14b). In these examples the divine name is linked with the events of salvation and the day of holiness; the final time the divine name appears it concludes the literary unit on a word of completion, authority, and confidence that the divine word will come to pass. In 58:2 another divine name, 'lhyw and 'lhym, appears in the word of accusation initiating the reasons and causes for a judgment of the people's actions, whereas the uses of YHWH in 58:8b,9a,11a,13b,14a,14b demonstrate the ways of sharing in God's salvation.[13] Second, the concentration of six of the seven occurrences of YHWH in 58:6-14 can serve as a structuring device separating the words of judgment in vv. 1-5 from the words of redemption in vv. 6-14.[14] The numerous repetitions in 58:6-14 function to highlight the message of hope with the reappearance of the divine name, the only One who bestows the great gifts of salvation; the continued recurrences of the divine name act as a way of reminding one that it is YHWH who protects (v. 8b) and guides (v. 11a) his

---

13. MAGONET demonstrates the difference between the literary setting of 'lhym and YHWH in the book of Jonah showing how literary contexts employ different names of the divinity as a structuring device to distinguish scenes or complementary images of God. Cf. Form and Meaning, 33-38.

14. Several authors show how the divine name serves as a structuring device; cf. CERESKO, "A Poetic Analysis," 29; FREEDMAN and HYLAND, "Psalm 29," 241: MUILENBURG, "A Study in Hebrew Rhetoric," 106. The significance and function of the divine name in 58:5 is considered later in this chapter.

people, who answers their call (v. 9a), and who is their true delight (v. 14a). Thus the uses of YHWH in 58:6-14 strengthen the salvific thrust of these verses by their frequent return to the central idea that it is the Lord who redeems, who comes to bring salvation.

The five times that the verbal root qr' appears, it is evenly distributed throughout the literary unit (58:1a,5c,9a,12b,13b). In 58:1 qr' begins the poem on a strong note of proclamation, to acknowledge to the people their sins. This same motif is found in v. 5c following the description of the fasting observances, asking if the people acknowledge (tqr') these practices as a fast. In 58:12b the observance of the fasting which God chooses brings the acknowledgment (wqr' lk) of a new name, "mender of the breach". In 58:13b one of the conditions for sharing in the salvific blessings is the acknowledgment (wqr't) of the sabbath as a delight. A different sense of the word is found in 58:9a where it is a synonym for prayer or beseeching the Lord. Thus the opening word of the literary unit begins a motif of "acknowledging" on four different levels: the people's sins, the proper observance of a fast, a new name, and the description of the sabbath. Though loosely connected the recurrences of qr' recall the strong tone on which the literary unit begins and carries through with a motif of crying out and acknowledging.

The word npš appears five times in the literary unit (58:3a,5a,10aa,10ab,11a), thrice in tandem with ^{c}nh (58:3a,5a,10ab). Four of five times npš refers to a person who practices fasting (vv. 3a,5a,10aa,11a) and the other time toward an individual who is not fasting (v. 10ab).[15] Specifically in v. 10aa, the motif of "one's self" is brought into contrast with the motif of "another individual" (v. 10ab) and emphasizes the relationship of one person to another.[16] In the instances that npš and ᶜnh are together, twice (vv. 3a,5a) the words refer to the act of humbling one's self while the other (v. 10ab) speaks of an individual who is already humbled. Thus, there is an opposition in the literary unit between "one's self" and "another individual," and more specifically between the person who humbles himself (vv. 3a,5a) and the individual who is in the state of having been humbled (v. 10ab). The importance of npš is corroborated by its five uses at various intervals in the poem, recalling the motif; a more detailed analysis of its function is developed in the Close Reading of the microstructures.

Several points argue for the overall unity of Isa 58: the inclusion with yᶜqb and the recapitulation of four words distinguish typical signs of framing a poetic unit which is further strengthened by the contrasts among the elements of inclusion and recapitulation; the seven repetitions of ywm, ṣwm, and YHWH signal key words whose placement in the poem shows them appearing in patterns and functioning as structural clues for a reading of the poem; and the five uses of qr' and npš mark off two further words whose employment throughout the unit point out motifs related to "acknowledging" and "the self."

---

15. Examples of fasting in a manner that God does not accept are explained in vv. 3a, 5a while the manner that God chooses and its effects are in vv. 10a,11ab.

16. In v. 10a the repetitions of npš present the twofold command to pour out one's self and to satisfy the self of another individual.

B. Delimitation of the Strophes

The opening verses of Isa 58 do not demonstrate the verbal signs which suggest a strophic division. While in vv. 1-4 second per. masc. sing. verbs dominate (vv. 1,3a-4b), examples of third per. masc. pl. (vv. 2a,2c), third per. masc. sing. (v. 2b) and first per. pl. vary the style. Here one senses a kind of narrative progression calling for the announcement of sinfulness to the people (v. 1), God's descriptions of their actions (v. 2), the question of the people to God (v. 3a), and God's response accusing the people of a wrong practice of fasting (vv. 3b-4).

Despite the shifting verbal system an inclusion at 58:1ab (hrm qwlk) and 58:4bb (bmrwm qwlkm) sets off vv. 1-4; to support the strength of this inclusion, the placement of these words at the end of their respective bicola locates them in a distinctive position. The pronominal suffixes on qwl distinguish between the call to an individual to lift up his voice (qwlk) in 58:1a, and the warning to a group that their voice (qwlkm) is not being heard on high in 58:4b. Thus the repeated words specify the characters of the poem in a play on the idea of "lifting up the voice": an individual is called to lift high his voice (hrm qwlk, 58:1a) like the shophar so as to inform the people that their fasting is not making their voice heard on high (bmrwm qwlkm, 58:4b). While Muilenburg suggests a division between 58:3a and 3b, one can argue that the flow between the question (v. 3a) and the answer (vv. 3b-4) should not be interrupted; the question and answer of vv. 3-4 work together to present a whole idea, responding to the inquiry to explain why their fasts are ineffective. Also the double expletives of 58:3b,4a (hn) serve to heighten the crescendo of the strophe, not calling for a division. The triple recurrence of hpṣ (58:2a,2c,3b) unites the strophe culminating with the sarcastic response that carrying out one's own pleasure is not a religious practice connected with fasting.

In 58:5 two examples of structured repetitions come into view in the first and third bicola of the verse. First, in vv. 5a,5c the demonstrative pronoun introduces the bicola with an interrogative h-, hkzh and hlzh. The strong character and function of zh is explained by Gesenius as alerting the reader to someone or something new while focusing it into the present moment.[17] In this literary context the function of the demonstrative pronoun can be related to both the question of whether this is the kind of fasting God chooses and also the hint that a new understanding of fasting is about to be disclosed in the following verses; note the use of zh in v. 6a specifying the kind of fasting God chooses. Thus the double use of zh emphasizes a "connecting" or "bridge" character in 58:5 moving the text from a former way of fasting to its new expression according to what God decrees.

Also, the roots ṣwm and ywm occur twice in a similar position, one in each colon of vv. 5a,5c. This double occurrence demonstrates another pattern distinctive in this verse separating it from the preceding verses where ṣwm and ywm are in the same colon. Also the close proximity of these words to the middle of their bicola gives the effect of a rhyme with the repeated -ôm sound, emphasizing the words and their similar placement toward the middle of the bicolon in both vv. 5a,5c.

---

17. Cf. GKC, 442 §136 a,b.

A final observation addresses the separation of v. 5 from v. 6. With those who deal with the question of meter, there is agreement as to the overall thrust of a 3+3 rhythm.[18] The one break in the rhythm is at v. 6a. Such a rupture in the general flow of the rhythm can serve as a signal that something new is beginning, that there is a change taking place in the movement of the text, or that something important is being introduced.[19] After the questions in 58:5, a new set of questions begins and continues with hlw' at vv. 6a,7a indicating a turn in the text to an explanation of the fasting that God chooses; these considerations all point to the separation of v. 6 from v. 5.[20]

Regarding 58:5, both Muilenburg and Hanson offer similar comments about its function in the literary context. In designating the second strophe as 58:3b-5, Muilenburg also notes that it has two segments, vv. 3b-4 and v. 5; he then goes on to say that v. 5c serves as an excellent transition to the verses that follow.[21] Hanson comments on 58:5 in saying that it summarizes the previous words of judgment while also serving as a bridge to what follows.[22] Despite the fact that they both distinguish 58:5 as a transition verse, Muilenburg connects it to vv. 3b-4 and Hanson to vv. 6-7 as part of a larger series of bicola which form

---

18. Cf. MUILENBURG, "The Book of Isaiah," 677; TORREY, The Second Isaiah, 437.

19. Cf. MUILENBURG, "Form Criticism," 12.

20. One could argue that the interrogative h- in vv. 5a,5c,6a,7a links these bicola and suggests strophic unity; though he does not mention it, this could be part of Hanson's delimitation of a strophe into vv. 5-7. Though the interrogative h- can be taken as a means of consolidating vv. 5-7, the other signs suggesting a division at v. 6a appear stronger to this writer.

21. Cf. MUILENBURG, "The Book of Isaiah," 680.

22. Cf. HANSON, The Dawn of Apocalyptic, 110.

a strophe. Based on the structured repetitions in 58:5a,5c and the rhythmic break in v. 6a, v. 5 stands as a transition verse connecting an old (vv. 2-4) and a new (vv. 6-14) interpretation of true fasting and a day of observance.

Several indications mark how 58:6-14 can be partitioned into strophes according to patterned indicators. Muilenburg stresses the importance of the ordering and placement of particles and other repetitions to give a sense of direction to the movement of the passage;[23] in 58:6-14 one notes the occurrences of several such indicators. In vv. 6a,7a there is the repetition of the negative question formed by hlw'; this is followed in vv. 8a,9a by the adverb 'z.[24] Then in vv. 13a,14a the text moves from the conditional particle 'm to the adverb 'z.[25] Similar to the pattern of vv. 13a,14a is the recurrence of 'm in v. 9b; however, one notes the absence of the particle 'z. But one can argue that the opening word of v. 10b (wzrḥ) substitutes for 'z with the similar opening sound of zayin.[26] Even beyond their placement in vv. 6-14, these vocal gestures point to a relationship between the salvific blessings (with 'z) and the conditions

---

23. Cf. MUILENBURG, "The Linguistic and Rhetorical Usages," 135.

24. The movement from hlw' to 'z also appears in Jer 22:15-16; there the elements emerge as a chiastic pattern accenting the movement from a particular action (doing just and righteous deeds) to a blessing (then things go well with one), showing the cause for blessing is to enable him to know the Lord God.

25. Several examples attest to the general movement of an 'm condition to an 'z consequence, while also employing an imperfect verb; cf. 1 Sam 6:3; Job 9:30-31; 11:13-15; Prov 2:4-5.

26. The zayin is a distinctive sound in this poem for other than the three occurrences of 'z in vv. 8a,9a,14a, the only other times a word contains that consonant are in vv. 2b (^{c}zb), 10b (wzrḥ), and 11c (ykzbw). Especially occurring at the opening of the verse, it repeats a sound similar to 'z as the text moves from a set of commands to the salvific effects promised to those who observe them.

(with hlw' and 'm) upon which they are dependent.[27] The healing, guidance, and answer to prayer in vv. 8-9a are redemptive gifts which come from a fasting which shatters every yoke (v. 6) and provides for the needs of others (v. 7). Likewise in the turning away of another's yoke (v. 9b) one comes to know the Lord's guidance (v. 11); and finally, if one keeps from doing his own pleasure on the sabbath (v. 13), then he will delight in the Lord and share in the inheritance of Jacob (v. 14). Based on the particle indicators hlw'/'m and 'z, the natural movement from "condition" to "result" distinguishes the strophes in 58:6-14 as vv. 6-9a, 9b-12, 13-14.[28]

Now that the strophes are delimited another aspect shows an element of unity in each strophe. It has been pointed out already that the verb qr' appears five times in 58. According to the proposed strophic plan, qr' appears once in each strophe: in 58:1-4, qr' (v. 1a); in the transition/bridge verse 58:5, tqr' (v. 5c); in 58:6-9a, tqr' (v. 9a); in 58:9b-12, wqr' (v. 12b); in 58:13-14, wqr't (v. 13b). The same verbal root which begins the literary unit carries throughout and establishes links between the different strophes.

The strophic plan for 58 divides the text into vv. 1-4, 5 ,6-9a, 9b-12, 13-14. The recurrence of verbal roots and particles orders Isa 58 in a way that shows its unity and cohesiveness, and its development from an improper to a proper observance of fasting and the Lord's holy day.

---

27. Cf. KOSMALA, "Form and Structure," 75; MUILENBURG, "The Book of Isaiah," 680-81; SCULLION, Isaiah 40-66, 163.

28. This follows the plan proposed by MUILENBURG for vv. 6-14; cf. "The Book of Isaiah," 677, 680-86.

II. CLOSE READING

A. Isaiah 58:1-4 -- Reasons for Judgment

The opening verse of 58 begins the literary unit in an intense fashion with four imperatives: qr', 'l-tḥśk, hrm, whgd. The first three imperatives explain the manner in which the announcement is to be made and the final verb in 58:1b gives the order to proclaim the transgressions to God's people; the w of whgd connects the verb to the preceding bicolon giving force to the sense of proclamation as something important, to be done in full voice without holding back. The alliteration of the l for l^{c}my and wlbyt y^{c}qb and the final -am with pš^{c}m and ḥṭ'tm serves to bring together those who are addressed and what is announced to them, their sins.[29] A distinguishing character of the parallel words for sin is that pš^{c}m is in the form of a singular noun with a plural suffix indicating a collective notion of transgressing, while ḥṭ'tm is in the form of a plural noun with a plural suffix indicating several sins. The root pš^{c} also appears at 57:4c where it carries the connotation of the nature behind sinful acts; for example, in 57:3-5 the sins of idolatry are shown to manifest a nature of mockery and deceit against God. There pš^{c} represents something other than the naming of a specific sin, but rather points to the essential character of rebellion in a particular act, what lies at the heart of a wicked deed, the fundamental evil in a sin. These observations rest until more can be discerned from the analysis of other microstructures at work in this strophe.

---

29. The words ^{c}my and byt y^{c}qb do not appear elsewhere as parallels in Isa 56-66.

The w of w'wty in 58:2a connects it with 58:1; despite their sin and transgressions, it is the Lord (w'wty) they seek daily. The bond established between 58:2a and 58:1 begins the literary unit on a note of inconsistency: the people sin and yet it is God they daily seek. Despite the usual w which links the bicola together, the whole of v. 2 is held together by two structural patterns: in 58:2a,2c the repetiton of yḥpṣwn frames the verse; the roots ṣdqh and mšpṭ form a chiasm in 58:2b,2c.

The framing of 58:2 with yḥpṣwn is supported by the additional third per. masc. pl. verbs in v. 2a (ydršwn) and v. 2c (yš'lwny); the verbs of v. 2b (third per. masc. sing.) describe the people of v. 1b. With the recurrence of yḥpṣwn as the last element of the bicola in vv. 2a,2c, emphasis falls on the final verb of v. 2b as the focus of the framing; an ABA pattern occurs.

(A) - yḥpṣwn (58:2a)

(B) - l' ᶜzb (58:2b)

(A) - yḥpṣwn (58:2c)

In patterns where there is a center element, it serves as a focal point in the interpretation. In this example of 58:2, the significance of yḥpṣwn is appreciated more as the strophe continues; in 58:3b ḥpṣ appears again. After questioning God as to why he is not responsive to their fasting (v. 3a), the response comes in 58:3b that on the day of their fast they find pleasure (tmṣ' w-ḥpṣ); it is apparent that taking pleasure in such practices is not what is intended and does not win God's attention. This negative connotation of ḥpṣ in v. 3b contrasts with its uses in v. 2 where God describes the people taking pleasure in both knowing God's ways (v. 2a) and drawing near to him (v. 2c); but v. 3b places v. 2 in perspective by clarifying that activities directed toward God are not to be directed toward pleasure for oneself. Ironic overtones prevail in v. 2 as the pleasure the people find in their practices later becomes their condemnation in v. 3b; their search for God's favor only turns him away from them. In v. 2a the emphatic pronoun w'wty (but me) heightens the incongruity by beginning the verse with a focus on God but then moves away to explain that their pursuit of God is, in fact, a pursuit of their own pleasure. The AA elements describe a pleasure which is not an authentic manifestation of what it suggests; in effect, the people do not know God's ways (v. 2a) nor draw near to him (v. 2c) if they do it for themselves. The focal point in B, while describing a righteous and just nation, suggests that the inauthentic seeking and knowing of the divinity is rather a forsaking of God; though a comparison of this people is made with a just nation that does not forsake its God ('lhyw l' ᶜzb), the point is that when a people claims to seek and know its God and in the end achieves its own pleasures, it strays from its goal, it abandons its God.

The chiasm with ṣdqh and mšpṭ spans two bicola and lies within a shift of the verbal speaker.

(A) ṣdqh (v. 2b)

  (B) wmšpṭ

  (B) mšpṭy (v. 2c)

(A) ṣdq

The description of a nation acting in righteousness comes in v. 2b with third per. masc. sing. verbs, while v. 2c notes the demands for justice made by those taking pleasure in drawing near to God with third per. masc. pl. verbs. The inversion of the words moves with the change in verbs from v. 2b to v. 2c, showing a consistency and balance in the progression of the pattern. The ABBA structure strengthens the irony already demonstrated in the previous paragraph, for here the description of the righteous and just nation in v. 2b then moves to describe an unrighteous nation asking for justice.[30] This chiasm emphasizes the notions of justice and righteousness and highlights the understanding that the house of Jacob is not to be counted among the just, though expressions of external actions may lead one to believe this.[31] Beyond its function as a chiasm, the roots ṣdqh and mšpṭ bring together the first two elements of the ABCB pattern of 56:1 which initiates the section 56-59. The recollection of this motif again focuses attention on the call to practice justice and righteousness because of the Lord's imminent coming (56:1) and complements it with an example describing what it means to be such a nation (58:2b) while at the same time showing the house of Jacob to be deficient in this pursuit. The placement of this chiasm close to the beginning of this literary unit of Isa 58 accents the motif and looks forward to a resolution of the initial call to embrace the ways of righteousness.

A change occurs in 58:3a with a new internal structure governing the bicolon.

	V. 3aa		V. 3ab
(A)	lmh	(A')	(lmh understood)
(B)	ṣmnw	(B')	ᶜnynw npšnw
(C)	wl' r'yt	(C')	wl' tdᶜ

---

30. Cf. HANSON, The Dawn of Apocalyptic, 110; SCULLION, "ṢEDEQ-ṢEDAQAH," 343.

31. Commentators note the function of chiasm can direct attention to a shift or movement in the text; cf. CERESKO, "The Function of Chiasm," 2-3; TALMON, "The Textual Study," 358.

The interrogative lmh (A) functions also for A' carrying the question through both cola of v. 3a. The BB' elements bring together the actions of "fasting" and "humbling oneself"; the similar verb forms with a triple terminal -nû unite the words by a recurring sound motif. Other examples of these two acts of mortification appear elsewhere together in the Scriptures suggesting that fasting is an act of humbling oneself.[32] The CC' elements repeat the negative wl' and combine two verbs, "seeing" and "knowing"; in Isa r'h and yd^{c} appear several times as a parallel pair denoting a sense of recognition.[33] Here the double negative emphasizes that the people in question receive no recognition by God for their practices.

The root yd^{c} appears twice in 58:2a,3a. In 56:9--57:2 the parallel pair yd^{c}//byn unites the two strophes addressing the lack of discernment in the leaders of Israel. The recurrence of yd^{c} in 58:2a,3a provides a new aspect of this motif. In 58:2a the people are said to take pleasure in a knowledge (wd^{c}t) of God's ways; in 58:3a the people question God as to why he is lacking in a knowledge (wl' td^{c}) of their acts of humility. These two uses of yd^{c} touch upon two levels of incongruity: the people take pleasure in knowing God's ways when in reality they do not understand, for they sin; they accuse God of lacking knowledge when it is they themselves who are without understanding. As 56:9--57:2 describes the leaders of Israel without knowledge, 58:1-3 similarly characterizes the house of Jacob wanting in knowledge. This lack of discernment brings judgment upon the leaders of Israel for they fail to

32. Note similar examples found in Ezra 8:21; Ps 35:13.

33. For further examples of the parallel pair r'h//yd^{c} see Isa 29:15; 41:20; 44:9.

comprehend how a concern for their own ways separates them from God (56:10-11). In like manner, the house of Jacob believes it knows the ways of God and even questions whether God is aware of their ritual practices (58:2-3a). Without an understanding of what true fasting entails, judgment comes upon the people as an individual receives the commission to announce their sins to them. Both passages dealing with a lack of knowledge are set in a context of judgment where an articulation of their actions brings forth an indictment.

The question in 58:3a receives its response in 58:3b-4a; the change from first per. pl. and second per. masc. sing. verbs in v. 3a to second per. masc. pl. verbs in vv. 3b-4a accents the shift from inquiry to response. The interjection hn draws attention to the words that follow and sets off the responses to the questions in a forceful manner.[34] The double use of hn at the beginning of vv. 3b,4a displays the reasons why God remains unmindful of the people's observances: they find pleasure on the fast day, they tyrannize their workers, and they fast only to contend, quarrel, and strike another individual. A chiastic sound pattern occurs in vv. 3b,4a further drawing attention to these bicola.[35]

v. 3b) ṣmkm tmṣ'w-ḥpṣ

v. 4a) wmṣh tṣwmw

In each opening cola the radicals ṣ and m invert; building on the importance of fasting (ṣwm) as a key idea in the strophe, the sound recurrence heightens the

---

34. Cf. MUILENBURG, "Form Criticism," 14-15; "The Book of Isaiah," 679.

35. For further examples see note 77 in Chapter Three on p. 132.

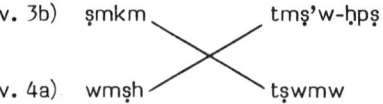

intensity with which the violations of it are pronounced. The transposition of key sounds witnesses to the transposition of ideas: on your fast day, you find pleasure; you contend and quarrel, and yet you fast. The double particle and the chiastic sound pattern mark off the bicola listing the offenses by accentuating devices of assonance.

The listing of the offenses committed on the fast day recalls the initial verse of the strophe and the careful distinction made between "their transgression" (pš^{c}m) and "their sins" (ḥṭ'tm). It has been shown that 58:2b, in the description of the upright nation, casts aspersions on the house of Jacob for not acting in righteousness and justice. In discussing the meaning of the root pš^c, G.H. Livingston describes it as fundamentally "a breach of relationship [. . .] between two parties."[36] A. Gelin distinguishes pš^c as a word less apt to have a sense of precision for designating a particular fault belonging to a list of sins; rather pš^c represents "the mystery of sin," the heart of the revolt.[37] The ABA pattern in 58:2 centers the verb l' ^{c}zb; while saying that the upright do not forsake the justice of their God, these words suggest that the unrighteous do just that. In the opening verses of the book of Isa, the text brings these two words together.

> Children I have reared and brought up,
> but they have rebelled (pš^{c}w) against me. [. . .]
> They have forsaken the Lord (^{c}zbw 't-YHWH),
> they have despised the Holy One of Israel,
> they are utterly estranged. (Isa 1:2b,4c)

---

36. Cf. LIVINGSTON, "pš^c," 741.

37. Cf. Albert GELIN and Albert DESCHAMPS, Sin in the Bible (Charles Schaldenbrand, trans.; New York: Desclée, 1964) 17-18.

In Isa 1, without specifying a catalogue of transgressions, pšᶜ and ᶜzb distinguish the revolt against God, namely, forsaking him. Similarly in 58:2b attention is not focused on specific deeds but on acting righteously and not forsaking God's justice; such a line of thought represents right relationship with God. The referent of pšᶜm in v. 1b appears in v. 2 where it characterizes the injustice, unrighteousness, and the forsaking of God.

In 58:3b,4a the people are accused of wrong deeds: they find pleasure on the fast day, they oppress their workers, they fast only to contend, quarrel, and physically strike another person. Both Gelin and Livingston speak of ḥṭ' as a failure to meet a norm or an expectation.[38] The most frequently used word for sin in the OT, ḥṭ' carries numerous different applications; however, it often carries the nuance of disobedience against God or his law.[39] In 58:3b,4a the list of wicked deeds displays what this people does on the day of its fasting, what actions accompany its day of religious observance; it is obvious the people miss the goal of what fasting should accomplish by proliferating wickedness. Thus the reference to "sins" in the opening verse of this chapter later specifies their evil deeds in vv. 3b-4a.

The placement and ordering of pšᶜm and ḥṭ'tm in 58:1b carry more weight than two parallel terms for "sin" initiating the poem. Rather they guide the reading of the first strophe to distinguish first the nature of the people's

---

38. Cf. GELIN and DESCHAMPS, Sin in the Bible, 17; G.H. LIVINGSTON, "ḥṭ'," TWOT 1, 277.

39. Cf. GELIN and DESCHAMPS, Sin in the Bible, 17; G.H. LIVINGSTON, "ḥṭ'," 277.

transgression in v. 2, and then move on to specify the sins of vv. 3b-4a, forming an ABA'B' pattern in the strophe.

(A) their transgression (v. 1ba)

(B) their sins (v. 1bb)

(A') forsaking God's justice (v. 2)

(B') finding pleasure, oppressing, quarreling, contending, and striking another person (vv. 3b,4a)

Thus the announcement to the people of their trangression reveals their lack of justice and righteousness in forsaking God (v. 2) and the declaration of their sins enumerates the various acts nullifying an authentic fast (vv. 3b-4a).

The emphasis given to the double l' in the question at 58:3a returns in 58:4b where both l' and ṣwm repeat. Taken together, the uses of l' work collectively to show a shift in thought in these final verses of the strophe; the question in v. 3a suggests that God neither sees nor has knowledge of their fasting, while in v. 4b the people are told that they do not fast in a manner which affords God's hearing. When the negatives which are repetitions of vv. 3a,4b are set in relief, they set off the main point of the question and answer.

v. 3a) Why do we fast and you do not see it [. . .] or know it?

v. 4b) You are not fasting [. . .] to make your voice heard on high!

In effect, what these people do is not fasting, not fasting according to what God expects.

Hanson comments that v. 4b concludes these words of judgment with the warning that their day of fasting does not enable their voice to be heard by

God.[40] In the context of the judgment language which calls for the announcement of their sins (v. 1) and an accusation of their ignoble deeds (vv. 2-4a), this final verse explains the situation to the people telling them what they bring upon themselves; God's ear is closed to the prayer issuing from unrighteous deeds. These people sentence themselves to an unresponsive God by a day of fasting which is to their own pleasure (v. 2) and to their neighbor's harm (vv. 3b-4a).

The general movement of the strophe is governed by an explanation of the transgression and sins of the people, first announced in 58:1; the words pš^{c}m and ḥṭ'tm distinguish between the internal and external manifestations of the people's wickedness. Two structures overlap in 58:2 with an ABA pattern governing the whole verse and a chiastic pattern in vv. 2b-c; both patterns work to bring out the incongruity of what at first appears to be righteous activities before God. The strophe builds in intensity with the "question-answer" dialogue between the people and God culminating in the response that their fasting practices are not efficacious for being heard by God. The recurrences of ṣdqh, mšpṭ, and yd^{c} recall motifs from previous poems establishing links among the literary units of 56-59.

B. Isaiah 58:5 -- A Question of Fasting on an Acceptable Day

The repetitions of zh, ṣwm, and ywm in vv. 5a,5c reveal several aspects of structure at work in 58:5.[41] Though important to note how these

---

40. Cf. HANSON, The Dawn of Apocalyptic, 106-107.

41. These repetitions are noted on p. 187.

patterns distinguish 58:5 from what precedes and follows it, the function of the structure needs further clarification.

The repetitions in vv. 5a,5c frame v. 5b disclosing an ABA pattern based on the structure of the bicola in 58:5.

(A) hkzh [. . .] ṣwm [. . .] / ywm [. . .] (v. 5a)

(B) hlkp k'gmn r'šw / wśq w'pr yṣy^{c} (v. 5b)

(A) hlzh [. . .] ṣwm / wywm [. . .] (v. 5c)

This kind of pattern throws emphasis on B, the middle element in v. 5b, as the focus of attention. Each colon in v. 5b presents a different aspect of the topic under consideration.

In v. 5bb the mention of sackcloth (wśq) and ashes (w'pr) recalls traditional instruments associated with the practice of fasting found in different biblical writings. The following examples show how the signs of fasting are representative of sorrow and repentance in the observance of Israelite religion.

> And in every province, wherever the King's command and his decree came, there was great mourning among the Jews, with fasting (wṣwm) and weeping and lamenting, and most of them lay in sackcloth (śq) and ashes (w'pr). (Esth 4:3)

> When I made my soul mourn with fasting (bṣwm),
> it became my reproach.
> When I made sackcloth (śq) my clothing,
> I became a byword to them. (Ps 69:10-11)

> Then I turned my face to the Lord God, seeking him by prayer and supplications, with fasting (bṣwm) and sackcloth (wśq) and ashes (w'pr). (Dan 9:3)

> And the people of Nineveh believed God; they proclaimed a fast (ṣwm) and put on sackcloth (śqym), from the greatest to the least of them. Then tidings reached the king of Nineveh, and he arose from

> his throne, removed his robe, and covered himself with sackcloth (śq) and sat in ashes (ᶜl-h'pr). (Jonah 3:5-6)

These examples enable one to see how the practice of fasting (ṣwm) related directly to the use of sackcloth (śq) and ashes ('pr); an association then exists between vv. 5aa,5bb, and 5ca where these words appear. In the previous verses the fasting of the people is criticized because of the wicked deeds they do on the day of observance (cf. vv. 3b-4b), while in v. 5bb traditional practices related to fasting are questioned as to whether these acts are what God chooses.

The expression hlkp k'gmn r'šw of v. 5ba occurs nowhere else in the Bible; the verb kpp appears only five times in the OT (cf. Pss 57:6; 145:14; 146:8; Isa 58:5; Mic 6:6). In Pss 57,145 and 146, the root kpp describes a state of being bowed down in distress and humiliation;[42] the complement to this condition in 145:14 and 146:8 is being raised up by the Lord.[43] In Isa 58:5ba it is not a situation of being bowed down but rather of bowing one's head as a sign of humility.[44] This description in v. 5ba forms an association with the question concerning a day in which one practices acts of humiliation in v. 5ab. The connection lies in seeing the relationship between the question as to whether fasting is a day when a person humbles oneself in v. 5ab and the description of one bowing one's head like a reed in v. 5ba. As in v. 5bb, v. 5ba describes a particular manifestation of fasting which is questioned as to whether God chooses such practices.

---

42. Cf. BDB, 496; Zor, 370.

43. In both Pss 145:14 and 146:8 the verb zqp expresses the Lord's gesture of raising them. In Mic 6:6 kpp is an action of worship or homage before the lofty God.

44. Cf. ALONSO SCHÖKEL, "Isaias III," 357.

In v. 5b the two infinitives stand at the extremes of the bicolon, accentuating their job of describing both the manner of humbling one's self and the manner of fasting questioned in v. 5a. The infinitives fill out the acts of fasting and humility with an account of what is done: the bowing of the head like a rush and lying on sackcloth and ashes. The significance of the B in the ABA pattern is to focus attention on the actions which constitute both the people's fast and their single day observance. In v. 5b the customary fashion of how these people fast is brought into question. In v. 5b the acts of humiliation and sorrow are given; but following upon the enumeration of wicked deeds in vv. 3b-4b, the manifestations of repentance in v. 5b display the sham of their observances for while they externally show signs of being contrite (v. 5b) their other deeds expose their lack of true sorrow (vv. 3b-4b). The traditional practices of fasting both blind their vision of what God chooses and assuage any guilt in harming their neighbor. A strong hint of the impact of the practices recounted in v. 5b is revealed in v. 5c when the final question of the verse is posed, "and this you call a fast, and a day acceptable to the Lord?" In point of fact, neither are the actions of v. 5b what God chooses nor are they to be called a fast or a day acceptable to the Lord.

Though the ABA pattern governs the verse, the repetitions and the descriptions of fasting and humility show another structure at work in the movement through the individual cola of v. 5. The following diagram presents the movement from colon to colon.

(A) - question regarding the kind of fast (ṣwm) God chooses (v. 5aa)

(B) - question continues to ask about a day (ywm) when one humbles one's self (v. 5ab)

(B') - question related to an act of humbling one's self (v. 5ba)

(A') - question related to the traditional manner of fasting (v. 5bb)

(A) - question as to whether these practices are to be called a fast (ṣwm) (v. 5ca)

(B) - question as to whether these practices are to be called a day (ywm) acceptable to the Lord (v. 5cb).

In v. 5a, the two cola each contain a motif: fasting (v. 5aa) and a day of humbling one's self (v. 5ab). The ordering of the motifs is inverted in v. 5b as the text speaks of bowing one's head like a rush (a sign of humility, v. 5ba) and then of lying upon sackcloth and ashes (an observance related to fasting, v. 5bb). Finally in v. 5c the motifs reverse again in speaking of the fast (v. 5ca) and the day acceptable to the Lord (v. 5cb).

v. 5a (A) ṣwm ⟶ / (B) ywm ^{c}nwt

v. 5b (B') hlkp k'gmn r'šw ⟶ / (A') wśq w'pr yṣy^{c}

v. 5c (A) ṣwm ⟶ / (B) wywm

A clear thought pattern emerges in reading the AA'A elements separately to see how they function together: is this the fast I choose, [. . .] is it to lie on sackcloth and ashes, is this what you call a fast [. . .] ? Likewise, the BB'B cola present a cogent progression of thought: do I choose a day when a person humbles one's self, is it to bow one's head like a rush [. . .] is this what you call a day acceptable to the Lord? The change from colon to colon highlights the distinction being made between ṣwm and ywm in the literary context. The six uses of these two words in vv. 1-5 characterize them as key motifs in Isa 58, and their placement in v. 5 further shows their distinct uses. In 58:5 "fasting" and "a day" set up a network of interrelating elements which move back and forth between the two ideas, in effect separating them; underlying this separation one understands from the literary context that neither their traditional practices associated with fasting nor their relegation of religious observance to a one-day time period fulfills the expectations of God. The impact of v. 5 unfolds as the text progresses to distinguish the kind of fast God chooses (vv. 6-12) and to specify the day that is holy, the sabbath (vv. 13-14).

Hanson and Muilenburg speak of 58:5 as a bridge or transition verse.[45] But in line with what is noted in Chapter Three, v. 5 holds the characteristics distinguishing a hinge verse.[46] To first consider those elements which look back in the text, the repetitions ṣwm and ywm in v. 5 recall the earlier use of these words as the people question whether God sees their fast in v. 3a and how God accuses the people of wicked deeds performed on their fast days. In 58:5a ᶜnwt echoes the motif of humility earlier employed as the people ask why they humble themselves (ᶜnynw npšnw) and why God does not know it in v. 3a. Then anticipating the coming verses, ṣwm and ywm look forward to a new understanding of the fasting God chooses (v. 6) and proper observance of the holy day (v. 13). As ᶜnwt in v. 5a recalls its earlier use so also does it await a change which shifts the focus of fasting from concern of one's self to that of the one who is already humbled (wnpš nᶜnh) in v. 10a. The question of v. 5a anticipates the response beginning in v. 6a employing the same verb, 'bḥrhw. And

45. For the earlier discussion of this, see pp. 188-89.

46. Cf. Chapter Three, pp. 132-33, 137.

finally, in v. 5cb the divine name YHWH appears for the first time with six subsequent occurrences in vv. 6-14. Characteristic of a hinge verse, the words of 58:5 employ vocabulary both preceding and following it, showing its transitional nature to move the text forward into new material. The function of this hinge is to show that the authenticity of the day relegated to fasting and the practices carried out on it are questionable; both their wicked deeds of vv. 3b-4b and the traditional acts of v. 5b are not what God chooses. The questions posed in v. 5 await answers in the verses that follow.

C. Isaiah 58:6-9a -- A Fast the Lord Chooses

The repetitions of hlw' (vv. 6a,7a) and 'z (vv. 8a,9a) indicate the general movement of the strophe. The rhetorical questions introduced by hlw' specify the kind of actions which accompany authentic fasting; following upon this, the particle 'z moves into the effects coming from the practice of a fast which the Lord chooses. Two characteristics distinguish the impact of hlw'. The employment of hlw' as a rhetorical question elicits an affirmative or a negative response;[47] here the literary context expects an affirmation of the enumerated deeds. One can see a parenetic character in this literary device where, by means of questioning, the new way of fasting is presented.[48] While true, it is also apparent that the combination of hlw' with 'z shows the instruction in vv. 6-7 to have a conditional character for only when the people perform these actions do

---

47. Cf. CONROY, Absalom, Absalom, 137; GKC, 476 §151a.

48. ALONSO SCHÖKEL discusses the parenetic character of vv. 6-7, 9b-10a,13; cf. "Isaias III," 356.

the redemptive effects of authentic fasting come to them;[49] the reception of the salvific gifts in vv. 8-9a is contingent upon the performance of a fasting God prefers. Thus both an instructional and a conditional character mark the new words about fasting. In vv. 6-9a one finds not only a new teaching on the practice of fasting but also its effects in the lives of those who follow it; where the former way of fasting brings judgment, the new way promises salvation.

With 58:6a the strophe begins by looking back to v. 5a where similar vocabulary occurs but also forges ahead with the explanation of the kind of fasting God demands for those who are his people. The internal structure of v. 6 shows a patterned construction. In 58:6ba,6bb,6ca an infinitive initiates the cola emphasizing the actions which constitute true fasting; the consistent use and placement of the infinitives unite the cola. The break in the pattern at 58:6cb draws attention to itself with the repetition of mwṭh but this time with wkl, and the verb at the end of the colon. A culmination takes place at v. 6cb when read in relation to the preceding cola: in vv. 6b,6ca the infinitives describe the loosening, unfastening, and freeing while v. 6ca, with the second per. masc. sing. verb, orders the shattering of every yoke.[50] The recurrence of mwṭh bespeaks a motif of "bondage" which is countered by a motif of "liberation" in the infinitives.[51] The recollection of bondage is at the very heart of the exodus experience of Israel; in this literary context the call to liberate others is to keep

---

49. Cf. MUILENBURG, "The Book of Isaiah," 681.

50. The sense of culmination in v. 6cb is well expressed in the TOB with the translation, "bref, que vous mettiez en pièces tous les jougs!".

51. Other uses of mwṭh attest to the motif of bondage that the word carries; cf. Jer 27:2; 28:10,12,13,13; Ezek 30:18; Nah 1:13.

alive the redeeming activity of God toward his people.[52] As the Lord had once released the Hebrews from slavery in Egypt and continued to deliver them, so now are his elect ones to carry on that work of redemption toward one another. The final word in the description of ways to liberate peaks in v. 6cb with the piᶜel verb stating, you are to shatter not only the thongs of the yoke but indeed every yoke (wkl-mwṭh). From the very outset the fasting God chooses is presented as a means of liberation according to the magnanimous way that the Lord saves Israel; from the very roots of Israel's identity in relation to Yahweh is there to be a movement which continues the process of liberation. As the Lord demonstrates to Israel how their liberation manifests salvation, so are they to carry on God's own redemptive action in their liberation of one another.

In 58:6b the repetition of ršᶜ calls for reflection upon its prior use in v. 4a. Among the reasons for God's unattentive reaction to the people's fasting is their striking another with a wicked fist (b'grp ršᶜ); following this information, v. 4b announces that such fasting does not cause one's voice to be heard on high. The instruction on fasting begins in v. 6b with a call to loosen the fetters of wickedness (ḫrṣbwt ršᶜ); the strophe then concludes in v. 9a with the promise that if one heeds the fasting according to God's design, then when the individual calls out the Lord will answer, his voice will be heard. The recurrence of ršᶜ links the two strophes and shows the movement in the passage from an old mode of behavior to a new one abolishing wickedness. The use of ršᶜ in 58:4,6 reinforces the pejorative connotations which it carries in bringing the literary unit 56:9--57:21 to a striking close (cf. 57:20-21). The motif carries through the

---

52. Cf. WESTERMANN, Isaiah 40-66, 337.

two literary units and looks forward to its abolition in the coming of God's redemption.

58:7 does not possess signs of a consistent internal structure which marks v. 6. However, the negative at the beginning of v. 7a and the close of v. 7b unites the bicola with a repetition at their extremes. The cola of v. 7a each conclude with a reference to what fasting calls them to share with others: their bread and their house.[53] Muilenburg demonstrates how the particle ky, in concert with ’z (v. 8a), accentuates ’z as the point toward which the passage is moving;[54] in v. 7b the particle pushes the text forward and signals a change that is about to take place.[55] In this literary context the particle ky draws attention to the final bicolon which concludes the conditions of authentic fasting and looks toward the promises which ensue. Similar to 58:6cb, v. 7bb slows down in rhythm with only two beats in the final colon of the verse. This accents the colon and brings the verse to a stronger sense of conclusion.

The particle ky at the beginning of the bicolon and the slowing down of the rhythm at the end distinctively mark the final colon of v. 7. Yet it seems anticlimactic to have a reference to caring for your own flesh or kinfolk after the preceding cola have stressed an all-encompassing concern for the hungry, the

---

53. The text of 58:7ab is emended to read bêteka instead of bayit based on the readings from the LXX, Syriac, Targum Jonathan, and Vulgate versions and also the parallelism with the pronominal suffix to the corresponding word of the bicolon (lḥmk). This emendation is observed by BJ, NEB, RSV; cf. also M. DAHOOD, "The Chiastic Breakup in Isaiah 58:7," Bib 57 (1976) 105.

54. Cf. MUILENBURG, "The Linguistic and Rhetorical Usages," 141.

55. Cf. Johannes PEDERSEN, Israel: Its Life and Culture, vol. 1-2 (Aslaug Møller, trans.; London: Oxford University Press, 1946-47) 118.

wandering, and the naked.[56] In the context of Isa 56-66 the root bśr appears six times (58:7; 65:4; 66:16,17,23,24); in 65:4 and 66:17, bśr refers to the flesh of swine while in 66:16,23,24 it is an expression for humanity. The expression in 66:16,23,24 is kl-bśr, referring to all humanity in the three stances of awaiting judgment, worshipping the Lord, and looking in abhorrence on those who have rebelled against God.[57] Though the expression kl-bśr is not used in 58:7, its literary context suggests an openness to provide bread, lodging, and clothing to anyone who needs it. The instruction in v. 7 expands beyond the realms of blood ties or legal bonds to establish a relationship which exists among human beings.[58] Thus the two bicola of 58:7 culminate with a message building on the need to provide food, shelter, and clothing for those in need, and conclude with a final demand of availability in not hiding from any person in want. One senses here a crescendo effect in the buildup of imagery describing the involvement with others in the fasting God prefers. In v. 7, a progression develops in what are known as the necessities of life: food, shelter, and clothing. Important as each of these things is, they are external manifestations. The climax of this short list comes in v. 7bb where, beyond these, the challenge calls for a personal self-involvement (tt^{c}lm, in hithpa^{c}el) in sharing of oneself. Thus this final colon gives direction to a kind of fasting which looks for an internal giving of self to accompany one's actions.

---

56. A translation similar to "kinfolk" is followed by BJ, NEB, and TOB. DAHOOD translates it "meat" to form a parallel with "bread" of v. 7aa; cf. "The Chiastic Breakup," 105.

57. In Isa 40-55 the expression kl-bśr also expresses the idea of "all humanity" in 40:5,6; 49:26.

58. Cf. WOLFF, Anthropology, 29.

The particle _'z_ introduces a movement in the strophe away from the rhetorical questions to the promises God offers to those who fast according to his decrees. The internal organization of 58:8 shows a repeated structure breaking from the patterns of the previous two verses.

v. 8a)	'z ybq^c	kšḥr	'wrk	/	w'rktk	mhrh	tṣmḥ
	(A)	(B)	(C)		(C')	(B')	(A')
v. 8b)	whlk	lpnyk	ṣdqk	/	kbwd	YHWH	y'spk
	(A)	(B)	(C)		(C')	(B')	(A')

In 58:8a the two verbs frame the bicolon and designate AA'. Moving toward the center of the bicolon the next element in each colon describes the action of the verbs in a comparative (v. 8aa) and adverbial (v. 8ab) manner joining BB'; the BB' elements intensify the verbs with imagery depicting the redemptive coming as rising light which breaks the darkness and ushers in recovery with accelerated urgency. The two remaining elements in the center of the bicolon are the subjects of the verbs, further connected by the second per. masc. sing. pronominal suffix and designated CC'.[59]

In 58:8b the verbs similarly frame the bicolon distinguishing AA' at the extremes. The BB' elements distinguish two images of the divinity where God's deliverance precedes in front of (_lpnyk_) the people in their trek (v. 8ba) and the divine name _YHWH_ stands in construct with _kbwd_ (v. 8bb). Then the middle elements _ṣdqk_ and _kbwd_ form CC' as the subjects of their respective verbs.[60] Thus the internal structure of vv. 8a,8b demonstrates a chiastic ordering.

---

59. These middle elements are further united by assonance with repeated _'_, _r_, and _k_ in a progressive order.

60. Cf. SCULLION, "_ṢEDEQ-ṢEDAQAH_," 343.

With chiastic structures as found in v. 8, the elements at the extremes and the middle distinguish the primary and secondary points of focus. In v. 8a the AA' elements portray the movement toward salvation as an upward one;[61] light breaks forth like the dawn where the sun ascends into the sky and healing rises up. The BB' elements (your light, your healing) bring together two ideas which may not at first seem connected while their parallel construction suggests their relationship. Though employing different vocabulary, the imagery of Mic 3:20 (MT) echoes a similar relationship.

> But for you who fear my name the sun of righteousness shall rise with healing in its rays. You shall go forth leaping like calves from the stall. (Mal 3:20, MT)

In Mic the rising of the sun brings forth healing rays; in Isa 58:8a the people's light breaks forth like the dawn and their healing rises up. Together the images suggest that from the rising light there comes a healing which ascends over the people; as they shatter every yoke that holds others oppressed (v. 6c) so does light break forth upon them and bring healing to their broken relationship with God (vv. 8a,9a).

In 58:8b the verbs (AA') recall the trek through the desert to the land of promise (cf. Exod 14:19; Isa 52:12). Here the notion of salvation depicts a pilgrimage led and protected by God; the redemption promised is not a transport to a totally new world of blessing, but rather a journey guided by God into the salvific gift of deliverance and healing.[62] To the extent that authentic fasting

---

61. LACK comments that bq^{c} in v. 8a portrays the breaking forth of light like the dawn as a salvific image. Cf. La symbolique, 135.

62. Cf. WESTERMANN, Isaiah 40-66, 338-39.

liberates others (58:6) does it become the means of entry into a new freedom for the one who practices it (58:8) for there the Lord provides for his people. This is especially evident in the BB' elements of v. 8b; the parallel character of ṣdqk and kbwd shows the sense of ṣdqk to be salvific instead of moral as seen in 58:2. As 56:1 plays between the moral and salvific character of ṣdqh in its repetition, in 58:2,8 a similar relationship occurs. When the people practice a fast that is founded in God's own righteousness (ṣdqh; see also vv. 6-7) then the Lord's deliverance (ṣdqh, v. 8b) becomes their portion by his saving presence among them (kbwd YHWH, v. 8b).[63]

In v. 9a the particle ʾz appears again and the internal chiastic order of the previous two bicola alters. As the strophe comes to a close the change in the internal structure accents v. 9a. Each of its cola has a similar twofold movement from the people's calling out to God to the Lord's response. The literary context of the strophe shows that God's answer to the people's plea is redemptive; in v. 3a the people questioned why God had withdrawn from them, unaware of their fasting and acts of humiliation. When God departs, the people are found to be in judgment; in v. 4b they are told that their manner of fasting will not bring them a hearing from God. But in v. 9a the promise extends to those who heed God's instruction for authentic fasting, for when they cry out the Lord will be present, he will say "here I am." The continuing dialogue between the community and God is contingent upon the way it relates to others; the salvific character of God's answer to prayer is the assurance of the divinity's presence and guidance in the pilgrimage of life.

---

63. Cf. SCULLION, "ṢEDEQ-ṢEDAQAH," 343.

The verbal root *^{c}nh* appears five times in Isa 58, four times meaning "to humble" (vv. 3,5,7,10) and once meaning "to answer" (v. 9). Hebrew poetry and prose are full of examples in which the same verbal root repeats while having different meanings in the same literary context; these recurrences of the same verbal root can provide a way of cleverly linking different motifs or ideas together.[64] This kind of wordplay is a form of paronomasia, already discussed on pp. 162-63 of the previous Chapter. The question in 58:3, why do we humble ourselves (*^{c}nynw*) and God does not know it, is answered in 58:5 with the hint that fasting is not only concerned with humbling (*^{c}nwt*) one's self; in contrast to this, 58:7a points out that in opening one's house to humbled wanderers (*w^{c}nyym mrwdym*) is the way that one's prayer is answered by the Lord (*wYHWH y^{c}nh*, v. 9a). The initial question of a person's humbling of self and not being acknowledged turns upside down to showing that to be answered by God one should care for the individual who is already in a humbled state. Thus the network in which *^{c}nh* recurs moves from question to answer, from dilemma to resolution.

In v.9a *y^{c}nh* is connected to v. 4b in an example of distant parallelism with *lhšmy^{c}*. Even in the context of the division Isa 56-66 the roots *^{c}nh/šm^{c}* are found in a consistent parallel pattern.

When I called you did not answer *(wl' ^{c}nytm)*,
when I spoke you did not listen *(wl' šm^{c}tm)*.
(65:12b)

Before they call I will answer *(w'ny '^{c}nh)*,
while they are yet speaking I will hear *(w'ny 'šm^{c})*.
(65:24)

---

64. Cf. J.M. SASSON, "Wordplay," 969-70.

Because when I called no one answered (w'yn ᶜwnh),
when I spoke they did not listen (wl' šmᶜw).

(66:4b)

The distant parallelism strengthens the bonds between the ends of two strophes where one ends with the reasons for not being heard on high (v. 4b) and the other which concludes with an answer from YHWH (v. 9a) showing the way to be heard (vv. 6-7).

A final observation considers the vocabulary initiating the description of salvation in 58:8. The word 'wrk recurs thrice in 60:1, initiating the section which announces the marvelous acts of redeeming love toward Israel; again in 60:19 'wr appears thrice as the image of God's saving action toward his people (cf. also 60:20). Parallel to 'wrk in 60:1 is wkbwd YHWH, also found in 58:8. Muilenburg calls kbwd the central word of Isa 60, expressing the fullness of the divine presence and its manifestation in redemptive deeds.[65] The placement of these words in tandem at the announcement of salvation in 58:8 presents a glimpse of the key imagery opening the eschatological poems of 60:1--63:6; these repetitions support a sense of congruity among the various images of salvation appearing in 56-59 and 60:1--63:6. The accumulation of similar images and recurring vocabulary in these two sections strengthens the ties between them showing how they relate to one another and demonstrate the unity within 56-66.

The imagery of light in 58:8 seems to depict God himself. The context of vv. 1-5 portrays a situation where God has departed from the presence of the people. They acknowledge the Lord's absence by their questions

65. Cf. MUILENBURG, "The Book of Isaiah," 697-98.

asking why the divinity does not see or acknowledge their fasts and humiliations (v. 3). And in reply the answer comes that fasting tinged with wickedness does not enable one to be heard on high (v. 4b). But then in v. 8, in response to those activities displaying the fast God chooses, the people's light breaks forth like the dawn; as they share in breaking the bonds which hold others captive, so then light breaks forth for them accompanied by healing and deliverance (v. 8). To a people participating in God's action of loosing yokes, light comes and shatters the darkness. In the same strophe announcing the breaking forth of light, God becomes present in responding to those who cry out (v. 9a). The divine presence restores itself and actively engages in dialogue with those who follow the new instructions. The expression "your light" (ʼwrk) carries a tone of relationship, designating the light as their own, namely their God who breaks forth like the dawn. As noted in the preceding paragraph, the kbwd YHWH also distinguishes the fulness of divine presence, which in 58:8b protects them from behind in their pilgrimage. Though somewhat elusive, the image of light in v. 8a can serve to depict the coming of the Lord among his people, a presence renewed when his word is acted upon.

After the initial question of v. 6a, this strophe moves from the answer to that inquiry (vv. 6b-7), to the redemptive effects of such actions (vv. 8-9a). The call to liberate (v. 6) and to serve one's neighbour (v. 7) both end in a climactic manner broadening the scope of the kind of fasting the Lord prefers. The chiastic ordering of the bicola in v. 8 emphasizes the process toward salvation under God's care and protection resulting from fidelity to God's word. The literary devices of paronomasia and distant parallelism in v. 9a bring the strophe to a note of resolution in relation to what has preceded (cf.

58:3b,4b,5a,7a). And finally the description of salvation employed in v. 8 glimpses the forthcoming eschatological poems beginning in Isa 60, employing similar imagery and vocabulary.

D. Isaiah 58:9b-12 -- The Way to Salvation

The overall literary character of this strophe is similar to the preceding one. As the negative questions of vv. 6-7 move to an explanation of their consequences in vv. 8-9a, so do the conditional statements of vv. 9b-10a progress toward the announcement of their results in vv. 10b-12. The analysis proceeds to consider the microstructures at work in the strophe.

The mood of 58:9b changes from what precedes it with the opening words ’m-tsyr; the text returns to further instructions about the manner of fasting God chooses. The bicolon structure presents two segments: a call to put away the yoke from their midst, and two examples of oppressive yokes. The opening verb governs the bicolon and the participial constructions distinguish the yokes that are to be abolished. The words mwṭh and šlḥ are also found in vv. 6b,6c respectively, and here at v. 9b they recall the motif of liberation from oppression. However, these repetitions in v. 9b remind the reader of the motif but then go on to specify in a concrete manner what v. 6 speaks of in a general fashion. In v. 9b the specification of the reproaching finger and the evil word present gestures of condemnation, malediction, and corrupt talk.[66] Both of

66. Cf. MUILENBURG, "The Book of Isaiah," 682; WESTERMANN, Isaiah 40-66, 339.

these ideas portray measures which show that a fasting which leads to redemption cannot be something negatively affecting another individual; the reproaching finger and the evil word only tighten yokes instead of shattering them. Thus v. 9b displays and specifies the yokes of v. 6 that must cease.

Though united to 58:9b by the w of wtpq, 58:10a exhibits a different pattern for this bicolon.

v. 10a)	wtpq	lr^{c}b	npšk	/	wnpš	n^{c}nh	tśby^c
	(A)	(B)	(C)		(C)	(B')	(A')

The AA' elements are the verbs framing the bicolon; their correspondence to one another shows two ways of service in giving of one's self and in satisfying the need of another. Two groups of those in want are expressed in the BB' elements; the hungry and the humbled person recur in v. 10a from an earlier occurrence in v. 7a. The CC elements, in using the same root word, refer to one's self and to another individual.[67] The chiastic pattern ABCCB'A' first stresses the outer elements of the bicolon and distinguishes verbs emphasizing service to others. The middle elements present the function of inversion which is typical of chiasm; the change from npšk to npš signals a movement in the text from giving of one's self to satisfying the needs of the other. Though several commentators suggest that npšk should follow the LXX and Syriac to read lḥmk (your bread), the parallelism of the middle elements would be diminished and would not expand

---

67. Though these two occurrences of npš refer to two distinct groups (the self and the other individual), the repetition of the same root designates the parallelism of CC, not CC'.

upon what is already stated in v. 7a;[68] the inverted parallelism expands and broadens the call to give bread to the hungry to now give more than bread--to give of yourself, which is both more demanding and yet more precious than bread. This call for greater self-involvement in giving continues from v. 7bb.

In 58:9b-10a the two motifs of liberation and service, initially found in vv. 6-7, repeat and develop in ways which are more specific: concrete examples of the kinds of yokes that are to be turned away and the gift of self which is to be given to others. Thus in the progression of the strophes, an intensification of the original demands emerges in 58:9b-10a.

The change from the conditions to the results of authentic fasting in 58:10b brings back the initial motif of light inaugurating the salvation imagery in v. 9a. A parallel movement appears in both cola progressing from darkness to light, from obscurity to high noon. In 58:8a the k acts as a comparative particle expressing the light breaking forth like the dawn (kšḥr); in parallel with 'wrk, the particle k returns in v. 10b to visualize obscurity rising like high noon (kṣhrym).[69] As in vv. 9b-10a, 58:10b shows an intensification of the earlier imagery; the breaking forth of the dawn gives way to the use of contrast with darkness and light, with obscurity and high noon. The image in v. 8a begins with

68. Those who encourage a reading of the LXX and Syriac include MUILENBURG, "The Book of Isaiah," 682-83; PAURITSCH, Die neue Gemeinde, 78; PENNA, Isaia, 570-71; WESTERMANN, Isaiah 40-66, 332; WHYBRAY, Isaiah 40-66, 217.

69. This reading of the bicolon takes the initial verb wzrḥ for both cola.

the first signs of light breaking forth and moves to its full display of brilliance at high noon. The representation of light breaking forth in v. 8 grows in poignancy as it reaches its peak display of radiance in v. 10b.

Third per. masc. sing. verbs and three recurring pronominal suffixes show 58:11a-11ba working together to describe the Lord's salvific action toward the people; he guides, satisfies, and makes strong. The change to a second per. masc. sing. verb in 58:11b and the <u>ka</u> comparative particle in vv. 11bb-11c tells of the blessings by means of different images of water; they are like a saturated garden and a spring whose sources do not fail. The six cola of 58:11 thus divide into two tricola (vv. 11a-11ba,11bb-11c). The break in the basic bicolon structure of the poem draws attention to these verses; they specify a new aspect of the salvific promise God offers. The further considerations of the vocabulary explain the significance of the imagery used in v. 11.

The words of 58:11ab repeat the verbal roots of vv. 10ab in an inverted pattern.

v. 10ab) wnpš [. . .] tśby^{c}

v. 11ab) whśby^{c} [. . .] npšk

The chiasm focuses attention on a relationship between "if" and "then" cola within the strophe; if a person satisfies the need of a humbled individual, then the Lord will satisfy the giver's needs. The use of a chiasm to underscore a "turn of events" which is taking place is typical of its literary function;[70] the repetition of the words in reversed order highlights the change that is taking

70. Cf. Chapter Three on 57:1-2, pp. 120-21.

place. This example in v. 10ab and v. 11ab shows concretely how the "if" and the "then" segments work together to build the strophe as a thought-unit which develops an idea both structurally and stylistically. Here the concept which is developed has a definite direction in calling the collective people Israel away from a concern about themselves toward a concern for others, which is later complemented by the promise that if they do this, then God will care for them.

The roots *śbᶜ* and *npš* in 58:10ab,11ab recall their earlier use in 56:11 telling of the irresponsible leaders in Israel. The shepherds of Israel are described as having an insatiable appetite (*ᶜzy-npš*) and yet not knowing satisfaction (*l' ydᶜw śbᶜh*, 56:11a); in 56:11c they are described further as each turning in his own way, each of them covetous for his own gain. In contrast to this, the chiastic structure of 58:10ab,11ab says that it is when an individual pours out one's self to satisfy his neighbor's need that the Lord satisfies him; thus 58:10a demonstrates the kind of activity which is charged with redemption and emphasizes how human individuals share in the salvific work of God by carrying out actions of liberation and service toward others.

In 57:18b, *w'nḥhw* is part of a series of verbs describing God's saving action toward Israel despite her undeserving response to God; although the people have walked turning in their own way, the Lord will guide them (*w'nḥhw*). Once again the motif of the Lord's guidance appears, now in 58:11a (*wnḥk YHWH tmyd*).[71] In both examples, 57:18b and 58:11a, the gift of God's guidance comes from literary contexts emphasizing the ways of God as opposed to any other way.

71. KSELMAN remarks on the tie between 57:18 and 58:11 in "A Note on *w'nḥhw*," 542 note 9.

The six occurrences of drk in 56:9--57:21 distinguish between the ways of humanity and the ways of God.[72] The "if-then" aspect of Isa 58:6-14 brings into focus an understanding of salvation which is intimately linked with following the ways of God, his teaching; if one is willing to turn away the yokes of wickedness, then he can expect the ever-present guidance of the Lord. The uses of nḥh in 57:18 and 58:11, similar in their contexts, represent a link between the literary units.

In 58:12b several expressions need further clarification. The expression wqr' lk shows a way of designating a new name for those who are addressed. But the particular manner in which the verb qr' is used with the inseparable preposition l is a way of expressing a blessing endowed by God to his people in the literary context of 56-66; the following examples witness to this.

> And they will call you (wqr'w lk) City of the Lord,
> Zion of the Holy One of Israel. (60:14b)
>
> That they may be called (wqr' lhm) oaks of righteousness,
> the planting of the Lord, that he may be glorified. (61:3c)
>
> And you will be called (wqr' lk) by a new name
> which the mouth of the Lord will give. (62:2b)
>
> But you shall be called (ky lk yqr') "my delight is in her,"
> and your land "married." (62:4b)
>
> And they shall be called (wqr'w lhm) the holy people,
> the redeemed of the Lord;
> And you shall be called (wlk yqr') "sought out,"
> a city not forsaken. (62:12)

These five examples demonstrate a pattern in which one aspect of God' salvation is manifested, in the giving of a new name symbolizing both a change in the

72. Cf. Chapter Three, pp. 97-98.

people and the entry into a new era of salvation.[73] Important to note here is the same manner of bestowing blessing by means of a new name in the context of 60:1--63:6 is also used in 58:12b. This example adds to the other expressions and images of salvation initiated in 58 which appear in the succeeding sections, linking them by similar literary expressions.

Several commentators suggest an emendation in 58:12bb from ntybwt (paths) to ntyṣwt (ruins), stating that it forms a natural parallelism with gdr prṣ.[74] However, another use of ntb in this literary section provides an alternate way of interpretation, keeping the text as it stands. In 59:8 the bicola build on the idea of drk as a modus operandi already seen in the previous and the present literary unit; parallel vocabulary for the two uses of drk include bm^{c}glwtm (courses) and ntybwtyhm (paths). These words of 59:8 express a way of life that has been chosen by the people who are addressed; there is no justice in their courses, their paths are crooked, and those who walk in them do not know peace (59:8). The expression ntybwt lšbt in 58:12bb is similar to another with the same root in Job 24:13b, yšbw bntybtyw; once again the noun is in parallel with drkyw and refers to a way of life opposed to God's ways.[75]

> They are among those who rebel against the light;
> they do not recognize his ways (drkyw)
> and do not remain in his paths (wl' yšbw bntybtyw). (Job 24:13)

---

73. Cf. BONNARD, Le Second Isaïe, 377-78, 427; MUILENBURG, "The Book of Isaiah," 718; WESTERMANN, Isaiah 40-66, 376, 379.

74. Cf. G.R. DRIVER, "Linguistic and Textual Problems, Isaiah XL-LXVI," JTS 36 (1935) 405; HANSON, The Dawn of Apocalyptic, 103 note (g); MUILENBURG, "The Book of Isaiah," 684; PENNA, Isaia, 570 note 12; WESTERMANN, Isaiah 40-66, 322; WHYBRAY, Isaiah 40-66, 217-18.

75. Cf. E. DHORME, A Commentary on the Book of Job (Harold Knight, trans.; London: Nelson, 1967) 365; Edward J. KISSANE, The Book of Job (Dublin: Browne and Nolan, 1939) 158.

Both from its other uses in 59:8 and the similar expression from Job 24:13b, ntybwt in 58:12b can be interpreted in a metaphorical manner referring to a way of life that is put into practice. Such an explanation for this final colon of the strophe brings the message about the kind of fasting that God chooses to a fitting conclusion; the one who has turned away the yoke and given of himself will be called the restorer of the paths in which to abide, that is, the restorer of God's ways which lead to life and salvation. This understanding of ntybwt lšbt relates back to the words of instruction about fasting, suggesting that these precepts are to become a way of life, the manner in which one abides with others. To be given the name "restorer of the paths in which to abide," designates a mission for the house of Jacob, a charge which rests in their name; they are to be the ones who show others the way to salvation by the manner of life they lead. Those who share in God's own action of liberation can expect to experience the Lord's guidance and protection, he will be the One who satisfies their needs and makes them strong (v. 11). Those who live according to God's word and put it into practice will be known as the restorers of his paths, his ways.

This strophe is characterized as being very similar to the previous one in the general movement from an instruction on fasting (vv. 9b-10a) to its salvific consequences (vv. 10b-12). However the strophe is further distinguished by its expansion on the earlier motifs; the examples of liberating and serving others are more concrete and specific. As the previous strophe has four bicola of instruction (vv. 6b-7) and three oriented toward salvation (vv. 8-9a), a stronger emphasis on salvation is found here with six bicola (vv. 10b-12) but only two of instruction (vv. 9b-10a); the pattern of emphasis on authentic fasting in the first strophe is reversed to an expanded account of God's redemptive action. The chiasm of 58:10ab,11ab demonstrates the relationship between the "if" and "then" segments of the strophe. The recurrence of the roots śbᶜ and nḥh recalls motifs from the previous literary unit and establishes links fostering the unity of the section. The expression wqr' lk of v. 12b is found in the eschatological poems of 60:1--63:6 and displays one of the blessings of salvation as the bestowal of a new name by God.

E. Isaiah 58:13-14 -- The Holy Day

The movement of this strophe, similar to the previous one, goes from protasis in v. 13 (initiated by 'm) to apodosis in v. 14 (initiated by 'z). Despite the commentators who cut these verses from the rest of the poem,[76] the elements of inclusion and recapitulation in vv. 1-2,13-14 argue for its integrity as an essential strophe which functions with the whole literary unit.[77]

One way that Hebrew poetry builds a motif or theme is the repetition of words in a step-wise pattern in successive cola or bicola.[78] The recurrence of the same roots slowly advances an idea and brings emphasis to certain words as they are repeated; the synonymous character in the series of reappearing words

---

76. See note 2 of this Chapter.

77. In addition to the elements of inclusion and recapitulation, the following words in vv. 13-14 appear elsewhere in 58: qr' (vv. 1,5,9,12,13); kbd (vv. 8,13,13,14); dbr (vv. 9,13,13,14); YHWH (vv. 5,8,9,11,13,14,14) 'z (vv. 8,9,14); mṣ' (vv. 3,13).

78. ALONSO SCHÖKEL speaks of this kind of parallelism as a "chain figure" possessing a flow of links by means of repetition; cf. Estudios de Poética Hebrea, 247-50.

echoes what has preceded but also moves the idea forward augmenting it with a new set of modifying and surrounding words. An example of this step-wise movement is found in 58:13.

58:13a)	(A)	mšbt	(B)	bywm qdšy		
58:13b)	(A)	lšbt	(B)	lqdwš	(C)	mkbd
58:13c)					(C)	wkbdtw

In 58:13a a sabbath motif is introduced into the literary unit; with a series of repetitions in each successive bicolon the motif is expanded and developed. The mention of the sabbath is developed further by the end of the bicolon in v. 13a in speaking of it as a holy day, a day set apart. The sabbath then is called a delight and is again called holy, a day set aside in honor. The honorable aspect of the day is recalled and leads into an explanation of how the day is to be observed; the verb wkbdtw (if you honor it) governs the movement of the whole bicolon. The repetitions bring into focus the significance of the sabbath as a day which is both holy and honorable, a day which is both set apart as being special to the Lord and given proper respect.

Participial forms of the verbal root ᶜśh are found in 58:13a,13c. In v. 13a, ᶜśwt ḥpṣyk recalls a motif initiating the literary unit and also serving as part of the recapitulation (vv. 2a,2c); the development of ḥpṣ in 58:2,3b shows that seeking one's pleasure is not a way to draw near to God. Here in v. 13a the same sense is preserved in explaining the proper conduct for the sabbath: one is to keep from carrying out his own pleasure on the Lord's holy day. In v. 13c mᶜśwt drkyk brings to mind the motif of the people delighting to know the ways of God (drky) from v. 2a, while in fact they do not understand his wishes;[79] rather what the people do is to follow their own ways. With regard to sabbath observance, a similar notion appears again in v. 13c warning against acting in one's own way. The recurrence of ḥpṣ and drk with the same root brings together these two motifs in v. 13 regarding the sabbath in the opening and closing bicola of the 'm segment of the strophe; what had been presented in an ironic manner in v. 2 is clarified and developed--you are not to seek your own pleasure, you are not to follow your own ways on the Lord's holy day.[80] The repetitions serve not only as part of the recapitulation but also as a means of contrast; the message that emerges once again is that an authentic religious observance depends upon following the ways of God not one's own pleasure.

The repetition of the verbal root ᶜśh in vv. 13a,13c, the three occurrences of mn in vv. 13a,13c, and the pronominal suffix -ka in each colon of vv. 13a,13c function to frame the protasis of the strophe. In these two bicola the concern is to describe what should not be done: not to trespass,[81] not to carry out your pleasure, not to follow your own way, not to find your own pleasure or speak continually. In contrast to this, v. 13b presents a positive approach to sabbath observance: to call it both a delight and the Lord's holy day

79. Here mn shows a movement away from a way of acting; its use is similar with mšbt in v. 13a and mmṣw' in v. 13c. Cf. GKC, 382 §119v,w.

80. The emphasis on not practicing your pleasures and your ways is further brought out by the pronominal suffix -kā on both of the words related to the participle. The pronominal suffix also appears with rglk (v.13a) and ḥpṣk (v. 13c).

81. The expression tšyb mšbt rglk in 58:13a is explained as an action of trespassing; cf. WHYBRAY, Isaiah 40-66, 218.

in a spirit of honor.[82] The basic movement of the protasis is ABA, beginning with negative instructions (A) in v. 13a, centering the positive admonitions (B) in v. 13b, and finishing with negative instructions (A) in v. 13c.

In 58:10a,11a the repetition of the roots npš and śb^{c} in a chiastic ordering establishes a relationship between cola of the protasis and apodosis in the strophe. Though not as intricate, the repetition of ^{c}ng in vv. 13b,14a similarly shows a connection between the protasis and apodosis segments: one calls the sabbath a delight, then he shall take unspeakable delight in the Lord. But even beyond this means of concretely linking protasis and apodosis, another pattern is at work in the strophe involving ^{c}ng with ḥpṣ. Though these words do not appear as parallels in the Bible, they are part of a vocabulary depicting joy. Their placement in the context of vv. 13a-14a follows a regular pattern of alternating words in the successive bicola.

v. 13a)	(A)	-	ḥpṣyk
v. 13b)	(B)	-	^{c}ng
v. 13c)	(A)	-	ḥpṣk
v. 14a)	(B)	-	tt^{c}ng

The two occurrences of ḥpṣ warn against following one's own pleasures on the sabbath; the two occurrences of ^{c}ng distinguish what is to be called one's delight and how that leads to taking delight in the Lord. The function of the ABAB pattern and the significance of the words can be viewed from two perspectives. 1) The two words differentiate between inappropriate (ḥpṣ) and appropriate (^{c}ng)

---

82. The use of mn with wkbdtw does not carry the negative sense of separating one's self from certain activities; DAHOOD points out that its use in v. 13b carries the sense of separation better expressed with the preposition "in" denoting the special manner of referring to the Lord's holy day, in honor.

joys which either lead away from or toward God's redemptive blessings. The Lord's holy day is not a time to seek one's own pleasures (vv. 13a,13c). And even in the larger context of the literary unit taking pleasure in a knowledge of God's ways (v. 2a) and drawing near to him (v. 2c) are inappropriate joys when they lead to oppression (v. 3b) and contention with others (v. 4a).[83] To call the sabbath a delight (ᶜng), a holy day of the Lord, leads to taking unspeakable delight in the Lord himself; in this literary context an appropriate joy leads to blessing.[84] 2) From a literary point of view the alternation between ḥpṣ and ᶜng serves as a way to heighten the movement of the strophe back and forth between the inappropriate observance of the sabbath and the way that leads to blessing. In viewing the extremes of the pattern it moves from a warning against seeking one's own pleasure to taking delight in the Lord; the movement is away from self and toward YHWH. Similarly as the previous strophe stresses a direction away from self and toward one's neighbor, this final strophe continues the orientation away from self, but now culminating in the Lord.

---

83. These examples of ḥpṣ are similar to the other five occurrences of this root in 56-66. In 56:4, the Lord's blessings come to those who do things that are pleasing to him (ḥpṣty); the emphasis is on God's pleasure not on those of the people. In 62:4b,4c again the accent is on God's pleasure both in the name that is given and in his delight in the people. In 66:3,4 condemnation and judgment are pronounced because the people take pleasure in abominations and choose things in which God does not delight. The examples distinguish between the things which please God and inappropriate pleasures which do not promise salvation.

84. The root ᶜng is not an often-used root, appearing only twenty times in the OT, four times in Isa 56-66. In 66:11, ᶜng describes the blessing of drinking deeply with delight from Jerusalem's abundance. In 57:4 the root is in the hithpaᶜel and has a pejorative sense of mocking or making sport of someone. Thus the use of ᶜng is not totally consistent in 56-66, but does express a delight in the things of God in 58:13b,14a; 66:11.

The announcement of blessing begins in 58:14a introduced by the particle 'z as also found in vv. 8a,9a. Following the hithpa^cel second per. masc. sing. verb in the opening colon, the successive two cola change to hiph^cîl first per. sing. verbs. The character of the hiph^cîl verb is causative with a declarative and intensive sense.[85] The movement from second to first per. throws attention on the speaker God and, coupled with the use of the hiph^cîl, accentuates what redemptive act he is going to accomplish in leading the people to authentic delight. Further, the Lord will bring them to the heights of the land ('rṣ) and to nourish them with the inheritance (nḥlt) of Jacob; this promise recalls a similar motif at 57:13c. The expression ynḥl-'rṣ in 57:13c accrues as a blessing to those who take refuge in God (whḥwsh by); in both 57:13c and 58:14 the emphasis on the land touches upon a key motif which runs through the whole of the Bible, for the land is one of God's most precious gifts to the people. In Deut 32 similar language is used to express the careful guidance of the Lord in the desert experience of the exodus.

> The Lord made him ride on the high places of the earth,
> and he ate the produce of the field;
> And he made him suck honey out of the rock,
> and oil out of the flinty rock. (Deut 32:13)

This reference in Deut describes the trek through the lands before entry to Canaan, while 58:14 distinguishes the land of promise in the mention of the inheritance of Jacob their father. Thus the delight in the Lord, which is announced, is intimately tied to the long-lasting promise to the ancestors of Israel's faith, a promise and blessing which still perdures. This pledge is climaxed with the divine self-affirmation ky py YHWH dbr concluding the

---

85. Cf. GKC 144 §53b-g.

literary unit in a solemn manner and a positive expression of hope that the word will come to pass.[86]

A final comment shows a relationship between these verses and 56:1-8. The basic movement of the three strophes at vv. 6-9a,9b-12, and 13-14 demonstrates that the actualization of God's promises functions in relation to his decrees; in following the instructions on the fasting God chooses does one come to share in the blessings promised. Similarly one finds the "if-then" motif in relation to the eunuchs and foreigners invited to become part of Israel; by holding fast to the given covenant precepts does one gain entry into the people of God. Within the framework of 56-59 the demand for fidelity to God's instruction walks hand-in-hand with the reception of blessings; but lest one become lost in rituals and laws, the decrees call for a love of God, his name, and his day (56:4,6;58:13) while also a liberation of one's neighbor (58:6-7,9b-10). Nonetheless, the conditions of God's word distinguish the ways of partaking in the gifts of salvation.

Following the protasis-apodosis schema of the previous strophe, several literary devices distinguish its microstructures. 58:13 has both a chain-figure and an ABA pattern which respectively develop the motif of sabbath and how it is to be observed. The ABAB pattern with ḥpṣ and ᶜng shows a clear relationship between the protasis and apodosis by means of repetition and also distinguishes between appropriate and inappropriate expressions of delight. Finally, the blessings of v. 14 recall the motifs of the land and serve as another link between the two literary units.

---

86. Cf. MUILENBURG, "The Linguistic and Rhetorical Usages," 147.

III. APPLICATION OF A LITERARY DEVICE TO ISAIAH 58:1-14

The analysis of both the macrostructures and the microstructures of Isa 58 shows the numerous repetitions of words in the literary unit supporting its integrity and continuity. It is in the literary contexts where these repetitions occur that one finds their interworkings in synonymous, antithetical, and synthetic ways. Not only does repetition focus the themes and motifs of the poem, but it also builds and expands them to provide a fuller appreciation of what the world of the text has to say; the recurrence of a word gathers a thought or idea which was previously expressed and brings it into dialogue with new aspects of corresponding thought.[87] Seemingly different and unrelated segments of a poem are linked together by means of a common word which carries a special nuance in its literary setting. The commingling of related ideas can be harmonious or discordant, but in their relationship to one another new ideas develop and display themselves in a literary context. For example, the five uses of npš not only show the interplay between one's self and another (v. 10a) but also the effect of that action on another human being (v. 11a); when read in a theological context, the fuller message with its components presents both a challenge and a promise.

The search for a literary device attempts to identify a plan by which a literary unit can be read and interpreted. Often more than one structure is at work in a poem; the clarification of different patterns can distinguish certain points of emphasis individually and sometimes the overlapping of structure can

---

87. Cf. MUILENBURG, "A Study in Hebrew Rhetoric," 99.

highlight together certain ideas. The numerous repetitions in 58 suggest the pattern found below.

(A) Declare to the house of Jacob their transgressions (58:1b)

(B) Yet me day after day they seek, a knowledge of my ways they take pleasure in, like a nation which has acted in righteousness [. . .] (58:2)

(C) Why [. . .] do we humble ourselves and you do not know it (58:3a)

(D) Behold, you fast [. . .] to strike with a wicked fist (58:4a)

(E) Is this the fast I choose [. . .] (58:5a)

(F) Will you call this a fast, a day acceptable to the Lord (58:5c)

(E) Is not this the fast I choose? (58:6a)

(D) To loose the bonds of wickedness (58:6b)

(C) And the self of the humbled one you satisfy (58:10a)

(B) If you turn back your foot from the sabbath, from doing your own pleasures on my holy day [. . .] If you honor it by not acting in your own ways [. . .] (58:13)

(A) And I shall nourish you with the inheritance of Jacob your father (58:14b).

This structure is called a concentric pattern. It follows the basic chiastic structure but is different in having a center point which is not part of either side of the chiasm.[88] This form of chiasm is sometimes called an "odd chiasm" because of the uneven number of its elements;[89] it is the middle odd element which is the focal point. The isolated point is taken as the dominant idea and the key thought to the development of the poem. Parunak describes the middle figure:

---

88. Cf. PARUNAK, "Oral Typesetting," 165.

89. Cf. PARUNAK, "Oral Typesetting," 165 note 24.

> The uniqueness of this location makes it suitable for emphasizing whatever is placed there. This method of emphasis uses the intrinsic shape of the structure to focus the reader's (or hearer's) attention on the item of interest [. . .] a deviation from a regular structural pattern (whether alternating or chiastic) can give emphasis. In this case, the emphasized item is highlighted precisely because it does not fit into the expected symmetrical scheme.[90]

Based on the analysis of macro- and microstructures presented thus far, a consideration of the concentric pattern begins with the alternating elements and concludes with the center or middle figure.

The AA elements focus on y^{c}qb from two standpoints: the house of Jacob and the inheritance of Jacob. In Hebrew poetry a name connected with the deep roots of the biblical tradition often serves to focus a point of relationship between God and the people.[91] In 58:1 the people are called the house of Jacob; the command is to announce to them their sins and transgressions. To a people loved and guided by the Lord, a harsh word of judgment initiates the literary unit. The converse comes into view at 58:14 where the inheritance of their father Jacob is promised. A pledge of the land with its produce for eating is reminiscent of Gen 28:13-15 where a similar promise is made to Abraham and to Jacob and his descendants.[92] As in Genesis, Isa 58:14 focuses on the magnitude of God's word of promise to their ancestors in faith; the promise remains firm through the ages, now to the house of Jacob. The beginning and end of the literary unit bring together through the name of the patriarch a movement from a commission to announce to the people their

---

90. Cf. PARUNAK, "Oral Typesetting," 165.

91. Cf. MUILENBURG, "A Study in Hebrew Rhetoric," 106.

92. Cf. MUILENBURG, "The Book of Isaiah," 686.

censoring acts, to a solemn promise that the age-old blessings promised their ancestors will be theirs; the opening and closing verses demonstrate a word of judgment and a word of salvation. To go one step further one can see a relationship between the words of judgment and salvation for in announcing the people's sins to them it opens the way to redemption in a call to reform. The words of judgment do not stand as a final utterance but lead to instruction offering salvation. Though affronting and challenging, the heart behind the message of judgment is an invitation to conversion and to redemption.

The BB elements bring together the words ywm, drk, ḥpṣ, and ᶜśh each of which displays a relationship in its recurrence while also working together in concert. The double use of ywm in 58:2 describes the people's search for God as a daily endeavor; couched in the irony of this verse, this daily effort is of little avail because what they do as observance is neither what God chooses nor is it truly righteous. The day-to-day attempts to exercise justice and to practice a fast day give way to understanding in 58:13 of what is "the day" par excellence, the sabbath, the Lord's holy day.[93] A play on the notion of ywm develops in three stages in the literary unit. 1) The daily practices which distinguish the righteous are found to be inauthentic; the people are "like" a nation which does these things, but in reality are not. 2) The notion of a fast day gives way to the idea that true fasting cannot be assigned to a day or a time --it is a way of life (vv. 6-7, 9b-10a); the liberation of others and the service of one's neighbor are responses to situations in life at a moment's notice, not a seasonal

93. To further support the importance of ywm in 58:13, one recalls this is the seventh and last time the word appears in this literary unit, a literary device for expressing perfection; see pp. 177-78. Also bywm qdšy is parallel with mšbt, signalling their relationship in the opening bicolon of 58:13.

or periodic reply. The fasting God chooses transcends a day's observance. 3) But when it comes to the observance of a special day, the sabbath stands as that which is to be revered; it is the day set apart, holy to the Lord. Rituals related to righteous observances and fasting delegated to one day are not what enable one to draw near to God; rather putting aside one's own ways and delighting in the Lord's holy day bring blessing. Thus, the movement of ywm in the chiasm moves away from wrong daily practices to a call for distinguishing the sabbath day as important.

The recurrences of drk in B echo the motif of 56:9--57:21 where the opposition between the ways of God stand apart from those of humanity. In 58:2 the people are said to delight in knowing the ways of God while it is their own ways they follow. In 58:13 a corrective to this comes with relation to the sabbath observance, that a person is to honor it in not acting in his own way. Once again there is the movement away from pursuing one's ways when they stand in opposition to God's word.

Much has already been said about ḥpṣ in this literary context.[94] Suffice it here to note the pleasure the people take in their religious observances (v. 2), in opposition to the word of instruction warning against personal pleasure on a day of observance (v. 13). This same development takes place in relation to ʿśh. By reference to the activities of the just in v. 2, their unrighteousness is exposed; in v. 13 the protasis explains that the sabbath is honored by not acting (mʿśwt) according to one's own ways. A wrong mode of

94. See pp. 226-29.

activity in v. 2 is given direction in v. 13 with emphasis directed toward concern for the Lord instead of one's own pleasure.

In 58:2 the daily practices done in the name of seeking and drawing near to God are called into question. In contrast to such diurnal exercises, the sabbath is esteemed as the day set apart for concern of God and not of self-centered practices. The general movement of B shifts away from a preoccupation with one's personal pleasures, and toward a way leading to delight in the Lord.

The CC elements touch on the practice of fasting itself; the parallel structure of the cola in v. 3a situates the verbs for fasting and humbling together. The question proposed focuses on the individual and the act of humbling one's self, trying to understand why God does not acknowledge it. In the explanation of the practice God chooses the tables are turned and it is clearly stated that fasting is not an act of humbling one's self but rather one of satisfying the need of a person who is already humbled. Once again the focus is a shift away from the self, and now toward an individual in need of help. This idea resonates with elements in B, calling for a proper concern for what relates to God. The combination of BB and CC stresses an esteem for what pertains to the Lord, solicitude toward another in need, and selflessness toward one's own person. Thus here one finds the heart of the law calling for an authentic love of God and neighbor.

The DD elements discuss two aspects of wickedness.[95] In the explanation of why the people's fast is a cause for their prayers not being heard by God, it is said they strike with a wicked fist; instead of their observance leading them in the ways of righteousness (v. 2b) it brings forth acts of violence. But what brings an answer to their prayer (v.9a) is the loosening of the fetters of wickedness (v.6b), fostering deeds of liberation and freedom. Thus in relation to the practice of fasting, rš^{c} represents a manner of acting which keeps one from communion with God, while its abolition leads to the kind of fasting warranting a divine response.

The EE elements move from a question to a response regarding the kind of fast which God chooses. After confronting the abuses of the manner in which the day is observed, the question arises as to whether this is what God desires; it culminates the abuses with a striking question. A very similar repetition in v. 6a launches the enumeration of a series of practices which God desires and blesses. The EE elements in 58:5aa,6a function as a summarizing question and initiation of a new teaching. V. 5a questions the abuses rehearsed in the name of a righteous fast and v. 6a initiates the corrective explanation of the manner of fasting God chooses.

And finally the middle point of the concentric pattern in the F element brings together the three words recurring seven times each in the literary context: ṣwm, ywm, and YHWH. This is the only time they all appear in

---

95. This motif recalls the closing verses of 57:20-21 where the wicked ones are described as being unable to rest and a people without peace. Here the motif of "wickedness" repeats and develops in another manner.

a single bicolon together. With the uses of ṣwm and ywm six times at this point and only once more in v. 6a (ṣwm) and v. 13a (ywm), the F element in v. 5c represents the turning point in the literary unit; now the rest of the literary unit will be directed to explaining what is a true fast, the benefits its proper practice brings one, and likewise what the true day of observance entails and the blessings coming to those who keep it. Also the bicolon initiates the use of the divine name YHWH found in the succeeding verses in contexts relating to the Lord's redemptive leadership (v. 8b, 11a) and response in times of need (v. 9a). The F element in v. 5c stands on the brink of announcing the way of salvation and its effects for those who follow it; in the poem, it is a point of transition from an old way to a new way of life.

Also part of the F element is the expression "a day acceptable to the Lord". The articulation of this expression in 58:5cb poses a question to the reader as to "what is an acceptable day to the Lord." The answer to this inquiry comes in vv. 13-14 as it becomes clear that observing the sabbath makes it the acceptable day. Keeping the Lord's holy day will bring blessing. A concern for the keeping of the sabbath recalls a similar motif in 56:2,4,6. Akin to its employment in the opening unit, again in 58:13-14 the proper observance of the sabbath becomes an avenue to blessing. Listed among the practices identifying those holding fast to the covenant (56:4,6), fidelity to the sabbath promises blessing and fellowship with the community of Israel. So also in 58:13-14, honoring the holy day leads one toward finding one's true delight in the Lord and receiving the promised blessings of the land as an inheritance. Thus one discovers the day acceptable to the Lord in observing the sabbath and sharing in the redemptive promises these actions bring.

A concentric pattern displays the symmetrical design of a poem and highlights key words. The pattern moves in a step-wise fashion and reaching its focal point progresses toward its end in reversing the order of key words. The inversion of words in the structure signals an inversion of ideas, as is apparent in Isa 58. Furthermore, a concentric pattern offers a way of seeing a literary unit as a whole in concert with its various parts. The F element at 58:5c is the pivot point dividing the unit into two basic segments, a judgment message (vv. 1-5b) and an instruction leading to salvation (vv. 6-14). What remains consistent in the reading of the concentric pattern is a sense of transformation between each of the recurring words in the figures. The harsh word of judgment toward Jacob which begins the unit becomes a promise of blessing with the heritage of Jacob in AA. The day after day pursuit of ways leading to unrighteousness changes to an observance of the Lord's holy day according to the ways of God in BB. The concern for self alters to call for actions of service toward one's neighbour in CC. The outward manifestation of wickedness gives way to a deed of liberation in DD. The account of a fast which God does not choose opens up to a new way of fasting in EE, one that is according to God's design. The concentric pattern unifies the poem by bringing into dialogue vocabulary from judgment and salvation contexts; the reversed pattern of key words guides the reader through a modification of a "former" to a "renewed" manner of fasting, from a word of judgment to an instruction for sharing in salvation. Thus the basic movement in the literary unit builds around the transformation of a people (the house of Jacob), a spiritual practice (fasting), and a religious institution (the sabbath); its emphasis is a movement away from self concern to a proper regard for God and neighbor.

IV. SUMMARY

Isaiah 58 is replete with rhetorical devices opening up an appreciation for its construction and interpretation. The seven occurrences of ṣwm, ywm, and YHWH both demonstrate the key motifs and offer a means of understanding the structure of the literary unit. The interworking of the motifs of fasting and sabbath also point to the themes of judgment and salvation in showing how the abuse of these practices turns away God's presence (vv. 3a,4b) while their observance brings the dawning of the Lord's guidance (vv. 8,11) and care (vv. 9a,12). The divine name YHWH further associates God's protection with his redemptive presence in vv. 6-14. The repetition of ywm serves to show the importance of vv. 13-14 as an integral part of the poem, dismissed by several commentators as being incongruous with the basic development of the poem. Rather the interest and attention given the sabbath at the end also plays on the idea that fasting is not to be relegated to a single day, but that the one day to be set apart is the sabbath.

The device of repetition not only serves to establish the major themes and motifs of the literary unit, but also develops them in a way which enhances their contextual meaning. The recurrence of npš centers on the "self" and then in v. 10a plays this idea against being concerned for another person in need. As a structuring device and a recurring motif, qr' weaves its way through the poem centering on the different aspects of acknowledging. The elements of inclusion and recapitulation in vv. 1-2,13-14 demonstrate the contrast in motifs with which the poem begins and concludes.

On the level of the microstructures there are numerous examples which show the careful construction of the poem and how it progresses with points of climax, with the rise and fall of ideas. The inclusion in the first strophe (vv.1a,4b) begins the unit with the command to lift up one's voice to proclaim to the people their sins, and concludes the strophe telling these same people their voice is not being heard on high. The examples of the fasting God chooses are enumerated in vv. 6,7 and build to a striking point in the last colon while a slight break in the rhythm signals a slowing down and completion of an idea. Also the general movement from protasis to apodosis in vv. 6-14 signals the conditions which lead to the blessings of salvation, and shows the basic rhythm of the second part of 58 which moves from "conditions" to "results" in each of the three strophes.

The overall thrust of the renewed sense of the fasting practices and the sabbath observance touches on a teaching of biblical faith: a mode of living which continually calls one to concern both for God and for neighbor, and less preoccupation with the self. In a concern and respect for such sacred institutions as the sabbath, one finds delight and blessing in the Lord. Also, the awareness of the needs and cares of others brings the promise that the Lord will care for them when they serve as the instruments of his liberating goodness and mercy.

CHAPTER FIVE

A RHETORICAL ANALYSIS OF ISAIAH 59:1-20

Translation Isaiah 59:1-20

1 BEHOLD the hand of the LORD is not too short to *SAVE*,
nor his ear too DULL to HEAR.
2 BUT RATHER your PERVERSITIES were causing a separation
between you and your GOD;
And your SINS have hidden the Face,
keeping him from HEARING you.
3 FOR your PALMS are defiled by BLOOD
and your fingers by PERVERSITY;
Your lips SPEAK DECEIT,
your tongue MURMURS dishonesty.

4 NO ONE pronounces suit RIGHTEOUSLY,
and NO ONE is JUDGED in honesty:
Confiding in emptiness and SPEAKING falsehood,
CONCEIVING distress and giving birth to WICKEDNESS.
5 They HATCH adders' EGGS
and they weave the spider's WEBS.
The one who feeds on their EGGS will DIE,
and if one is broken, it HATCHES a viper.
6 Their WEBS will not serve as a GARMENT,
one cannot cover oneself with their WORKS.
Their WORKS are WORKS of WICKEDNESS
and acts of violence are upon their PALMS.
7 Their feet rush to EVIL
and they hasten to shed innocent BLOOD.
Their THOUGHTS are THOUGHTS of WICKEDNESS,
devastation and misfortune are in their highways.
8 The WAY of PEACE they do not KNOW
and THERE IS NO JUSTICE in their courses
They have made crooked their own paths,
each one MAKING HIS WAY there does not KNOW PEACE.

9 Therefore, JUSTICE is FAR from us
and RIGHTEOUSNESS does not REACH us.
We LOOK for light, but BEHOLD darkness,
brightness, but walk in obscurity.
10 We GROPE like the blind for a wall,
like those WITHOUT EYES we GROPE.
We STUMBLE at high noon as if at twilight;
among the vigorous, we are like the DEAD.

11 We all growl like bears,
MURMUR and MURMUR like doves.
We CRY OUT for JUSTICE, but there is NONE,
SALVATION, but it is FAR from us.
12 FOR many are our TRANSGRESSIONS before you,
our SINS testify against us;
FOR our TRANSGRESSIONS are with us,
and we ACKNOWLEDGE them, our PERVERSITIES:
13 TRANSGRESSING against and denying the LORD,
TURNING AWAY from following our GOD.
SPEAKING oppression and revolt,
CONCEIVING and MURMURING DECEITFUL WORDS
from the heart.

14 Thus JUSTICE is TURNED AWAY
and RIGHTEOUSNESS stands AFAR.
FOR TRUTH STUMBLES in the public square
and uprightness is unable to COME.

15 Thus the TRUTH has been lacking
and the one veering away from EVIL makes himself prey.
The LORD SAW and it was EVIL in his EYES
that THERE WAS NO JUSTICE.
16 He SAW that THERE WAS NO man
and was appalled that THERE WAS NO ONE to intercede.
Then his own arm brought him SALVATION
and his DELIVERANCE sustained him.
17 And he PUT ON DELIVERANCE as armor
and SALVATION as a helmet upon his head.
He PUT ON GARMENTS of vengeance as covering
and wrapped himself in zeal as a mantle.
18 ACCORDING to their DEEDS, so ACCORDINGLY will he REPAY
them:
fury to his OPPRESSORS, RECOMPENSE to his enemies,
to the coastlands he will REPAY RECOMPENSE.
19 And thus they will fear the name of the LORD from the west
and his GLORY from the rising of the sun.
INDEED, he COMES as an OPPRESSED stream
which the breath of the LORD drives onward.
20 And he COMES to Zion, the *Redeemer*,
to those in Jacob who turn away TRANSGRESSION.
An oracle of the LORD.

I. OVERVIEW

A. Indications of Unity in Isaiah 59:1-20

Similar to the previous literary units, numerous examples of repetition link the strophes and recall motifs throughout 59:1-20. The key words studied below appear at least four times in this literary context: YHWH (the Lord), mšpṭ (justice), ṣdqh (righteousness), yšᶜ (to save), dbr (to speak), and hgh (to murmur).

The six uses of YHWH (vv. 1,13,15,19a,19b,20) occur, for the most part, in the second half of the poem. Typically, the divine name appears at the beginning and end of the literary unit;[1] it occurs three times in construct form and presents different images relating to the Lord (yd-YHWH v. 1; šm-YHWH v. 19a; rwḥ-YHWH v. 19b). The hand of the Lord is an image of redemptive strength (v. 1); the name of the Lord is the object of fear or reverence as God comes in glory (v. 19a); the breath of the Lord describes God's power as it impels a stream forward (v. 19b). The opening and conclusion paint a portrait of the Lord in might and awe; the final word of the literary unit closes with the attestation that this is an oracle of the Lord, n'm YHWH (v. 20), a common way

---

1. Cf. MUILENBURG, "A Study in Hebrew Rhetoric," 106.

of ending a literary unit. Following the long description of offences, v. 13 identifies the rebellion as a denial against YHWH;[2] in v. 13ab 'lhynw is parallel to YHWH, showing the personal nature of the revolt as being against our God. In v. 15b the divine name introduces the Lord as the One who sees that there is no one to intercede for the cause of justice; the Divine Warrior then dons the garments of salvation to bring deliverance with his own arm.[3] The divine name YHWH appears primarily in contexts relating the absence (v. 1) and the coming of God's saving power (vv. 15-20), but also showing the transgressions of the people as revolt against the Lord.

A key word which repeats six times throughout the literary unit is mšpṭ (vv. 4 [nšpṭ], 8,9,11,14,15). A distinguishing characteristic is the use of 'yn with mspṭ to function as a refrain-like expression, "there is no justice."

v. 4a	-	w'yn nšpṭ
v. 8ab	-	w'yn mšpṭ
v. 11ba	-	lmšpṭ w'yn
v. 15bb	-	ky-'yn mšpṭ

Two other examples of mšpṭ echo the same idea: justice is far from us (v. 9a); justice is turned away (v. 14a). Thus the recurring idea that "justice is absent" weaves its way through the poem.

---

2. Commentators note the appearance of the divine name in v. 13; the literary context highlights the notion that sin is a direct transgression against the Lord. Cf. BONNARD, Le Second Isaïe, 390; SCULLION, Isaiah 40-66, 167-68; WESTERMANN, Isaiah 40-66, 349.

3. A few commentators discuss the traditional imagery used to describe the Divine Warrior in vv. 15-20. Cf. BONNARD, Le Second Isaïe, 392-93; HANSON, The Dawn of Apocalyptic, 124-27; MUILENBURG, "The Book of Isaiah," 694-95.

Two kinds of literary context distinguish the five uses of ṣdqh (vv. 4 [bṣdq], 9,14,16,17). Similar to mšpṭ, ṣdqh laments the disappearance of righteousness in vv. 4,9,14. There is no one who enters into a lawsuit righteously (v. 4); so distant is righteousness (v. 14), that it is unable to reach those who search for it (v. 9). Different from these examples, ṣdqh is also a salvific image of deliverance.[4] In vv. 16b-17a the Divine Warrior is sustained by ṣdqtw and puts on ṣdqh as his armor for battle. This interplay between the two meanings of ṣdqh as a virtuous way of acting and also as an expression of deliverance is earlier noted in 56:1.[5]

> Thus says the Lord:
> Keep justice and practice ṣdqh,
> For soon is my salvation to come,
> wṣdqty to be revealed.

Similarly in Isa 58, ṣdqh refers both to the nation that acts in righteousness (v. 2), and to the deliverance that leads and protects those who fast properly (v. 8).[6] The two meanings of ṣdqh in 59 point both to an absence of righteousness and to the coming of God's righteous deliverance.

The theme of salvation frames the literary unit; the coming of the Redeemer in v. 20 remedies its absence in v. 1. The progression from a "lack" to "fulfillment" of salvation also characterizes the four occurrences of the root yšᶜ (vv. 1,11,16b,17a). The absence of the Lord's saving hand in v. 1 resonates with the description of salvation as being far away in v. 11. Contrasting the situation

---

4. Cf. SCULLION, "ṢEDEQ-ṢEDAQAH," 345.

5. Cf. SCULLION, "ṢEDEQ-ṢEDAQAH," 342; see also pp. 56-57 in Chapter Two.

6. Cf. SCULLION, "ṢEDEQ-ṢEDAQAH," 343; see also pp. 212-13 in Chapter Four.

of v. 1 with a similar image in v. 16, the Lord's own arm brings salvation in response to the disappearance of justice and no person to intervene. Among the garments of the Divine Warrior is yšwᶜh as the helmet upon his head.

The root dbr appears four times (vv. 3,4,13ba,13bb). Twice it occurs in concert with šqr to describe speech which is deceitful: your lips speak deceit (dbrw-šqr, v. 3b); conceiving and murmuring deceitful words from the heart (dbry-šqr, v. 13bb). As these two examples stand several verses apart, v. 13b echoes an early motif in the poem. In v. 3 the reason for God's unwillingness to hear is blamed on the people's deceitful and dishonest speech; the next appearance of the expression in v. 13 is in the context of a confession of transgressions. The recurrences of dbr with šqr progress from an accusation of deceitful speech to an acknowledgment of it by those reproved. The other two occurrences of dbr (vv. 4b,13ba,13bb) are in the same bicolon with hrh (to conceive).

v. 4b - Confiding in emptiness and speaking falsehood (wdbr-šw'),
conceiving (hrw) distress and giving birth to wickedness.

v. 13b - Speaking oppression (dbr-ᶜšq) and revolt,
conceiving (hrw) and murmuring deceitful words from the heart.

These examples of dbr and hrh are infinitive absolutes in both instances, suggesting the oft-continued performance of these actions.[7] The imagery of hrh with dbr presents the words of falsehood and oppression (vv. 4b,13b) as coming from the inner recesses of the accused: the birth of wickedness is first

7. Gesenius speaks of them as having a historical sense, describing actions that are still being performed; cf. GKC, 346 §113ff.

conceived in distress (v. 4b); the murmuring of deceitful words is initially conceived in the heart (v. 13b). Similar to the occurrences of dbr with šqr, the indictment of v. 4b culminates in the acknowledgment of transgression in v. 13b.

Complementary to the motif of deceitful speech are the four occurrences of hgh (vv. 3b,11a,11a,13b). In v. 3b, the "tongue that murmurs (thgh) dishonesty" is parallel to the "lips that speak (dbrw) deceit." Likewise in v. 13b, the "murmuring (whgw) of deceitful words" is parallel to the "speaking (dbr) oppression and revolt." The image of doves that murmur and murmur in v. 11 has as many interpretations as it has commentators, and remains a question for the Close Reading of the verse. It is sufficient for this Overview to note how dbr and hgh function together to distinguish the "speech" motif as a transgression against the Lord.

The parallel words mšpṭ//ṣdqh form a pattern which spans several verses in the poem.

v. 4a - No one pronounces suit righteously (bṣdq);
no one is judged (nšpṭ) in honesty.[8]

v. 9a - Therefore, justice (mšpṭ) is far from us,
and righteousness (ṣdqh) does not reach us.

v. 14a - Thus justice (mšpṭ) is turned away,
and righteousness (wṣdqh) stands afar.

---

8. In 59:4a bṣdq and nšpṭ are not, strictly speaking, in "parallel construction" as the term has been employed thus far. However, those specialists in biblical poetry who use the expression employ a certain latitude in discussing parallelism. In 59:4a the suggested parallels are repeated elsewhere in the literary unit and are part of a theme of justice in the poem; for these reasons, they are taken as parallels in this literary context.

The distances between vv. 4a,9a and vv. 9a,14a are nine bicola each, suggesting a careful placement of these parallels as a structuring device.[9] In reading through the literary unit, a refrain-like character comes to the reader as a reminder of the absence of justice and righteousness. The initial words which begin this division in 56:1 call the people to keep mšpṭ and to practice ṣdqh; but the Sitz im Text of 59 reports that righteousness and justice are not observed by anyone (v. 4) and have disappeared (vv. 9,14).

A literary device with the same words recurring three times in close proximity to one another (vv. 6,12-13a,17,18) appears four times in 59.[10] Amidst rather cryptic imagery in v. 6, ᶜśh is an aid to comparing the uselessness of webs as garments to the futility of the people's wicked actions.

Their webs will not serve as a garment,
a person cannot cover oneself with their works (bmᶜśyhm).
Their works (mᶜśyhm) are works of wickedness (mᶜśy-ʾwn). (Isa 59:6)

With the addition of pšᶜ, a new term expands the "sin" vocabulary of vv. 1-11 (ᶜwn, vv. 2,3; ḥṭʾ, v. 2; ʾwn, vv. 4,6,7).

For our transgressions (pšᶜynw) are many before you,
our sins testify against us;
For our transgressions (pšᶜynw) are with us
and we acknowledge them, our perversities:
Transgressing (pšᶜ) and denying the Lord,
turning away from following our God. (Isa 59:12-13a)

---

9. MUILENBURG cites several examples where the repetition of key words acts as a structuring device; cf. "A Study in Hebrew Rhetoric," 103-104, 107.

10. MUILENBURG notes several examples where patterns of triple repetition emphasize a motif; cf. "A Study in Hebrew Rhetoric," 108.

The donning of garments by the Divine Warrior draws attention to both a clothing of redemption and punishment.

> And he put on (*wylbš*) righteousness as armor,
> and salvation as a helmet upon his head;
> He put on (*wylbš*) garments of vengeance as a covering (*tlbšt*),
> and wrapped himself in zeal as a mantle. (Isa 59:17)

This final example draws a clear line between the notion of "one's deeds" and "one's recompense" according to their deeds by the interchanging use of *gml*.

> According to their deeds (*gmlwt*) will he repay them:
> fury to his oppressors, recompense (*gmwl*) to his enemies,
> to the coastlands he will repay recompense (*gmwl*). (Isa 59:18)

These examples of triple recurrence in close proximity focus attention on a particular point in the progression of a poem studded with other repetitions. Because of their nearness to one another in the rhythmic movement of the bicola and one tricola, they stand out as signposts of a motif to be given special attention. The employment of this device in both 56:1-8 and 59:1-20 demonstrates another aspect of style common to 56-59.

In concluding the remarks about the oft-repeated vocabulary, one notes the verbal similarity between 56:1 and 59:1-20. The emphasis given to *mšpṭ*, *ṣdqh*, and *yšᶜ* suggests a link between the initial words of the section and the final literary unit in that section. Further clarification of this vocabulary and of its function in 59 continues in the analysis.

B. Delimitation of the Strophes

A quick glance at the different strophic arrangements for 59 reveals the lack of consensus on this question. The BJ, NAB, NEB, and RSV are similar to Penna (vv. 1-8;9-15a;15b-20).[11] Fohrer and Whybray agree in their groupings (vv. 1-4; 5-8; 9-15a; 15b-20).[12] Variations on the plan of Fohrer and Whybray include that of Bonnard (vv. 1-3; 4-8; 9-15a; 15b-20),[13] JB (vv. 1-4; 5-8; 9-11; 12-14; 15-20), Muilenburg (vv. 1-4; 5-8; 9-11; 12-15a; 15b-17; 18-20),[14] and Westermann (vv. 1-3; 4-8; 9-11; 12-15a; 15b-20).[15] Most divergent in his reading of the poem as two large strophes is Hanson (vv. 1-8; 9-20).[16] As Ceresko suggests in his study of a strophic plan for Ps 105, the variety of arrangements may suggest that there are overlapping structures dependent upon the method of analysis one employs.[17]

Three elements of rhetorical style suggest the careful construction of vv. 1-3. First, an ABA'B' pattern of parallel images is found in vv. 1,3. The complaint about God's seeming absence is centered on two anthropomorphic features in v. 1: his hand which does not save and his ear which does not hear.

---

11. Cf. PENNA, Isaia, 572.

12. Cf. FOHRER, Das Buch Jesaja, 214; WHYBRAY, Isaiah 40-66, 220-25.

13. Cf. BONNARD, Le Second Isaïe, 381-83.

14. Cf. MUILENBURG, "The Book of Isaiah," 687-95.

15. Cf. WESTERMANN, Isaiah 40-66, 342-45.

16. Cf. HANSON, The Dawn of Apocalyptic, 113-17.

17. Cf. CERESKO, "A Poetic Analysis," 25.

In v. 3 a relationship is established with v. 1 by means of parallel images which explain the cause for the Lord's restrained redemption: their palms and fingers are given to perversity, and their lips and tongue speak deceit. The yd-YHWH (A) does not save those who use their palms and fingers (A') for wickedness, nor does ’znw (B) hear the lips and tongue (B') which issue dishonesty. Second, vv. 1,2,3 each begin with particles which highlight the opening of the poem in an emphatic manner; the initial hn and the repetitions of ky set the verses apart and indicate a dramatic beginning.[18] Third, after the opening bicolon, the interest shifts away from YHWH and focuses on those being addressed. This shift carries through vv. 2-3 with the pulsating sound of the pronominal suffix -km in each cola; the diagram displays the recurrences in each bicolon.

v. 2a	-	’m-ᶜwntykm	/	bynkm [. . .] ’lhykm
v. 2b	-	wḥṭ’wtykm	/	mkm
v. 3a	-	kpykm	/	w’ṣbᶜwtykm
v. 3b	-	śptwtykm	/	lšwnkm

The repeated -km demontrates, by means of the recurring "your," how the emphasis shifts from the Lord in v. 1 to the people being addressed in vv. 2-3.

An inclusion with ’yn špṭ balances the second strophe in vv. 4a,8a.

v. 4a - No one pronounces suit righteously,
w’yn nšpṭ in honesty.

v. 8a - The way of peace they do not know,
w’yn mšpṭ in their courses.

---

18. Cf. MUILENBURG, "The Linguistic and Rhetorical Usages," 149.

The opening line of the strophe laments that no one is judged in honesty, and then echoes similar sentiments toward the end with the acknowledgment that there is no justice in the paths they walk. A second point arguing for the beginning of a new strophe in v. 4a is the pair bṣdq//nšpṭ. As noted on pp. 249-50, the recurrence of the pairs in a consistent pattern suggests they may be a structuring device; here the parallels begin a strophe. And finally, the device of repeating a pronominal suffix as a structural element in the previous strophe continues here, now with the third per. pl. suffixes -hm/-m. Though not so evenly distributed as in vv. 2-3, eleven recurrences in the strophe distinguish its importance.

v. 5b	-	mbyṣyhm	/	
v. 6a	-	qwryhm	/	bm^{c}śyhm
v. 6b	-	m^{c}śyhm	/	bkpyhm
v. 7a	-	rglyhm	/	
v. 7b	-	mḥšbwtyhm	/	bmslwtm
v. 8a	-		/	bm^{c}glwtm
v. 8b	-	ntybwtyhm [. . .] lhm /		

After the initial announcement that there are no individuals who make righteous pronouncements and honest judgments, the poem proceeds to enumerate their deeds; the descriptive imagery keeps recalling for the reader that it is their eggs which bring death (v. 5), their webs which are useless as clothing (v. 6), their works and thoughts of wickedness (vv. 6,7), their feet that run to evil (v. 7), and their courses in which there is no justice. A description of the transgressors' ways pervades this strophe.

A shift in the speaker takes place in 59:9 and carries through to v. 13 with the first per. pl. pronominal suffix and verb forms suggesting the third strophe; following the descriptions of wickedness in vv. 4-8, a confession of sinfulness takes place in vv. 9-13.[19] The repeated sounds of the prefix n- and the suffix -nw carry through the strophe accentuating the acknowledgment of their actions and subsequent consequences.

v. 9a	-	mmnw	/	tśygnw
v. 9b	-	nqwh	/	nhlk
v. 10a	-	ngššh	/	ngššh
v. 10b	-	kšlnw	/	
v. 11a	-	nhmh [. . .] klnw	/	nhgh
v. 11b	-	nqwh	/	mmnw
v. 12a	-	pšᶜynw	/	wḥṭ'wtynw [. . .] bnw
v. 12b	-	pšᶜynw 'tnw	/	wᶜwntynw ydᶜnwm
v. 13a	-		/	'lhynw

The final pronominal suffix of v. 13a concludes this series of first per. pl. suffixes in a climactic manner with "our God," admitting their actions have been a denial of Yahweh and a turning away from 'lhynw. The parallel pair of mšpṭ//ṣdqh occurs in the first bicolon of the new strophe, repeating the pattern of the previous strophe in v. 4a.

19. Commentators generally acknowledge here an admission of guilt resembling the genre of a community lament; cf. BONNARD, Le Second Isaïe, 326, 388; HANSON, The Dawn of Apocalyptic, 119; FOHRER, Das Buch Jesaja, 219; MUILENBURG, "The Book of Isaiah," 690; PAURITSCH, Die neue Gemeinde, 102; WESTERMANN, Isaiah 40-66, 348; WHYBRAY, Isaiah 40-66, 223.

The commentators and the translations do not indicate a new strophe beginning at v. 14 (cf. p. 251); their divisions suggest v. 14 belongs to vv. 9-13 with a new strophe beginning at v. 15 or v. 15b. However, commentators do not account for the sudden shift from the first per. pl. to the third per. sing. verbs beginning in v. 14, nor the possibility of the mšpṭ//ṣdqh pair as a structuring device in Isa 59. Beginning in v. 14 the third per. sing. verbs appear through to v. 20, with the single exception of v. 19a, where it describes the fear of the people at the Lord's coming. Vv. 14-20 relate the situation which stirs the Divine Warrior to intervene (vv. 14-16a) and then portray the manner of his coming (vv. 16b-20). While one admits that vv. 14-16a are related to the confession of vv. 9-13, the general style of the poetry changes and suggests a subtle shift may be taking place and directing attention to something about to happen in the poem. For the purpose of this Overview it suffices to note that a new strophe could well begin in v. 14 by reason of the speaker change and the repetition of a pattern which similarly initiates strophes II and III.[20] The function of v. 14 is further discussed in the Close Reading of the text.

As in the delimitation of the strophes for the previous units, the task is not always easily and immediately perceived but rather demands further reflection in the Close Reading. Nevertheless, the suggested division into vv. 1-3, 4-8, 9-13, and 14-20 presents a distribution of bicola which are proportionately related with slight variation.

---

20. The shift in speaker plays an important role in the discernment of strophes; the study of 57:3-13 points this out on p. 104. SCULLION comments on the alternation of speakers in Isa 59; cf. Isaiah 40-66, 166.

vv. 1-3:	5 bicola
vv. 4-8:	10 bicola
vv. 9-13:	10 bicola
vv. 14-20:	11 bicola and 1 tricola

Even a slight variation on the above arrangement displays a balanced and well-proportioned literary unit. The careful shifts by means of pronominal suffixes and speakers, coupled with the recurrence of key words throughout argue for the careful construction and literary unity of Isa 59.

II. CLOSE READING

A. Isaiah 59:1-3 -- Salvation Delayed

In deciphering the first strophe's length, the three particles serve as a structuring device, initiating vv. 1,2a,3a. What now remains to be done is to discern their function in the literary context.

The hn of v. 1 is a demonstrative particle which begins the literary unit on a note of exclamation, giving emphasis to the opening bicolon.[21] The construction of v. 1 follows a parallel pattern, drawing ties between the two cola.

v. 1 -	hn l'-qṣrh	yd-YHWH	mhwšy^c	/	wl'-kbdh	'znw	mšmw^c
	(A)	(B)	(C)		(A')	(B')	(C')

21. Cf. GKC, 469-70 §147b-c.

After the demonstrative particle the verbs of each colon appear in a negative construction with l' (AA'), followed by corporal images related to God (BB'), and concluding with participial forms representing separation or remoteness (CC'). Beyond the parallel structure and placement at the end of each colon the repetition of the opening m, š, ō, and aᶜ in mhwšyᶜ and mšmwᶜ draws these words together in linking sound patterns. V. 1 brings into play a relationship between the absence of salvation and the withdrawal of attentiveness on the part of God.[22]

The ky of v. 2 introduces an adversive clause which functions in a deictic fashion to move the text forward and to comment on what precedes.[23] The ABCA'B'C' pattern of v. 1 continues here, but in an extended way between v. 2a and v. 2b.

v. 2a	-	ky 'm-ᶜwntykm (A)	hyw mbdlym (B)	/	bynkm (C)	lbyn 'lhykm; (D)
v. 2b	-	wḥṭ'wtykm (A')	hstyrw pnym (B')	/	mkm (C')	mšmwᶜ (D')

---

22. The motifs of "being heard" and "being saved" are found together in the psalms.

The poor man called and the Lord heard (šmᶜ),
and saved him (hwšyᶜw) out of all his troubles. (Ps 34:7)
The Lord fulfills the desire of all who fear him,
he hears (yšmᶜ) their cry and saves them (wywšyᶜm).
(Ps 145:19)

Both of these examples show that it is in having one's voice heard by the Lord that his saving action comes to the individual or community. 59:1 resonates with this idea, but in a negative sense: the Lord's hand is not saving nor is his ear hearing, thus God's deliverance has been withdrawn.

23. Following upon a negative (as v. 1) the ky can signal a manner of contrast which explains the preceding negatives; here the particle also serves as a connective ("but rather" in translation) between the verses. Cf. GKC, 500 §163a-b; MUILENBURG, "The Linguistic and Rhetorical Usages," 140.

Beginning each of the bicola, the elements AA' emphasize first that sinfulness has brought about the situation of v. 1 (note the repetition of mšmw^{c} in vv. 1,2b); the repeated pronominal suffix -km gives force to these opening words by placing blame on those addressed. The placement of two different words for "sin" as the first elements of the bicola emphasizes the impact of wrong-doing in bringing about a separation from God. The BB' expressions mutually use a vocabulary of segregation, explaining that their sins have brought about a separation from God and have hidden the Face. The CC' and DD' elements categorize the disunity existing between the addressed (CC') and the God whose hearing is sought (DD'). Thus v. 2 highlights a movement away from centering on the apparent lack of God's saving response to an explanation for the withdrawal of the Lord's hand and attentive ear: their sins and perversities are the cause.

The ky of v. 3 repeats the deictic function of the particle in v. 2 to move the text forward and specifies the causes for the withdrawal of God's saving presence. The bicola resemble a parallel ordering, but with variations.

v. 3a	-	ky kpykm (A)	ng'lw (B)	bdm (C)	/	w'ṣb^{c}wtykm (A')	b^{c}wn (C')		
v. 3b	-	śptwtykm (A)	dbrw- (B)	šqr (C)	/	lšwnkm (A')	^{c}wlh (C')	thgh (B')	

In v. 3a AA' are both parts of a hand; the repeated pronominal suffix -km also unites the words as the people's instruments of evil. The B element serves as the verb for both cola. The CC' elements describe the palms and fingers (AA') in a pejorative sense; these elements are united by the b performative on bdm and b^{c}wn. In v. 3b AA' are both organs of speech; the repeated pronominal suffix

-km functions similarly to v. 3a. In the final colon the B' and C' elements are reversed while still maintaining the parallel relationships between the vocabulary.[24] The BB' elements are verbs describing an utterance and the CC' elements further particularize the verbs as issuing falsehood in deceit and dishonesty. The palms defiled by blood and fingers by perversity in v. 3a prevent the hand of the Lord from saving in v. 1aa; the lips that speak deceit and the tongue that murmurs dishonesty in v. 3b keep his ear from hearing their pleas in v. 1ab. The deeds and words of the people ward off God's listening and redemptive action.[25]

The opening words of this unit also echo motifs from previous units by the repetition of vocabulary in a similar literary context. The reiteration of motifs strengthens the continuity of thought moving through the poems of 56-59. Aware that 59 is the final literary unit in the proposed section 56-59, such reappearances here may be especially significant to recall motifs of the poems in concert with one another.

The final elements of each colon in 59:1 not only bring together the ideas of "being saved" and "being heard," but also resonate with earlier motifs. In 56:1 the opening words of the section announce the imminent approach of salvation (yšw^{c}ty) as an impetus for the practice of justice and righteousness.

24. Examples of where the parallelism is complete but the order broken often serve to emphasize the latter words. This is true in v. 3b where, after following a patterned parallel ordering in vv. 1-3a, it breaks the pattern and draws attention to itself.

25. MUILENBURG notes the parts of the body and associates them with sins of action and word; cf. "The Book of Isaiah," 688.

While the succeeding poems employ both imagery and vocabulary of salvation, the root yšc does not appear again until 59:1; here the recurrence of mhwšyc signals the retardation of salvation because of sin. The tie of 59 with 56:1 is strengthened with the three reiterations that mšpṭ and ṣdqh are absent from the people (cf. 59:4,9,14). The use of these words in 59:4,9,14 explains the disappearance of that which is demanded in 56:1: to keep justice and practice righteousness. From this understanding one recognizes that the retardation of salvation comes about when uprightness vanishes. Also the four repetitions of the root yšc in 59:1,11,16,17 attest to its importance showing it to be a word recurring throughout the poem and resonating with the earlier use in 56:1.

In 58:4b the people are told that their fasting practices are not the kind of activities that win God's hearing (lhšmyc). In 59:1-2 the people are told that the Lord's ear is not too dull to hear (mšmwc) their pleas, but that their sins have brought about a separation from God. The repetitions of šmc echo a similar motif of the people's desire to be heard by God, and yet in both instances their sinfulness removes them from what they seek. While in 58 the problem revolves around inauthentic fasting, the vocabulary in 59 suggests a different yet related problem. As Hanson shows, the reference to pnym (the Face) in 59:2b may suggest a cultic issue at stake;[26] the employment of this term often carries the sense of divine presence encountered in worship. The vocabulary in 59:3 furthers this imagery while showing a relationship between the cult in which the people participate and their lives. Their palms (kpykm), associated with prayer in an uplifted position at worship, are defiled by blood (59:3a); their lips

26. Cf. HANSON, The Dawn of Apocalyptic, 121.

(śptwtykm), directed to the praise of God in cult, are marked as instruments of deceit (59:3b).[27] To be heard by God in the cult, one's life needs to be in right accord with precepts of justice; deeds related to murder and deceit turn God away even if the external manifestations of the cult are practiced. Thus the literary contexts of šmc look at two religious practices within the life of Israel (fasting and worship) and show that these observances can only achieve their end when they accompany a life of righteousness.

The blame levelled against God for supposedly not hearing (mšmwc) the people's pleas in 59:1 also resonates with the complaints of 58:3 that he does not see (wl' r'yt) nor acknowledge (wl' tdc) their acts of humility.[28] When the three complaints of not seeing, not knowing, and not hearing are taken as a whole, they present an interesting example of irony when read in the larger context of Isa; in the inaugural vision of the prophet he is told to proclaim an enigmatic message to the people.

> And the Lord said, "Go and say to this people:
> 'Hear and hear (šmcw šmcw), but do not understand (w'l-tbynw).
> See and see (wr'w r'w), but do not perceive (w'l-tdcw).'
> Make the heart of this people fat,
> and their ears heavy (w'znyw hkbd, cf. 59:1) and shut their eyes,
> Lest they see (pn-yr'h) with their eyes,
> and hear (yšmc) with their ears,
> and understand (ybyn) with their hearts,
> and turn and be healed." (Isa 6:9-10)

The very command God tells the prophet to announce to the people, the people level against God as charges in 58:3 and 59:1. Reading 58:3 and 59:1 within the

27. Cf. BONNARD, Le Second Isaïe, 386.

28. Cf. ALONSO SCHÖKEL, "Isaias III," 361.

larger context of Isa, these two passages strike a note of incongruity, for while the people charge God with failing to see, hear, and understand, it is they who fall short in comprehending the ways of God and putting them into practice; the word of judgment against the people shows that in their accusations against God, they accuse themselves.

In 59:2-3 two motifs recur from an earlier context in Isa 57. In 57:17a God reacts to the perversities (b^{c}wn) of the people's covetousness by hiding himself (hstr) from them; the Lord withdraws his presence. In 59:2 the perversities (^{c}wntykm) of the people bring about a separation from God, their sins hide the Face (hstyrw pnym), the divinity's presence. Both uses of ^{c}wn are in concert with str, distinguishing the absence of God in the presence of perversity. In addition, the motif of deceit (šqr) appears in both 57:4 and 59:3. In 57:4 zr^{c}-šqr expresses the deep-rooted nature of deceit in the people; they are descendants of a spurious generation. In 59:3 the enumeration of sins which cause separation from God specify "deceitful speech" (dbrw-šqr) (cf. also v. 13). The repetition of this motif underscores both the long-standing commitment to falsehood and its expression in words of deceit within the context of 56-59.[29]

A tone of judgment pervades the opening strophe. Having borne the charges of neither saving nor hearing the people's supplication, the charges against God are reversed and the people are indicted for their sinfulness; they are the cause of Yahweh's apparent withdrawal. This strophe opens the poem by turning the table on those who accuse God and issuing judgment against them for

29. The only other use of šqr in Isa 56-66 is 63:8.

their evil deeds and sham participation in the cult. In their judgment of God they bring judgment upon themselves.

B. Isaiah 59:4-8 -- The Collapse of Righteousness and Justice

The varied uses of imagery have led commentators to numerous interpretations of these verses. Westermann speaks of the "odd character" in which these verses are constructed,[30] and Torrey calls vv. 5-6 a "whimsical parenthesis" in the midst of an eloquent poem.[31] The task is to see if the construction of this strophe is as odd and whimsical as some commentators suggest.

In v. 4a the strophe begins with the repetition of the negative ’yn/w’yn at the beginning of each colon; the internal structure follows a parallel ordering of its elements.

v. 4a	-	’yn-qr’	bṣdq	/	w’yn	nšpṭ	b’mwnh
		(A) (B)	(C)		(A)	(B')	(C')

The AA elements show a cause-effect relationship: since no one pronounces suit righteously, the result is that no one is judged honestly. This relation also carries through in the BB' elements where the movement is from the "pronouncement" to the "being judged." Similarly the CC' elements bring together the unrighteous suit which gives way to dishonest judgment. The pronouncement of a suit and an arbitration lacking in honesty paint a portrait of

30. Cf. WESTERMANN, Isaiah 40-66, 347.

31. Cf. TORREY, The Second Isaiah, 186.

a trial scene; even beyond the accusations, which create a judgment scene, the vocabulary suggests the setting.[32]

A series of infinitive absolutes in v. 4b unites the cola and carries forward the thought of v. 4a. Note the cause-effect relationship apparent in v. 4bb; generative language expresses the movement from conception to giving birth (hrw, whwlyd).[33] The cause-effect relationship is apparent in vv. 4a,4bb, but the imagery of v. 4ba is not so easily discernible; however, a pattern runs through this verse clarifying the interpretation of v. 4ba. Following v. 4a, vv. 4ba and 4bb stand independent without a w to connect them; but each colon in v. 4b contains a w (wdbr in v. 4ba; whwlyd in v. 4bb). To isolate the uses of w in v. 4 displays a pattern at work and suggests that the function of w in vv. 4a and 4bb may also be at work in v. 4ba.[34]

---

32. In the previous literary units at 56:9-12, 57:3-13, and 58:1-5, the vocabulary and imagery depict a tone of judgement at the outset. Isa 59 follows that pattern beginning on a note of judgement.

33. There are other examples in biblical poetry where the infinitive absolute demonstrates a cause-effect relationship.

> For the company of the godless is barren,
> and fire consumes the tents of bribery.
> They conceive (hrh) mischief and bring forth (wyld) evil,
> and their heart prepares deceit. (Job 15:34-35)

In Job, the same generative vocabulary occurs to express the resulting evil from what is first conceived in mischief. The book of Proverbs provides another example.

> Taking out (hgw) the dross from silver,
> and coming out (wyṣ') for the refiners, a vessel;
> Taking out (hgw) the wicked from before the King,
> and established (wykwn) in righteousness is his throne.
> (Prov 25:4-5)

The removal of dross from silver results in a vessel, so the removal of the wicked from the King's presence produces a throne founded on righteousness.

34. Note a similar pattern in Prov 25:4-5, where the repeated word initiating both verses (hgw) is without a connective, while the cause-effect elements are united by w (wyṣ' in v. 4, and wykwn in v. 5).

v. 4a	-	'yn	[. . .]	w'yn	[. . .]
v. 4ba	-	btwḥ	[. . .]	wdbr	[. . .]
v. 4bb	-	hrw	[. . .]	whwlyd	[. . .]

Such a consistent structure suggests that v. 4ba also be read in the same cause-effect manner of vv. 4a,4bb. The sense of v. 4ba then reveals that trusting in vanity and emptiness (^{c}l-thw) results in destructive speech; such an idea suits the literary context, further describing the lack of righteous pronouncements in v. 4a and exposing another aspect of sinful speech found in v. 3b.

57:4 presents a threefold progression of cause-effect relationships. The opening bicolon states that unrighteous pronouncements lead to dishonest judgments. Vv. 4ba,4bb explain the testimony of the preceding bicolon as a progression from "empty trust" to "destructive speech," and from an "origin of distress" to "full-grown wickedness." Thus vv. 4ba,4bb amplify the magnitude of evil which v. 4a suggests.

A series of repetitions in vv. 5a-6a presents a pattern for the organization of the imagery used here.

(A) - byṣy, bq^{c}w (v. 5aa)

 (B) - wqwry (v. 5ab)

(A) - mbyṣyhm, tbq^{c} (v. 5b)

 (B) - qwryhm (v. 6a)

The opening A and B elements of v. 5a introduce two images: the hatching of eggs and a spider's web. The second A of v. 5b repeats vocabulary from v. 5aa;

the second B of v. 6a repeats a word from v. 5ab. The result is an ABAB pattern for the three bicola of vv. 5a-6a.

Examples of alliteration and assonance support the divisions of the ABAB pattern. The word for "adder" has the repetition of the ṣ in the opening elements; even the placement of this reiterated sound hints at the hissing of a venomous viper. Similarly the plosive sounds of b and q in the repeated bq^{c} (vv. 5aa,5bb) have a stopped quality similar to the ṣ. Distinct from this, the spider/web imagery has a recurrence of û, and ō in v. 5ab, which is then reiterated with a threefold û, twofold ō, and a twofold terminal -hm in v. 6a; the timbre of these sounds is soft and breathy. With these examples of onomatopoeia, the sibilate and plosive sounds of vv. 5aa,5b describing the serpent's eggs form a contrast with the open vowels and soft -hm tone of vv. 5ab,6a depicting the spider's web.

In isolating the two nouns of the ABAB pattern, byṣh and qwr distinguish the products issuing from the activities of the adder and serpent. But in v. 5a metaphorical language narrates the work of the unrighteous (v. 4); both the images of the adder and the spider focus on the end result of their endeavors, an egg and a web. This common focal point of v. 5a, supported by the repetitions in vv. 5b,6a, centers the thought of the ABAB pattern on the fruit of their work, the consequences of their activities. The first image (A) speaks of the spiders/unrighteous who hatch adder's eggs (v. 5a); these eggs bring forth death for those who eat them (v. 5ba) or engender another dangerous viper.[35] The

35. The ʼp^{c}h of 59:5a occurs elsewhere only in Isa 30:6 and Job 20:16. It is in a land of trouble and anguish that the viper dwells (Isa 30:6); the

metaphorical language describes the disastrous results of the evil ones' sinful activity and the consequences it brings to those who partake in it: death or more danger.[36] The second image (B) portrays the spiders/unrighteous who weave webs (v. 5ab); the webs, however, are useless as a garment or an article of covering (v. 6a).[37] The metaphors here expose another aspect of the fruits of the unrighteous ones' endeavors: its futility. The sum of the parts displays a bleak picture of the effects brought about by the unjust: useless works, more peril, and death. The final word in v. 6a (bmᶜśyhm) occurs twice in v. 6b (mᶜśyhm mᶜśy), linking the description of their useless works to what follows, and emphasizing their "labors in wickedness" by means of repetition.

The repetition of ʾwn in vv. 6b,7b unites these cola; the similar internal construction of these cola with ᶜśh and ḥšb, ending with ʾwn, further strengthens their unity. The placement of vv. 6ba,7ba frames v. 7a and shows an ABA pattern in vv. 6b-7b.

(A) - mᶜśyhm mᶜśy-ʾwn (v. 6ba)

(B) - rglyhm lrᶜ yrṣw / wymhrw lšpk dm nqy (v. 7a)

(A) - mḥšbwtyhm mḥšbwt ʾwn (v. 7ba)

An ABA pattern focuses attention of the B element. The AA elements frame the center, and here bring together the understanding that both the works (v. 6b) and thoughts (v. 7b) of the people are wicked (ʾwn).

---

tongue of the viper (Job 20:16) kills the wicked man. Both the literary contexts suggest it to be an animal that is dangerous.

36. Cf. PENNA, Isaia, 574.

37. Cf. ALONSO SCHÖKEL, "Isaias III," 361-62; PENNA, Isaia, 574.

In reading v. 7a, note the structure of the bicolon and the way it stresses two points.

v. 7a - rglyhm lr^c yrṣw / wymhrw lšpk dm nqy.
(A) (B) (B') (A')

First, in the BB' elements the verbs are brought close together and the terminal *û* repetition unites them; both verbs express frenzied movement toward an object. Second, the recurring *l* (AA') emphasizes the objects of the driving movement: they rush *to* evil (*lr^c*) and hasten *to* shed (*lšpk*) innocent blood.

Both A and A' echo previous motifs from the larger context of 56-59 and this immediate chapter. In the A element *lr^c* occurs twice earlier in 56:2; 57:1. In the opening instructions of 56:2, the final exhortation of the macarism warns against doing any evil at all (*kl-r^c*); in sharp contrast, 59:7 pictures the people rushing toward evil. Instead of refraining from evil as ordered in 56:2, 59:7 describes the advance toward evil. In 57:1-2, the righteous one is taken away from the presence of evil (*ky-mpny hr^{c}h*) and enters into peace (*šlwm*). An opposing portrait is painted in 59:7-8 by the repetition of vocabulary as the unrighteous rush to evil (*lr^c*) with a concluding comment that they do not know the way of peace (*šlwm*, v. 8a).

In A', *lšpk dm nqy* resonates with the earlier reference to blood in 59:3; though it is difficult to determine the exact sense of *dm* in 59:3, the surrounding imagery and vocabulary of the strophe suggest that the shedding of innocent blood in 59:7a refers to killing: in v. 5b, those who eat the adders' eggs will *die*; in v. 6b, their words are called *acts of violence*; in v. 7b, their thoughts are described as devastation and destruction.[38] Thus in v. 7a the AA' elements function together to portray the rush to evil as one of the most insidious and violent crimes, the shedding of innocent blood.

In the ABA pattern of vv. 6b-7b the repeated 'wn in AA recalls the motif initiating the strophe in v. 4bb: the unrighteous conceive distress and give birth to wickedness ('wn). The repeated ᶜśh (v. 6b) and ḥšb (v. 7b) with 'wn present an example of merism, focusing attention on the extent of wickedness; "works" and "thoughts" display a word pair spanning both inward and outward ways to manifest evil.[39] This merism functions to show how wickedness pervades the unrighteous, both externally and internally. Thus this ABA pattern establishes a strong statement with the expression of immersion in the ways of wickedness (AA), framing their hot pursuit of evil and shedding of innocent blood (B).

In v. 6b the root ᶜśh recurs and reiterates the motif of "works" which carries through 56-59. Its threefold use in 56:1-2 opens the section with a command to practice righteousness, to practice sabbath observance, and to keep from doing any evil. In 57:12, the sarcastic threat to proclaim Israel's righteousness and actions is an indictment of their unrighteous actions. The same motif of acting in righteousness at 58:2 unfolds into an exposé of the house

---

38. Cf. PENNA, Isaia, 574-75. Beyond the immediate literary context, lšpk dm nqy appears in 2 Kgs 21:16; Joel 4:19; Ps 106:38; and Prov 6:17 as an expression of homicide.

39. The word pair ᶜśh//ḥšb also appear in 66:18 where they express involvement of evil bringing harsh judgment. These opening words of 66:18 are read with v. 17; cf. PENNA, Isaia, 627; WESTERMANN, Isaiah 40-66, 422.

of Jacob's need for a renewal of their observances according to the desires of God. Again in 58:13 the reminder to honor the Lord's sabbath requires that one not act in his own ways, but observe it as a holy day. The uses of ᶜśh play back and forth between the command to act according to the Lord's commands (56:1-2; 58:13) and the reproof of the people for their failure to act in righteousness (57:12; 58:2). Now the indictment in 59:4ff exposes their words and v. 6 labels their actions "wicked"; despite the Lord's instruction, their words bear fruit in wickedness.

The fourfold š (thrice with b) in v. 7b links together the repetition of "their thoughts" with "devastation and destruction."[40] Torrey points out that the pair šd wšbr functions in 51:19 and 60:18 as an example of sonant emphasis which displays the double consonance by a similarity in sound and a complementarity in thought.[41]

In v. 6ab, at the conclusion of an ABAB pattern in vv. 5a-6a, bmᶜśyhm announces a motif that follows immediately in the ABA pattern of vv. 6b-7b; the repetition of ᶜśh links the two macrostructures and moves the poem forward. Similarly in v. 7bb bmslwtm, its final element, announces a motif that follows immediately in vv. 8aa with drk and carries through the verse.[42]

---

40. McCREESH shows how the repetition of sounds not only brings emphasis to a line of poetry, but also serves as a means of effectively joining words by the recurring intonations that the ear naturally connects: cf. "Poetic Sound Patterns," 63-64.

41. Cf. TORREY, The Second Isaiah, 194.

42. For further examples of the parallel pair drk//mslh, see Isa 40:3; 62:10.

Three repetitions in vv. 8aa,8bb frame the two middle cola; the motif of "a way" begun in v. 7bb, repeated in both vv. 8aa,8bb, is also present in v. 8ab (bm^c^glwtm) and v. 8ba (ntybwtyhm). V. 8 forms a clear pattern which moves through each colon reiterating the motif of "a way."

(A) - drk šlwm l' yd^c^w (v. 8aa)

(B) - bm^c^glwtm (v. 8ab)

(B') - ntybwtyhm (v. 8ba)

(A) - kl drk bh l' yd^c^ šlwm (v. 8bb)

In this ABB'A pattern the outer elements are more important; the repetition of drk, šlwm, and l' yd^c^ stresses the relationship between AA. V. 8a states that the unrighteous ones described above do not know peace; then as a conclusion to the structure, v. 8bb states that each person (kl) who walks in the crooked paths of the unjust (bh) also does not know peace. In using synonymous words for drk, the BB' elements bring out another aspect of their way of living. V. 8ab states their courses are devoid of justice; v. 8ba goes one step further to clarify that their crooked paths are of their own making. Thus the final structure of the strophe concludes the indictment emphasizing that the unrighteous and those who follow them do not know peace, and that their unjust way of life is their own creation.

In v. 8bb there is a recapitulation of three words from v. 8aa. These recurrences highlight words that have appeared in earlier literary units and here recall their motifs. The verb yd^c^ occurs again in 59:12; but for drk and šlwm, this is their final use in 56-59.

In the context of 56-59 drk occurs ten times: six repetitions in 56:9--57:21, two in 58, and two in 59. In 56:9--57:21 the modus operandi of Israel's leaders (56:11) and the people's idolatry (57:10) contrast with the path of God's way (57:14,14); the way of Israel's heart (57:17,18) leads toward perversity and eventually needs the healing and comfort of God to restore life to a broken people (57:18). Among the elements of inclusion in 58:2,13, drk emphasizes the transformation which needs to take place in the people's knowledge of what God's ways truly are (58:2) and then to carry them out (58:13); as the "if-then" movement displays, it is in the pursuit and fulfillment of God's ways and not one's own that the blessings of salvation are found.[43] Finally, 59:8 speaks of the drk šlwm which is not known by the unrighteous. Bringing these two words together in construct also recalls the references to šlwm in 57:2,19,21. The literary context of 57:1-2 associates peace with the righteous, and its absence with the presence of evil (ky-mpny hr^{c}h); similarly 57:19-21 promises peace to those who are not wicked (hrš^{c}ym). From the context of 57:1-2, drk šlwm echoes the way of righteousness; here in 59:8 the motif reappears, but in a negative fashion. Even the strophe begins and ends on these two descriptions of the people: in v. 4 there is no one who pronounces suit righteously (bṣdq), and in v. 8 they do not know the way of peace (drk šlwm). The modus operandi to which this people is called is absent; once again, the way of peace in God is contrasted with humanity's movement away from peace.

The second strophe continues the theme of judgment found in vv. 1-3. The absence of righteousness in v. 4 builds in the subsequent verses presenting an

---

43. The "way" motif also occurs in 58:12 with ntybwt where it uses "paths" as an image of a manner of right living; ntybwtyhm also appears in 59:8ba. For a fuller explanation of 58:12, refer to pp. 222-23.

indictment of their pervasive wickedness. With the imagery of the adder and the spider, vv. 5-6a present a charge against the people for actions whose results threaten death and produce a worthless outcome. The wicked deeds and thoughts of the people (vv. 6b-7) focus on v. 7a charging them with the pursuit of evil and with the shedding of innocent blood. As at the outset (v. 4ab), the people's lack of justice is reiterated at the end (v. 8ab). They charter crooked paths and do not know the way of peace. The repeating third per. pl. pronominal suffixes keep reminding one of the indictment taking place; their works, their thoughts, their feet, and their courses move in the way of evil. The strong incriminations in this strophe portray a decree of judgment which exposes not only crimes but a rootedness in the ways of injustice and unrighteousness.

In concluding, one recalls the comments of Westermann regarding this strophe.

> There is no progress from part to part in the description of the transgressors given in vv. 5-8. It represents an accumulation. The various verses hardly bear any relationship to one another.[44]

The rhetorical analysis presented above shows the careful progression from microstructure to microstructure in the strophe; the links and progression can be noted in the following diagram.

		I	II	III	IV
a)	vv. 4a-4b	’yn nšpṭ	’wn		
b)	vv. 5a-6a			bm^{c}śyhm	
c)	vv. 6b-7b		’wn	m^{c}śyhm	bm^{c}glwtm
d)	vv. 8a-8b	’yn mšpṭ			drk

44. Cf. WESTERMANN, Isaiah 40-66, 347-48.

The beginning and end frame the strophe stating the absence of justice (I); the birth of wickedness touches both works and thoughts (II); the image of the spider's useless works leads into a consideration of the wickedness of their works and thoughts (III); the highways of destruction usher in the concluding message about the paths of injustice (IV). Far from scattered, the repetitions and parallels move the reader deliberately through the strophe touching on different aspects of their lack of righteousness and justice and its effects. Beyond this, the progression of the microstructures exhibits a pattern.

vv. 4a-4b = 2 bicola
vv. 5a-6a = 3 bicola
vv. 6b-7b = 3 bicola
vv. 8a-8b = 2 bicola

The opening and closing bicola which tell of the lack of justice and the departure from the way of peace each constitute two bicola, while the description of their works and effects each have three bicola. The above observations argue for the strophe's unity of thought, clear progression of ideas, and a balance in construction.

C. **Isaiah 59:9-13 -- Lament and Confession**

The new strophe begins with ^{c}l-kn; this particle often expresses the result of what is previously stated.[45] The relationship between the new strophe and the preceding one is further brought out in the repetition of the same words at their outset; the placement of these words at the beginning of the two strophes highlights their importance.

45. Cf. MUILENBURG, "The Linguistic and Rhetorical Usages," 137.

v. 4a - No one pronounces suit righteously (bṣdq)
and no one is judged (nšpṭ) in honesty.

v. 9a - Therefore, justice (mšpṭ) is far from us
and righteousness (ṣdqh) does not reach us.

When placed in relief these bicola show a cause-effect relationship: the consequence of unrighteous pronouncements and dishonest judgments results in the absence of justice and righteousness. The ᶜl-kn also functions in a deictic manner to move the poem forward into this strophe; thus the particle acts as a bridge between the description of the wicked deeds of vv. 4-8 (set in the third per. pl. verbs and pronominal suffixes) and the personal acknowledgment of the situation in vv. 9-13 (in the first per. pl. verbs and pronominal suffixes).

A series of word repetitions and the internal patterning of bicola form a concentric pattern in vv. 9-11.

(A) - ᶜl-kn rḥq mšpṭ mmnw / wl' tśygnw ṣdqh (v. 9a)

(B) - nqwh l'wr whnh (v. 9ba)

(C) - ngššh kᶜwrym qyr / wk'yn ᶜynym ngššh (v. 10a)

(D) - kšlnw bṣhrym knšp / b'šmnym kmtym (v. 10b)

(C') - nhmh kdbym klnw / wkywnym hgh nhgh (v. 11a)

(B) - nqwh lmšpṭ w'yn (v. 11ba)

(A) - lyšwᶜh rḥqh mmnw (v. 11bb)

From the beginning of this literary unit, salvation is linked to justice and righteousness; the absence of God's redemptive hand (v. 1) is due to the unrighteousness of the people. In the AA elements a motif of "distance" is introduced by the recurrence of rḥq and mmnw, and the single use of tśygnw;[46] the nouns used with this motif in AA are mšpṭ, ṣdqh, and yšwᶜh. Once again the relationship among salvation, righteousness, and justice comes forward, this time cloaked in the motif of "distance." The understanding that God's salvation is intimately connected with the exercise of justice and righteousness recalls the opening words of the third division of Isa in 56:1.

> Thus says the Lord:
> Keep justice and practice righteousness,
> For soon is my salvation to come
> and my righteousness to be revealed. (Isa 56:1)

While 56:1 calls for the observance of righteousness and justice because of the coming of salvation, 59:9a,11b ties the remoteness of salvation to the absence of justice and righteousness. Beyond the development of this relationship in 59, the repetition of vocabulary and contextual similarity in themes links this final unit with 56:1.

The BB elements are united not only by the repetition of the opening nqwh in vv. 9ba,11ba, but also the internal structure of their cola moving to the object of their hope (both with l) and concluding with its disappointment (noted by w as a connective for antithesis). The repeated nqwh is obscure in this literary context with its usual translation, "to wait"; the uses of nqwh in vv. 9ba,11ba are also set in contexts with differing imagery suggesting a possible dual meaning of the word. It can be argued that in 59:9b nqwh is better rendered "we look for."[47] The literary context of v. 10a uses a simile to compare the

---

46. The parallel pair rḥq//śwg also occurs in 59:14a.

47. J.E. Hartley discusses a secondary meaning of qwh as "to look for"; cf. "qāwâ," TWOT 2, 791.

speakers to those who are blind and without eyes; a motif of "vision" appears to be at work here.[48] The development in thought is clear as they look for light, walk in obscurity, and grope like the blind without eyes.[49] But the situation appears quite different for nqwh in v. 11b. In v. 11a the people describe themselves with a motif of "sound," like growling bears and murmuring doves. A.R. Ceresko shows that in several places the root qwh can mean "to cry out."[50] If one looks at the literary setting, there is something more vigorous than "waiting" at stake in these verses. The images of groping (v. 10), stumbling (v. 10), and growling (v. 11) portray the struggle to come into contact with redemption, and yet to find frustration in its absence. Furthermore, it is possible that this repeated word carries two connotations, both expressing aspects of the anticipation for some sign of redemption; they look to the light and cry out for justice, waiting for salvation to no avail. A dual translation of the same word, based on differing examples of imagery in their contexts, enriches the sense of longing which this lament portrays; such a representation of paronomasia draws attention to these words as descriptive elements in the structure.

---

48. In Job 3:9 qwh is parallel to r'h (to see); consider the literary context where these verbs appear.

Let the stars of its dawn be dark;
let it look for light (yqw-l'wr), but have none,
nor see (w'l-yr'h) the eyelids of the morning. (Job 3:9)

The context of Job 3:9 is somewhat similar to Isa 59:9b in the contrasts between light and darkness; in Job 3:9, the frustration in looking for light is complemented by the situation which enables them to see the first streaks of dawn. This example from Job, though in another literary context, demonstrates that qwh can be understood in the sense of "looking for". Cf. DHORME, Job, 28.

49. For those also reading nqwh as "we look for" in 59:9b, see HANSON, The Dawn of Apocalyptic, 114; KISSANE, The Book of Isaiah, 243; RSV; NEB.

50. Cf. CERESKO, Job 29-31, 94.

The similar internal structure of the BB elements in vv. 9ba,11ba establishes a relationship between the cola and offers a means of clarification for the metaphorical language in v. 9ba. The search for light in v. 9ba is frustrated by the presence of darkness; similarly the search for justice in v. 11ba is frustrated by its absence (w'yn). The parallel construction of the cola unite l'wr with lmšpt, and whnh-hšk with w'yn; thus the image of light is related to justice, and darkness to the absence of justice.[51] Two other examples of the same metaphors in close proximity to 59 present a similar interpretation of these images. In 58:10ba the rising of light ('wrk) from darkness (bhšk) is an image which depicts the coming of the Lord with salvation in response to the activity which is demanded by God (cf. also 58:8); if ('m) the people will turn away the yoke, the reproaching finger and the evil word, and give of themselves to satisfy the hungry and humbled ones, then darkness will give way to light.[52] Also in 60:1-2, the opening words of the eschatological poems (60:1--63:6) employ the imagery of light and darkness in the description of God's coming.[53] The people are told to arise and shine for their light ('wrk) has come, the glory of the Lord has risen upon them (60:2). 60:1-2 relates the coming of light to God's visitation of the people; while his coming in light is further described in the salvific language of blessing, the gathering of nations, and the righteousness of Israel

---

51. As noted on pp. 246-47, mšpt and ṣdqh are connected with the theme of salvation in the context of Isa 59: further in v. 11b, lmšpṭ is parallel with lyšwᶜh which strengthens their ties in this context.

52. For a fuller discussion of these images in their context of Isa 58, refer to pp. 214-15, 218-19 of the previous Chapter.

53. The parallels l'wr//lnghwt of 59:9b are also found in Isa 60:3,19 as metaphors of salvation.

(60:1-22), the rest of the earth and its people remain in darkness.[54] In the context of 56-59, the image of light in 58:8a,10b looks forward to the redemptive coming of God's salvation in 60 where there will be an end of darkness (60:2), and where blessings and righteous behavior walk hand-in-hand (60:19-22). In 59:9b,11b the darkness which keeps the light remote paints a scene of judgment where justice and salvation are sought (nqwh) but remain far off; the absence of light depicts the absence of the Lord's presence. While both 58:8,10 and 59:9,11 can be viewed in relation to 60, their contexts express two aspects of the "light" and "darkness" motifs: 58:8,10 anticipates the end of darkness and the breaking forth of salvation's light, the Lord God among the people who heed his word; 59:9,11 looks for the light of justice but can only lament the darkness of judgment that comes upon them because of the Lord's absence in the face of unrighteousness.

The internal structure of the bicola and the use of simile unite the CC' elements. The verbs in vv. 10a,11a do not recur as in vv. 9b,11b, but the beginning and end of the respective bicola are linked by an example of repetition in v. 10a (n^{e}gaš^{e}ša, n^{e}gaššēša) and rhyme in v. 11a (neh^{e}meh, nehgeh). The repetition of gšš in v. 10a furthers the image of "walking in obscurity" found at v. 9bb; v. 10a highlights the uncertainty with which they walk, comparing themselves to the blind and those without eyes. In v. 11a the rhyming words at the extremes of the bicolon bring together two different verbs but nonetheless both express a motif of "speech": we growl, we murmur. The placement of nhmh and nhgh as framing elements suggests they are the key words for

54. Cf. MUILENBURG, "The Book of Isaiah," 697-99.

interpreting the imagery. To demonstrate the full effect of the people's spoken response to their situation, v. 11a uses a merism to express both its intensity (we all growl like bears) and duration (we murmur and murmur like doves). The similes of v. 11a present extremes in the animal world with a growling bear and a murmuring dove;[55] and yet such polar images bring together a vividness in expression that is hard to capture with a single statement.[56] Together the elements of the merism demonstrate an intense and continual calling out in the expectant hope that redemption may come, but to no avail.

The D element is the middle point or focus of the concentric pattern; there are several poetic devices at work here. First, the series of verbs in vv. 9b-10a presents a gradual buildup which climaxes in v. 10b: the people look for light but are in darkness (v. 9a); they walk about yet are in obscurity (v. 9bb); they grope, they feel for a wall like a blind person (v. 10a); and finally at high noon when light is at its peak, they stumble as if it were twilight (v. 10b). In the context of a lament about their pitiable situation, the people explain their plight in the imagery of a blind individual. The progression of the verbs paints a scene which is already hopeless from the start because they look for light but find darkness; even their attempts to walk and grope for something end in defeat when they stumble (v. 10b). The suspense of the blindman's walk breaks in v. 10b and turns to the image of a growling bear in v. 11a.

---

55. Cf. ALONSO SCHÖKEL, "Isaias III," 362.

56. Cf. HONEYMAN, "Merismus," 17.

Second, in the D element kmtym repeats a verbal root from v. 5b (ymwt). In his recent study of stylistic devices in judgment speeches, P.D. Miller cites numerous examples where the repetition of words establishes a basis of correspondence relating the fate that falls upon an individual as a result of his deeds.[57] The common biblical metaphor which expresses this idea is the seed which is sown in corruption and yields a harvest of wickedness (cf. Prov 22:8; Hos 8:7; Mic 6:15), while what is sown in mercy yields righteousness (Ps 126:5; Prov 11:18; Hos 10:12; 2 Cor 9:6; Gal 6:8; Jas 3:18). The repetitions of mwt in vv. 5b,10b show a similar relationship. In v. 5b the activities describing the unrighteousness of the people are set in metaphorical language; the unjust are described as hatching adders' eggs which bring death to those who feed on them. The thrust of the metaphor shows that the labors of the wicked produce a result that offers death to those who partake in it. In v. 10b as the unrighteous describe their situation they speak of themselves as being like the dead among those who are vigorous; walking in obscurity, groping like the blind, and stumbling about at high noon, they are like those who have no life in them. They who have sown the seeds of death now reap its harvest. What is striking about the development of mwt in this literary setting of a judgment scene is the movement from a description/accusation in v. 5b to the acknowledgment by those accused in v. 10b: the accused announce their own sentence in describing themselves like the dead, acknowledging a situation which they have created and brought upon themselves.[58] These considerations of mwt strengthen a reading of

57. Here MILLER builds on K. Koch's theory of "menschlicher Tat entspringendes Schicksal" to explain the retribution one finds, particularly in the prophetic writings. Cf. Sin and Judgment, 5.

58. PAURITSCH speaks of vv. 9-12 as a self-accusation before Yahweh; cf. Die neue Gemeinde, 90.

the D element as the structure's focal point, showing not only how the movement of the chiasm climaxes on the acknowledgment of their own death, but also establishing a tie with the previous strophe which links their deeds with their final fate.

The particle *ky* introduces the remaining bicola beginning in v. 12a, similar to the particle in v. 9a which initiates the strophe and chiastic structure. In v. 12a, *ky* functions in a deictic manner to move the text forward; as vv. 9-11 express the people's lament over their situation, the particle in v. 12a ushers in the confession of sinfulness which dominates through v. 13. The slowing down of the meter to a 2+2 and the alliteration of *-nû* in each element stress v. 12b;[59] here the *ky* heightens the opening of the bicolon as a "vocal gesture" to draw attention. Muilenburg notes that the successive appearance of particles, similar to those of 59:12, accentuate the bicola and underscore their importance in the literary context.[60] Thus in v. 12 the particles signal the transition from lament to confession and emphasize the acknowledgment of sinfulness.

The triple recurrence of *pš*^{c} unites vv. 12-13;[61] *pš*^{c} also introduces a new word into the already developed "sin" vocabulary of Isa 59. In v. 12aa the people confess that their transgressions are many before God (*ngdk*); similarly in

---

59. MUILENBURG notes the change in meter as a means of emphasis; cf. "Form Criticism," 11.

60. Cf. MUILENBURG, "The Linguistic and Rhetorical Usages," 148.

61. The triple repetition of a word as a means of emphasis is discussed earlier in Chapter Two (pp. 50-51) and in this Chapter on pp. 250-51. In addition, a triple occurence of *'yn* appears in vv. 15-16a.

v. 12ba they admit their sins remain with them ('tnw). Here the people acknowledge the dual affect that their transgressions have in relation to God and to themselves. The internal construction of the bicola in v. 12 places both ḥṭ' and ^{c}wn as parallels with pš^{c}. This internal structure suggests that pš^{c} is a broader or more expansive word for sin, subsuming both ḥṭ' and ^{c}wn as parallels.[62] In v. 13aa pš^{c} begins a series of six infinitive absolutes which enumerates rebellious acts of transgression.

A closer look at vv. 12-13 reveals several repetitions which link these verses to the opening strophe in vv. 1-3; consider the following chart.

1)	YHWH	v. 1	v. 13a
2)	'lhym	v. 2a	v. 13a
3)	^{c}wn	vv. 2a,3a	v. 12b
4)	ḥṭ'	v. 2b	v. 12a
5)	dbr	v. 3b	vv. 13b,13b
6)	šqr	v. 3b	v. 13b
7)	hgh	v. 3b	v. 13b

These recurrences of vocabulary fall into three categories: a) the divine names (no. 1,2); b) a vocabulary of "sin" (no. 3,4); and c) a motif of "deceitful speech" (no. 5,6,7). Each of the categories is considered to discern the function of the repetitions.

62. C.H. LIVINGSTON comments that pš^{c} as a term for sin "is a collective which denotes the sum of misdeeds and fractured relationship." This conception resonates with the use of pš^{c} in the literary context of Isa 59; cf. "ps^{c}," 741.

In vv. 1-2 the absence of the Lord's saving hand and his separation from the people come as a result of their sinful actions. Similarly in v. 13a the divine names are in a context where transgression describes separation from God: they acknowledge denying and turning from following him.

In vv. 2-3 the description of perversities and sins demonstrates the cause of God's absence; he withdraws his saving hand (v. 1). Similarly in v. 11b, salvation is far away from the people because of their transgressions (v. 11b); and yet their perversities and sins remain to testify against them. In both literary contexts, sin prevents the arrival of redemption.

And in v. 3 deceitful speech is named as one of the offences retarding the coming of God's salvation. In the confession of transgressions v. 13b repeats the murmuring of deceitful words. Both contexts note dishonest speech as a transgression.

The repetitions of these seven words and similar contextual uses link vv. 1-3 and vv. 12-13. The confession of sinfulness in vv. 12-13 attests to the earlier indictment of vv. 1-3. In v. 13 not only do the people acknowledge their oppressive speech, but also that their transgressions are a denial and turning away from God. Thus the repetitions function to establish ties between the opening words of accusation in vv. 1-3 and the people's confession of sin in vv. 12-13; these links within the poem further confirm its careful construction.

In v. 12b yd^{c}nwm governs the six infinitive absolutes of v. 13.[63] As

63. Cf. GKC, 340 §113d.

the people admit to their wrong-doing the strophe reaches a new point in its progression; the meter and alliteration attest to this already. Beyond this, the previous strophe concludes on a word of indictment regarding the lack of knowledge in the accused; in v. 8, following from the metaphorical description about the reign of wickedness in thought and deed, the people are said to be without a knowledge of the way of peace, and also those who walk in their crooked paths.[64] But in 59:12 the people admit to their perversities.

Beyond the importance of yd^{c} in this immediate literary context, the motif of "knowledge" weaves its way through three successive units. In 56:10-11, the leaders of Israel are charged as being without knowledge and discernment; then in 57:1, a general regret is voiced that there is no one with discernment (b'yn mbyn).[65] In 58:2-3, yd^{c} functions in literary contexts that are clothed with sarcasm and irony. The people accused of transgression in v. 1 are described in v. 2 as those who delight in a knowledge of God's ways; these people are contemptuous because they actually take pleasure in the belief that they understand the course of God's justice and yet truly are lacking a knowledge of it, as the succeeding verses go on to tell.[66] In v. 3a the irony builds as the self-righteous believe they understand God's ways and question God's lack of knowledge regarding their practices of humility. While they claim to know God's

---

64. From the larger literary context the path of peace is reserved for those who walk in righteousness and uprightness (57:2), while the wicked are excluded from a share in peace (57:20-21).

65. For a discussion of the parallel pair yd^{c}//byn, see pp. 115-16 in Chapter Three.

66. This motif is developed in the discussion of 58:2 on pp. 195-96.

ways they judge him as one lacking knowledge about them. Then in Isa 59 after the indictment charging the people and their followers with not knowing the way of peace (v. 8), they acknowledge their transgression (v. 12).

Though it stands beyond the intention of the present study, the importance of ydᶜ in 56-59 is further supported by its occurrences at significant positions in the book of Isaiah: the opening words of the book lament the lack of knowledge and discernment among God's people (Isa 1:2-3); the inaugural vision of the prophet gives a mission related to the people's understanding and discernment (6:9-10); J.C. Exum shows the relationship among hearing, instruction, and knowledge in Isa 28-33;[67] Isa 40-55 treats different aspects of how God's redemption of Israel leads to a knowledge of his ways (40:21,28; 41:20) and of the divinity himself (43:10; 45:3,6; 49:23,26; 52:6); the coming of God to Jerusalem and the turn of events will bring Israel to the knowledge of Yahweh as Savior in 60:16. Thus the motif of "knowledge " in 56-59 complements the other uses of this motif throughout the Book of Isaiah.

The third strophe continues the theme of judgment but in the style of a confession or self-accusation. The key words mšpṭ, ṣdqh, and yšwᶜh all appear here accenting the distance of those redemptive qualities sought by those who lament their situation. A point of climax is found in v. 10b where the people acknowledge their situation as being similar to those who are dead; those who are charged with crimes relating to death (vv. 5b,7a) now experience the consequence of their actions (v. 10b). As the strophe draws to a close, several

67. Cf. EXUM, "Whom Will He Teach Knowledge," 110-11, 120-21, 133-35.

words from vv. 1-3 recur and link the opening accusations of the poem with the acknowledgment of sin in vv. 12-13; these repetitions connect the strophes and reinforce the judgment theme by employing the vocabulary of the accusations (vv. 1-3) to affirm the indictment by the accused themselves (vv. 12-13). They acknowledge their sinfulness and describe its effects; the words of judgment are proven true by the self-accusation of those indicted.

D. Isaiah 59:14 -- The Situation Reviewed

Three characteristics of 59:14 distinguish it from what precedes and follows it. The consistent use of the first per. pl. verbs and pronominal suffixes ceases and the third per. sing. begins. Note also the perfect tenses of v. 14 change to a series of imperfect tenses in vv. 15-17. And the internal chiastic structure of the bicola in v. 14, with the verbs as framing elements and their subjects meeting at the middle, is not found in vv. 13b or 15a. These distinct features of 59:14 suggest it may stand apart from what precedes and follows.

Eight of the twelve words in v. 14 are repeated in the context of the poem, as noted in the following diagram.

		Before v. 14	After v. 14
(1,2)	whsg ’ḥwr	v. 13a	
(3)	mšpṭ	vv. 4a,9a,11b	v. 15b
(4)	ṣdqh	vv. 4a,9a	vv. 16b,17a
(5)	mrḥwq	vv. 9a,11b	
(6)	ky-kšlh	v. 10b	
(7)	’mt		v. 15a
(8)	lbw’		vv. 19b,20

These words can be divided into three groups: a) those that recall previous motifs (no. 1,2,5,6); b) those that look forward to new ones (no. 7,8); and c) those that are part of both the previous poetry and what is yet to come (no. 3,4). The following paragraphs consider each group separately.

Among those words which recall previous motifs, they all appear in the preceding strophe (vv. 9-13).

(no. 5) justice is far from us (v. 9)
salvation is far from us (v. 11)
righteousness stands afar (v. 14)

(no. 1,2) turning away from following our God (v. 13)
justice is turned away (v. 14)

(no. 6) we stumble at high noon (v. 10)
truth stumbles in the public square (v. 14)

In no. 5 what is as important as the repetition of rḥq is the triad of nouns occurring with it: mspṭ, yšw^{c}h, ṣdqh. These are key words recurring several times in 59 and here are united by the motif of distance. Beyond their importance in 59, these words initiate this section of Isa in an ABCB pattern at 56:1. The triad appears in 59 as a literary structure, united by rḥq, and functions like a refrain repeating the remoteness of justice, salvation, and finally righteousness in v. 14. The vocabulary of no. 1,2,6 places on the lips of the people expressions of their lamentable situation in v. 10b and their confession of sin in v. 13a; these same verbs relate the assessment of the sin-filled situation in v. 14.

The recurrences of 'mt (no. 7) in vv. 14b,15a reiterates the demise of truth. In v. 15a the waw consecutive imperfect verb with h'mt changes the temporality of the contexts where "truth" is used; where v. 14b describes a present situation of ’mt, v. 15a describes a past-to-present situation. The infinitive lbw’ (no. 8) continues the motif of distance in v. 14bb where uprightness is described as being unable to come; the absence of these virtues explains the withdrawal of God's saving hand. But the demise of virtue (v. 14) looks forward to a reversal in vv. 19b-20 with the coming of the Redeemer to Zion, clothed in righteousness and salvation.

The absence of justice (no. 3) appears as a motif throughout the literary unit; both before and after v. 14 there is the refrain, ’yn mšpṭ (cf. vv. 4a,8a,15b). In v. 14a ṣdqh once more recalls the disappearance of justice (vv. 4a,9a); but in vv. 16b-17a, the Lord sustains and clothes himself with ṣdqh. The dual meaning of ṣdqh as a virtue and as deliverance is consistent in this section of Isa.[68] Moreover, the literary context in 59:14, where ṣdqh is described as being afar, looks to its return in the coming verses; when justice and righteousness disappear, the Lord alone can intervene to establish a way of life according to his decrees.

A final observation on this hinge verse looks at the addition of a new word in this unit and even section, ’mt (truth). The vocabulary in vv. 12-13 collects words already employed and brings them together as a kind of cluster of terms describing the sin of the people. Similarly in v. 14, the disappearance of virtue brings together three words already used (mšpṭ and ṣdqh are often used,

68. Note the two uses of ṣdqh in 56:1a,1b and 58:2,8b.

and nkḥh appears in 57:2); but 'mt draws attention to itself by reason of its infrequent use. Several examples of distant parallelism in this study show how parts of a poem are united by reason of word pairs; the pair 'mt//šqr (truth//deceit) occurs presenting an example of antithetical parallelism.[69] As noted in the Overview of this Chapter, šqr occurs in this unit (vv. 3b,13b) and also in 57:4 describing Israel as an offspring of deceit. In 59:3b,13b the people stand accused and acknowledge their deceitful speech which contributes to the demise of justice and the absence of salvation. Then in reviewing the sorry state of affairs at v. 14, the description of truth stumbling in the public square has referents in vv. 3b,13b; truth fumbles in the presence of deceit. The repetition of 'mt in v. 15 reiterates the lack of truth in the face of deceit.[70] Thus the example of distant antithetical parallelism with 'mt//šqr in vv. 3b,13b and 14b,15a explains the addition of 'mt in v. 14 and gives a sense for how it functions in the literary context. With the other repeated words 'mt recalls the transgressions of dbry-šqr (v. 13b) and looks forward to a remedy of the lamentable situation (v. 15a).

V. 14 collects vocabulary which both recalls the past confession of sin but also anticipates the defeat of evil and the coming of the Redeemer. In this way v. 14 functions as a hinge verse bringing together motifs which are already enunciated, but which function to summarize what is stated while also employing vocabulary which "sets the stage" for its resolution.[71] Thus while the absence

---

69. For examples of the parallel pair 'mt//šqr, see Prov 11:18; 12:19.

70. A sense of balance is achieved in seeing how both 'mt and šqr each appear twice in the unit.

71. For a discussion of the hinge verse, see Chapter Three, p. 133 and note 75, and Chapter Four pp. 205-206.

and distance of justice, righteousness, truth, and uprightness review the effects of transgression, the assessment of the situation looks forward to an act of salvation which God alone can accomplish.

E. Isaiah 59:15-20 -- The Coming of the Redeemer

The waw consecutive imperfect dominates in vv. 15-17 with a translation of the verbs in the past. As Muilenburg points out, the "prophetic perfect" is often employed in Isa 40-66 where an act of forthcoming redemption is shown to be certain by already speaking of the event as if it happened in the past.[72] After the lament and confession of sin in vv. 9-13, v. 14 presents the state of affairs which springs from the previous verses while also anticipating their reversal; in v. 15 wthy shifts into the past and begins the new strophe. The repetition of h'mt in v. 15a links the description of this past situation to the state of affairs in v. 14: as truth stumbles in the street, so also has its presence been lacking. In vv. 15b-16a, the Lord views the situation and in vv. 16b-17a he responds by acting with salvation and deliverance. One can thus see how the waw consecutive imperfect in vv. 15-17 unites a threefold movement from a statement of the situation (v. 15a), to its assessment by the Lord (vv. 15b-16a), and finally to his active response to the predicament by effecting salvation with his own arm (vv. 16b-17b).

The following diagram shows the pattern of repetitions which unite vv. 15-16a in their respective bicola.

---

72. Cf. MUILENBURG, "The Book of Isaiah," 694; also see GKC, 312 §106n.

v. 15a			/	mr^{c}
v. 15b	wyr' wyr^{c}		/	ky-'yn
v. 16a	wyr'	ky-'yn	/	ky-'yn

The repetition of r^{c}, r'h, and ky-'yn are explained to show their interrelatedness and function here and in the larger context of 56-59.

The recurrence of r^{c} shows the pervasiveness of evil at hand: in v. 15a an individual turning away from evil is plundered, and in v. 15b there is neither justice nor any person to intercede in this situation. In v. 7a the portrayal of the unrighteous as rushing toward evil complements v. 15 where evil has taken over; as the unjust ones scurry toward evil so has it become established among them and they do not know peace (v. 8a). Similar in imagery and vocabulary is 57:1-2 where the righteous and merciful ones are taken from the presence of evil (ky-mpny hr^{c}h) and enter into peace. The opening and closing literary units are brought into contrast with an initial call to keep one's hand from doing any evil (m^{c}śwt kl-r^{c}) in 56:2, while 59:7,15 paint a portrait of a people who rush toward evil and are enmeshed in its death-dealing effects (cf. also 59:9-11).

In vv. 15,16a the Lord saw (wyr') that there was no justice nor any individual to intercede in the situation; after seeing this the Lord then turns to effect salvation with his own arm.[73] Here, there is a relationship between "no

73. The repetition of wyr' in vv. 15b-16a emphasizes the Lord's act of seeing; when he sees the situation he turns to effect a change, i.e. he brings salvation (vv.15-20). In contrast to this, the people lament that they are like the blind, groping about as persons without eyes (v. 10); they are unable to change the circumstances which their sins bring upon them (vv. 9-11). By the use of

individual to intercede" (v. 16a) and the plundering of anyone who turns from evil (v. 15a). Any agent of justice would fall prey to the power of evil at work, thus the Lord stands alone to bring redemption. A similar image occurs in 57:18 where, despite humanity's perversity which leads God to anger and punishment, the Lord sees (r'yty) these feeble ways and turns to bring healing and full comfort. Then in 58:3, the people accuse God of not seeing (wl' r'yt) their fasting practices, while obviously their manner of fasting does not bring them a hearing (v. 4b). On the contrary, Yahweh reminds the people in v. 7b that when they see (ky-tr'h) a naked person they are to clothe him. Thus it is not for God to be observant, for the divinity sees all and acts in righteousness; but rather it is for humanity to see the needs of others and to act upon the vision which extends God's mercy toward them. These examples of r'h depict an image of God who sees into situations that are replete with the tragedy of a broken relationship through sin and his response is to turn with the offer of deliverance to those unable to save themselves, while calling humanity to share in these righteous deeds.

The triple use of ky-'yn in vv. 15b-16a highlights the absence of justice and of any individual to intercede; there are other examples of triple repetition which heighten the dramatic effect and add a note of the superlative to the expression.[74] This is especially applicable to mšpṭ since its employment in v. 15b completes its third occurrence with 'yn (cf. also vv. 4ab,8ab); the full

---

similar imagery, the powerlessness of the people contrasts with the might of Yahweh. See also in 56:10 that "blindness" characterizes Israel's irresponsible leaders.

74. Cf. POPE, "Number," 564. For further examples, see Isa 6:3; Jer 7:4; 22:29; Ezek 21:27.

concert of ʼyn with mšpṭ as it reaches its third and last heralding in v. 15b announces the humiliation and extinction of justice from among the people. The added particle ky with the three negatives stresses the buildup and sets the stage for the Divine Warrior's battle with the forces of evil. Thus it can be seen that the concert of elements in vv. 15-16a introduces this final strophe in a forceful manner: the repetition of hʼmt from v. 14b briefly brings into focus the sad state of affairs; the pervasiveness of evil is stressed; and the threefold negation shows the pre-eminence of the wickedness that has taken over.

In vv. 16b-17 the text describes the actions taken by the Divine Warrior. As in the previous three bicola, here also a series of repetitions bind these verses together. A chiasm unites vv. 16b-17a with wtwš^{c}: wṣdqtw:: ṣdqh: yšw^{c}h. The wylbš begins vv. 17a,17b. These overlapping structures unify the movement of thought in vv. 16b-17.

v. 16b)	(A) wtwš^{c}	(B) wṣdqtw				
v. 17a				(C)	wylbš	
	(B) ṣdqh	(A) yšw^{c}h				
v. 17b)				(C)	wylbš, tlbšt	

The repetitions in vv. 16b-17 show two movements of transition taking place. The chiasm moves from the announcement of salvation's coming (note the hiph^{c}îl in wtwš^{c}, having the causative sense of bringing about salvation) in v. 16b, to the garments which signify that redemption in v. 17a. The repetition of wylbš then links together what might best be called the garments of redemption, described as both deliverance (v. 17a) and punishment (v. 17b).

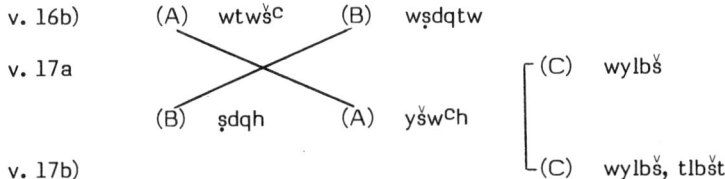

The implications of such an analysis carry a theological impact to the understanding of salvation in this context. The links between the bicola in vv. 16b-17 show that the Lord's establishing of salvation carries with it a dual notion of both deliverance and punishment. The coming of God is prompted by the utter lack of justice (vv. 15b-16a); thus it is that his redemptive act is to establish mšpṭ and this he does in the figurative image of clothing. To further establish the relationship of deliverance and punishment, one notes the other two occurrences of nqm in the context of Isa 56-66.

> To proclaim the year of the Lord's favor,
> and the day of vengeance (wywm nqm) of our God. (Isa 61:2a)
>
> For the day of vengeance (ywm nqm) was in my heart,
> and my year of redemption has come. (Isa 63:4)

In both 61:2a and 63:4 the "day of vengeance" stands in a position of parallel contrast to a year of the Lord's favor and redemption.[75] These examples are similar to 59:17 where the garments of vengeance are in a structured position with the armor of righteousness and helmet of salvation; the two examples of nqm bring the concept of vengeance into relationship with an aspect of God's redemption. When one is willing to accept the text as it stands, a consistent image of nqm prevails where vengeance is part of God's act of deliverance. In 59:16b-17 the chiasm occupies two bicola where the vocabulary of righteousness and salvation is more forceful because of its repetition. Also in 61:2a and 63:4 a

---

75. Some commentators attempt to soothe the harshness of nqm in 61:2 by citing Ugaritic examples where a cognate root carries the implication of "to rescue, to requite"; cf. MUILENBURG, "The Book of Isaiah," 710-11; WESTERMANN, Isaiah 40-66, 367; On the other hand, some add a note of reprisal to 63:4 by changing g e'ûlay to g emûlî to express the idea of retribution as a parallel to nqm; cf. MUILENBURG, "The Book of Isaiah," 727; WESTERMANN, Isaiah 40-66, 383.

motif of "time" is found comparing the year of favor and redemption to the day of vengeance; the greater length of time is given to the period of the Lord's favor and redemption, while the shorter prevails with vengeance. In these contexts where nqm appears, the salvation imagery is predominant. Thus the literary contexts of nqm support the structure of 59:16b-17 which describes God as the One who cannot do other than restore total justice in his acts of salvation and deliverance, which means making right all that is wrong in his eyes (59:15).

The structure of vv. 15-17 forms a set of two three-bicola segments (vv. 15-16a, 16b-17) within this strophe. A change occurs in v. 18 with the employment of a tricolon, breaking the previous series. The internal ordering of the elements in v. 18 shows a pattern as given in the following diagram.

v. 18) $k^{c}l$ gmlwt $k^{c}l$

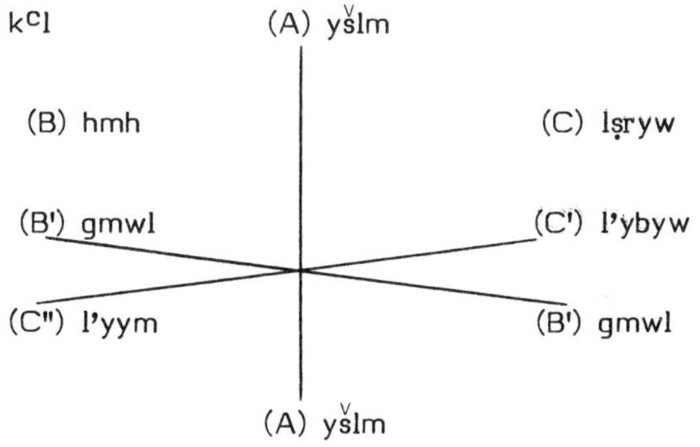

The opening colon, through the repetition of $k^{c}l$, establishes a relationship between "deeds" and their "recompenses"; reading $k^{c}l$ in a causal sense makes a link between the actions performed and a proper repayment based on the deeds themselves.[76] The repetition of yšlm (A) marks the conclusions of the opening

76. For $k^{c}l$ as a causal substantive, cf. GKC, 375-76 §118s[2]; 492 §158b. TORREY reads $k^{c}l$ as the Aramaic $k^{c}n$ (a temporal adverb) with a

and closing cola, emphasizing the motif of "recompense." In v. 18ab a series enumerates both the recompense (B) and its recipient (C);[77] but in v. 18ba the order of "recompense-recipient" is inverted, then ending the tricola with yšlm (A). A. Mirsky studies the literary device of inverting final elements within the internal structure of a series;[78] the reversal in the last members of a series is a way of articulating an alternation in the elements themselves and indicating a conclusion.[79] The alternation of the elements in 59:18ba distinguishes between two groups in the structure: the oppressors and enemies, and the coastlands. The repetition of yšlm in v. 18ba closes the tricolon on the motif of "recompense." The observations of Mirsky for final alternating elements resonate with the pattern in 59:18 and emphasize the movement from images of deliverance in vv. 16b-17 to their implementation in the issuance of just recompense in v. 18.

The final inquiry into the interpretation of v. 18 seeks to discern the two groups that are distinguished by the structural pattern. Despite the literary context of 59, Westermann argues that the oppressors and enemies of v. 18 are the foes of Israel; the description of God's coming in vv. 15-20 relates the saving

---

phonetic variation close to the Syriac kēl ; cf. The Second Isaiah, 442. MUILENBURG accepts Torrey's emendation of the text; cf. "The Book of Isaiah," 695. However, the literary context argues for an appreciation of the clear ties formed between "deeds" and "recompense" by the repetition of k ͨl.

77. The l alliteration draws attention to the recipients (C).

78. Cf. Aharon MIRSKY, "Stylistic Device for Conclusion in Hebrew," Semitics 5 (1977) 9-23.

79. Cf. MIRSKY, "Stylistic Device," 12-15.

of God's people and the destruction of its outside adversaries.[80] However, when one looks at the progression of thought in 59, the introduction of a motif related to the "outside enemies of Israel" at the end of a whole poem dealing with the evil committed by God's people does not correspond to its general thrust. Rather one sees the Divine Warrior taking up the armor of salvation and the garments of vengeance in response to the absence of justice, which the people have already confessed (59:9a,11b). It is the people who prevent the saving hand of the Lord from coming to them because of their sins (59:1-3); their unrighteous actions manifest wickedness in both thought and deed (59:6b,7b). It is Israel who revolts against God and ruptures the relationship of friendship which leads to their denial and turning away from him (59:13a).[81] The notion that Israel is referred to as the enemies of v. 18 is further strengthened by 59:20 which states that the Redeemer comes to Zion for those who turn away transgression; the promise of deliverance presumes that its recipients reverse the injustice and unrighteousness of sin so that truth and uprightness may abide among those in Jacob (59:14,20). The use of l'yym in v. 18b remains a puzzle to numerous commentators.[82] However, within Isa 56-66 it appears in 60:9; 66:19; both of the literary contexts suggest that 'yym refers to those distant regions to which

80. Cf. WESTERMANN, Isaiah 40-66, 350. MUILENBURG suggests outside foes to Israel, but does not definitely rule out another interpretation of who the enemies include; cf. "The Book of Isaiah;" 695.

81. Cf. BONNARD, Le Second Isaïe, 393-94; VERMEYLEN, Du prophète Isaïe, 468-69. HANSON also argues that the enemies are within the community; however, his concern with the Sitz im Leben specifies two warring factions in Judah, which a literary study such as this does not attempt to define. Cf. The Dawn of Apocalyptic, 125.

82. Cf. MUILENBURG, "The Book of Isaiah," 695; WESTERMANN, Isaiah 40-66, 351; WHYBRAY, Isaiah 40-66, 227.

the Lord's salvation will extend at his coming.[83] Furthermore, within the context of 56-59 the expansive character of God's offer of salvation is demonstrated. In 56:6c, the words of instruction to the foreigners broaden the invitation to include all keeping (kl-šmr) the sabbath; following in 56:7, God promises that his house will be called a house of prayer for all peoples (kl-h^{c}mym). So the reference in 59:18 to the coastlands does not stand in isolation here, but has several referents within 56-66 that also reveal the sweeping offer to share in redemption to those outside Israel. Thus the announcement of recompense is understood to be directed to those within Israel and those outside its confines.

At v. 19a the attention momentarily shifts away from the description of the Divine Warrior's acts to the fear of the people at his coming, with a third per. pl. verb. wyyr'w. Then in v. 19b a third per. sing. verb with ky focuses the thought back on the Lord who will come. The ky in v. 19b functions primarily in a causal manner to interpret the preceding utterance: the people fear for the Lord comes as an oppressed stream. The particle also functions in a climactic sense both with the announcement of the Lord's advent and as a means of dramatically concluding the poem.[84] The repetition of wb' in v. 20 extends the description of the Lord's coming on a note both hopeful and sobering: the Lord comes as Redeemer, but to those who turn away transgression. The opening

---

83. Cf. MUILENBURG, "The Book of Isaiah," 695, 771.

84. MUILENBURG discusses and cites examples where ky follows a dramatic utterance and serves in both a causal and emphatic manner; cf. "The Linguistic and Rhetorical Usages," 149.

verbs of each bicolon in vv. 19-20 highlight the progression of thought in this conclusion to the final strophe:

v. 19a) They will fear

v. 19b) for indeed he will come

v. 20) And he will come to Zion, the Redeemer.

The emphasis in vv. 19-20 is clearly in the Lord's advent, coming as a Redeemer, like an oppressed stream, instilling awe in those from east to west.

An apparent wordplay on the root ṣwr (to oppress) unites vv. 18 and 19. The recompense described in v. 18 notes that God's fury comes to his oppressors (lṣryw) because of their deeds. Then the portrayal of God's advent in v. 19b announces his arrival in the imagery of an oppressed stream (knhr ṣr). As Yahweh bears the burden of being oppressed, so does that oppression break loose in the form of a pent-up stream. In combat with the Lord God, those who oppose his decrees can look forward to the same opposition that they inflict. This eschatological image of the Lord's coming to Zion paints a portrait of the divinity having been forestalled in his arrival and now breaking forth with the power of an unleashed stream; forestalled by transgressions (pš^{c}, v. 20), the Redeemer comes to establish righteousness in Jacob, to issue recompense.

The repetition of bw' in vv. 19b-20 emphasizes the context of the Lord's coming, especially with ky in v. 19b. The movement of this final strophe places the event of the Lord's coming at the close; emphasis is given to his arrival by its placement at the end, climaxing the Divine Warrior's intervention with salvation, vengeance, and just recompense. But beyond this buildup in the strophe, the repetition of *bw'* highlights two aspects in the general movement of the larger division of Isa 56-66.

First, the announcement of Yahweh's coming as Redeemer in v. 20 fulfills the opening pronouncement of 56:1b that soon God's salvation was to come. Structurally this is further achieved by the distant inversion of words which also describe the change in events.

56:1ba)	yšw^{c}ty	lbw'
59:20)	wb'	gw'l

The section 56-59 has moved from a call to observance because of the approach of salvation in 56:1, through a series of judgments and promises of deliverance (56:9--59:20), and now finally arrives at the coming of the Redeemer; that which had been announced is now realized in 59:19-20.[85] The whole movement of the literary units following the opening announcement of a forthcoming salvation hints at different aspects of God's promised redemption: the Lord will gather many peoples (56:8); he offers peace and healing to those near and far (57:19); the Lord will lead the people with righteousness and his glory as a rear guard (58:8). Yet these suggestions of a future deliverance do not specify the Lord's coming until 59:19-20 when it is announced that indeed he comes (*ky-ybw'*) as an oppressed stream driven forward by the breath of the Lord, yes he comes to Zion as Redeemer.

---

85. Karl ELLIGER comments on the relationship between 56:1 and 59:20 noting that only those who are rightly prepared share in the glorious coming of the Redeemer. Cf. "Der Prophet Tritojesaja," *ZAW* 49 (1931) 122.

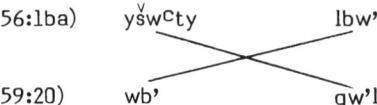

Second, the repetition of bw' in 59:19-20 also has an anticipatory function in this literary context, looking forward to Isa 60. The opening words of 60:1 reflect the coming of the Lord in the image of light: qwmy 'wry ky b' 'wrk. The importance of this motif related to the Lord's coming is verified by the eleven uses of bw' in Isa 60.[86] The rhetorical preparation for Isa 60 in 59:19-20 is also seen in other repetitions which reflect the predominance of salvation motifs that run through 60:1--63:6; consider the following diagram which shows the vocabulary of 59:19-20 also found in Isa 60.

1) šm-YHWH (59:19; 60:9)

2) zrḥ (59:19; 60:1,2)

3) kbwd (59:19; 60:1)

4) ṣywn (59:20; 60:14)[87]

5) gw'l (59:20; 60:16)

6) y^{c}qb (59:20; 60:16)

In their literary contexts, each of these words portrays different aspects of the description of the Lord's coming salvation. Thus, 59:19-20 serves not only to conclude the section begun in 56:1 with the fulfillment of the initial announcement, but also it anticipates the glorious acts of God's salvation which carry into the following Chapter, Isa 60.

---

86. Cf. Isa 60:1,4,4,5,6,9,11,13,17,17,20.

87. References to Zion/Jerusalem occur in 56-59 in examples of metonymy (hr-qdšy in 56:7; 57:13c) with the exception of 59:20 where Zion is explicitly mentioned. Thus the employment of lṣywn this one time just before the beginning of Isa 60 anticipates a greater emphasis given to it as a place of honor (cf. Zion at 60:14; 61:3; 62:1,11; and Jerusalem at 62:1,6,7) in the following section.

The description of the Lord's coming in 59:19b employs a simile in likening his arrival to an oppressed stream (knhr ṣr) which the breath of the Lord drives onward. In his Estudios de Poética Hebrea, Alonso Schökel draws attention to the diverse images of water used in Isa to describe different events, effects, and situations.[88] More recently, this same author shows how the image of water can define the structure and unity of Pss 42-43.[89] Though it is not the intention of the following brief observation to imply that the structure of 56-59 can be discerned by its images of water, there are three such examples which portray a description of three distinct characterizations.

In 57:20-21 the wicked are portrayed as an agitating sea that is unable to rest; their tumultuous character is further strengthened by the image of waters flinging mire and slime.[90] Immediately preceding in v. 19 is the contrasting description of the Lord's magnanimous offer of peace and healing; yet v. 21 comments that for those wicked, compared to the destructive sea, there is no peace. Thus the exposé of the wicked is a characterization which specifies them as a people of tumult, unable to rest, and devoid of peace.

In 58:11 those who put into practice the Lord's understanding of a true fast are likened to a well-watered garden and a spring of water that does not deceive, that is, it satisfies thirst (58:11a). The imagery here portrays the

---

88. Cf. ALONSO SCHÖKEL, Estudios de Poética Hebrea, 282-94.

89. Cf. Luis ALONSO SCHÖKEL, "The Poetic Structure of Psalm 42-43," JSOT 1 (1976) 4-11.

90. Cf. ALONSO SCHÖKEL, Estudios de Poética Hebrea, 290.

just individual as one who is life-giving, fecund, and not deceptive.[91] To those who put into practice what God commands there are the signs of vitality, growth, and truth.

Finally, the portrayal of the Lord as a pent-up stream driven onward by the rwḥ-YHWH carries a sense of power and determination. Here one imagines a raging current of water that has been pent-up and now rushes forth to follow its course; not only does it break forth from its hold, but it is compelled forward by the force of the Lord's own breath. The water imagery in 59:19b paints a portrait of the Lord resolved to run the breadth of his course until his task is accomplished. Thus, the three images of water used in 57:20-21, 58:11, and 59:19 distinguish the three main characterizations which predominate in this section: the wicked, the righteous, and the Lord of salvation.

This final strophe moves away from the previous developments of the judgment theme to that of salvation. The whole of vv. 15-20 looks forward to an act of restoration about to take place as the Divine Warrior draws near to intervene in a situation torn apart by the loss of justice and righteousness.[92] The vocabulary of vv. 16b-17a announces the coming of salvation (yšw^{c}h) and deliverance (ṣdqh) as Yahweh prepares for battle against the forces of evil (v. 15). The Lord's arm of salvation (v. 16) brings about a transformation to usher in recompense according to one's deeds (v. 18) and reverence for his glory and his name (v. 19). But as it is seen in the previous literary units, the

91. LACK discusses 58:11 as a "vegetal" motif, indicative of true justice and the blessings of salvation. Cf. La symbolique, 136-37, 244.

92. Cf. HANSON, The Dawn of Apocalyptic, 132-33.

description of the approaching redemption touches upon the need for a renewal in the way one accepts the Lord's commands and then puts them into practice; the Redeemer comes to those who turn away transgression.[93] Similarly in 57:19-21 and 58:6-14, the promises of salvation emerge in a context emphasizing the movement away from wickedness and inauthentic practices to a pathway charted by God's word of command. Furthermore, this understanding of salvation resonates with the opening command of 56:1 where the word issues that the people are to practice justice for salvation is coming soon. As pointed out in the study of 56:1 with the play on the repetition of ṣdqh, the practice of righteousness (ṣdqh) is intimately connected with the promise of deliverance (ṣdqh); in 59 this same employment of ṣdqh as righteousness (vv. 4,9,14) and deliverance (vv. 16,17) shows the same notion at work in this unit, echoing 56:1 in a more developed manner. Redemption comes for those who turn away transgression (59:20), who keep justice and practice righteousness (56:1).

In 59:21 the repetition of ʼmr YHWH at the beginning and end of the verse plus the change from poetic to prose verse structure suggest that it stands apart; as noted earlier, some commentators speak of v. 21 as a bridge between 59 and the series of eschatological poems that follows in 60:1--63:6.[94] Though 59:21 is not part of the literary unit under consideration, a brief word about its placement and vocabulary may aid in understanding its function.

---

93. The translation of lšby (59:20) in its participial construction emphasizes with a metaphorical image the active manner of "pushing back, turning away" transgression. While the RSV and NAB render it "turning away from transgression," such a translation does not carry as active and dynamic a quality for the participle.

94. See Chapter One, p. 27.

In 59:21 the Lord announces that his covenant is with them (probably related to v. 20, those in Jacob who turn away transgression). The word bryt (covenant) appears only in 56:4,6 and 61:8 in the context of 56-66. In 56:4,6 attention focuses on adherence to prescribed precepts, with a promise of blessing; the message in 61:8 echoes a similar understanding of covenant with concern for justice and the assurance of faithful recompense by giving them renown among the nations.

> For I the Lord love justice (mšpṭ)
> I hate robbery and wrong;
> I will faithfully give them their recompense,
> and I will make an everlasting covenant (wbryt ^{c}wlm) with them.
> Their descendants shall be known among the nations,
> and their offspring in the midst of the peoples;
> All who see them will acknowledge them,
> that they are the people the Lord has blessed. (Isa 61:8-9)

The relationship between "just deeds" and "promise of blessing" touches on the uses of bryt in 56-66; God's covenant with the people highlights both aspects of living according to his decrees and sharing in the assured benefits announced by the Lord. In 56:4,6 and 61:8 the contexts where bryt recurs highlight the relationship between the faithful promise made by Yahweh and the importance of fidelity to God's message for full participation in the bonds of bryt. In 59:21 the bestowal of covenant brings to the faithful people God's spirit (rwḥy) and words (wdbry); these words shall not depart from the mouth of his people from this time forward (v. 21). The presence of God's word assures both living according to his covenant precepts and sharing in the benefits of that treaty. With the appearance of bryt in 56:4,6 and 61:8 resonating a similar message, 59:21 recalls the word of instruction and promise and also anticipates this motif within the eschatological poems of 60:1--63:6. Furthermore the recurrence of rwḥ in 59:21 echoes its use in 57:15-16 where God promises a revival to life by the spirit proceeding from himself; rwḥ also anticipates the bestowal of the spirit of the Lord God in 61:1 to share in the mission of redemption.

Though sketched in broad strokes, one can see how 59:21 bears the characteristics of a hinge verse, reviving the "covenant" and "spirit" motifs of 56-59, while also looking to their further development in the subsequent chapters.[95] As D.R. Jones points out, the placement of bryty in 59:21 opens one to the fuller awareness of the marvelous covenant promises about to unfold in Isa 60;[96] as 60:1 begins by echoing the salvific images of light, glory, and Yahweh's coming among the people, there is a greater appreciation of the bonds of unity with 56-59. 59:21 prepares the way for an understanding of 60:1--63:6 as a further expansion of God's offer of salvation in covenant.

III. APPLICATION OF A LITERARY DEVICE TO ISAIAH 59:1-20

Throughout the rhetorical analysis of 56-59 examples of repetition both argue for the coherence of the individual literary units and demonstrate networks of correspondences. Beyond these elements of continuity within each poem, there are also recurrences of words among the literary units which link them together by a similarity of motifs. More recently H.V.D. Parunak proposes that there are ways of distinguishing emphasis and order in the biblical texts by

---

95. See note 71 of this Chapter.

96. Douglas Rawlings JONES, Isaiah 56-66 and Joel (Torch Bible Paperbacks 20; London: SCM Press, 1971) 64.

means of different structural features;[97] among the devices, repetition plays a key role. Parunak notes that as contemporary modes of printing today direct a reader's or listener's attention by means of a table of contents, chapter headings, section titles, and paragraph divisions, the biblical texts also have means by which devices guide one through these ancient writings.[98] The clues to perceiving these indicators of structure are not similar to what characterize contemporary ways of exposing the whole and its component parts; the different means of emphasis employed by the ancients call for an approach to the text which surveys the diverse ways of ordering the biblical texts. This final consideration of Isa 59 builds on the principle that the repetitions of words and word pairs is a way that the biblical texts can be structured.[99]

It is noted on pp. 249-50 that the word pair mšpṭ//ṣdqh, located at the opening of the second and third strophes and at the pivot in v. 14, recalls the opening words of the section in 56:1a. But also, the word pairs yšw^{c}h//ṣdqh of vv. 16b-17a recall 56:1b where they appear as parallels. These occurrences in Isa 59 reflect the ABCB pattern of 56:1 both by the repetition of word pairs and by their ordering in the Chapter; the following diagram distinguishes the similar structural elements in 56:1 and 59.

---

97. Cf. PARUNAK, "Oral Typesetting," 153-55.

98. Cf. PARUNAK, "Oral Typesetting," 153-55.

99. For an affirmation of this principle, see the comments of EXUM, "Promise and Fulfillment," 44-45; PARUNAK, "Oral Typsetting," 56-57.

Isa 59		Isa 56:1	
v. 4a	- bṣdq//nšpṭ	mšpṭ//ṣdqh	: AB elements of 56:1a
v. 9a	- mšpṭ//ṣdqh		
v. 14a	- mšpṭ//ṣdqh		
v. 16b	- wtwšᶜ//wṣdqtw	yšwᶜh//ṣdqh	: CB elements of 56:1b
v. 17a	- ṣdqh//yšwᶜh		

The ordered occurrence of the AB and CB elements in 59 suggests a relationship between the ABCB pattern of 56:1 and the whole of Isa 59. The repetition of word pairs, their key positions throughout the poem, and the two blocks of ordered AB and CB elements in Isa 59 reflect a literary situation which resonates with the initial command of 56:1a and the announcement of 56:1b. As Muilenburg emphasizes, the repetition of vocabulary is part of a literary style in the Bible which seeks to demonstrate continuity and synthesis;[100] here in Isa 59, the elements of the ABCB pattern of 56:1 give a literary structure which develops the initial themes of the division and provides a sense of closure to the section. Beyond the repetitions in the word pairs, the ABC elements also occur separately and in another pair: cf. mhwšyᶜ in v. 1a; mšpṭ in v. 15b; and lmšpṭ//lyšwᶜh in v. 11b.

The repetitions of the ABC elements in Isa 59 hint at the significance of the opening words in 56:1, both in terms of their structure (exhortation and salvation announcement) and their interpretation in this literary context. An analysis of the recurrences of mšpṭ, ṣdqh, and yšwᶜh in Isa 59 attempts to show how these words function in their literary context.

---

100. Cf. MUILENBURG, "A Study in Hebrew Rhetoric," 99.

In the opening verse of Isa 59 mhwšy^c appears for the first time since 56:1b where it announced God's approaching salvation (yšw^{c}ty lbw'). In 59:1-3 the absence both of the Lord's saving hand and attentive ear is a sign of the separation that comes between the people and God because of their sins. The first use of yšw^{c}h since 56:1 harkens one back to that initial statement about the coming of salvation. God's deliverance walks hand-in-hand with the exercise of justice and righteousness. In contrast to the message of 56:1, the broad references to sinfulness in 59:2 and the specific violations in 59:3 demonstrate the demise of justice and hence, the absence of God's saving hand and attentive ear.

The first AB pair comes in 59:4 with bṣdq//nšpṭ; the two points expressed here show the lack of righteousnes and its effects in the injustice shown others. Set in imagery depicting a courtroom scene with pronouncements and judgments, the succeeding verses of the strophe describe the negative effects of the wicked on others.[101] Their words result in death (v. 5b), the shedding of innocent blood (v. 7a), and useless products (v. 6a). Those who follow in the footsteps of the unjust come to the same end--they are without peace (v. 8). The imagery of vv. 4-8 evokes a harsh word of judgment against the unrighteous for the far-reaching effects which threaten the peace, well-being, and life of those they afflict.

A transition takes place in v. 9 which is suggested by the inverted order of the AB elements in vv. 4a, 9a.

---

101. Even though the imagery remains obscure (i.e. the serpents and spiders), there is little doubt that the effects of the evildoers on others are negative.

v. 4a) bṣdq — nšpṭ

v. 9a) mšpṭ — ṣdqh

The repetition of ṣdqh and mšpṭ unites the pronouncement of unrighteousness and injustice in v. 4a with the people's lament over the absence of justice and righteousness in v. 9a. But what is noteworthy is the turn of events which takes place between the second and third strophes: in lamenting their situation, they acknowledge the fate which they have created for themselves (vv. 9ff). The repetition and inversion of these key words in vv. 4a,9a highlight the inherent relationship between deeds and consequences; the stifling of righteousness and justice portrayed in vv. 4-8 has produced a situation where these qualities of life they seek are far off (vv. 9-12). The connection between "actions" and their "results" is also shown in the repetition of mwt in vv. 5b,10b. Using metaphorical language, v. 5b shows the wicked one produces something which leads to death for those who eat it; in v. 10b the people describe themselves as being like dead individuals among the vigorous. A similar end comes to those who inflict their death-dealing activities upon others; the labors of injustice toward others now return to their originators. The above examples of repetition demonstrate the transition that takes place in the second and third strophes as the people lament the lot which they have brought upon themselves by their own unrighteousness.

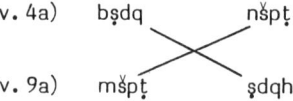

To further clarify the sense of mšpṭ in the third strophe, consider the repetitions in vv. 9aa,11bb. As explained on pp. 276-77 the recurrence of rḥq(h) and mmnw with mšpṭ and lyšw^{c}h form the A elements in a chiastic structure. These A elements unite the motifs of justice and salvation in a lament about their distance; these motifs are also joined in an internal relationship between the cola of v. 11b by the preposition l. The blending of these two motifs shows their interrelatedness, explaining that the remoteness of salvation is due, at least in part, to the remoteness of justice.[102] The opening bicolon of the strophe in v. 9a notes that both justice and righteousness are unapproachable: the final bicolon of the chiasm in v. 11b concludes the segment by affirming the absence and the distance of salvation. The elaboration of the effects of unrighteousness in vv. 9-11 reaches its conclusion in v. 11bb with a statement about the remoteness of redemption. The interrelatedness of righteousness//justice and salvation recalls the beginning of this section in 56:1 where the command for its observance springs from the announcement of God's forthcoming deliverance; now 59:9a,11b builds on this concept to affirm the absence of salvation because of injustice and unrighteousness.

The motif of remoteness from vv. 9-13 is repeated in v. 14 with mšpṭ and ṣdqh. In v. 14a, rḥq appears for its third and final time in Isa 59. In noting its other occurrences in vv. 9a,11b, there is a buildup of vocabulary which is described as being far away.

v. 9aa - ᶜl-kn rḥq mšpṭ mmnw

v. 11bb - lyšwᶜh rḥqh mmnw

v. 14ab - wṣdqh mrḥwq tᶜmd

The three nouns portrayed as remote are the ABC elements of the ABCB pattern from 56:1. At this turning point in the poem, all that was called for and

102. Cf. SCULLION, "ṢEDEQ-ṢEDAQAH," 344-45.

announced in 56:1 is far off: the observance of righteousness and justice are distant, the anticipated salvation remains remote. The use of <u>mšpṭ</u>, <u>ṣdqh</u>, and <u>yšwᶜh</u> with <u>rḥq</u> paints a picture of the alienation brought on by sin. Following upon the confession of vv. 12-13, the assessment of the ravages of transgression in v. 14 shows how humanity, figuratively speaking, keeps away the practice of justice, and in effect, stifles the approach of salvation. As Muilenburg points out, the admission of revolt in v. 13 possesses an antithetical character to the debilitated virtues of v. 14.[103] With <u>mšpṭ</u>, <u>yšwᶜh</u>, and now <u>ṣdqh</u> far from the scene, the stage is set for the Lord's deliverance.

The change from the AB to CB pairs in v. 16b initiates the process of restoring redemption; the arm of the Lord brings about salvation. The change is further supported by the example of distant parallelism with <u>yd//zrᶜ</u> in vv. 1aa,16ba and the repetition of <u>yšᶜ</u>.[104]

v. 1aa) hn l'-qṣrh <u>yd-YHWH</u> <u>mhwšyᶜ</u>

v. 16ba) <u>wtwšᶜ</u> lw <u>zrᶜw</u>

The intervention of the Lord's redemptive action in v. 16b resonates with the opening words of the poem; a turn of events takes place as the absence of the Lord's hand in v. 1 changes to a mediatory action with his arm bringing about salvation in v. 16b. The word pair in v.16b, <u>wtwšᶜ//wṣdqtw</u>, shows the source of salvation to be grounded in the Divine Warrior: <u>his</u> arm brings about salvation,

---

103. Cf. MUILENBURG, "The Book of Isaiah," 693.

104. For further examples of the parallel pair <u>yd//zrᶜ</u>, see Deut 4:34; 5:15; 7:19; 11:2; 26:8; 2 Sam 22:35; 1 Kgs 8:42; 2 Chr 6:32; Pss 18:34; 89:13,21; 136:12.

his righteousness sustains him. Vv. 15b-16a indicate that there is no one to intercede so that the task of establishing deliverance rests alone with him.[105] The same emphasis on the Lord as the source of salvation is reflected in the announcement in 56:1b where the pronominal suffix is repeated in yšwᶜty and wṣdqty; there in 56:1b the Lord speaks and specifies that the salvation and righteousness which are approaching belong to him.

What one sees in Isa 59 is a literary unit which reflects the opening words of the section in 56:1 both structurally and thematically. Isa 59 enlivens the importance of the opening command and proclamation of salvation in 56:1. To use another image, 56:1 is the skeletal message of the relationship between right and just actions and salvation, while 59 is the flesh and blood which enlivens the impact of that kernel message with literary development. As 56:1a issues the order to practice justice and righteousness, 59:1-14 explains the impact brought on by the decline of righteousness and justice. As 56:1b announces the coming of God's salvation, 59:15-20 portrays the arrival of redemption in the image of the Divine Warrior. As 56:1a states the fundamental components for sharing in God's salvation, 59:1-14 describes the absence of the Lord's redeeming power when right and just ways are abandoned. As 56:1b emphasizes that God's own deliverance (yšwᶜty, wṣdqty) is drawing near, 59:15-20 affirms that the power to redeem rests in the Lord alone who comes in glory.

As a whole, Isa 59 portrays the word of God as a medium of communication which is faithful and true, holding firm to what it announces. As

---

105. Cf. HANSON, The Dawn of Apocalyptic, 124; MUILENBURG, "The Book of Isaiah," 694-95; SCULLION, "ṢEDEQ-ṢEDAQAH," 345.

56:1 calls for the keeping of righteous and just ways in order to share in God's deliverance, Isa 59 attests to the truth of those words by showing how the absence of virtue keeps God's saving hand at a distance. Isa 59 is a confirmation of the necessity of righteous living if one hopes to partake in the benefits of the Lord's saving help. To the very end of the poem this notion is upheld, with the concluding thought that, "yes, the Redeemer comes to Zion, but to those who turn away transgression from their lives." Though 59:19-20 leads into the description of God's eschatological coming, the call to right living remains the fundamental word for participation in the Lord's saving strength.

Thus the whole of Isa 59 concludes the first section of this division by enlivening and expanding upon the opening words of 56:1. Isa 59 points back to the significance of the initial message of 56:1 and also brings those words to pass in announcing the coming of the Redeemer to Zion for those who turn away transgression in their lives.

IV. SUMMARY

Isa 59 gives indications of being a poem well-constructed and strong in its different uses of imagery. The absence of God's saving hand at the beginning changes with a conclusion describing the arrival of the Redeemer to Zion. The repetition of key words like YHWH, yš^{c}, mšpṭ, and ṣdqh forms a network of interweaving themes that show how the lack of righteousness and justice prevent the Lord's deliverance from coming to the people who seek it.

The pronouncement of sinfulness and the description of wicked deeds build the theme of judgment in vv. 1-8. But the usual "sentencing" is here replaced by a lament and confession in vv. 9-13. And yet the vocabulary and imagery continue the emphasis on judgment already begun in vv. 1-8; the people accuse themselves and show how their deeds have already sentenced them to a dreadful fate. The death they had inflicted on others (vv. 5b,7a) now falls back upon themselves (v. 10b). But the judgment scene gives way to hope as vv. 15-20 announce the coming of salvation in the image of the Divine Warrior. This movement from judgment-to-salvation is similar to the basic structure of the two preceding literary units (cf. 56:9--57:13 and 57:14-21; 58:1-5 and 58:6-14), and thus shows a continuity in the construction of the literary units.

The change in speakers through the course of Isa 59 distinguishes the delimitations of the strophes. The pronominal suffixes also highlight the different emphases in the progression from strophe to strophe: attention is drawn to "your" sins in strophe I, to "their" deeds in II, to "our" transgressions in III, and to "his" mighty actions in IV. The hinge at v. 14 functions as the turning point in the poem, describing the utter absence of virtue, which leads into the Lord's intervention to rectify the situation.

The different macrostructures within the strophes are distinguished by the numerous repetitions of words, particles, and points of grammatical syntax in close proximity to one another. These recurrences articulate the motifs clearly and argue for the unity of the poem.

In several ways, Isa 59 brings the whole of 56-59 to a sense of closure or completion. First, the repetitions of vocabulary with similar contextual meaning from the three previous literary units bring these motifs forward for consideration a final time before the text moves into the eschatologial poems of Isa 60:1--63:6. The motifs of "avoiding evil" and "the right practice of deeds" in the Introduction (56:1-8) recur again in Isa 59. The earlier motifs of "the way," "knowledge," "peace," and "transgressions" are integral parts of the development of this poem. These motifs establish ties between the poems and argue for the integrity of the section (56-59).

Second, the emphasis on the Lord's coming salvation, which begins the section in 56:1, finally reaches its fulfillment in 59:19-20. The promised salvation arrives as a Redeemer for Zion.

Third, the opening ABCB pattern of 56:1 is also the literary structure which governs the concluding literary unit. The placement of the AB and CB elements in an ordered structure in Isa 59 establishes the ties between the beginning and end of the whole section. The use of the ABC elements is integral to the interpretation of the whole poem; the whole chapter functions as a commentary on the initial command and announcement of 56:1.

Several theological themes are developed in the poem. Isa 59 points out the effect of sinfulness, showing its devastating influence both on those who are unjust and those whom their injustice reaches. The absence of salvation and God's intervention is recalled throughout, depicting a situation which is at its breaking point. Two images of God emerge. First, there is the all-powerful Lord who is the only One who can reverse the pitiable state in which these people find themselves; salvation cannot exist without his strong arm to bring it about. Second, there is the Lord who in his deliverance is totally just, and in bringing redemption also distributes recompense according to one's deeds. The Lord who demands justice of his people also binds himself to show total justice to all, both deliverance and recompense.

CHAPTER SIX

CONCLUSIONS

This study of Isa 56-59 demonstrates the various strands of unity working together in the literary units, strophes, macro- and microstructures. On several levels rhetorical criticism shows how the poetry in this section of Isa operates as a unified whole. This concluding Chapter sketches broadly the recurring patterns distinguishing prominent poetic devices, the thematic structure of 56-59, and the motifs and themes constituting its religious teaching.

I. POETIC DEVICES

Numerous poetic devices are demonstrated in the analysis of Isa 56-59 including alliteration, assonance, chiasm, contrast, delayed identification, distant parallelism, functions of particles, hendiadys, hinge verse, inclusion, merism, metonymy, onomatopoeia, paronomasia, recapitulation, repetition, rhetorical question, rhyme, rhythm, and uses of <u>waw</u>. The four devices of repetition, chiasm, distant parallelism, and hinge verse stand out as recurring and unifying poetic techniques in this section of Isa.

Most of the structures presented in this study are built on the understanding that repetition is a unifying principle. Lest this notion be confined to root words, the analysis shows that the repetition of sounds, images, particles, and motifs strengthens the bonds of unity in individual poems and among the whole ensemble. For example, the repetition of sounds in a regular pattern establishes ties between 57:14 and 57:19b; also the recurring combination of ṣ and m in words throughout 58 subtly rcalls the motif of fasting (ṣwm). The images of light and darkness in 58:8,10 and 59:9 describe the promixity and distance of salvation in a contrasting manner. This present study shows the numerous ways that repetition is used in structuring Hebrew poetry, employing it as a technique for establishing continuity and development of thought in Isa 56-59.

Different styles of chiasm are found in the poetry under consideration; examples of inverted word pairs, semantic-sonant patterns, and concentric design recur several times throughout. Governing the limits of the section is the inversion of elements in 56:1b and 59:20 first announcing the coming of God's salvation and concluding with the message that the Lord comes as Redeemer; the shifting of words in 56:1b and 59:20 signals the change that occurs, moving from an initial proclamation to its fulfillment. The concentric design in 58 exhibits how a chiastic structure alters ideas in the transposition of words (for the diagram see p. 233); this structural device highlights the transformation from a former to a renewed manner of fasting. Scholarly opinion supports the varied forms of chiastic style in ancient writings as a frequently employed device;[1] its recurrent use in Isa 56-59 witnesses to this convention as a means of structure and interpretation.

1. A. STOCK presents a summary article discussing the manner of education among ancient civilizations where chiasm played a fundamental role in both oral and written rhetoric; his article shows the subsequent influence on literary style. Cf. "Chiastic Awareness and Education in Antiquity," BTB 14 (1984) 23-27.

The examples of distant parallelism show it to be a device which fosters a greater sense of unity within and among the literary units. Referring back to the inverted word pair in 56:1b and 59:20, yšw^{c}ty//gw'l marks off the limits of the section. Two examples where word pairs serve as inclusions (lbw'//mqbṣ in 56:1,8, and mhwšy^{c}//gw'l in 59:1,20) distinguish the convention as a means of delimiting a unit. And the distant parallels 'tyw//ybw' in 56:9 and 57:2, and yd^{c}w//mbyn in 56:10 and 57:1b argue for the ties between two strophes which several commentators distinguish as unrelated. Further examples of this device hopefully will encourage exegetes to search for more illustrations of this unifying device.

The three samples of hinge verses in 57:6, 58:5, and 59:14 present a technique of transition becoming better known by those interested in devices of structure. By means of repeated words the hinge functions to recall previous motifs and to anticipate new ones. In 58:5 and 59:14 the hinge stands at the turning points of the poems where the theme of judgment is concluding and that of salvation is about to begin. In both 58:5 and 59:14 the literary contexts describe a situation in need of reform and look forward to a remedy; these verses await a change where the Lord's instruction (58:6-14) and intervention (59:15-20) offer a promise of redemptive resolve. Then in 57:6 the hinge verse shifts attention with a change of speaker to prepare for the descriptive account of Israel's idolatry in vv. 7-10, while describing their allotment for the wicked deeds previously portrayed. These examples of hinge verses exhibit the refined way in which the poetry of Isa 56-59 ushers the reader into a new development by reviving old motifs and hinting at new ones.

The various poetic devices displayed in Isa 56-59 not only reveal the careful literary construction of the poems but aid in conveying a message. Beyond their artful and aesthetic qualities, the rhetorical features serve as keys to unlocking the treasures of ancient texts which discuss fundamental principles of religious faith.

II. THE THEMATIC STRUCTURE OF ISAIAH 56-59

The aim of this consideration is to show the thematic patterns which constitute the major building blocks of a linear reading of Isa 56-59. Having completed a detailed analysis, the discussion of the overall structure can be brief, paraphrasing the thematic developments and movements which characterize the individual units and the whole complement.

The introductory character of 56:1-8 is established both by the ABCB pattern carrying through from 56:1 to the succeeding chapters and the internal inclusion of 56:1-8 and 66:18-24 forming bookends in this final division of Isa. Beyond these rhetorical devices, an interplay between themes of observance and salvific promise takes place in vv. 1-8. The opening verse issues the command to practice justice, followed by the announcement of God's approaching deliverance. The message to the eunuchs and foreigners imitates 56:1 by an instruction for holding fast to the covenant (vv. 4,6) and immediately is succeeded by a promise of the favors coming to those who observe God's decrees (vv. 5,7). Thus the opening literary unit of the section mingles the themes of observance and salvific promise, highlighting the understanding that a share of God's deliverance expects adherence to his decrees.

The second literary unit (56:9--57:21) breaks the thematic pattern of "observance-promise of salvation" in 56:1-8 and initiates a new pattern which continues through the three subsequent poems. The progression of themes moves from a word of judgment to a promise of salvation. In 56:9--57:21 the opening two stanzas present a message of judgment by a double indictment directed against the irresponsible leaders of Israel (56:9--57:2) and those practicing idolatry (57:3-13). A promise of salvation (57:14-21) follows the double word of judgment. The offer of redemption in 57:14-21 looks forward to a revitalization of the humble and contrite, a pledge of guidance and comfort to those smitten by God, and an assurance of peace and healing for those who are not wicked. The thematic movement in 56:9--57:21 is from judgment to salvation.

In 58:1-5 there is a transition back to the theme of judgment as the transgression and sins of the house of Jacob are enumerated. These verses present the charges which God brings against his people for their lack of righteousness and their wicked actions accompanying their day of fasting. Then in vv. 6-14 Yahweh explains the kind of fasting he chooses and lists the salvific gifts accompanying such actions. The people complain that God is unattentive to them (v. 3); but the ensuing instruction by God shows them how to fast so as to be heard and responded to (v. 9b). Salvation will come to the house of Jacob when it shares in the Lord's own deeds of liberation toward others, forsaking the ways of wickedness (vv. 6-7). The thematic movement in 58:1-14 progresses from a word of judgment to a promise of salvation.

The theme of judgment returns and pervades 59:1-13. The people are told that their sinfulness is the cause of their separation from God (vv. 1-3). The judgment theme carries special weight in the second and third strophes where the repetition of mwt (death, vv. 5,10) establishes a relationship between their deeds and the consequences of those deeds; the accused people who have sown seeds of death now reap a harvest of death. The fate they bring upon themselves comes as a result of their own actions. The hinge verse in 59:14 portrays the demise of virtue and sets the stage for the arrival of Yahweh, the one who can transform the situation. The theme changes in 59:15-20 as the Divine Warrior brings salvation and deliverance; the Lord's advent is portrayed in solemn fashion, his name and his glory provoking fear in all the people of the earth. Thus the thematic movement in 59:1-20 proceeds from a word of judgment to an announcement of salvation.

Based on the patterns discussed above, the following diagram sketches a thematic structure in Isa 56-59.

1) Introduction: Observance ⟶ Promise of Salvation

2) Judgment ⟶ Salvation

3) Judgment ⟶ Salvation

4) Judgment ⟶ Salvation

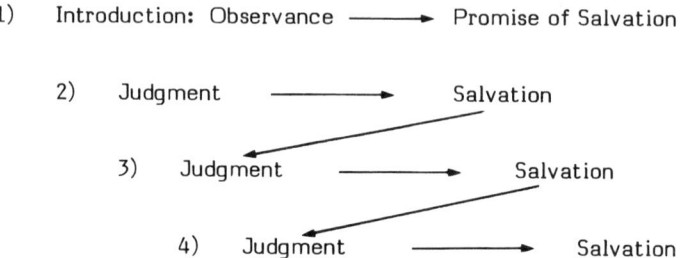

Reading Isa 56-59 in a linear fashion with its thematic content in full view exhibits a recurring pattern. Following the Introduction, the three succeeding poems demonstrate a thematic arrangement moving from a word of judgment to a promise of salvation.[2] The consistent pattern of these three units separates them from the Introduction and suggests a unity of style which brings the themes of judgment and salvation into relationship with one another. (The significance of the juxtaposition of these two themes is discussed in Section III of this Chapter.) An appreciation for the overall similar structure of units 2,3,4 further establishes the introductory unit as distinct from the others; while a detailed analysis shows the Introduction is connected to the poems that follow, it is also distinct.

A further point underscores a common basis of integration in all four units: the theme of salvation. The opening exhortations in 56:1-8 appear as instructions showing the way to share in redemptive blessings. The succeeding three literary units show that though the word of judgment is present, it is not the final word; rather the structure shows that the word of judgment eventually gives way to an instruction for sharing in salvation.

Such a schematization of basic themes has its drawbacks when following upon a verse by verse analysis; this kind of Overview can tend to diminish the unique character of each unit by broadly subsuming varied motifs under general categorizations. On the other hand, attention to broad internal movement can enable one to see a way in which units resemble one another, form a pattern, and distinguish themes. Furthermore, the discovery of a pattern in Isa 56-59 may help in recognizing other similar or contrasting structures in

2. W. VOGELS shows a similar thematic pattern occurring in Hos 1-3; cf. " 'Osée - Gomer' car et comme 'Yahweh - Israël,' Os 1-3," NRT 103 (1981) 719-20.

60-66 or earlier parts of Isa. Even in Isa 56-59 the consistent attention to salvation provides a context for appreciating the predominant redemptive motifs and images in 60:1--63:6 which immediately follows.

III. MOTIFS AND THEMES IN ISAIAH 56-59

This final section of the Conclusion distinguishes the major motifs and the themes which appear several times in Isa 56-59. The recurrence of root words and the juxtaposition of thematic patterns within the individual units exhibit different aspects of subject matter which together give the section its unique character. Arising from the rhetorical analysis of Chapters Two through Five, the discussion of motifs and themes displays the continuity of thought and the development of theological topics in Isa 56-59.

A. Righteousness and Justice

As Muilenburg points out, the positioning of key words in strategic places of literary units often directs the reader to its major motifs;[3] this observation holds true in Isa 56-59 as the opening words call for the keeping of justice and the practice of righteousness. The positioning of this word pair in other key places in a stylistic manner demonstrates the importance of mšpṭ//ṣdqh throughout the section.[4]

---

3. Cf. MUILENBURG, "Form Criticism," 16-17.

4. The word pair appears in a chiastic ordering in 58:2 and also begins the strophes in 58:4,9, and the hinge verse in 59:14.

The initial command of the section is a call to practice justice and righteousness, but pulsating through the poems is the lamentable demise of these virtues. Each context where these words appear describes a scene of judgment where the actions of the people are specified (58:2; 59:4; cf. also 57:12) and the consequences of their deeds are mourned (59:9,14). The opening command of 56:1 sets off a chain of motifs repeating that justice and righteousness have vanished among the people.

From the literary context, how can one discern the sense of justice and righteousness in these chapters of Isa? To begin a consideration of this question, reference is made to Gerhard von Rad's discussion of righteousness; he writes,

> There is absolutely no concept in the Old Testament with so central a significance for all relationships of human life as that of ṣdqh. It is the standard not only for man's relationship to God but also his relationship to his fellows, reaching right down to the most petty wranglings--indeed, it is even the standard for man's relationship to the animals and to his natural environment. Ṣdqh can be described without much ado as the highest value in life, that upon which all life rests when it is properly ordered.[5]

As other authors note, mšpṭ similarly often expresses the connotation of relationship.[6] Taking a lead from von Rad, one can see how pervasive the idea of relationship is in the contexts where these words appear. In 57:12 the mocking threat to announce the harlot Israel's righteousness arises from a broken union with God because of idolatrous practices. The feigned practices of justice

---

5. Cf. G. von RAD, Old Testament Theology, vol. 1 (D.M.G. Stalker, trans.; New York: Harper and Row, 1962-65) 370.

6. Cf. F. BÜCHSEL and V. HERNTRICH, "krinō," TDNT 3, 926.

and righteousness before Yahweh while simultaneously oppressing one's neighbor in 58:2-4 describe a ruptured relationship with both God and humanity. In 59:4 the lack of righteous dealings and their unjust consequences inflict others (59:4-8) and bring about separation from God (59:1-3). And in 59:9-11 the demise of righteousness and justice portrays humanity's alienation from itself; that for which the people search is unattainable because the fractured relationship with God and man forestalls the arrival of salvation. Thus in seeing the larger context of Isa 56-59 one can better understand the implications of the call to practice justice and righteousness in 56:1; it is a summons to embrace the ways of right relationship with God and with neighbor.

The text points to concrete manifestations of right relationship on both levels. Toward God, righteousness expresses itself in trust and confidence that Yahweh is the only One who can save (57:13); this implies that one finds their strength in nothing but the Lord God who holds the power to revive and renew (cf. 57:8,10,15-18). Also right relationship with God calls for adherence to his word of instruction (58:6-14) where he teaches his people to share in his redemptive ways of liberation. Toward one's neighbor, righteousness is practiced in the gift of self (58:7b,10a) in addition to caring for the necessities of life (58:6-7). In establishing right relationship with God and with neighbor, one lives the essential message of the call to justice and righteousness.

B. The Ways of God and of Humanity

The manner in which the ten occurrences of drk distinguish between the ways of God (57:14,14; 58:2) and of humanity (56:11; 57:10,17,18; 58:13;

59:8,8) echoes a motif very familiar in the Bible. To note only one example, the opening poem of the Psalter distinguishes that there are two paths of living, according to the way of the righteous and of the wicked; the way of the righteous leads to God's care and that of the wicked to destruction.[7] A similar pattern is found with the uses of drk in Isa 56-59. The irresponsible leaders who walk in their own way of covetousness bring a harsh judgment upon themselves (56:11); also the untiring efforts of harlot Israel, walking in the ways of infidelity, fail to assure her the deliverance she seeks from her gods (57:10-13). However the way which Yahweh prepares for his people points out the paths leading to redemption (57:14-16).

The importance of the "way" motif is also seen in its relationship to the Introduction at 56:1-8. The opening unit is interspersed with exhortations (56:1-2,3-4,6) emphasizing a call to observe just and righteous practices and to hold fast to the covenant. The repetitious manner in which drk recurs keeps before the reader the ways of true justice according to God's word and those of unrighteousness according to man's wishes. As the exhortations in 56:1-8 show that adherence to God's word promises blessing (56:2,5,7) so do the references to drk complement this idea (57:14-16) but also show the judgment and punishment coming to those who walk in their own ways (56:11; 57:17; 59:8). Thus the teaching in 56:1-8 that observance of righteousness leads to blessing is complemented in the following poems by the varied references to the ways of God and of humanity.

---

7. Cf. A.A. ANDERSON, The Book of Psalms, vol. 1 (New Century Bible Commentary; London: Oliphants, 1972) 63.

C. Transgression

Among the words that constitute the vocabulary of "sin" in 56-59, <u>pšc</u> appears most regularly in each of the three units after the Introduction. In each of its contexts, "transgression" is presented in a distinctive manner. In 57:4 the people are distinguished as part of a long line of sinners, children of transgression. As the structure of 57:3-5 reveals in the analysis, the heart of their transgression is expressed as a jeering mockery of God; they practice sorcery and idolatry, deceiving Yahweh. The exegesis of 58:1-4 shows that the reference of "their transgression" (58:1) again points to a revolt against God; they forsake him by feigning practices of justice and righteousness (58:2). And finally in 59:12-13, the people acknowledge that their transgressions are known both before God and before themselves, and they proceed to describe them as a denial of the Lord and a turning away from their God.

The contexts where "trangression" appears explain the reason for judgment: the house of Jacob is steeped in its revolt against God. The contexts of judgment where this term recurs express the abandonment of God's way of righteousness and a pursuit of deeds that manifest their alienation from the divinity. Reading 59:14 in relation to what precedes it in vv. 13-14, one sees the effects of transgression as v. 14 portrays the situation in bleak terms; the power of transgression is shown in the demise of justice and righteousness. Thus the contexts where "transgression" recurs demonstrate its gravity and potential for destruction of a way of life which can offer redemption; Israel's transgression is forsaking God and his ways of justice.

D. Knowledge

The knowledge motif in Isa 56-59 has a quasi-narrative character where one can follow its development from a lack to a fulfillment of knowledge. The leaders of Israel are said to be men without knowledge (56:10,11,11). As watchmen over the people they fail to fulfill their function as guards; like mute dogs they are unable to alert the oncoming danger. Likewise the shepherds are like dogs with an insatiable appetite; they are guardians without discernment who care only for their own gain. They are leaders without a sense of proper relationship to those entrusted to their care; they lack righteousness. A similar lack of knowledge resides in the house of Jacob; while accusing God of being without knowledge of their fasting practices (58:3a), it is they who need to become aware of the manner of fasting that God chooses (58:6a). Following the metaphorical description of the people's wicked deeds, the unrighteous are said to be a people who do not know peace, and furthermore anyone pursuing their path of life lacks this same knowledge (59:8). But there is a reversal when, after a lament of their situation, the people acknowledge their iniquities and enumerate their various transgressions (59:12b-13). The people create a situation in which righteousness is ignored and thus God's saving hand is absent (59:1,11); caught in the consequences of their injustice, they come to a knowledge of their sinfulness.

The lack of knowledge of God's ways displayed in Isa 56-59 is reminiscent of two passages of importance in Isa. The opening verses of the Isaian corpus, inaugurating the sixty-six chapters, touch on the people's ignorance of God's ways despite the care shown them.

> Hear, O heavens, and give ear, O earth;
> for the Lord has spoken:
> "Sons have I reared and brought up,
> but they have rebelled against me.
> The ox knows its owner
> and the ass its master's crib;
> But Israel does not know,
> my people does not understand." (Isa 1:2-3)

In the call of the prophet, the commission to announce the word of God becomes the cause for their lack of knowledge; their rejection of God's ways, i.e., their lack of knowledge, hastens the onslaught of judgment.

> And the Lord said, "Go and say to this people:
> 'Hear and hear, but do not understand;
> see and see, but do not perceive.'
> Make the heart of this people fat, and their ears heavy,
> and shut their eyes;
> Lest they see with their eyes, and hear with their ears,
> and understand with their hearts,
> and turn and be healed." (Isa 6:9-10)

The motif describing the lack of knowledge in Isa 56-59 reflects the same message as found in Isa 1 and 6: knowledge is founded on an understanding of the ways of God and without this perception one progresses toward judgment. The similarity in recurring motifs like this one encourages the search for greater signs of unity in the Isaian corpus.

E. The Lord Who Sees

The language and imagery describing the divinity in Isa 56-59 present one who gives life (57:15-16), who instructs (58:6-14), and who engages in combat with the forces of evil (59:15-18). One common description of God occurring in three literary contexts portrays his sight. In 57:18 and 59:15,16 the Lord sees the ways of humanity and what this mode of action has done to them. Similar to the motif of knowledge in 58:3, the people ask why God does not see their fasting.

A further consideration of the root r'h (to see) shows an added dimension of their interrelatedness in Isa 56-59. In noting where it specifically states that God sees. the texts proceed to describe that God takes a course of action: he sees and he saves. The portrayal of Yahweh in 57:17 is of one who, in seeing the wayward wanderings of his people, turns to heal, lead, and comfort them. Similarly in 59:15b,16 the Divine Warrior sees that there is no justice and no one to intervene in the situation; his own arm establishes salvation and his will to deliver sustains his redemptive action. Both instances make evident that Yahweh, though a Deus absconditus in the face of unrighteousness, is a God who saves, whose intention is to bring deliverance to those held captive by their own failure to establish justice and righteousness. And yet also Yahweh appears as the divine One held captive by his love for his creatures and his intent to save them; not only does he free them but also guides, heals, and comforts (57:17) as witness to the power and strength of his salvation.[8]

F. The Lord Who Comes To Redeem

Isa 56-59 is framed by the motif of the coming of salvation (with bw', cf. 56:1b; 59:19b,20). While the repetitions of bw' are not numerous in these chapters, other images express the approach of redemption in varied ways. In 57:17-18, God hides his face from the people because of their covetous deeds;

8. Cf. S. TERRIEN, The Elusive Presence: Toward a New Biblical Theology (Religious Perspective 26; New York: Harper and Row, 1978) 265-66.

but despite his anger, Yahweh promises to return to wayward Israel and to bring healing, guidance, and comfort. In 58:3-5 God is described as unattentive to the people on account of their inauthentic fasting. However, if the people will transform these practices according to a manner that God chooses, Yahweh will break forth like the dawn, and will lead them with his deliverance and with his glory as their rear guard (58:8-9). In 59:1-3, the text explains that the sins of the people hide the Face and cause a separation from God. Yet in their desolation, the Divine Warrior brings salvation and deliverance for they stand alone without anyone to intervene for them (59:15-17).

Each of these examples demonstrates that the salvation which is announced is nothing less than Yahweh's own coming among the people. He is their healing, peace, and comfort (57:17-19); he is their light, deliverance, and glory (58:8-9); he is their warrior, salvation, and Redeemer (59:15-20). Apart from Yahweh, Israel stands outside the realm of redemption. As the motif develops in various ways in Isa 56-59, it comes to a splendid announcement of Yahweh's coming in Isa 60 where Jerusalem stands radiant in the light of salvation, in the light of its Lord. The God who approaches Israel comes to bring salvation in abundance.

F. From Judgment to Salvation

Underlying a major portion of Isa 56-59 is an interplay between the themes of judgment and salvation. This is stylistically shown in the numerous repeated words and motifs which express aspects of both themes; for example, in Isa 58 the name "Jacob" appears in a context of judgment where the prophet is told to announce to Jacob its transgression (v. 1) while the same name recurs in a context of salvation announcing the blessed heritage of Jacob for those who obey the Lord's commands (v. 14). There are many more similar illustrations in 56:9--59:20. The juxtaposing of the two themes suggests that their patterning also carries a message on the relationship between a message of judgment and of salvation.

In 56:9--57:21 the examples of paronomasia demonstrate the futility of idolatry in comparison with the promises of Yahweh who is the true Lord.[9] The concentric pattern of 58 presents a corrective for misguided deeds which need to be transformed into liberating acts for others if God is to be responsive to their pleas.[10] And the development of the ABCB pattern of 56:1 in 59:1-20 describes the demise of righteousness, hence the reason for judgment and the need for deliverance.[11] In each case, the thematic movement is toward salvation, but it is a progression through judgment toward redemption. From this one can see that the harsh words of judgment become the means by which the promises of salvation emerge.[12] The manner in which the offer of redemption appears in 56-59 takes the guise of an indictment looking forward to a change in

9. For an explanation of this literary device in its context of 56:9--57:21, see pp. 160-71.

10. For an explanation of this literary device in its context of 58, see pp. 232-40.

11. For an explanation of this literary device in its context of 59, see pp. 308-316.

12. J.J.M. ROBERTS notes examples in Isa where the Lord's "fiery judgment" against the people of Zion brings them to a change of heart; righteousness is restored and God's deliverance comes to the people. Cf. "Isaiah in OT Theology," 137-38.

attitude and action; by means of a threat both an instruction and a promise of deliverance call one to walk in the ways of Yahweh. Salvation comes to the humble and contrite (57:15), to those who reject wickedness (57:19-21), to those who liberate others and give of themselves (58:6-14), and to those who actively remove sin from their lives (59:20). The biting word of judgment is the catalyst revealing the Lord's continuing offer to save; even the indicting chastisement possesses a salvific dimension for its intention is to lead one to transformation, to walk the way of righteousness toward salvation.

Various motifs which recur in Isa 56-59 display consistency and development of thought, giving signs of its unity. The different ways of reiterating the motifs and themes work together to develop the message of these chapters. In his essay "The Music of Poetry," T.S. Eliot describes this kind of poetic technique by analogy to a symphonic piece of music whose integrity is understood by its careful interplay of motifs and themes.

> The use of recurrent themes is as natural to poetry as to music. There are possibilities for verse which bear some analogy to the development of a theme by different groups of instruments; there are possibilities of transitions in a poem comparable to the different movements of a symphony or quartet; there are possibilities of contrapuntal arrangement of subject matter.[13]

In the subtle shifts of timbre and the unobtrusive repetition of a melody, the composer directs the listener to the key musical expression of the composition; so also does the shift of theme and the repetition of motif direct the reader to the message of the poetic text. The heart of Isa 56-59 speaks a message that is

---

13. Cf. T.S. ELIOT, The Music of Poetry (Glasgow: Jackson, Son, and Company, 1942) 28.

universal and transcends the limits of time. God's call to embrace the ways of righteousness is an invitation to share in the gift of salvation; his are the ways of true justice and righteousness that lead to salvation.

BIBLIOGRAPHY OF WORKS CITED

I. Commentaries of Isaiah 56-66

ACHTEMEIER, E. The Community and Message of Isaiah 56-66: A Theological Commentary. Minneapolis: Augsburg Publishing House, 1982.

ALONSO SCHÖKEL, L. "Isaias III." In Profetas I: Introducciones y comentario. Edited by L. Alonso Schökel and J.L. Sicre Diaz, pp. 341-395. Madrid: Ediciones Cristiandad, 1980.

BONNARD, P.-E. Le Second Isaïe, son disciple et leurs éditeurs: Isaïe 40-66. Etudes bibliques. Paris: J. Gabalda, 1972.

DUHM, B. Das Buch Jesaia. Übersetz und erklärt. 4. Auflage. Göttingen: Vandenhoeck und Ruprecht, 1922.

FOHRER, G. Das Buch Jesaja, 3. Kapitel 40-66. Zürcher Bibelkommentare. Zürich: Zwingli-Verlag, 1965.

HANSON, P.D. The Dawn of Apocalyptic. Revised ed. Philadelphia: Fortress Press, 1979.

HERBERT, A.S. The Book of the Prophet Isaiah 40-66. The Cambridge Bible Commentary. Cambridge: Cambridge University Press, 1975.

JONES, D.R. Isaiah 56-66 and Joel. Torch Bible Commentaries 20. London: SCM Press, 1964.

KISSANE, E.J. The Book of Isaiah, 2. Dublin: Browne and Nolan, 1943.

McKENZIE, J.L. Second Isaiah. AB 20. Garden City, NY: Doubleday, 1968.

MARTY, J. Les chapitres 56-66 du Livre d'Esaïe. Paris: P. Geuthner, 1924.

MUILENBURG, J. "The Book of Isaiah, Chapters 40-66." In IB 5, pp. 381-773. Nashville, TN: Abingdon Press, 1956.

ODEBERG, H. Trito Isaiah (Isaiah 56-66): A Literary and Linguistic Analysis. Uppsala: A.-B Lundequistska Bokhandeln, 1931.

PAURITSCH, K. Die neue Gemeinde: Gott sammelt Ausgestossene und Arme. AnBib 47. Rome: Biblical Institute Press, 1971.

PENNA, A. Isaia. La Sacra Bibbia. Torino: Marietti, 1964.

SCULLION, J.J. Isaiah 40-66. Old Testament Message 12. Wilmington, DE: Michael Glazier, 1982.

TORREY, C.C. The Second Isaiah. New York: Charles Scribner's Sons, 1928.

VERMEYLEN, J. Du prophète Isaïe à l'apocalyptique: Miroir d'un demi-millénaire d'expérience religieuse en Israël. Tomes 1,2. Paris: J. Gabalda, 1977-78.

VOLZ, P. Jesaja 2. Kommentar zum Alten Testament 9. Hildesheim/New York: Georg Olms, 1932.

WESTERMANN, C. Isaiah 40-66. Translated by D.M.G. Stalker. Old Testament Library. Philadelphia: Westminster Press, 1969.

WHYBRAY, R.N. Isaiah 40-66. New Century Bible Commentary. London: Oliphants Press, 1975.

II. Additional Commentaries, Books, and Articles

ABRAMOWSKI, R. "Zum literarischen Problem von Jes 56-66." TSK 96/97 (1925) 90-143.

ALBRIGHT, W.F. "New Light on Early Canaanite Language and Literature." BASOR 46 (1932) 15-20.

----------. "The High Places in Ancient Palestine." VTS 4 (1957) 242-58.

----------. "The Song of Deborah in Light of Stylistics." VT 1 (1951) 168-80.

ALONSO SCHÖKEL, L. "Die stilistische Analyse bei den Propheten." VTS 7 (1959) 154-164.

----------. "Hermeneutical Problems of a Literary Study of the Bible." VTS 28 (1975) 1-15.

----------. "The Poetic Structure of Psalm 42-43." JSOT 1 (1976) 4-11.

----------. "Poésie hébraïque." DBSup. Vol. 8, cols. 47-90. Paris: Letouzey et Ané, 1972.

ANDERSEN, F.I. and FREEDMAN, D.N. Hosea: A New Translation with Introduction and Commentary. AB 24. Garden City, NY: Doubleday, 1980.

ANDERSON, A.A. The Book of Psalms, Vol. 1. New Century Bible Commentary. London: Oliphants, 1972.

ANDERSON, B.W. "The New Frontier of Rhetorical Criticism. A Tribute to James Muilenburg." In Rhetorical Criticism: Essays in Honor of James Muilenburg. Pittsburgh Theological Monograph Series 1. Edited by J.J. Jackson and M. Kessler, pp. ix-xviii. Pittsburgh: Pickwick Press, 1974.

----------. "Tradition and Scripture in the Community of Faith." JBL 100 (1981) 5-21.

ARISTOTLE. Rhetoric. Translated by L. Cooper. Englewood Cliffs, NJ: Prentice Hall, 1932.

AUERBACH, E. Mimesis: The Representative of Reality in Western Literature. Princeton: Princeton University Press, 1953.

BAKER, D.W. "Further Examples of the Waw Explicativum." VT 30 (1980) 129-136.

BAR-EFRAT, S. "Some Observations on the Analysis of Structure in Biblical Narrative." VT 30 (1980) 154-173.

BARR, J. "Reading the Bible as Literature." BJRL 56 (1973) 10-33.

BENTZEN, A. Introduction to the Old Testament, Vol. 2. Copenhagen: G.E.C. Gads, 1948-49.

BERGMAN, J.; HALDAR, A.O.; and WALLIS, G. "'hb." TDOT 1. 99-118.

BERLIN, A. "Grammatical Aspects of Biblical Parallelism." HUCA 50 (1979) 17-44.

BLACK, E. Rhetorical Criticism: A Study in Method. Madison, WI: University of Wisconsin Press, 1978.

BLENKINSOPP, J. "Stylistics of Old Testament Poetry." Bib 44 (1963) 352-58.

BOADT, L. Ezekiel's Oracles Against Egypt: A Literary and Philological Study. BibOr 37. Rome: Biblical Institute Press, 1980.

----------. "Isaiah 41:8-13 : Notes on Poetic Style and Structure." CBQ 35 (1973) 20-34.

BODELSEN, C.A. T.S. Eliot's Four Quartets: A Commentary. Copenhagen, Denmark: Rosenkilde and Bagger, 1958.

BRAULIK, G. Die Mittel deuteronomischer Rhetorik: Erhoben aus Deuteronomium 4:1-40. AnBib 68. Rome: Biblical Institute Press, 1978.

BRIGHT, J. Jeremiah: Introduction, Translation, and Notes. AB 21. Garden City, NY: Doubleday, 1965.

BROWN, F.; DRIVER, S.R.; and BRIGGS, C.A. A Hebrew and Aramaic Lexicon of the Old Testament. Oxford: Clarendon, 1907.

BRUEGGEMANN, W. The Land. Overtures to Biblical Theology 1. Philadelphia: Fortress Press, 1977.

BUBER, M. "Leitwortstil in der Erzählung des Pentateuchs." In Die Schrift und ihre Verdeutschung. Edited by M. Buber and F. Rosenzweig, pp. 211-38. Berlin, 1936.

BÜCHSEL, F. and HERNTRICH, V. "krinō." TDNT 3. 921-54.

BUDDE, K. Geschichte der althebräischen Literatur. Leipzig: C.F. Amelangs Verlag, 1906.

CASSUTO, U. A Commentary on the Book of Genesis. Translated by Israel Abrahams. Jerusalem: Magnes Press, 1961-64.

CERESKO, A.R. "A Poetic Analysis of Ps 105, with Attention to Its Use of Irony." Bib 64 (1983) 20-46.

----------. "Chiastic Word Patterns in Hebrew." CBQ 38 (1976) 303-11.

----------. Job 29-31 in the Light of Northwest Semitic: A Translation and Philological Commentary. BibOr 36. Rome: Biblical Institute Press, 1980.

----------. "The A:B::B:A Word Pattern in Hebrew and Northwest Semitic, with Special Reference to the Book of Job." UF 7 (1975) 73-88.

----------. "The Function of Chiasmus in Hebrew Poetry." CBQ 40 (1978) 1-10.

CHILDS, B.S. Memory and Tradition in Israel. SBT 37. London: SCM Press, 1962.

CLEMENTS, R.E. One Hundred Years of Old Testament Interpretation. Philadelphia: Westminster Press, 1976.

----------. "The Unity of the Book of Isaiah." Int 36 (1982) 117-29.

CLIFFORD, R. "Rhetorical Criticism in the Exegesis of Hebrew Poetry." In SBL 1980 Seminar Papers. Edited by P.J. Achtemeier, pp. 17-28. Chico, CA: Scholars Press, 1980.

----------. "The Function of Idol Passages in Second Isaiah." CBQ 42 (1980) 450-64.

CLINES, D.J.A. I, He, We, and They: A Literary Approach to Isaiah 53. JSOTSup 1. Sheffield: The University of Sheffield, 1976.

CONROY, C. Absalom, Absalom! Narrative and Language in 2 Sam 13-20. AnBib 81. Rome: Biblical Institute Press, 1978.

DAHOOD, M. "Hebrew Poetry." IDBSup., 669-72.

----------. Psalms: Introduction, Translation, and Notes. 3 Vols. AB 16-17a. Garden City, NY: Doubleday, 1966-70.

----------. "The Chiastic Breakup in Isaiah 58:7." Bib 57 (1976) 105.

----------. "The Language and Date of Psalm 48 (47)." CBQ 16 (1954) 15-19.

DELCOR, M. "Two Special Meanings of the Word yd in Biblical Hebrew." JSS 12 (1967) 230-40.

DEWEY, J. Markan Public Debate. SBLDS 48. Chico, CA: Scholars Press, 1980.

DHORME, E. A Commentary on the Book of Job. Translated by Harold Knight. London: Nelson, 1967.

DION, P.-E. "Did Cultic Prostitution Fall into Oblivion during the Postexilic Era? Some Evidence from Chronicles and the Septuagint." CBQ 43 (1981) 41-48.

DRIVER, G.R. "Linguistic and Textual Problems, Isaiah XL-LXVI." JTS 36 (1935) 396-406.

ELIOT, T.S. The Music of Poetry. Glasgow: Jackson, Son, and Company, 1942.

ELLIGER, K. "Der Prophet Tritojesaja." ZAW 49 (1931) 112-41.

EXUM, J.C. "Isaiah 28-32: A Literary Study." In SBL 1979 Seminar Papers, Vol. 2. Edited by P. Achtemeier, pp. 123-53. Missoula, MT: Scholars Press, 1979.

----------. "Of Broken Pots, Fluttering Birds and Visions in the Night: Extended Simile and Poetic Technique in Isaiah." CBQ 43 (1981) 331-52.

----------. "Promise and Fulfillment: Narrative Art in Judges 13." JBL 99 (1980) 43-59.

----------. "Whom Will He Teach Knowledge?: A Literary Study of Isa 28-32." In Art and Meaning: Rhetoric in Biblical Literature. JSOTSup 19. Edited by D.J.A. Clines, et. al., pp. 108-39. Sheffield: JSOT Press, 1982.

FEINBERG, C. God Remembers: A Study of Zechariah. Portland, OR: Mullnomah Press, 1979.

FISHER, L.R., Ed. Ras Shamra Parallels: The Texts from Ugarit and the Hebrew Bible. 2 Vols. AnOr 49-50. Rome: Biblical Institute Press, 1972-81.

FITZGERALD, A. "Hebrew yd = 'love' and 'beloved'." CBQ 29 (1967) 368-74.

FREEDMAN, D.N. "Pottery, Poetry, and Prophecy: An Essay on Biblical Poetry." JBL 96 (1977) 5-26.

----------. "The Poetic Structures of the Framework of Deuteronomy 33." In The Bible World: Essays in Honor of Cyrus H. Gordon. Edited by G. Rendsburg, pp. 25-46. New York: KTAV Publishing House, 1980.

----------. and HYLAND, C.J. "Psalm 29: A Structural Analysis." HTR 66 (1973) 237-256.

GELIN, A. and DESCHAMPS, A. Sin in the Bible. Translated by Charles Schaldenbrand. New York: Desclée, 1964.

GEVIRTZ, S. Patterns in the Early Poetry of Israel. Chicago: University of Chicago Press, 1963.

GITAY, Y. Prophecy and Persuasion: A Study of Isaiah 40-48. Forum Theologiae Linguisticae 14. Bonn: Linguistica Biblica, 1981.

GLUCK, J.J. "Paronomasia in Biblical Literature." Semitics 1 (1970) 50-78.

GOOD, E.M. "The Composition of Hosea." SEA 31 (1966) 21-63.

GORDIS, R. "The Structure of Biblical Poetry." In Poets, Prophets, and Sages: Essays in Biblical Interpretation, pp. 61-94. Bloomington, IN: Indiana University Press, 1971.

GREENWOOD, D. "Rhetorical Criticism and Formgeschichte: Some Methodological Considerations." JBL 89 (1970) 418-26.

HARRIS, R.L., Ed. Theological Wordbook of the Old Testament, Vol. 1,2. Chicago: Moody Press, 1980.

HARVEY, J. Le plaidoyer prophétique contre Israël après la rupture de l'alliance: Etude d'une formule littéraire de l'Ancien Testament. Bruges/Paris: Desclée De Brouwer, 1967.

HOLLADAY, W.L. Isaiah: Scroll of a Prophetic Heritage. Grand Rapids, MI: William B. Eerdmans Publishing Company, 1978.

----------. The Architecture of Jeremiah 1-20. Lewisburg: Bucknell University Press, 1976.

HOLMGREN, F. "Yahweh the Avenger, Isaiah 63:1-6." In Rhetorical Criticism, Essays in Honor of James Muilenburg. Pittsburgh Theological Monograph Series 1. Edited by J.J. Jackson and M. Kessler, pp. 133-48. Pittsburgh: Pickwick Press, 1974.

HONEYMAN, A.M. "Merismus in Biblical Hebrew." JBL 71 (1952) 11-18.

HOPPE, L.J. "Isaiah 58: 1-12, Fasting and Idolatry." BTB 13 (1983) 44-47.

IRWIN, W.H. Isaiah 28-33: A Translation and Philological Commentary. BibOr 30. Rome: Biblical Institute Press, 1977.

----------. " 'The Smooth Stones of the Wady'? Isaiah 57: 6." CBQ 29 (1967) 31-40.

JANZEN, W. "'ašrê in the Old Testament." HTR 58 (1965) 215-26.

JOÜON, P. Grammaire de l'hébreu biblique. Rome: Biblical Institute Press, 1923 (1965, corrected reprint).

KAISER, O. Isaiah 1-12. Translated by R.A. Wilson. Old Testament Library. Philadelphia: The Westminster Press, 1972.

KAPELRUD, A.S. "The Number Seven in Ugaritic Texts." VT 18 (1968) 494-99.

KESSLER, M. "A Methodological Setting for Rhetorical Criticism." In Art and Meaning: Rhetoric in Biblical Literature. JSOTSup 19. Edited by D.J.A. Clines, et. al., pp. 1-19. Sheffield: JSOT Press, 1982. Originally in Semitics 4 (1974) 22-36.

KIKAWADA, I.M. "Some Proposals for the Definition of Rhetorical Criticism." Semitics 5 (1977) 67-91.

KISSANE, E.J. The Book of Job. Dublin: Browne and Nolan, 1939.

KITTEL, B.P. The Hymns of Qumran: Translation and Commentary. SBLDS 50. Chico, CA: Scholars Press, 1981.

KNIGHT, D. "The Understanding of Sitz im Leben in Form Criticism." In SBL 1974 Seminar Papers, Vol. 1. Edited by G. MacRae, pp. 105-25. Cambridge, MA: Society of Biblical Literature, 1974.

KOSMALA, H. "Form of Structure of Isaiah 58." ASTI 5 (1967) 69-81.

KSELMAN, J.S. "A Note of w'nḥhw in Isa 57:18." CBQ 43 (1981) 539-42.

----------. "Design and Structure in Hebrew Poetry." In SBL 1980 Seminar Papers. Edited by P.J. Achtemeier, pp. 1-16. Chico, CA: Scholars Press, 1980.

----------. "Semantic- Sonant Chiasmus in Biblical Poetry." Bib 58 (1977) 219-23.

----------. "The ABCB Pattern: Further Examples." VT 32 (1982) 224-29.

KUGEL, J.L. The Idea of Biblical Poetry: Parallelism and its History. New Haven, CT: Yale University Press, 1981.

KUNTZ, J.K. "The Contribution of Rhetorical Criticism to Understanding Isaiah 51:1-16." In Art and Meaning: Rhetoric in Biblical Literature. JSOTSup 19. Edited by D.J.A. Clines, et. al., pp. 140-71. Sheffield: JSOT Press, 1982.

LABERGE, Léo. "The Woe-Oracles of Isaiah 28-33." Église et Théologie 13 (1982) 157-90.

LABUSCHAGNE, C.J. "The Emphasizing Particle gam and its Connotations." In Studia Biblica et Semitica in Honor of T.C. Vriezen. Edited by W.C. van Unik and A.S. van der Woude, pp. 193-203. Wageningen: H. Veenman, 1966.

LACK, R. La symbolique du livre d'Isaïe: Essai sur l'image littéraire comme élément de structuration. AnBib 59. Rome: Biblical Institute Press, 1973.

LAPOINTE, R. "Tradition and Language: The Import of Oral Expression." In Tradition and Theology in the Old Testament. Edited by D.A. Knight, pp. 125-42. Philadelphia: Fortress Press, 1977.

LIEBREICH, L.S. "The Compilation of the Book of Isaiah." JQR 46 (1956) 259-77; JQR 47 (1957) 114-38..

LIPINSKI, E. "Macarisme et psaumes de congratulation." RB 75 (1968) 321-67.

LIVINGSTON, H.G. "ḥṭʾ." TWOT 1. 277-79.

----------. "pš^{c}." TWOT 2. 741-42.

LOWTH, R. De Sacra Poesi Hebraeorum Praelectiones Academicae. Oxford: Clarendon, 1821.

LUND, N.W. Chiasmus in the New Testament. Chapel Hill, NC: University of North Carolina, 1942.

LUNDBOM, J.R. Jeremiah: A Study in Ancient Hebrew Rhetoric. SBLDS 18. Missoula, MT: Scholars Press, 1975.

MAASS, F. "ʾdm." TDOT 1. 75-87.

----------. "ʾnwš." TDOT 1. 345-48.

McCREESH, T.P. "Poetic Sound Patterns in Proverbs 10-29." Ph.D. dissertation. Catholic University of America, 1982.

McKENZIE, J.L. Dictionary of the Bible. Milwaukee: Bruce Publishing Company, 1965.

MAGONET, J. Form and Meaning: Studies in Literary Technique in the Book of Jonah. BBET 2. Bern: Herbert Lang, 1976.

MARCH, W.E. "Prophecy." In Old Testament Form Criticism. Edited by J.H. Hayes, pp. 141-77. San Antonio, TX: Trinity University Press, 1974.

MELUGIN, R.F. "Muilenburg, Form Criticism, and Theological Exegesis." In Encounter with the Text: Form and History in the Hebrew Bible. Semeia Studies 8. Edited by Martin J. Buss, pp. 91-100. Philadelphia: Fortress Press, 1979.

----------. "The Conventional and the Creative in Isaiah's Judgment Oracles." CBQ 36 (1974) 301-11.

MILLAR, W.R. Isaiah 24-27 and the Origin of Apocalyptic. HSM 11. Missoula, MT: Scholars Press, 1976.

MILLER, P.D. Sin and Judgment in the Prophets: A Stylistic and Theological Analysis. SBLMS 27. Chico, CA: Scholars Press, 1982.

MIRSKY, A. "Stylistic Device for Conclusion in Hebrew." Semitics 5 (1977) 9-23.

MOULTON, R.G. The Literary Study of the Bible. Boston: D.C. Heath and Co., Publishers, 1899.

MUILENBURG, J. "A Study in Hebrew Rhetoric: Repetition and Style." VTS 1 (1953) 97-111.

----------. "Form Criticism and Beyond." JBL 88 (1969) 1-18.

----------. "Poetry (Biblical Poetry)." Encyclopedia Judaica. Col. 670-81.

----------. "Teaching the Bible from the Literary Angle." CE 8 (Dec. 1924) 82-87.

----------. "The Linguistic and Rhetorical Usages of the Particle ky in the Old Testament." HUCA 32 (1961) 135-60.

----------. "The Literary Character of Isaiah 34." JBL 59 (1940) 339-65.

MURTONEN, A. "Third Isaiah--Yes or No?" Abrn 19 (1980-81) 20-42.

NIELSEN, K. Yahweh as Prosecutor and Judge. SJOTSup 9. Sheffield: University of Sheffield, 1978.

PARUNAK, H.V.D. "Oral Typesetting: Some Uses of Biblical Structure." Bib 62 (1981) 153-68.

----------. Structural Studies in Ezekiel. Ann Arbor, MI: University Microfilms International, 1979.

----------. "Transitional Techniques in the Bible." JBL 102 (1983) 525-48.

PEDERSEN, J. Israel: Its Life and Culture. Vol. 2. Translated by A. Møller. London: Oxford University Press, 1947.

POPE, M. "Number, Numbering, Numbers." IDB 3. 561-67.

----------. "Seven, Seventh, Seventy." IDB 4. 294-95.

PORTEN, B. "The Structure and Theme of the Solomon Narrative." HUCA 38 (1967) 93-128.

---------- and RAPPAPORT, U. "Poetic Structure in Genesis IX:7." VT 21 (1971) 363-69.

RAD, G. von. Old Testament Theology, Vol. 1. Translated by D.M.G. Stalker. New York: Harper and Row, 1962-65.

RICHTER, W. Exegese als Literaturwissenschaft: Entwurf einer alttestamentlichen Literaturtheorie und Methodologie. Göttingen: Vandenhoeck und Ruprecht, 1971.

RINGGREN, H. "ʾh." TDOT 1. 188-93.

ROBERTS, J.J.M. "Isaiah in Old Testament Theology." Int 36 (1982) 130-43.

RUMMEL, Stan, Ed. Ras Shamra Parallels: The Texts from Ugarit and the Hebrew Bible. Vol. 3. AnOr 51. Rome: Biblical Institute Press, 1981.

SASSON, J.M. "Wordplay in the OT." IDBSup, 968-70.

SAWYER, J.F.A. "A Change in Emphasis in the Study of the Prophets." In Israel's Prophetic Tradition: Essays in Honor of Peter Ackroyd. Edited by Richard Coggins et al., pp. 233-49. Cambridge: Cambridge University Press, 1982.

----------. From Moses to Patmos: New Perspectives in Old Testament Study. London: SPCK Press, 1977.

SCHOORS, A. I Am God, Your Savior: A Formcritical Study of the Main Genres in Is 40-55. VTS 24. Leiden: E.J. Brill, 1973.

SCULLION, J.J. "ŞEDEQ-ŞEDAQAH in Isaiah cc. 40-66." UF 3 (1971) 335-48.

----------. "Some Difficult Texts in Is 56-66 in the Light of Modern Scholarship." UF 4 (1973) 105-28.

STEK, J.H. "The Stylistics of Hebrew Poetry." Calvin Theological Journal 9 (1974) 15-30.

STOCK, A. "Chiastic Awareness and Education in Antiquity." BTB 14 (1984) 23-27.

TALMON, S. "The Textual Study of the Bible--A New Outlook." In Qumran and the History of the Biblical Text. Edited by F.M. Cross and S. Talmon, pp. 321-400. Cambridge, MA: Harvard University Press, 1975.

TERRIEN, S. The Elusive Presence: Toward a New Biblical Theology. Religious Perspectives 26. New York: Harper and Row, 1978.

THOMAS, D.W. "A Consideration of Some Unusual Ways of Expressing the Superlative in Hebrew." VT 3 (1953) 209-24.

TOURNAY, R. Review of Das Buch Jesaja, Kap 40-66, by Claus Westermann. RB 74 (1967) 120-21.

ULLMANN, S. Language and Style: Collected Papers. Oxford: B. Blackwell, 1964.

VIGANO, L. Nomi e titoli di YHWH, alla luce del Semitico del Nord-Ovest. BibOr 31. Rome: Biblical Institute Press, 1976.

VOGELS, W. "Diachronic and Synchronic Studies of Hosea 1-3." BZ 28 (1984) 94-98.

----------. " 'Osée-Gomer' car et comme 'Yahweh-Israël,' Os 1-3." NRT 103 (1981) 711-27.

WALSH, J. "Jonah 2:3-10: A Rhetorical Critical Study." Bib 63 (1982) 219-29.

WATSON, W.G.E. "Chiastic Patterns in Biblical Hebrew Poetry." In Chiasmus in Antiquity: Structures, Analyses, Exegesis. Edited by J.W. Welch, pp. 118-68. Hildesheim: Gerstenberg, 1981.

----------. "Further Examples of Semantic-Sonant Chiasmus." CBQ 46 (1984) 31-33.

WATTERS, W.R. Formula Criticism and the Poetry of the Old Testament. BZAW 138. Berlin: W. de Gruyter, 1976.

WEINFELD, M. "bryt." TDOT 2, 253-79.

----------. Deuteronomy and the Deuteronomic School. Oxford: Clarendon Press, 1972.

WEISE, M. "Jesaja 57:5f." ZAW 72 (1960) 25-32.

WEISER, A. Einleitung in das alte Testament. Stuttgart: W. Kohlhammer, 1939.

WELCH, J.W. "Introduction." To Chiasmus in Antiquity: Structures, Analyses, Exegesis. Edited by J.W. Welch, pp. 9-16. Hildesheim: Gerstenberg, 1981.

WHEELER, C.B. The Design of Poetry. New York: W.W. Norton, 1966.

WINTEROWD, W.R. Rhetoric: A Synthesis. New York: Holt, Rinehart, and Winston, 1968.

WESTERMANN, C. Basic Forms of Prophetic Speech. Translated by H.C. White. Philadelphia: Westminster Press, 1967.

WOLFF, H.W. The Anthropology of the Old Testament. Translated by M. Kohl. Philadelphia: Fortress Press, 1974.

ZIMMERLI, W. Ezekiel, 1. Translated by R.E. Clements. Hermeneia. Edited by F.M. Cross and K. Baltzer. Philadelphia: Fortress Press, 1979.

ZORRELL, F. and SEMKOWSKI, L. Lexicon hebraicum et aramaicum Veteris Testamenti. Rome: Biblical Institute Press, 1954.

INDEX OF AUTHORS

(Each reference is for the full bibliographical entry)

Abramowski, R., 12.
Achtemeier, E., 26.
Albright, W.F., 2, 70.
Alonso Schökel, L., x, 6, 7, 24, 138, 304.
Andersen, F. I., 5.
Anderson, A.A., 331.
Anderson, B.W., 3, 9.
Aristotle, x.
Auerbach, E., 2.

Baker, D.W., 69.
Bar-Efrat, S., 2.
Barr, J., 9.
Bentzen, A., 16.
Bergman, J., 45.
Berlin, A., 18.
Black, E., x.
Blenkinsopp, J., 8.
Boadt, L., 39, 85.
Bodelson, C.A., xi.
Bonnard, P.-E., 14.
Braulik, G., 39.
Bright, J., 130.
Brueggemann, W., 10, 146.
Buber, M., 2.
Büchsel, F., 329.
Budde, K., 12.

Cassuto, U., 178.
Ceresko, A.R., 18, 121, 148.
Charpentier, E., 14.
Childs, B.S., 96.
Clements, R., xi, 1.
Clifford, R., 3, 99.
Clines, D. J. A., 106.
Conroy, C., 37.

Dahood, M. J., 18, 62, 98, 114, 209.
Delcor, M., 139.
Deschamps, A., 197.
Dewey, J., 5.
Dhorme, E., 223.
Dijkstra, M., 12.
Dion, P.-E., 130.
Driver, G.R., 223.
Duhm, B., 10.

Eliot, T.S., 338.
Elliger, K., 302.
Exum, J.C., xii, 7, 9, 47.

Feinberg, C., 154.
Fischer, L.R., 18.
Fitzgerald, A., 139.
Fohrer, G., 16.
Freedman, D. N., 5, 9, 101, 178.

Gelin, A., 197.
Gevirtz, S., 55.
Gittay, Y., xii.
Gluck, J. J., 162.
Good, E. M., 5.
Gordis, R., 108.
Greenwood, D., 3-4.
Grelot, P., 12.

Haldar, A. O., 45.
Hanson, P. D., 12.
Hartley, J. E., 277.
Harvey, J., 126.
Herntrich, V., 329.
Holladay, W. L., 5, 99.
Holmgren, F., 16.
Honeyman, A. M., 110.
Hoppe, L. J., 25.
Hyland, C.F., 178.

Irwin, W.H., 18, 24.

Janzen, W., 50.
Jones, D.R., 308.

Kaiser, O., 116.
Kapelrud, A.S., 178-9.
Kessler, M., 1.
Kiesow, K., 12.
Kikawada, I.M., 9.
Kissane, E.J., 223.
Kittel, B.M., 39.
Knight, D., 7.
Knight, D.A., 10.
Kosmala, H., 25.
Kselman, J.S., 10, 56, 133, 154.
Kugel, J. L., 61.
Kuntz, J.K., 35.

Laberge, L., xii.

Labuschagne, C.J., 135.
Lapointe, R., 9.
Lack, R., 14.
Liebreich, L.S., xi.
Lipinski,E., 49.
Livingston, C.H., 284.
Livingston, G.H., 198.
Livingston, H.G., 132.
Lowth, R., 2.
Lund, N.W., 120.
Lundbom, J.R., 39.

Maass, F., 63.
Magonet, J., 28.
March, W.E., 104.
Marty, J., 12.
McCreesh, T.P., 117.
McKenzie, J.L., 12, 130.
Melugin, R.F., 4, 7, 12.
Merendino, R.P., 12.
Millar, W.R., xii.
Miller, P.D., 133.
Mirsky, A., 298.
Moulton, R.G., 179.
Muilenberg, J., 2, 3, 5, 12.
Murtonen, A., 11.

Nielson, K., 126.

Parunak, H.V.D., 9, 86, 133.
Pauritsch, K., 12.
Pedersen, J., 209.
Penar, T., 18.
Penna, A., 7.
Pope, M., 178, 179.
Porten, B., 9, 55.

Rappaport, U., 55.
Richter, W., 7.
Ringgren, H., 85.
Roberts, J.J.M., 87.

Sasson, J.M., 162.
Sawyer, J.F.A., xi.
Schoors. A., 12.
Scullion, J.J., 17, 20, 70.
Spykerboer, H.C., 12.
Steck, J.H., 179.
Stock, A., 322.
Stuhlmueller, C., 12.

Talmon, S., 18.
Terrien, S., 335.
Thomas, D.W., 138.
Torrey, C.C., 2.
Tournay, R., 15.

Ullmann, S., 37.

Vermeylen, J., 11.
Vigano, L., 101.
Vincent, J.M., 12.
Vogels, W., 9, 327.
Volz, P., 98.
von Rad, G., 329.

Wallis, G., 45.
Walsh, J., 35.
Watson, W.G.E., 11, 133.
Watters, W.R., 18.
Weinfeld, M., 48, 70.
Weise, M., 136.
Weiser, A., 12.
Welch, J.W., x., 61.
Westermann, C., 16, 44.
Wheeler, C.B., 40.
Whitman, C.H., 41.
Whybray, R.N., 16.
Wolff, H.W., 95.

Zimmerli, W., 49.

INDEX OF BIBLICAL PASSAGES (selected)

GENESIS

9:7 55, 56
27:29 55
28:13-15 234

EXODUS

14:19 212
31:14-17 49
31:17 49

LEVITICUS

19:26 130
26:12 68

DEUTERONOMY

4:34 314
5:15 314
7:19 314
11:2 314
18:10 130
18:14 130
23:2 72
23:3 68
23:4-7 68-69
25:1 126
26:8 314
32:9 105
32:13 230

I SAMUEL

6:3 189
15:12 70

II SAMUEL

18:18 70
22:35 314

I KINGS

8:42 314

II KINGS

21:6 130
21:16 270

ISAIAH

1:2-3 282, 334
1:2b 197
1:3 115, 116
1:4c 197
1:19-20 163
1:27 59
2:2 166
2:6 130
3:15 45
5:7 59
5:16 59
6:3 294
6:9-10 262, 282, 334
9:6 59
11:12 77
14:7 160
14:18b 118
16:5 60
19:4 45
26:9 60
27:13 166
28:14-22 67
28:17 60
29:15 195
30:6 267
32:1 60
32:16 60
33:5 60
34:1 126
40:1-11 23, 47
40:3 271
40:3-5 23
40:5 210
40:6 210
40:8 23
40:21 282
40:28 282
41:1b 126
41:20 195, 282
41:22c 101
41:23a 101
41:25 101
43:5 22, 51
43:10 282
44:7 101
44:9 144, 195
44:10 144
45:3 282
45:6 282
45:7 122
45:8 60
45:21 60
46:13 60
49:18 22, 51
49:23 282
49:26 20, 210, 282
51:1-16 105
51:5 60
51:6 60
51:8 60
51:12 63
52:6 282
52:12 212
53:5 156
54:17 45
55:1-13 23
55:10-11 23
55:12-13 23
56:1 22, 29, 30, 51, 56-57, 80, 261, 302, 309, 310-16, 322
56:1-2 52, 54, 55-64, 61
56:1-8 15, 23, 44,85
56:1b 19, 20
56:2 23, 81
56:3 53, 64, 67
56:3-7 54, 64
56:4 69
56:4-7 53, 66
56:5 70-72, 83
56:6 72-73, 83
56:7 29, 73-75
56:8 51, 76-79, 84
56:9 109-111, 116
56:9-12 12, 23, 109
56:9-57:2 101
56:9-57:13 24
56:10 25, 29, 94
56:10-11 114-15
56:11 25, 29, 97, 112-14
57:1 29, 30, 120
57:1-2 119-24
57:2 122-24
57:3 124-27
57:3-5 124-32
57:3-13 24, 103
57:5 130
57:6 132-37

Isaiah (cont'd)
57:6-8 138
57:7-8 140-41
57:7-10 137-42
57:8 139
57:9-10 138
57:10 29, 139
57:11 143-45
57:11-13 142-47
57:12 29, 146
57:13 146-47
57:13c 24
57:14 29, 147-48
57:14-19a 147-56
57:14-21 24, 107
57:15 148-50
57:16 151-53
57:17 25, 29, 97, 153, 263
57:18 29, 154-55, 157
57:19b-21 156-60
57:20 25, 94
57:20-21 158-60, 304
58:1 26, 29, 186, 191, 198-99, 234
58:1-4 186, 191-200
58:1-12 25
58:2 29, 30, 192-94, 235-36, 238, 247
58:3 29, 196, 262
58:4 186, 261
58:5 179-80, 182, 187, 188, 189, 200-206 238-39
58:6 207-209
58:6-9a 206-17
58:6-14 189
58:7 29, 209-10
58:8 21, 29, 211-13, 215-16, 247, 280
58:9a 213-15, 238
58:9b 217-19
58:9b-12 217-25
58:10 219-20, 280
58:11 220-22, 304-305
58:12 29, 222-24
58:13 29, 226-28, 235-36
58:13-14 25, 175-77, 225-31
58:14 26, 230-31, 234
59:1 26, 247, 257-58, 262
59:1-2 285
59:1-3 252-53, 273
59:1-14 15
59:1-20 26
59:2 258-59
59:3 259-60, 285
59:4 29, 30, 246, 253, 264-66
59:4-8 264-75
59:5 282
59:6-7 268-272
59:8 29, 272
59:9 29
59:9-13 255, 275-88, 289
59:10 282-83
59:11 29, 285
59:12 29, 285-87
59:12-13 283-84
59:13 29, 285
59:14 30, 256, 288-92
59:15 29
59:15-17 297-98
59:15-20 15, 292-304
59:16 29
59:16b-17 295-97, 309
59:18 298-300
59:18-19 301
59:19 19, 20, 300-301
59:19-20 21, 301-302, 305
59:20 19, 22, 26, 29 247, 302-304, 322
59:21 27, 306-308
60:1 21, 22, 74, 215, 303, 308
60:1-2 279
60:1-22 15, 21-22, 288
60:1-63:6 306, 307, 308, 328
60:2 279, 280, 303
60:3 279
60:4 22, 51, 303
60:5 22, 303
60:6 22, 303
60:7 87
60:9 83, 87, 299, 303
60:9b 74
60:10 23
60:11 22, 303
60:11b 74
60:13 22, 303
60:14 87, 303
60:14b 222
60:16 20, 282, 303
60:17 22, 303
60:19 215, 279
60:19-22 280
60:20 22, 215, 303
61:1 308
61:1-11 15
61:2a 296
61:3 303
61:3c 222
61:5 23
61:8 307
61:8-9 307
62:1 303
62:1-12 15
62:2 87
62:2b 222
62:4b 222, 229
62:4c 229
62:6 303
62:7 303
62:8 23
62:10 271
62:11 303
62:12 222
63:1 79, 86
63:1-6 15, 16
63:4 296
63:7 87
63:7-64:11 15, 16, 87
63:8 263
63:9 20, 22
63:12 83, 87
63:14 83, 87
63:16 83, 87
63:19 87
64:1 87
64:6 87
64:10 87
64:11 16
65:1 87
65:1ff 16
65:1-66:17 15
65:4 210
65:8-9 72
65:10 125
65:11 87, 125
65:12b 214
65:13-14 125
65:13-15 73
65:14 151

Isaiah (cont'd)
65:15 87
65:24 214
66:3 229
66:4 229
66:4b 215
66:5 84-5
66:11 229
66:14 73
66:16 210
66:17 210, 270
66:18 22, 51, 79, 84
66:18-24 15, 80, 81, 82, 85, 86, 87, 89, 324
66:18a 51
66:18b 81
66:19 299
66:20 81, 83, 84, 85, 86 166
66:20-23 83
66:22 82, 83, 84, 87
66:22-23 82
66:23 23, 82, 86, 210
66:24 81, 82, 210

JEREMIAH

2:8 144
2:20 130
3:6 130
3:16 166
5:19 105
7:4 294
7:23 68
9:2 129
9:4 129
12:7 111
12:7-9 111
12:8 111
12:9 111
12:10 111
12:10-13 111
22:15-16 189
22:29 294
27:2 207
27:9 130
28:10 207
28:12 207
28:13 207
29:11 122
31:33 68
33:6 156
48:9a 71
50:5 68

EZEKIEL

11:20 68
18:31 151
20:12-13 49
20:16 49
20:21 49
20:24 49
21:27 294
22:8 49
23:28 49
30:18 207
36:26 151
39:10 110
48:29 105

DANIEL

9:3 201

HOSEA

8:7 282
10:12 282

JOEL

4:19 270

JONAH

3:5-6 201-202

MICAH

4:2 166
5:11 130
6:6 202
6:15 282
7:2 95

NAHUM

1:13 207

HABAKKUK

2:18 144

ZECHARIAH

1:1-16 154
1:2 154
1:14-17 154
1:15 154
1:16-17 154
1:17 154
2:15 67,68
2:15a 67

MALACHI

3:20 212

JOB

3:9 278
3:13 160
3:25 101
3:26 160
9:30-31 189
11:13-15 189
15:34-35 265
20:16 267-68
24:13 223
24:13b 223,224
25:6 63,64

PSALMS

4:5 118
8:5 63,64
9:8 114
12:2 95
18:6 138
18:34 314
27:2 114
31:19 129
34:7 258
35:13 195
37:9 114
38:11 114
43:3 114
50:8 75
50:14 75
50:23 75
56:7 114
57:6 202
59:4 114
63:12 129
69:10-11 201

Psalms (cont'd)

89:13	314
89:21	314
106:38	270
107:23	114
109:2	129
120:2	129
122:4	166
126:5	282
136:12	314
145:14	202
145:19	258
146:8	202
147:2	77
147:12-13	77

PROVERBS

1:27	101
2:4-5	189
6:17	270
11:18	282,291
12:19	291
16:9	96
22:8	282
25:4-5	265

QOHELETH

4:17	75

CANTICLE OF CANTICLES

4:8	101
8:6	138

II CHRONICLES

4:5	160
6:32	314
33:6	130

EZRA

8:21	195

NEHEMIAH

13:15-18	49

ESTHER

4:3	201

MATTHEW

5:23-24	75

II CORINTHIANS

9:6	282

GALATIANS

6:8	282

JAMES

3:18	282

INDEX OF RHETORICAL DEVICES AND SUBJECTS

Alliteration, 48, 72, 108, 153, 191, 267
Alonso Sch ökel, influence of, x, 6-8
Alternation of verbal elements,to express conclusion, 298
Ambiguity, as a rhetorical device, 139 n. 90
Antithesis, 24, 94
Assonance, 118, 127, 148, 157, 267

Bondage, imagery of, 207-208, 217

Chiasm, 53, 54, 61, 66, 114-115, 120, 136, 149-50, 220, 322
Chiasm, an odd, 233-34
Chiasm, function of, 120-21, 220-21, 302
Chiastic sound pattern, 133, 196
Climactic verses, 76
Concentric structure, 14-15, 233, 240, 276
Courtroom scene, 126-128, 142-44

Delayed identification, 98 n. 8
Delimitation of literary units, 22-27
Diachronic exegesis, xi, 9, 9 n. 26
Distant chiastic parallelism, 20-21
Distant parallelism, 18-19, 18 n. 50, 22, 36, 54, 101, 120, 214, 323
Divine Warrior image, 30-31, 293-306

Emphatic particles, 5, 21, 135, 137 n. 85, 300 n. 84
Eunuch, 68-70

Gradation of imagery, 141, 210

Hendiadys, 70
Hinge Verse, 132-33, 137, 205-206, 288-92, 323-24

Inclusion, 4, 18-19, 23, 25, 26, 36, 53, 85-86, 88, 103, 160, 175-76, 253
Inclusion, external, 86
Inclusion, internal, 86-87
Isaiah 56-66, recent studies, 12-17
Isaian unity, viii-ix, 10-12

Justice, a motif, 58-61, 193-94, 198-99, 246-47, 249-50, 276-77, 289, 290, 294-95, 309-16

Knowledge, a motif, 31-32, 195-96, 285-87, 333-34

Liberation, imagery of, 207-208, 212, 217
Light, imagery of, 212, 215-16, 279-80

Macarism, 49 n. 8, 62
Macrostructures, 38
Merism, 110, 110 n. 30, 122, 158, 270, 281
Metaphony, 162-63
Metaphors, corresponding, 154-55
Method of analysis, 35-39
Metonymy, 134
Microstructure, 37
Motif, 28, 28 n. 76, 30
Muilenburg, influence of, xiii, 2-6

Onomatopoeia, 118

Parallel pairs, 20, 22, 30, 51, 63-64, 95, 101, 105 n. 21, 146, 151, 151 n. 104 and 105, 160 n. 117, 195 n. 33, 249, 258 n. 22, 270 n. 39, 271 n. 42, 277 n. 46, 279 n. 53, 291 n. 69
Paronomasia, 146, 162-63, 169, 278
Particle of surprise, 114
Patterns (word, grammatical, syntactic, structural, thematic),
- ABA, 63, 109, 131, 192, 201
- ABAB, 57, 113, 119, 199, 228, 266
- ABBA, 73-74, 115, 135, 148, 193, 272
- ABBAAB, 61, 203-204
- ABCABC, 151
- ABCACB, 148, 257, 264
- ABCB, 55-60
- ABCBA, 66, 67 n. 41, 71, 159
- ABCCBA, 211, 218
- ABCDABCD, 258

Pronouns, emphatic use of, 143-44, 152, 193

Qînа, rhythm, 103-104, 127

Recapitulation, 85-86, 176, 272
Repeated patterns with negatives, 102
Repeated sound patterns, 116-18, 253, 254, 255, 258, 271 n. 40
Repeated vocabulary, patterns of, 27-34, 50, 80, 106, 169, 177, 178-79, 246, 249, 250-51, 274, 284, 289, 293, 295, 297, 303, 303 n. 86, 310
Rhetorical criticism, ix-xiii, 1-10, 38 n. 92
Rhetorical questions, 104-105, 105 n. 20, 127-29, 143-44, 206-207
Righteousness, motif of, 55-56, 58-61, 99-100, 120-21, 145-46, 193-94, 247, 249-50, 270-71, 276-77, 328-30

Seven, patterns of, 178-79, 178 n. 8, 181, 183
Sin, cf. Transgression
Sitz in der Literatur, 7, 7 n. 20, 126 n. 56, 138
Sound-motif, 157, 182, 195
Superlative, use of in Hebrew, 137-38
Synchronic exegesis, xii, 9, 9 n. 26

Themes, 28, 28 n. 76, 324-28, 327 n. 2
Transgression, motif of, 29, 32-33, 128-32, 191, 197-99, 283-84, 332
Trial speech, cf. Courtroom scene
Tricolon, importance of, 110, 140

Water, imagery of, 304-305
"Way", imagery of the, 32, 97-98, 141-42, 153, 223-24, 273, 273 n. 43, 330-31
Waw emphatic, 65
Waw explicative, 69-70
Wordplay, 214, 301
Wordplay, function of, 170-71

Herbert W. Basser

MIDRASHIC INTERPRETATIONS OF THE SONG OF MOSES

American University Studies: Series VII, Theology and Religion. Vol. 2
ISBN 0-8204-0065-3 326 p. pb./lam. US $ 28.85
recommended prices - alterations reserved

This work provides a translation of, and a commentary to the text of *Sifre Ha'azinu.* Finkelstein's edition (1939, reprinted JTS 1969) and selected readings of the London manuscript of this midrash appear in translation with full notes covering textual observations, philological inquiries and exegetical problems. The following ideas are discussed within the course of the work: midrashic forms, the use of Scripture in midrash, the dating of the traditions and of the recording of this midrash, the use of apologetic and polemic in midrash. An *Introduction* and *Conclusion* have been provided which discuss the items in this midrash which are relevant to the academic study of Judaism. The literary aspects of this midrash on Deut. 32 are used to exemplify *midrashim* on poetic Scriptures.

Contents: Introduction discussing literary, theological, historical aspects of midrash - Translation and analysis of the midrash to Deut. 32. Sifre Deuteronomy - Conclusion summing up the findings in the work.

PETER LANG PUBLISHING, INC.
62 West 45th Street
USA - New York, NY 10036

Heinz O. Guenther

THE FOOTPRINTS OF JESUS' TWELVE IN EARLY CHRISTIAN TRADITIONS

A Study in the Meaning of Religious Symbolism

American University Studies: Series VII, Theology and Religion. Vol. 7
ISBN 0-8204-0164-1 156 pp. hardcover/lam. US $ 20.90
recommended prices – alterations reserved

The sudden disappearance of the twelve apostles from the pages of post-Easter Christian history is in B.H. Streeter's judgment 'one of the great mysteries of history'. The purpose of this publication is to shed some new light on this mystery and to examine, on the basis of the available New Testament evidence, the claim that the earthly Jesus himself had appointed the twelve. The book opens (Part I) with a redaction-critical inquiry into those New Testament writings which advance this claim, touching on both the origin and setting of the source materials used by the evangelists to support it. The question of how and why firmly established traditions are still suggestive enough to inspire visions entailing their reformulation on new levels of meaning is treated in this part. The book goes on (Part II) to discuss the role played by the symbolic number twelve in Hellenistic and Jewish milieux, concluding with the description of the substance and power added to early Christianity by the use of this prestigious number. The publication will be of benefit mostly to specialists and graduate students interested in deriving historical knowledge from religious materials.

Contents: The Twelve in Luke's Theology – Luke's Sources Revisited – Traces of the Twelve in the Source Q, the pre-Markan and the pre-Pauline Tradition – The Interpretive Power of the Twelve in Hellenistic culture, in Judaism and early Christianity.